Small-town Boy, Small-town Girl

Small-town Boy, Small-town Girl

GROWING UP IN SOUTH DAKOTA,

1920–1950

ERIC B. FOWLER & SHEILA DELANEY

Edited and with an Introduction by

MOLLY P. ROZUM

SOUTH DAKOTA STATE HISTORICAL SOCIETY PRESS

Pierre

This book is funded, in part, by the Great Plains Education Foundation, Inc.,
Aberdeen, S.Dak.

Library of Congress Cataloging-in-Publication data
Fowler, Eric B.
Small-town boy, small-town girl : growing up in South Dakota,
1920-1950 / by Eric B. Fowler and Sheila Delaney ; edited and with an
introduction by Molly P. Rozum.
p. cm.
Includes bibliographical references and index.
ISBN 978-0-9798940-7-7
1. Fowler, Eric B.—Childhood and youth—Anecdotes. 2. Delaney,
Sheila, 1927—Childhood and youth—Anecdotes. 3. Milbank
(S.D.)—Social life and customs—20th century—Anecdotes. 4. Mitchell
(S.D.)—Social life and customs—20th century—Anecdotes. 5. Fowler
family—Anecdotes. 6. Delaney family—Anecdotes. I. Delaney, Sheila,
1927- II. Rozum, Molly Patrick. III. Title.
F659.M54F69 2009
978.3'0320922—dc22
2009037630

The paper in this book meets the guidelines for permanence and durability
of the committee on Production Guidelines for Book Longevity of the Council
on Library Resources.
Text and cover design by Rich Hendel
Please visit our website at http://www.sdshspress.com

Printed in the United States of America
13 12 11 10 09   1 2 3 4 5

Small-town Boy, Small-town Girl

GROWING UP IN SOUTH DAKOTA, 1920–1950

ERIC B. FOWLER & SHEILA DELANEY

Edited and with an Introduction by

MOLLY P. ROZUM

SOUTH DAKOTA STATE HISTORICAL SOCIETY PRESS

Pierre

This book is funded, in part, by the Great Plains Education Foundation, Inc.,
Aberdeen, S.Dak.

Library of Congress Cataloging-in-Publication data
Fowler, Eric B.
Small-town boy, small-town girl : growing up in South Dakota,
1920-1950 / by Eric B. Fowler and Sheila Delaney ; edited and with an
introduction by Molly P. Rozum.
p. cm.
Includes bibliographical references and index.
ISBN 978-0-9798940-7-7
1. Fowler, Eric B.—Childhood and youth—Anecdotes. 2. Delaney,
Sheila, 1927—Childhood and youth—Anecdotes. 3. Milbank
(S.D.)—Social life and customs—20th century—Anecdotes. 4. Mitchell
(S.D.)—Social life and customs—20th century—Anecdotes. 5. Fowler
family—Anecdotes. 6. Delaney family—Anecdotes. I. Delaney, Sheila,
1927- II. Rozum, Molly Patrick. III. Title.
F659.M54F69 2009
978.3'0320922—dc22
2009037630

The paper in this book meets the guidelines for permanence and durability
of the committee on Production Guidelines for Book Longevity of the Council
on Library Resources.
Text and cover design by Rich Hendel
Please visit our website at http://www.sdshspress.com

Printed in the United States of America
13 12 11 10 09   1 2 3 4 5

Contents

Introduction

MOLLY P. ROZUM

young Eric Fowler made his way along the blocks toward Main Street in Milbank, South Dakota, little sister by his side. Conversation back and forth about the purchase occupied the walk. He ran a hand through his wavy auburn hair. The two had seen the nickel-plated electric toaster in the windows of the Bleser drugstore. Odd jobs had provided the funds, and they carefully counted their coins. Assisted by the storeowner, who knew the Fowler family, the two youngsters selected well. It was absolutely "tops," Eric thought on the way home, blue eyes crinkling as he pictured his mother's surprise at the birthday gift. It was the 1920s. Appliances had appeared everywhere; electricity lightened loads *and* toasted homemade bread precisely—formerly a struggle on the cast-iron coal stove.[1]

Sheila Delaney's red hair flew off her forehead as she pedaled five blocks down Sixth Avenue toward Main Street in Mitchell, South Dakota. She made a left and headed to the office building. She was ten years old with a job to do every Saturday afternoon. Lugging and huffing the bike into the elevator, she thought over her instructions as the cage ascended to the third floor: dust, sweep, empty, organize, and sterilize. She closed the lids of her hazel eyes, thinking. All instruments must show metal-shine clean. The Delaney Medical Office would be in fine shape on Monday when her father opened the doors for his first patients. It was the 1930s. Her father might be paid in produce, a butter crock, or not at all.[2]

Sheila Delaney and Eric Fowler have written lively memoirs of their youths in eastern South Dakota towns in the years between World War I and World War II and on into the 1950s. Often, memoirs from the grasslands region focus on the farm, rural life, and agriculture, and for a state with a population that did not tip urban until 1990, accounts of the rural and the agricultural have enduring value.[3] Nevertheless, it is also true, as historian John Miller has asserted, that no matter "whatever else it may be," South Dakota "is a state that is defined by its small towns, and there, more than anywhere else, is where its identity is to be found."[4] These two memoirs are significant because they allow for a deep consideration of the experiences of young people in thriving, modern American small towns during the time that broad economic changes began to transform them. While Delaney and Fowler did not know small-town life without automobiles, they still lived their youths within a railroad dominion and at a time when a workhorse or buggy pony could still need a livery stable.

As these compelling narratives show, the region's twentieth century has a far richer base than that covered in the most popular tales of the Great Plains—memories of the 1930s Dust Bowl.[5] Delaney and Fowler lived through the dust and depression of the 1930s, but their stories include the 1920s, 1940s, and 1950s, decades that are also intimately connected to the choices made and paths followed in their long lives. Written after they retired, their histories convey perspective both on how the Great Depression immediately influenced their lives and on how it receded into an indelible cultural lesson. When Delaney and Fowler recall their youths in Mitchell and Milbank, they remember the depression, but they dwell on the joys of childhood discovery, the sorrows of illness and uncertainty, and the complexity of family dynamics and human relationships. Their stories illuminate how South Dakota and the post-frontier region were linked to the modern world, urban as well as rural. In the end, these small towns fostered the movement of their young into the broader nation, yet called them back home again in these memoirs.

Both Milbank and Mitchell were established during the Great Dakota Boom (1878–1887), when the Chicago, Milwaukee, & Saint Paul Railroad (the Milwaukee Road), the Chicago & North Western Railroad, and other lines built "a lattice work of track" on the face of South Dakota east of the Missouri River.[6] Hundreds of towns sprouted in eastern southern Dakota as over twenty-four million acres, nearly every corner and crevice save the land set aside for American Indian reservations, were peopled with immigrants from Europe, Canada, and other parts of the United States. Enough people arrived so that after Congress enabled Dakota Territory to separate into two states in 1889, South Dakota boasted a population of 328,808. It had been around 13,000 in 1870.[7] Eastern South Dakota would maintain its population density, as people settled themselves on 160-acre family farms and in railroad-siding villages platted at ten-mile intervals, then in the towns that grew into small cities such as Mitchell and Milbank.

By the time Fowler and Delaney lived in Milbank and Mitchell, these county seats had distinguished themselves as more than railroad country towns,[8] although the Milwaukee Road had platted both communities in 1880. Mitchell had been named for railroad company president Alexander Mitchell, while Jeremiah Milbank, a director of the road, gave his name to Milbank. The Hastings & Dakota Division of the Milwaukee Road reached Milbank by way of Ortonville, a small town situated on the Minnesota side of Big Stone Lake. Railroad town-site agents chose a homestead about twelves miles southwest of Ortonville over the presumed division point at Dakota Territory's Big Stone City, rather than pay the high price demanded by that town. South and west of Milbank, the Milwaukee Road platted Mitchell near the point at which Firesteel Creek poured into the James River but well above the flood-level village named for the creek. Both towns also won county-seat battles over the towns that had lost the railroad advantage, Mitchell defeating Firesteel to become the county seat of Davison County and Milbank spoiling Big Stone City's hopes of becoming the Grant County seat. In addition, the federal government named Mitchell as the land office where the processing of homestead and other land-grant programs would take place for a ten-county surrounding area. From the start, Milbank and the railroad expected to benefit from distribution of government annuities to the nearby Lake Traverse Indian Reservation. These unique service opportunities gave competitive advantages to each town.[9]

The success of both Mitchell and Milbank can be further attributed to their geographic location. As a goose flies across South Dakota in autumn, roughly one hundred fifty miles separate Milbank and Mitchell, both now the largest "cities" in their respective counties. From this bird's-eye-view, grasslands ripple below, pockmarked by glacial lakes or depressions that once held water. The two towns sit atop the same rich and fertile ground, the same black soils. Both Grant and Davison counties lie east of the 100th meridian, the classic line of demarcation that separates arid and humid agricultural zones. West of the line, sparse precipitation confounds farming, but Davison County is 75 miles east of the line, while Grant County is 135 miles east. The dark clouds that contained dust, not rain, and the dry, cracked lakebeds that Fowler recalls from the 1930s seem to challenge this broad humid-zone classification. Nevertheless, both Mitchell and Milbank experience an average of between eighteen and twenty-two inches of precipitation annually. Grant County temperatures average a little cooler than those of Davison County, and the Milbank area, which is farther north, has a shorter growing season if frost makes an early appearance and stays long, but agriculture has become a durable economic base for both counties.[10]

The eastern part of Grant County bordering Minnesota, what Fowler calls the "low prairie," formed out of the aftermath of an antique version of the modern Red River. An eroded, elevated plateau, the Coteau des Prairies, or what Fowler calls the "hills," rose up in the western part of the county. Six-hundred-million-year-old granite bedrock outcropped here, and developers exploited this "mahogany granite" for graveside monuments, the carving of which marked part of Fowler's early working life. Big Stone Lake, twenty-five miles long and one mile wide, began as a glacial lake spillway; it became a major feature of recreation in Fowler's childhood.[11] The Sisseton and Wahpeton Dakotas, who once lived near the lake, had been removed to the Lake Traverse reservation, part of which occupied western Grant County, long before Eric Fowler's parents moved to the United States. Few if any of these eastern Sioux lived in Milbank during Fowler's time, although enough of them lived in the area in 1928 so that Indians "playing Indians" joined with Swedes "playing Swedes," Germans "playing Germans," and so on for the town's fiftieth-anniversary "pantomime pageant."[12]

Davison County lies west and south of the Coteau de Prairies in the James River Valley. Fifty miles wide and two hundred miles long, this glacial swath, layered in drift, till, and loess deposits often hundreds of feet thick, constitutes, as Delaney writes, "one of the richest farming areas" in the country. The flat, sometimes dry or nearly dry James ("Jim") River flows south with a slight eastward tilt through the entire state, joining the Missouri River in the southeast corner. In the early 1920s, the city of Mitchell dammed Firesteel Creek, tributary to the James, to supply the growing town with water (making it a "two water tower" town, notes Delaney) and to create a six-hundred-acre recreational lake. During Delaney's childhood, archeologists began to excavate a prehistoric occupation site on the banks of Lake Mitchell; these Middle-Missouri villagers were ancestors of the Mandan Indians who lived in the region in the eighteenth century when European settlers first came in contact with them. By Sheila Delaney's day, the Nakota and Lakota Indians, or middle and western Sioux who claimed and traveled through eastern South Dakota in the modern era, had lived on reservations over one hundred miles from Mitchell for decades.[13]

If, as some historians suggest, the 1920s "constituted the high tide of . . . existence" for most small towns in the region, then Fowler and Delaney grew to adulthood in an era when these small towns buzzed with activity.[14] In both Mitchell and Milbank, a Milwaukee road depot and division-point roundhouse anchored Main Street. The depot complex shuffled passengers and greeters, while trains belched steam and coal smoke into the sky. The railroad was especially important to the Fowler family, for it was there that Eric Fowler's father worked. Over ninety businesses operated in Milbank's town center, over fifty of them founded in the 1920s, and Mitchell's retail district was much larger, with an adjoining warehouse district. Milbank acquired a Red Owl grocery in 1924, and Mitchell, a Piggly Wiggly; both chains competed with family grocery businesses. The national J. C. Penney Company had been serving Mitchell for ten years when it opened a department store in Milbank in 1927. A Maytag appliance store appeared in Milbank in 1928. In Mitchell, banks, doctors' offices — Dr. William Delaney's among them — lawyers' offices, bakeries, drugstores, cafés, hardware stores, and movie theaters all competed for the attention of a child traveling along Main Street's blocks. Both towns were trade centers for their counties. The steam trains that pulled boxcars full of appliances for the Bleser Drug Company in Milbank or the hardware store in Mitchell shipped out crates of "soda pop" from local bottling factories in both towns. They also carried corn, wheat, and cattle to distant commodity markets in Minneapolis, Omaha, and Chicago.[15]

The smell of one-horse buggies competed with the odor of fuel burnt by automobiles plying the muck of unpaved roads leading into town. Both kicked up dust and splatter. Draying businesses, carting ice or coal and supported by harness and blacksmith shops, worked Main Street. Automobile garages also sold cheap Model Ts and, later, Ford Model As, Chevrolets, Buicks, and a host of barely remembered makes and models—Whippets, Flints, Hupmobiles, Auburns, Jordans, Overlands, and Underslungs. Mitchell surfaced its first streets before the United States entered World War I, and by 1928, a Milbank promoter boasted, "The city has well-paved streets."[16] In the thirties, dealers already sold used vehicles and several garages and filling stations in each town kept vehicles operational.

By the twenties, telephone companies, water and sewer systems, and electric utilities had long served Mitchell. In Milbank, the Union Public Service opened in 1921 and a plumbing shop in 1923. Telegraphs still tapped out messages for Western Union across the miles, though the "two-lip" telegraph, as Fowler might say, could be faster in town and more private than the telephone. Both towns sported golf courses and hospitals. Mitchell had two, Saint Joseph's Hospital, the Catholic facility where Delaney's father practiced, and the Methodist Hospital. In Milbank, Saint Lawrence Hospital opened in 1920. Dakota Wesleyan University made its home in Mitchell and, during Sheila Delaney's time, consisted of the College Hall, a music hall, men's and women's dorms, and a gymnasium. Granite quarries enhanced Milbank's economy and its built environment. A grand, columned, three-story courthouse stood watch on Milbank's Main Street and kept time with the regular ring of a clock tower within hearing distance of the Fowler home. In Mitchell, the World's Only Corn Palace, an auditorium clad in multicolored corn and prairie grasses, oversaw Main Street, only five blocks west of the Delaney home.

Neighborhoods in both towns, a mixture of modest and distinguished houses, buffered Main Street from the countryside. Lumber, brick, cement, quartzite, and granite patterned and colored town space. Lilacs fashioned the avenues. By the 1920s and 1930s, mature oaks, elms, apple trees, box elders, hackberries, and cottonwoods cast shadows on neighborhood streets. As youngsters, both Delaney and Fowler could easily survey town boundaries. They knew where grain fields and pastures began. They walked at their ease among the towns' nearly all-white population, which included significant populations of German, Scandinavian, English, Irish, and Canadian-born immigrants. For brief periods, handfuls of African Americans, American Indians, and Chinese lived in Mitchell.[17] Delaney's parents came from Iowa and fit the pattern of the majority of both towns' residents, who migrated from nearby states, while Fowler's parents formed part of the English and Canadian migration to South Dakota.

Although the pace of Mitchell and Milbank seemed to quicken with the speed of the automobiles on town avenues in the 1920s, town businessmen— including Delaney's father—would have been concerned about troubles in agriculture that were placing the entire state's economy, as South Dakota historian Herbert S. Schell phrased it, in the "doldrums."[18] In the words of another state historian, "The rural prosperity bubble burst suddenly and completely in 1920."[19] In 1921, the bottom dropped out of commodity prices. Farmers had less cash to spend in town than they had in the World War I years when they had expanded operations to provide food for the allied effort and reap the profits of high demand. "Food Will Win the War" had been a popular federal slogan. Some farmers purchased new gasoline tractors and others more land, allowing them to increase production. Most purchases required trips to town for bank loans. A farmer's fix ensued: low prices encouraged increased crop sizes, which lowered prices, which led to foreclosure when debts and taxes went unpaid, which led to bank failures. In Milbank, the recession led to labor conflict on the Milwaukee railroad and to layoffs at the roundhouse. Soon, Fowler's father sought work out-of-state, with disastrous results for the family. By 1925, 175 banks had closed in the state.[20] The broader economic consequences of World War I mobilization now hung low on the region's agricultural horizon.

By the time the Great Depression began, South Dakota was already "highly vulnerable" economically. As foreclosures began to rise, land values and farm earnings dropped even more. By 1935, South Dakota land weighed in lightly at \$18.65 per acre, down from \$35.24 per acre in 1930, which already represented a drop of fifty-eight percent during the 1920s. State bank failures continued, eventually totaling almost seventy-one percent; by 1934, more than fifty percent of national banks operating in the state had also failed. In 1934, thirty-nine percent of South Dakota's population received relief—the "highest relief load for any state."[21] Meanwhile, in Milbank, it was so dry that the Milwaukee Road had to freight in the water it used for maintenance of trains at the roundhouse.[22]

Despite a depressed economy, Sheila Delaney and Eric Fowler went about a small child's and a young man's daily business in the 1930s. Fowler went on one of his first vacations—west to the Black Hills— at the dawn of the depression. One of the most memorable events of Delaney's childhood was her eldest sister's elaborate marriage in 1938. Delaney walked through many years of dust to Mitchell's Notre Dame Academy, where she contemplated the mysteries of the Holy Trinity, while Fowler, just out of high school, worked as a New Deal clerk in Milbank's courthouse.

At the same time, Mitchell's population remained stable at more than ten thousand, and Milbank's continued to rise to almost three thousand. Despite the economic conditions, Mitchell added new businesses to its Main Street; another general-merchandise store and a new jewelry store opened in 1936, and the Coca-Cola Bottling Company expanded twice in the 1930s. Milbank's two main banks weathered the 1930s storm, and another bank actually incorporated during the decade. Mitchell residents could watch feature films at two newly opened theaters, the Paramount in 1932, a favorite of Delaney's, or the Roxy in 1933. In Milbank, movies could be seen at the Bentley Grand Theater and the Defea Theater—the latter also built in the early 1930s. Indeed, observers of small towns across the nation have noted, with some irony, that it "was during the greatest economic crisis in the nation's history that many communities were able to accomplish more in the way of improving their infrastructure than in any previous comparable time period."[23] Mitchell received federal money to fund new water-main construction, sewer modernization, a high-school stadium, a recreation center, and a new courthouse. A center also opened in Mitchell to process cattle, purchased by a federal New Deal agricultural program, into canned products for the needy. Federal money in Milbank remodeled the public high school, built an athletic field, and improved the town's roads.[24]

Even if economic depression, dust, and eventually a war made life uncertain, small towns such as Mitchell and Milbank opened exciting avenues to the world for young people during this period. Delaney's regular 1930s movie attendance suggests the lure of popular culture and the wider world, as does her reading of magazines and newspapers while holed-up in the attic of her family home. The national reach of popular culture through touring musicians, who traveled to the Corn Palace and other state venues, exposed the state's young people to more than jazz and big bands. This performance culture provided what were likely the only links to racial diversity for many regional residents. Fowler's world connections came through the radio as he tuned in at "radio shack" gatherings of men and boys. Radio programming also connected this age group to national politics and policy in an immediate way, through Franklin Delano Roosevelt's "fireside" policy chats and Eleanor Roosevelt's weekly radio program. Both Delaney and Fowler recalled President Roosevelt's "Declaration of War" to Congress as read over radio waves in 1941. Delaney followed the course of the war, sobered and excited, thinking of her brothers and friends who served abroad.

Even though Fowler and Delaney grew into maturity connected to the world in new ways, the textures of their daily lives suggest two young people focused on home, family, play, and work. Few commercial toys make the pages of these memoirs. Fowler and Delaney recount independent wanderings out-of-doors and about town to make fun from chanced-upon "bits and pieces," as Fowler phrased it. Downtown Milbank's supply of fascinating cast-off objects seemed endless. Sheila Delaney specialized in creative personal spaces, from her own hiding places in and around the house, to neighborhood games of "hide and seek," to perches in tree branches.

They recall their houses almost as animate protectors. The hard-coal heater fought back at snow wind-blasted through the cracks of the Fowler home. Knowledge of the various sizes and types of coal— anthracite, bituminous, hard and soft, lump and nut, Montana and Pennsylvania—and the intensity and longevity of the heat they gave clearly became second nature to Fowler as he fed the heater and the stove. A fireplace and the massive brick of the Delaney house talked back to the "Banshee screams" of blizzard winds. In both homes, the family gathered close to the source of heat to keep warm in the main room, where Fowler read "many library books," or the den, where Delaney entered a "reading world." Though electricity lighted their homes, both Fowler and Delaney recall that the family frequently turned off the lights to sit together by a fire. Delaney stared "into the shapes in the hearth and flickering on the walls and ceiling," while Fowler recalled watching "the fire behind the isinglass windows." Blue-flamed coal through mica and waves of yellow-flamed wood suggest the tenor of small-town homes before television—a device neither author mentioned.[25]

Their stories are filled with family, friends, and people that a small-town boy and girl encounter when growing up. Nevertheless, when Fowler and Delaney reflected on what they had written, each wondered if his or her life story had been basically a summary of work experiences. A "travelogue of different work places," wrote Delaney. Work must seem to be his "middle name," speculated Fowler. "I wanted to work," Delaney wrote about her first post-college years. In reference to her first administrative job, she noted, "I liked the work." Fowler, too, had a staunch belief in the value of work. "Right or wrong, I have often wondered," he admitted, "but I worked twelve hours a day and often much longer" because laboratory research "demanded it."

Although Delaney was a child during the depths of the 1930s and Fowler a young man just out of high school, their mutual lifelong gravitation toward and driving desire to work suggest an era's unique mark. As they grew up, work was hard to find. In 1934 and 1935, the unemployment rate for those aged sixteen to twenty-four rose much higher than the national unemployment rate.[22] Delaney prayed hard for those farmers who paid her father with chickens and eggs. Her memory, too, of obtaining her Social Security card at the age of ten in 1937—the very year that South Dakota took action to comply with the federal program—is telling, but was it a symbol of achievement or security?[26] Events of the 1930s challenged both. Coming after a period in which notions of leisure and consumer culture first began to make inroads among the masses, the Great Depression seems to have given renewed meaning to *work*. The physical and economic necessity of work and the psychic costs of not being able to work formed deep social and cultural impressions on individuals that lasted entire lifetimes.

Yet, in Delaney's long working life can be seen something more: the struggle that women of her generation experienced with wide-spread assumptions about women's work. Women could vote; that came with the Nineteenth Amendment in 1920. In Delaney's day, too, women earned college degrees with comparative ease, although for middle-class women, pursuing college or occupational goals in lieu of college remained equally normative choices, especially for single women.[27] Shelia Delaney, the youngest in the family, desired the intellectual options she saw open to her brothers and men generally. Delaney's patients-first, hardworking doctor father had plans for his sons to follow in his footsteps, but he expected of his daughters only that they marry well. Delaney's father shared the attitudes of his class and generation. Her brothers may not have appreciated the pressure to conform to their father's desires, but they had secure futures outlined for them. Delaney's oldest sister who wanted to follow the same pattern, however, was discouraged into marriage, a less-secure future as divorce became more and more common. As a divorced single mother, Sheila Delaney worked to support herself and her daughter and struggled to find the opportunity to secure the education that gave her the "intellectual give and take" she had experienced at her childhood dinner table.

The limitations on women's economic opportunity in the interwar period were not hidden; they were unquestioned ideas held by many Americans, whether they lived in small towns or big cities. These assumptions hold as true in Fowler's memoir as in Delaney's. If a woman wanted to work, she taught, as one of Fowler's sisters did, or attended "business" school to prepare for a host of office positions, as Fowler's other sister and Sheila Delaney both did, or worked in the nursing and medical-service sector.[28] Eric Fowler himself briefly considered the medical-technician field, until, as he explained, one of his college professors "convinced me that I would always be competing for women's wages." The vulnerability of women is also apparent in Fowler's clear memory of the toll on his mother's spirit and body as a result of the hard menial work she performed to provide for a family after his father died. From his mother, he learned "what the lack of an education could mean" for her, but also for a man. If Delaney worked against circumscribed opportunities for women of the times, Fowler worked to find "sufficient money not to worry about tomorrow's breakfast" as he completed his college degrees.

Eric Fowler and Sheila Delaney eventually worked their way out of the small towns of eastern South Dakota. In this respect, their lives fit a pattern then emerging in the post-World War II United States, whereby small towns provided "a secure haven in which young people were reared and educated, but on reaching adulthood they left for greater opportunities than those available in their hometown."[29] By the middle of the twentieth century, about a decade after Fowler left Milbank and a decade before Delaney left South Dakota, national observers detected "an evident spirit of decay" in villages[30] and small towns due to "the problem of the future of the small town in an urban-industrial civilization."[31] These observers looked at the same modern innovations that had animated and enriched the small-town lives of Fowler and Delaney and found them destructive to "community" and to what they considered to be the distinctive cultures of small towns. Radio, the film industry, mass magazines, and especially the gasoline automobile, tractor, truck transportation, and highway proliferation spelled the end of "older rural predominance" in American life. By the end of the 1950s, these scholars claimed, New Deal "wages and hours legislation," which had ensured more leisure and financial resources for a broader popular participation in a bureaucratic "mass society," had diluted, if not extinguished, the authentic qualities of small towns in the United States. Further, 1930s federal farm legislation had encouraged larger farms and corporate agriculture, accelerating rural depopulation and, in turn, increasing the decline of small towns. In addition, factory jobs during World War II, extraordinary post-war economic growth, and increasing college enrollments pulled young adults to the cities.[32]

From a regional perspective, however, Mitchell and Milbank have never registered only as small towns. Mitchell and Milbank actually stabilized and grew as part of the rise of urban America. Since the mid-twentieth century, national observers noted a distinctive regional pattern in which towns considered small in the East would "likely . . . be the largest community in a considerable area—perhaps a whole county" in the West.[33] In 1950, a few years prior to Sheila Delaney's final move from Mitchell, the federal census recorded Mitchell's population at 12,123, making it one of only six cities with a population of over ten thousand in the state. When Delaney left, just over fifty thousand people lived in the state's largest city of Sioux Falls. Only two other South Dakota cities reached a population of over twenty thousand people (Rapid City and Aberdeen). In 1950, Milbank's population reached 2,982, making it one of the top fifteen urban centers in South Dakota. As cities in a regional context, Mitchell and Milbank attracted retail jobs, what industry there was to be had, and college students and/or tourists, all at the expense of nearby smaller towns, villages, and hamlets. Mitchell and Milbank, when compared nationally, earned city status by virtue of the lack of overall urbanization in the state and the Northern Great Plains region.[34]

Cities though they are by United States Census measures, Mitchell and Milbank have also remained small towns. At the middle of the twentieth century, one regional observer noted, "On the northern route, . . . between Minneapolis and St. Paul, and the Pacific coast cities, there was no important city."[35] As South Dakota historian John Miller explained, "Industry never became the large force in the state that it did elsewhere in the United States, and what industry did emerge was grafted onto the normal span of activities that occur in a primarily agricultural community." As the rest of the nation grappled with urbanization after 1920, slow growth "left most towns in South Dakota and the surrounding region grasping desperately to survive, let alone trying to become a little Chicago or new Denver."[36] Milbank and Mitchell seem to have taken root just inside the western edge of what scholars have identified as "the optimal place for the settlement, survival, and longevity of small towns," that is, a location "somewhere in the middle of the Midwest." The optimal town zone is marked by a not-too-arid location (so the environmental land base will support a concentration of population) and a not-too-close-to-the-metropolis location (to avoid incorporation into the city as a neighborhood or suburb).[37]

Leaving their small cities behind, Fowler and Delaney each pursued opportunity and eventually retired, coincidentally, in the American Southwest. Despite their personal reasons for leaving, Delaney and Fowler were in step with many in the national population, pursuing college degrees and looking to the nation's West for economic opportunity. Post-World War II economic growth and/or Cold War defense spending fostered Fowler's research career at the Los Alamos National Laboratory and Delaney's early employment in Santa Fe, the center of new cultural research initiatives.

At ninety-five years of age, Eric Fowler told me in 2009 that his hair is no longer auburn, but his recall is refined and sharp down to the smallest of details. He first drafted his memoir at least thirty years ago after taking a writing class in the 1970s. With the celebration of the nation's bicentennial in 1976, ancestry and family and local history came into vogue, and his children and grandchildren asked him to remember his life for them. In our 2009 conversations, Fowler seemed to remember his story as if he had written it the year before, a testimony to the significance of the incidents he recounts. Now unable to write for extended periods of time, Eric Fowler took the time to explain to me over the telephone terms and situations that suggest how different was his small-town experience from that of later generations. Telling me about relief barrels and a "time killer" in his clear voice, he helped me understand the intensity and distress of the 1930s. His knowledge of the intricacies of a steam thresher and radio construction suggest the value of his memoir: these elements of his Milbank boyhood distinguish it strikingly from later eras.

Just as Fowler's hair is not auburn today, Sheila Delaney no longer stands five-foot, eleven-inches tall. At eighty-two, she measures five-foot, nine-inches and is still taller than many women, clearly taking after her six-foot, four-inch father. When I spoke with Delaney, she consulted her copy of the manuscript on her computer, suggesting that her interest in communication media has not abated since retirement. Long interested in literature and writing, Delaney's autobiographical project, begun some ten years ago, seems to flow out of a long-held desire to express her creativity—though her grandchildren also began to demand family history from her. My conversations with her in 2009 made the subtle references to popular movie culture jump from the pages of her text, indicating how intense and transforming this new medium was for the generations that first experienced it. Enthralled since girlhood with movie plots and Shakespeare, she enrolled in many creative-writing courses in her adult life and wrote numerous newspaper feature stories and press releases. All this attention to language manifests in her lively and witty account of her life in Mitchell.

Although these memoirs make clear the importance of home-towns to Fowler and Delaney, their stories are equally about family and most especially about a father and a mother. As Delaney points out, her story could not be told without telling her father's story, too; his fierce drive, dedication, and intellect arched intensely over family life in that household. Although she clearly admired and loved him, Delaney could not unlock all her father's mysteries while he lived, and writing about him from the perspective of her own elderly years helped her assess his influence on her life. Similarly, Fowler's story could not be told without the lens of his mother, whose bits of wisdom punctuate his memoir. She was not the same woman after her husband died, but she was subtly and warmly at the center of things, conveying the same powerful parental presence as Delaney's father did. Fowler's mother percolates through his life story, and looking back as an older man, he clearly recognized her influence on his own life choices. Family cultures, as much as Main Street and economics, shaped the small towns in which the boy Fowler and the girl Delaney lived.

Eric Fowler and Sheila Delaney share the experience of growing up in South Dakota and its small towns during the first half of the twentieth century. They do not know one another, but today both live in Albuquerque, New Mexico. Although I have not met either one in person, I share their roots. I grew up in Mitchell, six blocks away from the Corn Palace, some forty years after Sheila Delaney did. I even remember roller-skating on the big brick porch of her home, owned by a different family during my day in the neighborhood, and also running countless times through what was once the Delaney backyard to play "Jail Break" or to get to my best friend's house.

The railroad, so much a part of Delaney and Fowler's town life, registered on my consciousness only as a defunct depot (now restored) at the end of Main Street, although the town's businesses and movie theaters did remain significant to my own experience of small-town life. My father owned a Ford dealership on Main Street, and I shopped at the J. C. Penney store downtown, but neither business remains on Main Street. Mitchell never grew suburbs, but many places of business moved to the outskirts, into malls or industrial parks along the highways leading into town. Milbank never developed suburbs, either. Both towns remained stable as county-seat service centers and the dominant cities of distinct trade areas that contained a host of smaller towns and villages. In the second half of the twentieth century, a federal interstate highway on the edge of Mitchell, still with its Corn Palace, and a major state highway into Milbank, still boasting its mahogany granite, have taken the place of the railroad that fostered town development in the first half of the twentieth century. Agriculture endures as the economic base of these communities.

History finds few people such as Eric Fowler and Sheila Delaney who have the "willingness to rethink home."[38] Everyone has a story to tell, but the writing down of it can be difficult as well as rewarding. The best storytellers layer experiences, feelings, and thoughts, willfully and unconsciously using memory to sift and shape a life's chapters and plot. Most of us simply recite our life narratives over and over to ourselves.[39] Voices such as Sheila Delaney's and Eric Fowler's are necessary to sustain community and the history of unique, but always historically fleeting, places such as the eastern South Dakota cities of Mitchell and Milbank, two American small towns.

Notes

My heartfelt thanks go to Shelia Delaney and Eric Fowler, whose memoirs have taught me much about South Dakota. The rewarding interview discussions I had with each of them left me an admirer of their generosity, thoughtfulness, determination, and work ethics. I thank Nancy Tystad Koupal for inviting me to join this project and for comments she made that improved the quality of this introduction. Also, I thank Nancy and Patti Edman for considerable assistance and work on editing and annotating these manuscripts. Conversations and emails with Tom Isern, Gary Frost, and Mark Orsag clarified for me various aspects of the history presented here. I thank Alan B. Carr at the Los Alamos National Laboratory for providing me with a report on nuclear accidents. Kim Jarvis and Phil Weitl, my colleagues along with Mark Orsag at Doane College, provided welcome criticism and helpful suggestions on an early draft and frequent comforting discussions throughout the project.

1. Eric Fowler tells the basic story presented here in Chapter 2, "The Home," of his memoir. All information related to and quotations attributed to Fowler in this introduction are from his memoir, *Small-town Boy*, published in this volume or from information from telephone discussions. In preparation for this project, I interviewed him by telephone on 17, 18, and 27 March 2009.

2. Sheila Delaney relates this basic story in Chapter 2, "A House for All Seasons," of her memoir. All information related to and quotations attributed to Delaney in this introduction are from her memoir, *Small-town Girl*, published in this volume or from my telephone interview with her on 27 March 2009.

3. For Dakota examples, *see* Robert Amerson, *From the Hidewood* (Saint Paul: Minnesota Historical Society Press, 1996), and Aagot Raaen, *Grass of the Earth* (1950; reprint ed., Saint Paul: Minnesota Historical Society Press, 1994).

4. John E. Miller, "Small Towns: Image and Reality," in *A New South Dakota History*, ed. Harry F. Thompson (Sioux Falls, S.Dak.: Center for Western Studies, Augustana College, 2005), p. 182.

5. *See*, for example, Lawrence Svobida, *Farming the Dust Bowl: A First-Hand Account from Kansas* (1940; reprint ed., Lawrence: University Press of Kansas, 1986). Studies highlighting the agricultural 1930s are also numerous; for example, *see* Donald Worster, *Dust Bowl: The Southern Plains in the 1930s* (New York: Oxford University Press, 1979).

6. [Rex Myers], "Transportation and Tourism," in *New South Dakota History*, ed. Thompson, pp. 487–89.

7. Ibid.; Herbert S. Schell, *History of South Dakota*, 4th ed., rev. John E.

Miller (Pierre: South Dakota State Historical Society Press, 2004), pp. 158–65, 219–22.

8. On the establishment of railroad towns, *see* John C. Hudson, *Plains Country Towns* (Minneapolis: University of Minnesota Press, 1985), and on their continuing development, *see* James R. Shortridge, *Cities on the Plains: The Evolution of Urban Kansas* (Lawrence: University Press of Kansas, 2004).

9. Milbank was originally named Milbank Junction. In the fashion of post-Civil War naming practices, Union general Ulysses S. Grant provided the latter county's title, while a now obscure business investor and landowner in the area—Henry Caleb Davison—gave his name to the former. Doris Louise Black, *History of Grant County, South Dakota, 1861–1937* (Milbank, S.Dak.: Milbank Herald Advance, 1939), pp. 22, 76–77; Bob Karolevitz, *An Historic Sampler of Davison County* (Virginia Beach, Va.: Donning Co., 1993), pp. 18–19, 22–26; Schell, *History of South Dakota*, pp. 158–65, 219–22.

10. Geographer Walter Prescott Webb designated the arid-humid dividing line at the 98th meridian. Mitchell is on the 98th meridian, and Milbank is about seventy miles east of it. John Wesley Powell, in his 1878 *Report on the Lands of the Arid Region* to Congress, however, named the 100th meridian as the line between a "dry" and "wet" United States. Webb, *The Great Plains* (1931; reprint ed., Lincoln: University of Nebraska Press, 1981), pp. 17–18; and Donald Worster, *A River Running West: The Life of John Wesley Powell* (New York: Oxford University Press, 2001), pp. 354–56.

11. [Edward P. Hogan], "Physical Environment," in *New South Dakota History*, ed. Thompson, pp. 16–18.

12. Black, *History of Grant County*, pp. 94–95. For more on the American Indians in Grant County, *see* ibid., pp. 11–16, 33–37, 86.

13. Hogan, "Physical Environment," pp. 18–19; *Mitchell Re-Discovered: A Centennial History* (Mitchell, S.Dak.: Mitchell Centennial History Committee, 1981), p.1; [Herbert T. Hoover], "Native Peoples," in *New South Dakota History*, ed. Thompson, pp. 40–46.

14. Richard O. Davies, Joseph A. Amato, and David R. Pichaske, eds., *A Place Called Home: Writings on the Midwestern Small Town* (Saint Paul: Minnesota Historical Society Press, 2003), p. 85.

15. This and subsequent paragraphs summarizing the businesses and infrastructure of Mitchell and Milbank are based on the following books, unless otherwise noted: Black, *History of Grant County*; A. James Dowd, comp., *The History of Grant County: Its Romantic Past, Its Progressing Present, Its Possibilities for the Future* (Milbank, S.Dak.: By the Compiler, 1928); *100 Years in Grant County, South Dakota, 1878–1978* (Milbank, S.Dak.: Grant County His-

torical Society, 1979); Karolevitz, *Historic Sampler of Davison County*; *Mitchell Re-Discovered*; M. Lisle Reese, *South Dakota: A Guide to the State* (New York: Hastings House, 1952); Miller, "Small Towns," pp. 182–93; and [Gary D. Olson], "Cities and Towns," in *New South Dakota History*, ed. Thompson, pp. 157–81.

16. Dowd, *History of Grant County*, p. 58.

17. The 1920 through 1950 United States censuses reveal little racial diversity in either Davison or Grant counties. In 1920, for example, seven Chinese lived in Grant County and nineteen in Davison County, while there were none in either county in 1930 and 1940. Seventeen American Indians lived in Davison County in 1940, but none in 1900, 1920, or 1930; the 1910 census listed four in Davison County. Grant County had no Indians living within its borders from 1900 to 1940 and only three African Americans in 1930. Blacks, however, were Davison County's largest minority population: eighteen in 1910; fifteen in 1920; sixty-three in 1930; and eleven in 1940, and all but one or two lived within Mitchell's city limits.

The greatest diversity occurred in the foreign-born populations. The largest groups in Grant County in 1920 came from Germany, Sweden, Norway, the Netherlands, and Canada, making up 15.7 percent of Grant County's 10,880 people. There were twenty-two English-born, including Eric Fowler's parents. By 1940, Grant County's population had dipped to 10,552 people, with the foreign-born populations mentioned above each reduced by at least half.

German, Norwegian, Swedish, Canadian, and English were the five largest foreign-born groups in Davison County in 1920, with a total foreign-born population of 8.7 percent among the total of 14,139 people. By 1940, Davison County's population had risen to 15,832, and its top five foreign-born populations showed losses similar to Grant County's. U.S., Department of Commerce, Bureau of the Census, *Fourteenth Census of the United States Taken in the Year 1920*, vol. 2, *Population* (Washington, D.C.: Government Printing Office, 1922); *Fifteenth Census* (1930), vol. 3, pt. 2; *Sixteenth Census* (1940), vol. 2, pt. 6; *Seventeenth Census* (1950), vol. 2, pt. 41.

18. Schell, *History of South Dakota*, p. 282.

19. [Lynwood E. Oyos], "Farming Dependency and Depopulation," in *New South Dakota History*, ed. Thompson, p. 230.

20. Schell, *History of South Dakota*, pp. 277; Michael P. Malone and Richard Etulain, *The American West: A Twentieth-Century History* (Lincoln: University of Nebraska, 1989), pp. 18–19.

21. Schell, *History of South Dakota*, pp. 282–84, 290, 292.

22. Black, *History of Grant County*, p. 84n23.

23. Davies, Amato, and Pichaske, *Place Called Home*, p. 214.

24. The New Deal Agricultural Adjustment Administration purchased an estimated forty-two percent of the state's cattle in 1934; some of the animals were destroyed, while the meat of healthy animals was either canned or distributed fresh to relief recipients. The Public Works Administration funded road construction and other infrastructure projects, providing forty-five percent of project funds with the remainder coming from loans or local bonds. The Works Progress Administration spent over $35 million in the state on new construction and remodeling and on amenities such as swimming pools and playgrounds. Schell, *History of South Dakota*, pp. 289, 292–93; Karolevitz, *Historic Sampler of Davison County*, pp.137–39; *Mitchell Re-Discovered*, p. 38; *100 Years in Grant County*, pp. 117, 232–33.

25. Television sets did not become common in the area until the mid-1950s.

26. Robert Cohen, ed., *Dear Mrs. Roosevelt: Letters from Children of the Great Depression* (Chapel Hill: University of North Carolina Press, 2002), p. 6; Schell, *History of South Dakota*, p. 296.

27. In 1940, forty percent of United States undergraduates were women, but in 1950 that number had dropped to thirty-one percent. Only fourteen percent of all women and men aged 18–21 attended colleges in 1940. After postwar government programs for returning veterans helped to grow attendance, twenty-seven percent of the age group attended college in 1950. In Milbank, only 80 people in 1950 reported four or more years of college, while in Mitchell that number was 270 people. An additional 595 persons in Mitchell had one to three years of college. Peter G. Filene, *Him/Her/Self*, 3d ed. (Baltimore: Johns Hopkins University Press, 1998), p. 262; *Seventeenth Census* (1950), vol. 2, pt. 41.

28. In the 1920s, the "overwhelming majority of female professionals" were teachers or nurses, while typists, clerks, and salespersons made up the category of businesswomen. By 1940, although three in ten women worked across the nation, they worked in "factory, domestic, and clerical work," not in business and professional positions (Filene, *Him/Her/Self*, pp. 129, 161). In 1900, women earned only about fifty percent of what men earned. The federal 1963 Equal Pay Act guaranteed equal pay for "identical work," but not "equal pay for comparable worth," even though most jobs remained sex-segregated, making "identical" work a rare situation. As late as 1970, full-time workingwomen averaged only fifty-nine percent of the median wage of men's earnings (Ellen Carol DuBois and Lynn Dumenil, *Through Women's Eyes: An American History with Documents* [Boston: Bedford/St. Martin's, 2004], pp. 588–89, 658).

29. Richard O. Davies, *Main Street Blues: The Decline of Small-Town America* (Columbus: Ohio State University Press, 1998), p. 139.

30. Lewis Atherton, *Main Street on the Middle Border* (Bloomington: Indiana University Press, 1954), p. 336.

31. Granville Hicks, *Small Town* (New York: Macmillan Co., 1947), p. 12.

32. Arthur J. Vidich and Joseph Bensman, *Small Town in Mass Society: Class, Power and Religion in a Rural Community* (Princeton, N.J.: Princeton University Press, 1968), pp. 319–27. *See also* Atherton, *Main Street on the Middle Border*, pp. 217–42, and Davies, Amato, and Pichaske, *Place Called Home*, pp. 213–16.

33. Hicks, *Small Town*, p. 195.

34. Indeed, Mitchell's population had reached about four thousand by 1890, already well past "urban" by federal census standards, which called for a population of twenty-five hundred. Lower on the urban continuum, Milbank did not pass the mark until 1940, two years after Eric Fowler left town, with a population of 2,745. (South Dakota's state population was 652,740 in 1950, up about ten thousand from 1940, but down from the 1930 census of 692,849.) The two counties did develop different patterns within their borders. Grant County (684 square miles in 1950 — 15 persons per square mile) is about one-third larger than Davison County (432 square miles — 38.2 persons per square mile). Davison County in 1950 had about forty percent more total population than Grant County. Mitchell, however, was four times the size of Milbank. Grant County's population was less concentrated in Milbank than Davison's was in Mitchell; indeed, Davison County had only two other towns of note (Mount Vernon and Ethan), each with more population than all but one of the eight other towns of any size in Grant County in 1950 (Albee, Big Stone City, La Bolt, Marvin, Revillo, Stockholm, Strandburg, and Twin Brooks). *Seventeenth Census* (1950), vol. 2, pt. 41; Karolevitz, *Historic Sampler of Davison County*, p. 29.

35. James C. Malin, *The Grassland of North America: Prolegomena to Its History* (Gloucester, Mass.: Peter Smith, 1967), p. 321.

36. Miller, "Small Towns," pp. 187, 191. The state was close to twenty-five percent urban in 1940; nineteen percent in 1930; and sixteen percent in 1920. The 1950 census recorded 248 towns with less than one thousand people. *Seventeenth Census* (1950), vol. 2, pt. 41.

37. Davies, Amato, and Pichaske, *Place Called Home*, p. 10.

38. Joseph A. Amato, *Rethinking Home: A Case for Writing Local History* (Berkeley: University of California Press, 2002), p. 6.

39. For how people remember, *see* Robert Butler, "The Life Review," *Psychiatry* 26 (1963): 65–76; Richard N. Coe, *When the Grass Was Taller: Autobiography and the Experience of Childhood* (New Haven, Conn.: Yale University Press, 1984); and Mary Hufford, Marjorie Hunt, and Steven Zeitlin, *The Grand Generation: Memory, Mastery, Legacy* (Washington, D.C.: Smithsonian Institution, 1987).

Small-town Boy

"He Who Lives Longest Will See Most and Know Least"

ERIC B. FOWLER

Contents

Preface

*T*here is an old tale, probably not true, of Stanley's search for Livingstone. Stanley knew that he was on Livingstone's trail because he (Stanley) had found an abandoned typewriter, and he knew the typewriter had been abandoned by Livingstone because the "I" was missing.[1] As *I* attempt to put these words together, *I* have a visceral feeling that *I* will be accused of the same conceit, for much of what follows will be in the first-person singular. But in truth, these *are* the years from 1914 as *I* lived them and as *I* saw them. In this humble attempt to reconstruct my life, for the benefit of my children and grandchildren, people, places, and events have been combined in various ways. I do not attempt chronology *in toto*. Rather, subjects are presented that characterized the period and determined the shape of life and living. Within each subject, I have attempted a chronology of events, and some cross-reference is inevitable between chapters, but each subject is intended to stand alone.

The Fowler family began in England, where their station was among the masses; they were craftsmen or laborers. My mother, a Pickersgill, was from the same class, and she never forgot that "station" should be remembered—always. There are few families that know essentially nothing about their heritage; the Fowler family is one of those. I learned what little I know around 1932. As the depression deepened, certain professors at Harvard University sought to maintain some income by doing genealogical research. They compiled the genealogy associated with family names, printed the part that related to family origin, and mailed the information to prospects. The initial work was underwritten by Harvard; for ten dollars, they would continue research on your specific branch of the family. But that was one month's living; we did not subscribe.

According to the prospectus, the originator of the Fowler line was a hunter who supplied the king's camp with edible birds at the time of the Norman invasion in 1066. Because he killed birds, or fowl, he was a fowler. One night while returning to camp from a spell at the local pub, the fowler detected the enemy preparing to attack the camp.

He rushed to sound the alarm and saved the day—or the night—for which he was knighted as Sir Richard, the Fowler. The ironical follow up is that later he was caught stealing the king's horses and was hung as a thief. From that auspicious beginning arose the Fowler family, whose coat of arms reads *Vigilate et Orate*—"see and tell." Because the story came from Harvard researchers does not mean that one should accept it, but it is interesting to contemplate. With her Irish wit, my mother would say, "Don't believe all you hear and only half of what you see."

From the eleventh century to the eighteenth is quite a distance to fly, but we Fowlers did just that. My family has traced birth and marriage certificates back to William Fowler, who had a son named John, my grandfather. John was a gardener for the greater part of his life; his only son William, my father, born in 1873, was a railroad man. In each traced generation, the Fowlers had only a single male offspring. My father married Jane ("Jennie") Pickersgill, about whose family little is known; Jane was born in 1880, also in England. At separate times, William and Jennie immigrated to North America in the early 1900s, coming at last to South Dakota, where I was born in 1914. So, the Fowlers and Pickersgills did not arrive on the Mayflower; they did not shape the grand course of history. They were poor laborers or craftsmen. Exempting Sir Richard, they were from hardy stock that knew how to survive. This story chronicles their survival in the United States.*

*I am grateful for the efforts of historian and editor Molly Rozum and South Dakota State Historical Society Press editor Patti Edman in bringing this document to its present form. I offer special thanks to my daughter Mary Fowler Worman, who first asked that I write a memoir for the children and later that I share it with a wider public.

hen discussing those close and dear to us, we are too often influenced by the good and too often neglect what is not good. But I can honestly say that I cannot recall any conflict between Father and Mother. They had been married only sixteen years when Dad was killed; I remember them only as a loving couple. I do not remember fights, not even cross words. Differences must have been discussed in the absence of the children.

I do recall that Mom would walk the floor on those occasions when Dad was called out by the call boy to help repair bridges, lay track, or remove railroad cars from ditches or rivers.[2] Hours later—sometimes days—Dad would rap at the back door and come in completely exhausted, wet to the skin or half frozen. His "Hello, Jane" was as casual as though he had just taken a stroll in the garden. Mother had warm "long johns" and clean clothes waiting and always a steaming cup of tea—"black as your hat and twice as strong." I remember one occasion when the return was sealed with a long—and probably passionate—kiss. There were no words.

My father was born in 1873 in the Bradford area of England. His father was a gardener, and his mother was in poor health. Father was the only son in a family of four children. The daughters were Mary (called Polly), Annis, and Elizabeth (called Liz or Lizzy). The family was orphaned at an early age. Dad and Aunt Elizabeth were placed in an orphanage. Dad went to work at about the age of twelve in the Sloan and Davidson Foundry, which still does business near Bradford. Dad received schooling through the third grade in the English system. Slightly later, Dad and Aunt Elizabeth moved to a police academy, where Elizabeth helped with the household chores and Dad acted as janitor after his day at the foundry. Conditions were not quite those of Dickens's *Oliver Twist*, but they were not much better.[3]

Dad became associated with the Oxford Place Chapel, where he eventually became a "side man"—a combination of deacon's assistant, usher, and so on. He was a Bible scholar, and for that and attendance, the chapel presented him with a Bible that I now own. He probably met Mother there, for she also passed on to me a hymn book that she had received from the chapel, also for attendance. When Dad was in his early to mid-twenties, a demand for settlers in central Canada led him to emigrate. With a few savings and help from the chapel, Dad set out for Moose Jaw, Canada. The land-development scheme involved a Swedish ship line, and Dad worked for partial passage as fireman, cook, deck swabber, and whatever else was necessary. He landed near Montreal, Canada, and made his way to Moose Jaw. When he presented himself to claim his land, he learned that the entire scheme was a fraud. He went to work in the woods as a lumberjack. While on that job, he suffered a series of boils that he treated by lancing them with a sharp knife and packing them with turpentine.[4]

Although Dad loved plants and the outdoors, he was a foundryman and, after about a year in the Canadian West, worked his way south into the United States, coming to rest in Grant County near Milbank, South Dakota. There he worked as a laborer on several farms, the primary one being Will Ackerman's tree claim. The Ackerman family became an important part of our lives. Eventually, they "adopted" Mother and Dad, so to speak, and came to consider all of us a part of their family.[5] Father saved his money for five or six years and sent it to England about 1906 for Mother's passage to the United States. She, however, had saved her own and would not use money from a man to whom she was not yet married. But when Dad said "come," mother came. They met in Minneapolis, Minnesota, on 1 April. Mother would not be married on All Fool's Day, so they were married on April second at Westminster Church, then located where Donaldson's department store later came to stand. Mother returned Dad's money, and they went out to the frontier of eastern South Dakota on the Milwaukee Road.[6] That was the railroad on which Dad was later to work and on which he would be killed.

Times were not good. There were droughts, grasshoppers, and wheat rust—and when wheat rust came, all was lost. But there was carpentry work and cattle. The latter were bad news for Dad, who was gored by a bull and was out of work for almost a year. He had always been bothered by a "hammer toe," the little one on his right foot bent as if a claw. As the bones mended from his goring and the gashes began to heal, the local doctor became interested in the toe, and one day, without the benefit of anesthesia, the toe was removed. Dad's slight limp may have been a gift from the bull, the loss of his toe, or an unnoticed injury in the foundry when he single-handedly removed a large iron beam that had fallen on two other workers. Dad never talked about it and never complained. I saw him bedridden only once, during the influenza epidemic of 1918–1919.[7]

After recovery, Dad found a job on the Milwaukee Road. On occasion, Dad would be called out at night to fire the boiler of some locomotive that had been in the roundhouse for repairs. Once he took me with him. We lived on First Street in Milbank at the time, and it was a short walk to the roundhouse. I must have been quite young, for Dad carried me home in the small hours of the morning. The firing of the boiler and the engineer's cab left a lasting impression on me, and I have never lost my fascination for steam. It was the power of the day, and no sound can compare with the whisper of steam as it goes about its business. Valves and levers were everywhere and are still there when I close my eyes and think on it. It seemed to take hours to get up a head of steam, and it seemed that the *scrape-swoosh, scrape-swoosh* of the shovel would never stop, but Dad's bare torso and perspiration eventually prevailed, and before dawn the gauge showed ample pressure. Then all the waiting became worthwhile. Dad climbed into the engineer's seat, put me in his lap, blew out the cylinders, released the brake, adjusted the inlet valve for reverse, and placed my hand with his on the throttle. A slight tug, a gentle whisper of steam, and that monster backed out of the house. The brake was set, and Dad climbed down, threw the switch, and *we* backed the locomotive onto a siding and parked her. At home, mother was waiting with the cup of hot tea and an anxious look that disappeared when I said, "I drove it."

Father loved his home, his new land, and his three children, but that love was not displayed with emotional outbursts; rather, he displayed his love by showing and doing. For me, my father built a farm wagon that was convertible from stake, to lumber, to dump. It was built to scale, and the stake set had a "bang board" and an adjustable reach. For my sister Dorathy, Dad built a dollhouse from a discarded battery box. It was built in our kitchen and was the occasion of a scowl on Dad's part. I knew that Dad had a glass cutter among his tools, and for some reason I wanted it. Dad had said "no," but as he worked, I rummaged in his tool box and came forward with the cutter. I held it up for him to see. Neither of us spoke, but Dad scowled and that was enough—the black-black hair, the bushy black eyebrows, the swarthy complexion, and the scowl. The cutter was replaced, and I left Dad to his work on the dollhouse.

For my sister Annis, Dad made doll clothes. He was fiercely independent and could back that up with his versatility. He could sew as well as, and perhaps better than, Mother. In the short time that I knew Dad, I never knew him to ask for help nor to hire a job done. "Menial" was not a word in his vocabulary. He dug the privy pit when necessary and moved the outhouse over it. He would cook, wash, and iron. When on the job, he would help to rebuild a trestle or drive a locomotive. Mother used to say, "Some day his independence will kill him." Perhaps it did.

Mother was quite different from father. She was not a world-beater as a cook (typically English), although her coffee bread and fruit cake were specialties that none could hold a candle to. Neither was she a seamstress, and someone else usually helped or produced garments. Mother had worked in the woolen mills, and she knew wool. She could "feel" a piece of wool and tell where it came from—the origin of the wool—if it were English. She delighted in looking at and feeling the bolts of cloth in the general store. Mother could knit and tat and crochet and produce pieces that won county fair prizes.

Except for shoes and overalls for me, we did not own much that was "store bought." And shoes lasted because Dad repaired them, uppers, soles, and heels. Mother would knit the mittens, the scarves, and the socks we wore. At the time of World War I, she was in great demand by the ladies' organizations that prepared boxes "for the boys." The product of her needles was letter perfect, and she could carry on a conversation and knit and knit and never look at what she was doing. Many cold winter nights, I held the skeins as Mother rolled the balls. The needles would fly and a pair of socks would be born before my eyes.

Mother was born in the Leeds, England, area in 1880. Her name was Jane Pickersgill, and she was probably one of the younger of the eight children of Miles Pickersgill. Her mother was not well, and so Jane had to fare for herself. She attended school through the third grade of the English system and then worked in a candy factory— probably not for long because she started work in the woolen mills at about twelve years of age. She worked in the mills until she came to the United States at the age of twenty-seven. In later years, she was bothered by a neck and shoulder problem that she attributed to the carrying of bolts of cloth, which she always carried on the left shoulder.

She was a pretty woman, quite small, weighing less than one hundred pounds when she was married. She had sky blue eyes and a massive head of hair; she could sit on the two braids that fell to the back of her knees when she stood. Until Dad's death, Mother was laughing, happy, with a wit that was faster than a jackrabbit. Her lack of education did not seem to be a handicap in *her* world. She could "sum" much faster and more correctly than we children. She had been born English. Somewhere in the background of the family, however, there were Irish genes. In the woolen mills, she had worked with many Scotch girls. As a result, Mother's accent was a peculiar mixture of Yorkshire and Scotch. Her Scotch-Irish-English accent was such that it was difficult to determine whether her grammar were correct or not.

After Dad's death, Mother changed. I saw the change, and my sisters must have seen it also, but we never discussed it. The "talk it out syndrome" had not yet become popular. Each of us seemed to be blest with the same instinct to be independent, and there was no advantage in discussing that which only added confusion to an already confused state. We worked out our own problems, right or wrong. For a period of time, Mother might discuss England, aunts, uncles, the happy times, and the hard times with us, but she gradually withdrew into herself and eventually would ignore questions about Dad and her homeland.

I slept on a couch, or daybed, in the living room next to the hard-coal heater. The two beds were reserved for Annis and Dorathy and for Mother. I awoke one night—probably early fall because the heater had been started—to hear Mother talking at the back door. She soon came back through the living room, and I heard her climb into bed. When I asked about her caller in the night, she hesitated and then looking at me—a look I had never seen before—told me that she had heard Dad's rap and had gone to the door. Dad was standing there and had said, "Don't worry, Jane, everything will be all right," and had then disappeared. Mother had a certain amount of Irish super-stition—or was it the family's guardian angel? You choose; I have never been able to. Mother was brave, but she cried often in private and softly at night. Although I heard her and I am sure Dorathy and Annis must have also, we said nothing; it would have been too embarrassing for Mother.

The summer after Dad's death, Mother had all her teeth removed in two sittings. I recall Mother making supper for us over the old three-burner coal-oil stove located in the attached shed. Supper, at least in part, was fried potatoes. She wiped the tears from her cheeks and the blood from her lips and said nothing. Mother was fitted with false teeth, which she put in immediately and never removed—at least, I never saw them removed. Mother was buried wearing the same set of teeth—worn thin but still "active" after thirty-seven years.

A year after her teeth were removed, Mother was in the hospital in Webster, South Dakota. She had been ill for some time, and Dr. Charles Flett[8] was sure that she had "stomach trouble—dyspepsia" or intestinal inflammation caused by all her worries. The case wors-ened, and Mother told the doctor that she was going to Webster. He told her that they would not admit her, and she said that she would sit on their front steps until they did admit her. Dr. Flett made the telephone call; Mother went to Webster. Surgery revealed a large tumor of solid tissue, called a "meat tumor." The doctor squeezed it into a two-quart Mason jar and sent it to Dr. Flett so that he could *see* what the problem had been.

During Mother's absence, I went to the Ackerman farm; Dorathy went to neighbor Gus Swanson's; and Annis went to a girl's camp. Mother gave Annis ten dollars, which she lost. She was supposed to use it to care for us when she returned from camp. Today, we take ten dollars to the "five and dime," but at that time it was a month's cur-rency for a family of four. One sad regret that I remember from that time was a horse-and-buggy trip to town. Grant Thomas, Grandma Ackerman's grandson, drove, and we went past Gus Swanson's house.

Dorathy was out in the yard, but we did not stop. Dorathy ran after us down Diggs Avenue and up First Street. All I said when she caught up with us was "hello." And my little sister stood there watching us as we drove back to the farm. Dorathy was alone; Annis and I were not. Why did I not say more or do something? I do not know. I have often cogitated on the thoughtlessness and selfishness of the young.

Unlike her former self, Mother now began to complain, to be bitter and even sarcastic on occasion. She did not punish us physically, but that would have been preferred to the punishment of her tongue. But as young as I was, I tried to understand in my own way. Here was a beautiful and still-young woman who had known little other than work. Fifteen years had been spent in the woolen mills; she had given those years to her mother's comfort. She had seen Dad seriously injured in a farm accident and for one year had nursed him back to health. She had watched as he struggled to find work because there was a depression, union organization, and a strike. And just as a brighter day was on the horizon, she had seen him die from a railroad accident. The need for teeth, the need for surgery, and even the loss of ten dollars were all too much. But she continued to be brave, continued to work at what she could, and continued to raise her family.

What Mother could do was wash and iron and scrub, and those she did for the wonderful people the good Lord sent her way. There were the Rawsons and the Hunters, the Germains, the Ackermans, and now and then others. We were humans in need, and I sincerely believe that as often as not "work was made"—it was productive work, but in truth these kind people did not *require* outside help.

But with all the help and with the meager pennies that we children earned, life was becoming more difficult. It was years later that I heard about another visit of our guardian angel. Eliza Rawson had stopped to see her husband, J. Charles Rawson, whom she called "Papa," at his coal-shed office, where he oversaw his coal and wood delivery business. She was pulling her own wagon filled with groceries. She had had a sudden feeling that Mother was in trouble, she told him, and she had loaded the wagon from her wonderful pantry and was on her way to see "Jennie." Papa sent her on her way with, "You'd better hurry." When she arrived at our house, she found Mother alone and crying. We had no food and no money. Mother had reached the end of her rope—even the knot at the end was gone.

Life did improve for Mother, but it was never easy. Annis went into teaching in 1927—fresh out of high school with a Normal Certificate.[9] As I remember, she was paid forty dollars a month; she paid her own board and room and transportation and helped the family. Mother was more relaxed now, and on occasion we all laughed. But Mother would be released from trials only by death. She worked less as we worked more, but she continued to wash and iron and scrub for others. I have vivid recollections of the times I came home from work and found her standing at the front door with a broom in her hand. She had swept, or was about to sweep, the slivered, wooden front porch and had stopped to gaze into the western sunset. Even at a distance, I could see that the gaze was fixed on her beloved Will and a kinder life somewhere out there.

A few years later, Annis was married, Dorathy was working as a secretary in Minneapolis, and I was in school at Kansas State.[10] An occasional letter mentioned that Mother had fallen, or that she had bumped into the door at Shad's Bakery, or that she had dizzy spells and had been up to see Dr. John W. Pay—an osteopath and surgeon. I discovered that she had high blood pressure on one occasion when I was home and found her taking nitroglycerine pills. She was probably having minor strokes and would sometimes say about my graduation from college, "You'd better hurry." Bless her, she had no background to realize that graduation could not be hurried.

The point came when she could no longer tolerate winters alone in Milbank and spent them with Dorathy in Minneapolis. On one such occasion, Mother suffered a paralyzing stroke; her left arm and leg became useless and her speech impaired. Dorathy was her night nurse, and church friends of Dorathy's acted as day nurses. Her speech improved, and she was encouraged to try a walker. Then her hip broke, and she was bedridden for five years. Her heart was brave but worn out from a life of struggle. Two months before her eighty-fifth birthday, she was returned to the hospital; her pericardial sac was filling with fluid. She died there while in a coma.

Mother was laid to rest in Milbank beside her Will. She had seen much and suffered much, but the suffering was over, and Dad no longer had to rap at the back door. She used to say that she would live a long life because Saint Peter did not want her and the devil would not have her. She lived a long life because she was stubborn, independent, and would not give up. Her Irish wit helped see her through her troubles. She had an expression for most occasions, and of her own long life, she might have said, "He who lives longest will see most and know least."

I had left home when I was twenty-one and was able to keep *my* body and soul together but could offer little help to mother. I had rebuilt her house, but that was little comfort in view of her other needs. I had spent twelve years getting an education; all of that time in need of money, clothes, and health care, but that was little consolation to mother, who needed help as much as I did. My visits home were too few and too far between and were dictated by finances. When at long last I was able to help, it was too late for Mother—but she had always encouraged us to get an education because that was something that no one could take from us. I hope she understood.

lose your eyes—no, leave them open so that you can better see my childhood home. Now select four rooms—three average size and a smaller one: a bedroom, a living room, a kitchen, and a small pantry. Under the house is a hole, perhaps ten-by-twelve and six feet deep, scooped out of the earth over which the house is placed. Add eight windows, two to each room, and a front door into the living room as well as a back door into a small shed that adjoins the kitchen. Now, take everything out of the rooms—I mean everything, including plumbing.

Place two beds in the bedroom. One bed is brass bound with the broken stringers between the bottom posts. The other bed is made from iron rod joined where necessary by cast-iron roses, all painted ivory. Place a dresser under the window between the beds at the head; place another dresser with mirror at the foot of the brass-bound bed. At the foot of the iron bed is a box built onto the wall. That is the clothes closet, which is closed with a flowered curtain hung on a string. A rag rug on the floor completes the bedroom. Dad and Mother slept in one bed, and Annis and Dorathy in the other until after Dad's death. My room was a corner of the living room.

In the living room, south of the bedroom, place a nickel-plated hard-coal heater against the north wall. The heater must have a hopper-feeder and a swivel top complete with a brass-harp finial. It must stand on nickel-plated legs, have nickel-plated removable side aprons and a nickel-plated ash door, behind which is the ash pan. The business section of the heater must be divided so as to have a larger upper belly and a smaller lower access. There will be four doors above and four doors below, and each will have many isinglass (mica) windows. All of the nickel plate is decorated with scrolls, and scrolls, and scrolls.

The hopper allows Pennsylvania nut anthracite to feed onto the bed of burning coal in the belly. The lower part has a shaker grate and a fire pot that is replete with many small Gothic windows at the bottom. The windows are access for the poker; the shaker grate permits the forced removal of ashes into the ash pan. Connect a stovepipe at the back and insert the upper elbow into the wall thimble, which gives access to the brick-lined flue. Make sure that the stovepipe has a damper; place a pan of water on the small shelf at the back to provide humidity; the house is ready for winter. Start the heater as late in the season as possible because, once started, the fire will not be allowed to go out until spring. Fill the hopper once or twice a day as required and take out the ashes on a similar schedule.

The heater is the most important piece of furniture in the room. On winter nights when the wind is blowing thirty to forty miles per hour and snow is drifting through unplugged cracks, sit in close and do school work, or make toys, or watch the fire. We had gotten electricity when I was about four or five years old, but on occasions when Mother would sit in her rocking chair and gaze into nothingness, we would turn out the lights and watch the fire behind the isinglass windows. Then after setting everything to rights, we would undress behind the heater and go to bed—run would be more nearly correct.

My iron-frame daybed sat beside the heater, and I would watch the few visible red coals and the many small blue flames from the hot coals (due to burning gas). I would think on Sunday's sermon about hell fire and brimstone, and I thought I knew what hell was like. That heater was a dear and comforting friend until morning when it was my job to shake and poke and run to the barn for another bucket of coal; then it was a hungry monster.

One year, Grandma Ackerman had spent the winter with relatives on the West Coast. Mother had a lifetime pass on the railroad, and in the spring, perhaps April, she left us in Annis's care and went west to bring Grandma home. Annis and Dorathy became ill; for some reason, I did not. When they could not get out of bed, I called Dr. Flett. When he came through the front door, he immediately demanded to know where the coal gas was coming from. The source had to be that hard-coal heater; I had not smelled the gas.

The house was opened, the fire was put out with water, and I climbed onto the roof with a rope that had a handleless hammer head tied on one end. By repeatedly dropping the hammer head down the chimney, I broke the plug loose. A bird had built a nest in the chimney, and the accumulation of loose mortar and fly ash had resulted in a plug. That was a close call, and when Mother heard of it upon her return, she had a fit. She would never leave us again. But the same would have happened whether she had been there or not.

But I must complete the room furnishings. Place a Congoleum rug (a painted floor cloth that predated linoleum) on the floor—before the heater is set up of course. It will not cover all the floor. In the corner to the right of the heater, place the daybed. You must make up the daybed every morning. Against the wall south of the door that leads from the living room to the kitchen, place an oak china closet. The cabinet drawers will contain Mother's linen tablecloths from England, tea towels, and a few silver-plated knives, forks, and spoons. Behind the upper glass doors will be two ceramic Kewpie dolls, male and female, and a huge ceramic sugar or cracker bowl with cover, decorated with real gold paint. That was a present to Grandma Ackerman and her husband that Grandma returned to Mother after Will Ackerman's death. Three china tea cups and saucers with red dragon decorations can also be found in the cabinet. The cups were a gift to Mother from one of her uncles, who brought them back from the Boer War in South Africa. There were other odd pieces—a beautiful glass cookie plate with iridescent purple surfaces, a cut-glass saltcellar, and a creamer and sugar set. Mother served tea with those when the minister called.

Place a large oak table in the center of the room; it has four turned legs, one of which I will later convert into a mallet. Place a rag rug on the floor and Mother and Dad's rockers wherever there is room. A small table will stand in one corner. The walls will be bare except for a tall picture of a little girl standing in a field of flowers, called *Spring*, and a picture of a robin, called *Robin*. A cardboard plaque on the wall will have a red-plush surface with white lettering that states, "Christ is the head of this house, the unseen Host at every meal, the Silent Listener to every conversation." There will be few books except for the Bible and some newspapers and magazines, which were from Mother's good friend Helen McGiven, who moved from the South after the Civil War. The magazines contained paper-doll cutouts for Annis and Dorathy. Before Dad was killed, he purchased a *Book of Knowledge* and a volume of World War I pictures.[11] One striking image was that of a shell burst and a photographer with a raised arm. The caption read, "Photographer and the shell burst that killed him." Another photographer had taken the picture. Step back—you now have the room in which I grew up and where I made many toys and later read many library books. It was also the room in which my father's casket stood on the day of his funeral.

The kitchen and pantry were made over from a one-room chicken coop and attached to the other two rooms. The roof sloped for drainage and the floor sloped, too, but not as much. The east wall was less than six feet high. There was little furniture in the room—a table with four chairs and a cook stove. Beside the stove was a trap door in the floor that gave access to the dugout below, and in back of the stove was the woodbox.

The stove was a marvel of ingenuity; I have never seen another like it. It had no legs but stood on a wooden box that had been constructed of two-by-twelve-inch planks. There was no back, but there was an oven with a thermometer (which did not work) in the door. A cast-iron cistern was on the right side, and a feeder door on the left. The cistern provided warm water when there was a fire in the fire box. There was a feeder door at the front and an ash door that closed over the ash pan. A clean-out below the oven door permitted the removal of soot with a wire-handled scraper, and there was a damper in the stovepipe. The latter entered the flue by means of an elbow and a thimble. There were four lids on the top; we charbroiled our toast on them. The collected soot would often catch fire, and we would watch the red flameless mass creep slowly through the damper. Wet cloths were placed on the stovepipe, and the fire would be allowed to burn out. We used both wood and coal depending on the need for heat in the house. The coal was often lump Montana Roundup.

The chairs were old spindle back, and the table was older. I made a drop-leaf table for Mother, but the legs were not well designed and it was shaky. It could only stand in one place because I made two of the legs shorter to accommodate the slope in the floor. We replaced it years later with a store-bought table and four chairs. A calendar hung behind the heavy homemade door. It showed phases of the moon, morning and evening stars, weather, and the best fishing days; the weather forecast was seldom correct. A coat rack also adorned the wall behind the door. Behind that door, I heard John Lewis, who owned an icehouse and delivery service, tell Mother about the war in Europe. Mother replied that the Germans would not last long with the English in the war. But they did. America would be involved and Mother would lose two brothers before the war was over.

Our meals came from that kitchen for many years. Mother canned vegetables and meat and baked bread there and ironed clothes on the kitchen table. The irons were boat-shaped pieces of cast-iron polished smooth on the bottom; the wooden handle was detachable. Mother heated them on the hot stove lids until her wetted finger sizzled when applied to the bottom surface. She clamped on the handle and pressed the clothes until the iron cooled, when it would be exchanged for another heated block. They were called sadirons because, Mother said, no one could be happy while ironing.[12]

After the house was electrified with plug and tube wiring, the feeder to the kitchen light came from the living room. Two wires woven together penetrated the wall, ran along the ceiling, and terminated in a ceramic disconnect. The single bulb socket hung on braided cord fitted with a pull-chain switch. We children were short and Mother was short; we had no problem with the hanging fixture. But when Mrs. Olson took care of us at the time of Dad's death, there were problems. She was tall and continually bumped into the light. She hung a strip of red cloth on the chain to warn her. There were no wall outlets; we had no use for them.

Eventually, we did own two electrical appliances: an iron made by General Electric with the model name Oak Leaf. It had an oak-leaf pattern stamped on the specification plate. Dad had purchased the iron just before his death. Later, Dorathy and I bought a toaster for Mother on the occasion of her birthday. I do not recall how old we were, but both of us were doing odd jobs and had saved a few pennies that did not go into Mother's apron pocket. We window-shopped at Bleser's drugstore downtown, and at long last, we told Mr. Bleser that we wanted to buy a present and that the nickel-plated electric toaster was tops. How much was it? Well, how much did we have? I do not recall the amount now, but it was probably less than a dollar. Surprise! that was exactly what it cost. Mother had a toaster, and no longer did we create charcoal on the stove lid. I am sure Mr. Bleser supplied the present; we may have paid a few percent of the cost.

Mother was using the toaster years later when I left home; it never required repairs.

Dorathy and I "bought" Mother another birthday present one year. She had an old vase that was cracked and crazed, and we thought it should be replaced. Dorathy and I went to see Lura Rodgers and her sister at their store downtown. They were craftsmen and artists who made and painted pottery, pictures, and knickknacks. Dorathy and I had spied a dark-ivory ceramic vase that we thought Mother would like. It was straight-sided with a bulge at the bottom and covered with blue-and-red beads and flowers. It must be expensive, we mused. Well, how much did we have, the sisters wondered. Whatever we had must have been a pittance, but . . . "That was just what it cost," they said. How kind those people were; how kind everyone was! We were not made to feel embarrassed; we purchased and paid for what we had selected.

The small pantry was north of the kitchen. It contained a kitchen cupboard for dishes and our tableware. The spoons had been plated, but the brass underplate was exposed, and when those foods containing vinegar were served, I could taste the copper or zinc acetates. Those were my first chemistry lessons. One drawer contained recipes that Mother never used and a copy of Mary M. Crawford and Thurston S. Welton's *Before the Doctor Comes*. What a world of information that book held! It included recipes for bread poultice and how to prepare the kitchen table for home delivery. Our supply of medicine was ensconced on one shelf—boric acid powder, liniment, turpentine, nerve tonic (I believe it was Dr. Miles's), Vaseline, and a special jar of lard for burns. The box of Arm and Hammer soda was kept with the medicines. There was also a small bottle of tincture of iodine.[13]

Another piece of furniture in the pantry was the lower part of a different type of kitchen cabinet. It had pull-down flour and sugar bins and two drawers. The top served as work space where anything relative to cooking was done. Also on the top was a pail of drinking water and a pail of cistern water; both froze in the winter, and the respective dippers were used to break the ice. There was no heat in the pantry. A slop pail or swill bucket, a household necessity, also resided in the pantry. It received liquid discard—including ours at night—and was emptied in the alley or poured into the privy pit each morning and night. Emptying the bucket was an assigned chore, and because girls did not do such work, the job fell to me, but Dorathy, Annis, and Mother did help.

Eventually, my workbench replaced the original kitchen cabinet in the pantry. The workbench was an important part of my life. I built it in manual training in school after receiving Mother's reluctant blessing. I believe the cost for lumber was about five dollars. The materials consisted of West Coast fir-plank two-by-sixes and two-by-fours with some white pine. Only bolts and screws were used as fasteners. The old flour-bin half-cabinet was removed from the pantry, and the bench took its place. The vise, a gift from H. C. Gilbert, my algebra teacher and Boy Scout master, was broken and repaired with strap iron. It served for many years. Mother used the bench top for food preparation.

The bench finally ended up in the dirt cellar, where it was the center of my entry into the business world. I could now make things for sale! I did make one sale—a pair of gessoed candlesticks painted green and brushed with gold paint and sold to Mr. Rawson for one dollar. I entered and left the field of business within a short time. I was no salesman, but I conducted many experiments and made many things on that bench, including horn bookends and a small clock of black walnut. After the bench was moved to the cellar, I spent many hours working in the dugout under the house. The five-dollar investment was repaid many times in pleasant hours.

The third piece of furniture in the pantry was the washstand on which stood a granite wash bowl (the ceramic wash bowl and water pitcher were kept in the bedroom along with the ceramic bedpan). A soap dish contained the lye soap, and a towel hung on a rack above the washstand. You will have lived in this home but a few days before realizing that you need a copper boiler—a wash boiler, that is—with lid; a galvanized tub; and a scrub board. Beware of the lye soap; it is a skinner. If you have the five dollars you may purchase a washing machine. The "peggy," or stirring mechanism, will be operated by a lever and a rack and pinion, and you may be fortunate to have a wringer—hand-cranked of course.

If you have been successful in following this re-creation, you now have a visual picture of our house. But it was more than a house, it was our home, where we laughed and cried and played. Annis, Dorathy, and I cleared the table and washed the dishes, the latter on the stove or in the pantry as the temperature dictated. I recall one time that we were clearing the table and Annis was passing things from the kitchen to me in the pantry. For some reason, she chose to toss a loaf of bread, Mother's bread, to me, and for some reason, I chose to stand aside. Now Mother's bread was solid with a hard crust, and the loaf hit the pantry window and sailed on into Bill Lewis's yard. Annis cried, but I quickly recovered and as quickly was outside to recover the bread. It was fully brushed by the time I was back in the house, where the loaf was put away for the next meal. Mother called her bread "Home Rulers for Old Ireland," and if you remember your history of the first Irish Revolution, you will understand what she meant.[14] I always saved bits and pieces, and from a bit of broken glass, I cut a square and had it tacked and puttied into place in jig time. I do not know if Mother ever knew of our horsing around.

To reconstruct further, now go out into the yard to build a privy — a three-holer (two big and one small) — and place it over the privy pit. Save a Sears, Roebuck or Montgomery Ward catalog.[15] You will need it. You can discard the remaining slick pages in the spring; they are useless. You will also have to dig a well near the back door and cover it with a plank to hold the pump. Also dig a cistern at one corner of the house to receive the runoff from the eaves troughs around the roof. The cistern must also have a cover and a pump. Add a wooden sidewalk from the house to the barn and privy. Provide garden space, and you are ready to move in.

The well might go dry — and it did; there might be no rain and no cistern water — both happened. We carried drinking water from Ed Johnson's sweet-water well, a well complete with rope, pulley, and bucket.[16] We also hauled water from the roundhouse, where the boiler blower fed into a barrel against the outside wall. We carried or pulled the filled buckets in the wagon or on the sled in winter, using the soft water for washing clothes, dishes, and ourselves. We took one bath a week in a wash tub in front of the kitchen stove. Wet shoes might be drying on the oven door — and smelling — but the hot water from the roundhouse did not smell as cistern water did. In winter,

Mother would have brought in the frozen long johns from the clothes line. And what a wonderful smell as the long johns thawed and dried in front of the hard-coal heater. We would dress and be clean, savoring the fresh smell of the out-of-doors.

Outside, father had built a play yard for his three children—a set of swings (one solid and one a car tire), a roly-poly horse, and a tee-ter-totter. All were constructed of pipe, chains, and heavy timbers, long before anyone thought to capitalize on such sets. Many years later, I converted the pipe from the swing sets into standards for a clothesline for my mother.

I rebuilt Mother's home before I left Milbank. I replaced the siding, the window trim, and the roof, removing the wood shingles in favor of rolled roofing. The house was completely rewired with receptacles and new fixtures, and the walls were papered and painted. The remodeled pantry featured built-in cupboards and a work surface with a sink. The sink drained through a one-and-one-half-inch line into a fifteen-foot bore hole in the garden. The hidden cesspool never filled to the best of my knowledge.

I plumbed the house for water, installed a pressure system, and redug the well. I could stand in the well but could not lean over, so the blue-clay bottom was chewed out with a homemade foot shovel. I almost smothered in that well, but Annis, Dorathy, and my guardian angel were watching. I dug through two feet of blue clay. It required two weeks, but I finally found sand, and Mother had water. I demolished the old shed and built a room, replacing the wooden steps and sidewalk with brick ones. I also used concrete to replace the front steps. I then filled, leveled, and planted the lawn.

During one period when Mother was absent, Dorathy and I traded in her living-room furniture and purchased a new chair and couch, although we retained Dad's desk. Mother, forgive us—we did not know what we were doing. When Annis heard about the trade-in, she bought Mother's rocking chair and Dad's chair back from the furniture store. Today, all these pieces are still in the family.

As the remodeling continued, the house acquired a coat of white paint to give it a clean look and a green-painted trim to match the roof. The chimneys were rebuilt and replastered—one on a hot July day. I was stripped to the waist, and the results of the sunburn can still be seen above my belt line. The cistern was dry, so I cleaned that and learned where the smell of cistern water originated. A half foot of muck crawled with live, dead, and dying worms. It was horrible.

I did all this work "after work" and sometimes until two and three o'clock in the morning. I was violently ill one time after drinking some canned grapefruit juice at about 3:00 A.M. and then going to bed. But I learned a lot, and Mother had a more comfortable home when I left Milbank.

W hy talk about food? Because it *was* different back then. My grandfather was a gardener by profession. Perhaps there is a gardening gene in the Fowler family, for my father was also much at home among growing things and the soil. I, too, have worked with soil, but my first recollection of gardening relates to when I was a toddler in rompers. Mother and Dad rented a large lot across the street from our house and planted a large garden. I recall "going to the garden" on summer evenings and watching Dad wield the hoe and Mother weed the rows. Dad knocked potato bugs into a can of coal oil and then burned the bugs by setting the coal oil on fire. The only crop I remember is potatoes—called "spuds" or Irish potatoes. The end product went into the dugout under the house for use throughout the winter. In the spring, the potatoes were de-sprouted and served until a new crop appeared—about July—and then the remaining withered tubers were cleaned out and dumped.

Potatoes were a mainstay, and a real meal always included them. They were boiled (English-style), fried, or, in the winter when the kitchen stove was used to heat the house, baked. Dad could do things with fried potatoes that Mother could not; when he cooked, he would add eggs or chopped liver. Dad's fried potatoes always tasted different from Mother's.

We later had a garden at Grandma Ackerman's place on Diggs Avenue, but we always had a kitchen garden at the back of the house. Elmer Thomas, who married Grandma's daughter Nell, plowed it for us a few times, and as I grew older, I spaded the plot with a garden fork. It was a small garden but a big job. We had horseradish plants, and on the west end there were hills of "strawberry red" pie-plant (rhubarb). A rare treat was pie-plant pie. The crust was made with home-rendered lard from Grandma Ackerman's farm. I recall the first boxed lard—Swift's Silverleaf brand.[17]

Peas and beans enter my memory at a later date and center on the Fourth of July. The menu for that holiday was standardized. We "robbed" the hills of new potatoes and picked new peas. Those would be boiled together and smothered with cream gravy—cream only in that it was white. A live chicken would be purchased from Paul Prisinger across the alley, killed, cleaned, and fried.[18] I learned to hold the chicken by its legs and wings and cut (chew) the head off with our notorious axe. It often required several chops to find the right place on the neck. At first I threw the beheaded chicken, but that resulted in much flapping of wings and squirting of blood, so I learned to hold the chicken at arm's length and watch the red stream of life squirt to a dribble. When the wing muscles relaxed, the chicken went into a pail of hot water and the plucking began. Creamed new potatoes and peas, a fried chicken, and sometimes a pie-plant pie—that was, and is, a repast fit for a king. And as always, Mother's grace ended with, "God bless the wee ones—wherever."

After frost in the fall, the fresh vegetables were no more until the next year. We had little meat except for soup bone and calf's liver—both were free for the asking. There was fish at times from our friend Ed Germain, and in later years I would catch yellow-belly bullheads in Whetstone Creek. In even later years when I did go hunting, we had pheasant and duck. I was never able to bring down a goose. Mother canned some of the birds for winter. We had salt pork and navy beans; it was not all that bad. Breakfast was cooked cracked-wheat or oatmeal with Mother's homemade bread charred on the hot stove lids (until, that is, we purchased the toaster for Mother). We had fresh milk from A. C. Grams—just down the alley. They had a couple of cows, and every day, we would buy a half-gallon pail of milk.

Lunch was a slice of Mother's bread with uncolored cocoa butter, Mother's jell, and a glass of milk. In the summer, vegetables were added—radishes for sandwiches and fresh tomatoes with salt. The evening meal was *the* meal. It might be boiled potatoes with flour-gravy, bread, and perhaps meat—the free liver would be fried. Hamburger is not new; we had hamburger at times.

Mother maintained her family, in part, by canning and preserving garden produce—quarts and quarts of vegetables, fruit, and pickles—just as my wife would keep her family going and keep me in school by canning and freezing fruit and vegetables in the 1940s and 1950s. The Christmas after Dad was killed, the small shed that was attached to the house was filled to overflowing with goodies supplied by sympathetic friends—chickens, ducks, geese, and slabs of meat, homemade bacon, and ham. I also well recall Mother's crying and my wondering why; after all, we had all that food. The supply lasted until spring, and we had ham for Easter.

We three children had noon chores—coal and wood in, ashes out—so we always came home from school at noon. When a storm was brewing, or had brewed, Mother would pack us a lunch and we would eat in the school room at our desks. We had to clean the desk and floor around us with a wet rag before we went outside for exercise. I have vivid recollections of the lunch—a slice of bread (I preferred the heel)—spread with lard. Dorathy did not seem to recall those lunches. Maybe Mother gave her a different type.

There were memorable occasions when Mother would give us a penny to spend on the way to school. Sometimes the penny was saved for future investment, but when the penny was too hot to keep in our pocket, we would buy two sticks of licorice root (real root) or two horehound sticks. The licorice roots would last for days because we could bite a small piece and chew it for hours; the remaining dry root went into a pocket for another day.

Mother's Christmas dinner would be elegant—how, I do not know. She always managed fruit cake and coffee bread. There was none like it. She served a roasted chicken, potatoes, and hot tea—always hot tea. One year, Mother made plum pudding. It was hard as it should be, and I can still taste the tallow as I think of it. Mother never made it again. I remember that I was disappointed, for there were no plums in the pudding.

Our Christmas stocking usually had an orange that came with Mother's statement, "In England we had to be dying to get an orange." Other fresh fruit in winter we did not have. Sometimes we would see it in the stores and wonder. I was probably sixteen before I saw grapefruit and then only as rinds thrown out with the slops in the alley behind Harry Boerger's. I did not know what they were but later learned that they were grapefruit—a wonderful cross of something and an orange—and they came from California. Visualize those empty yellow shells turned orange from the freezing, spread among other scraps from the table, and you will understand what I saw.

I was a senior in high school and taking biology before I heard of vitamins. I have wondered whether our lives might have been different if we had had those wonders in our childhood. I must have been nineteen or twenty before I ate in a restaurant and only then because I was not at home and because it was time to eat. When I was working in Arlington, South Dakota, a complete meal cost thirty-five cents. That was a lot of money; I often skipped lunch. By the way, that meal included soup *and* desert.

Preservation was accomplished by drying, salting, or cooking. In summer, we had ice from the icehouse. We "helped" prepare the ice and load it into the horse-drawn wagon. For that, we received the broken chunks. In the winter, we used the shed attached to the house, where the temperature was always freezing or below. The first refrigeration I saw was at Bob Hunter's house—a wonder of motor, compressor, pipes, and a huge box upstairs.

Do not get the impression that we starved or were underfed. We did not and were not. I do not recall ever being hungry, and I do not suffer from hunger now. Mother's simple grace, "For what we are about to receive, Lord make us truly thankful," accompanied each meal. She was English and her cooking, except for a few specialties, was not the greatest. But she struggled to feed us and to set a table before us. We ate and we cleaned our plate. When Mother said, "Finish your meal," we finished our meal. Working came first with Mother, and feeding ran a close second. I often wonder how she did it. She had little money, was often dog tired and alone, and yet she did feed us. To say, "I don't like that," or to leave anything on our plate would have been sacrilegious. Mother taught by example and not by threat. For her ability to provide food and her dedication to feeding us, she deserved a star in her crown. I am sure she was awarded one.

Although memory can take me back to the hazy age of two, and I can recall some events at the age of three vividly, early recollections of birth and death evade me. The influence of the Victorian Age was not too far removed from 1914 and into the 1920s. The niceties of that period did not permit discussion of sexual, prenatal, and natal topics. Women might talk among themselves; ladies did not. Gentlemen refrained from such discussions, and only the crass would discuss women as other than genteel.[19]

My first recollection of a reference to sex was not interpreted as such at the time. In fact it was years later, perhaps in adulthood, that the hidden meaning was revealed to me. The day was late spring and my age perhaps five. In those years, the eastern South Dakota sky could be as blue as my Mother's eyes. The building cumulus clouds were so white that the reflecting sunlight hurt the eyes. The aroma of plowed earth from near at hand filled the air, and male robins encouraged their mates with what we called their rain song. I often wonder whether later generations are awed by the hand of God moving over the landscape as each season fades into the next.

A ten-foot-by-ten-foot chicken-coop shed was attached to our chicken-coop kitchen. In warm weather, the wooden-tub washing machine was placed outside against the south wall of the shed. A handle operated the rack-and-pinion drive that drove the wooden "peggy" with its four wooden dowels—a pleasing wooden replica of a cow's udder. Grandma Ackerman was visiting us, having stopped to see *her* Jennie. Mother pushed and pulled the handle with my well-intended help, receiving a sliver in her finger. Grandma obtained a needle and retrieved the sliver as the conversation developed into how slivers of steel migrate through the body. Grandma climaxed the discussion with her story of how a young man received a sliver of steel in the palm of his hand, and it came out three weeks later in the leg of a girl in the next county. At the time, I was impressed with the mysteries of migration. The implication only dawned on me many years later. Be that as it may, the episode constitutes the only reference to sex that I remember in the Fowler household.

Birth took place in the home, and children were sent away for the event. A doctor was usually in attendance; a competent neighbor woman was always present, as was the threat of puerperal, or childbed, fever before the advent of antibiotics. When the children returned, they were told that their mother had been away and had brought back a baby brother or sister, as the occasion demanded. In the Fowler household, there was no discussion of storks or cabbage patches, nor was there any discussion of facts.

I vaguely recall Dorathy's advent but only because Mother was confined to bed and Dad did the cooking. I do remember the little red creature that seemed to keep Mother in bed. Dorathy was breast fed but did not progress. She was then given cow's milk, which she rejected, and was finally placed on goat's milk. I never saw Mother breast feed Dorathy. In fact, I never saw Mother other than fully clothed as that was the only appearance acceptable.

My older sister Annis married Max Kaden in 1933 and moved to a farm near Watertown, South Dakota. It was a sad occasion for many reasons. First, Mother was dead set against the marriage; second, the Great Depression was at its height, and farming was at its depth. We had come to depend on Annis as a mainstay, and we were losing that support. Birth and death both became very real to us one year later when Annis's first child was born dead—a stillbirth. Her stay in the hospital, the funeral, the debate about where Annis should recuperate—at her farm or at our home—the ever-increasing fear over Mother's dire predictions about Annis's marriage, all deepened the depression further. Birth and death became closely related to me, and the thought of birth did not conjure happiness. One of Mother's quips came to mind repeatedly: "Laugh at a funeral; cry at a wedding." Could it be true?

There were other births. Annis had four children, all alive and well. With time, distance, and success, the early trauma was relegated to the back burner. Birth became a biological event, and I understood the humor in the story of the little boy who was always biting his fingernails. In desperation, his mother told him that if he did not stop he would grow a paunch like Uncle Alf's—and Uncle Alf was over

paunchy. Johnny stopped biting but not thinking. Days later, a pregnant friend of his mother's was visiting, and as Johnny eyed her criti-
cally, he made the profound statement, "It's easy to see what you've
been up to." I understood the humor, but it still embarrassed me.

In due course, I married Dorcile Samuelson of Randolph, Kansas,
and we had children of our own. Mary was born in Ames, Iowa, in
1945. Dorcile went to the hospital late in the day; at about 8:00 P.M.
I was sent home—it was going to be a long wait. With an income
of only nine hundred dollars per year, taxi money was not all that
available, so I walked home. I juggled a full-time job, research, and
course work that occupied sixteen to eighteen hours of my day. I
was exhausted, but Morpheus, the god of dreams, was not kind that
night. A telephone call as I made coffee the next morning informed
me of a baby girl. I taxied back to the hospital—hang the twenty-five
cents—and found Dorcile in a room by herself, pale and exhausted
but happy. We sat there holding hands until the middle of the afternoon as Dorcile drifted in and out of sleep. I was again sent home;
Dorcile had had a hard time and needed complete rest. I marveled
at how this new mother bathed, bottled, and dressed Mary and was
embarrassed at my own fears. I had to steel myself even to pick the
baby up and hold her. I could beat hot iron at a blacksmith's forge,
but that little helpless girl made me shake with fright.

Ruth Ann was born in 1947, also in Ames. February weather was
not too bad that year, and much of the time I walked the three miles
to the campus. When weather was bad, I rode with a friend. I walked
home early that particular afternoon—perhaps three o'clock. I do not
recall that I had been called. Martha Samuelson, Dorcile's mother,
had arrived a few days earlier to take care of Mary when Dorcile went
to the hospital. One look at Dorcile as I came in the back door and I
did not need Mother Samuelson's urging. I called a cab and explained
the situation, and it was there pronto. Dorcile was in late labor as we
drove to the hospital; the imprint of her nails on my hand remained
for some time.

This time there was no long wait, although it seemed like hours.
My name was called in the waiting room, and I went upstairs to see
Dorcile—not so pale—and a new girl. Some of the fear had left me,
but the basic feeling was still present. Dorcile remarked, "Her little

hands and feet are perfect—and this time they didn't have time to give me an enema." I looked in the nursery at each visit, but Ruth Ann was always asleep. It was not until after she came home that I heard her cry. On the rare occasions when Dorcile was absent, I would be "out of my gourd" until she returned. We now had two lovely daughters, both blonds.

William was born in 1960, and many changes had occurred. I was out of school, had a good job in Los Alamos, New Mexico, and housing was not a problem. Dorcile was concerned about my feelings—another mouth to feed after thirteen years. I was more relaxed, but Dorcile was not. I watched the birth through a window; the doctor held up the baby, and there was no question but that it was a boy. The single boy in the Fowler family was repeated for the third generation. Dorcile insisted on the name William after his paternal grandfather. Her lone remark as we wheeled her back to her room was, "You didn't think I could do it, did you?" My unuttered thought was, "God bless you, I knew you could."[20]

Now all the unknown mysteries had answers. I had seen a birth and knew why, where, how, and when. It was a humble and thankful father who drove the old Hudson automobile to check the laboratory where I worked before going home. As I faced the church across the street, I muttered, "Thank You." Birth can be sad, I knew, but it could also be wonderful, and only God can put together the biological mechanisms that assure future generations a place in a wonderful world. Am I still afraid of the newborn? Yes, I am. William was baptized in that same church—the United Church of Los Alamos. I carried him up the aisle with Dorcile at my side as we presented him to God and to the minister. I was shaking like a leaf.

The subject of death, just like birth, was not discussed openly in the Fowler home. Milbank being a railroad center and Father being a railroad man brought us closer to death than life because so many railroad workers died as a result of violent accidents. We would hear people comment, "Frank has pulled his last freight," or "John has dead-headed home," and as children we knew what that meant. "Casey Jones," a popular song about the heroic railroad engineer for the Illinois Central Railroad who died in a crash, was a part of our small collection of Edison cylindrical records.

But the first death to touch us, and the first funeral I attended, was that of my own father. A combination of the depression of 1920–1923 and the union organization of the local railroad workers, which resulted in a strike, closed the Milbank section of the H & D Division. In disgust and as a matter of preservation, workers moved, and the Milbank section never recovered. Father worked as a car repairman on what was known as the Rip Track.[21] Out of work and with five mouths to feed, he took a job as janitor at the First National Bank. The strike continued, and when he was offered a job in Watertown, Wisconsin, that fall, he took it. We were to move in June when school was out. Father had picked out a two-story house with inside plumbing and a furnace—a far cry from our four-room house in Milbank, one half of which was a rebuilt chicken coop.

In April 1923, Mother was called to Wisconsin. Father had been injured while repairing a freight car. Mrs. Olson cared for the three of us while Mother was gone. The next message was that Father had died.[22] Annis was fourteen and old enough to be completely shattered by the news. I was nine and in school, and Dorathy was to be eight. We two children cried, probably because Annis cried, but the full impact did not hit us until the day of the funeral. Mother returned to Milbank with the body. The funeral was at the house and at the Congregational church. A large crowd came to pay their respects, overflowing the small living room and into the yard. The casket was opened at the house but not at the church. Led to the casket by Grandma Ackerman, Mother placed her hand on Father's head and said, "Oh, Will," and fainted. She was forty-three years old with four mouths to feed, no education, and not a penny to her name. There was a balance due on the house. The fragrance of carnations remains with me to this day, and the aroma calls forth a picture of Mother standing at the gray casket as I looked down on a chipped and worn Congoleum rug.

I returned to school, and although Father had always worked and I had not known him well, something had changed. I was alone—and life was never to be the same. Grandma Ackerman helped Mother select the cemetery lot. It had to have a tree on or near it because Dad loved trees. It was a half lot because the children would be gone and would not be returned for burial. The lot has since received Annis's

first child, Mother, and my sister Dorathy. The American elm continues to grow.

In 1933, Grandma Ackerman died, a victim of old age and diabetes. I possessed a 1920 Overland touring car and drove Mother to
the Ackerman farm four miles south of town. Ten years had passed
since Father's death, but I could not bring myself to enter the farm-
house. Mother paid her respects, and I shook hands with "Uncle"
Elmer, Grandma's son-in-law, out in the farmyard. Another world
had changed and I was alone again—and I could smell carnations.
The funeral was at the Congregational church. We were not really
relatives, so we sat with the congregation until "Uncle" Elmer and
"Aunt" Nell moved us to the mourner's pews. At the cemetery, the
same words were said, "Ashes to ashes and dust to dust," and again
the three small clods of earth dropped onto the casket. A great and
kind lady was gone.

Shortly thereafter, I do not recall the year, one of the few friends of
my boyhood died. As poor as we were, Leonard came from a family
that was poorer still. His father, Phill Bloomenrader, was a farmer
and horse trainer who had seen so many failures that he had ceased
to exist in a world where success could be possible. I had met Leonard
while at Grandma Ackerman's on some forgotten occasion. When the
Bloomenraders moved into town, after still another failure, I introduced Leonard to scouting. He became ill at about the age of fifteen
with some unknown sickness that lingered and worsened. I knew
nothing about driving a car, but I drove Leonard—in Phill's Model
T—to his aunt's who lived in Dell Rapids, about one hundred miles
south of Milbank. Leonard died about two months later, probably
from some form of cancer.

I was a pallbearer at his funeral. He was buried from the German
Lutheran church and in his Boy Scout uniform at his request. Rev.
Fred Wessler was of the old, old school, and the uniform was a no,
no. I was asked to intervene, which I did, but it was the townspeople
who told him what to do, and the uniform was accepted. I remember
only three words from the sermon, ". . . this young sinner . . . " and of
leaving the cemetery in A. C. Grams's car. It was becoming apparent
that being too close was also too painful.

Melvin Berkner died of leukemia about 1935. I was then in Brookings working for State Recreation with the Civil Works Administration and drove home to be a pallbearer. I had enjoyed many outings with Melvin and his wife Florence. We had seen the Black Hills, Yellowstone Park, and the West Coast together. We had fished and hunted Big Stone Lake, both summer and winter, one time on an all-night campout at forty-three degrees below zero. Melvin had a game left leg, and I a right. Two pair of shoes—one pair larger than the other—did for both of us. I helped him build his cabin on the lake shore near Kite's Island. Once more, I had seen a close and true friend laid to rest—and in private I cried. It became easier to don the hard mask; I sold my shotgun, and my hunting days were over.

In the following years, many friends and acquaintances died. I avoided funerals and weddings. But in 1952, my father-in-law Rudolph Samuelson died. We were in Ames; Dorcile was not well, but we packed the girls into the 1948 Oldsmobile and drove to Kansas. In Lincoln, Nebraska, a car in front of us stopped suddenly. I braked hard, and although that car's bumper was bent, other damage was not evident. However, Ruth Ann in the front seat hit the windshield with her head, and Dorcile rolled off the back seat and hit her head on decorative metal. The doctor pronounced all well enough to continue the trip, but Dorcile had two of the biggest black eyes I have ever seen, and Ruth Ann had a headache.

The funeral was at the Swede Creek Church, where we had been married ten years before. Dad Samuelson was highly respected; the church was overflowing. It was a respectful but stern procession that drove to the cemetery—a procession of Swedes and Germans. Embarrassed by the black eyes, Dorcile did not want to go, but she changed her mind. At the post-interment dinner, a new experience to me, everyone was so kind and thoughtful that I became confused about my own feelings. I am still confused.

Mother died in the spring of 1965, a few months short of her eighty-fifth birthday. With her British Isles wit, she had so often said, "When I go, I hope I go so fast I make the devil jump." She was not granted her wish. She spent her last years bedridden. Although she had seldom attended church after Dad died, she was a child of God and resigned herself to whatever fate might be. She was buried in

Milbank beside Dad, and her services were held at the Congregational church.

After Mother's passing, I began to recognize that my feelings were changing. Death for Mother came as a blessed release from a life filled with work, disappointment, heartache, and pain—and I could not cry. I could just stand mute and wonder. With Mother's passing, death put on a different robe, and when my sister Annis died in 1974, it also seemed a blessed release from a life of heartache, disappointment, unhappy marriage, pain, and all that had happened to one who had been our surrogate mother and teacher. She, who had given happiness to all the handicapped children who came through her classes, was an angel who asked for nothing in return. No sacrifice was too great—not even the red wool sweater that she had once given to me so that *I* would be warm while walking to school when I was on crutches. That was a garment that she had needed to keep *her* warm on the long cold days of teaching in a country schoolhouse. She had gone to her reward, and again I could not cry.[23]

There is pain at birth and pain at death, and both are voyages from the known to the unknown; it is the unknown that we fear. In truth, we start to die at the moment of conception. As long as anabolism continues at a rate higher than that of catabolism, we live and grow. When the two reach equilibrium we are in a steady state—maturity. When the two processes reverse—and they do for all living organisms—death is the result. The mortal coils unwind. Death is sad for the young; a life and its potential are lost. Death is a release for the aged and comes with an attitude of high expectancy—a release into a beautiful unknown. It is so easy to say. Is it easy to do?

*I*t will be as difficult for you, the reader, to understand the health and disease aspects of my early childhood, as it was for me to understand those of my parents' era, and as it will be for your children to understand those of your childhood. Just as death was considered inevitable, so was disease. Inoculation against smallpox with live vaccinia virus was the only effective preventive medical tool of my childhood. The hospital in Milbank was the place of last resort. It was generally believed that one went to the hospital to die, and that was true in many, many cases. So to keep healthy and away from the hospital, we dosed ourselves with tonics. After prohibition was repealed in 1933, the tonic for men was Bock beer, but for us as we were growing up, the tonic of spring was sulphur and molasses. In the thinking of the time, the blood had to be thinned after the winter thickening, and the innards needed to be purged. Hot cambric tea, which consisted mostly of milk and sugar with a bit of tea, and hot lemonade for colds were other parts of our home-health treatment.

The term "disease," however, was seldom used; a person had measles, chicken pox, scarlet fever, mumps, smallpox, croup, dyspepsia, or Bright's (kidney) disease. Or one might be bilious or sanguinal. In our area of the Midwest, the term disease served as a contraction of "social disease," which is now referred to as venereal disease. Most people "were sick" or had a specific condition, but a few "had a disease." Tuberculosis was called consumption if progressing at a normal rate and galloping consumption in those cases where death followed rapidly on the heels of diagnosis. Poliomyelitis, or polio, was called infantile paralysis because it was believed to be a disease of the young. Persons with liver dysfunction (alcohol-induced or otherwise) were bilious.

In the case of certain diseases, parents would make an attempt to expose their children so that they could get the inevitable out of the way at an early age. In reality, the parents were practicing in an uncontrolled way what the medics were later taught to practice in a controlled way. That was especially true for mumps and especially for boys. The concern related to the possible extension of the disease into the testes of mature males with all the dire consequences—real or imagined. Once a child contracted mumps or chicken pox, he or she recovered or not—and some did not. A child was confined to his bed at home; the mother waited. If the child recovered, he returned to living in society. If he did not recover, the family returned to living in society.[24]

The many infections that brought about an elevated temperature resulted in a sanguinary condition. Pneumonia or double pneumonia was one of those and was also known as chest congestion or hepatized lung (a term meant originally to describe the organ, that is, filled with fluid like the liver). Pneumonia was often fatal. The illness had a crisis period associated with a temperature pattern. Once the illness was contracted, there was nothing to do but wait and try to keep the patient's temperature down. If the temperature broke and the lungs began to discharge phlegm, the patient might recover. If the temperature continued to rise, the patient would go into a coma, and death was probable. The vigils were long as the doctor and family members waited for the outcome. Before antibiotics, nothing else could be done.

Blood poisoning was another sanguinary disease, and it was ever present in our rural community. The many wounds received in the unclean conditions of barnyard and stable resulted in infections that were treated with salt, turpentine, coal oil, horse liniment, and wool fat. Calomel was used externally as well as internally. How many mercury-containing drugs do you know of today? Even 606, or salvarsan, has passed away.[25] When the red streaks would start and progress up the arm or the leg, the doctor would lance and drain and hope. An appendage might be rendered useless, but a life would be saved.

Childbed, or puerperal, fever was a killer of the birthing woman, but it was rare in our community, where there was no lying-in hospital in which doctors might deliver baby after baby with the chance of serial infection spreading from one woman to another. In Grant County, babies were delivered in individual homes with clean preparation. But the disease was present, and at least one of my friends was motherless because of it.

Today, we have more types of flu than we have flies, but about the time of World War I, we had Spanish influenza and stomach disorders. I remember the epidemic—actually it was a pandemic—of 1918–1919. Ours was the last family in town to succumb, and Dad was the last member of the family to contract the illness. Mother was recovering when Dad took to bed, but the five of us recovered without a death in the family—not a miracle, perhaps, but something to be thankful for when one considers the high mortality rate.[26]

Post-infection, each family followed a cleansing ritual in the home. The floors were scrubbed, curtains washed, and bedding and dishes were boiled. The family then moved temporarily to a friend's house. Those were real friends! A fire was started in the kitchen stove. The last person out—usually the head of the household—spread flowers of sulphur or paraformaldehyde on the hot stove plates, left the house, and closed the doors. After a period of time, someone returned and opened the doors and later the windows to ventilate the place before the family returned to the fumigated home. Too bad it was all worthless.

On a cold, rainy spring day when I may have been about six years old, I rode on the back of the dump wagon for much of the day as Horton Mills, a retired farmer, set fence across the road. I went to bed with a cough and fever and was ill for a long time. Events and people came and went like flashes of a slow-timed strobe light. Dr. William J. Fergusen flickered in and out until he left for the state-side army camps and died there of flu. I slept a lot and recall waking one sunny afternoon to see Mother standing at the bedside. "So you finally woke up," she said. I had been asleep three days! Dr. Flett took over my care, and one day he came visiting with one of the Mayo doctors from Rochester, Minnesota. They went into the living room to tell Mother and Dad that I had infantile paralysis, whatever that was.[27] There was a treatment of sorts. My right leg, side, and arm were wrapped in cotton, and oil of wintergreen was poured on. The oil soaked through the cotton and stung my scrotum, but I could not talk about those parts, and so it had to sting. Mother rubbed my arm and leg and side, and that was the extent of the treatment. On the day I was allowed out of bed, I discovered that I could not walk. I crawled around the house on my left side.

I regained the use of my right leg, and I learned to walk for a second time. The right arm was more reluctant, and I learned to print with my left. I was probably eight years old before I began to print with my right hand, and nine when I began to write. My right leg and foot were short, and the ankle was of little use. The arm suffered less damage, and work at the forge and in the granite works helped me to develop an acceptable set of muscles. John Lewis's son had also had polio and was left with only one normal bone in his body—his skull. How fortunate I was! Over the years, I have had seven surgeries. In the last one, the doctor rebuilt the leg and fused the ankle, and forty some years of pain ended.

Too much detail? Probably, but it points out what the microbiologist and biochemist have achieved. Some years later, Dorathy also became seriously ill. She ran a fever, and her joints were swollen and painful. Dr. John W. Pay was called, and he tried to manipulate the joints and rub them. Dorathy screamed with pain. Eventually, the pain grew less, and Dorathy was up and about after a fashion. The infection was probably a strep, and it was systemic; it damaged her joints and probably her heart valves. One seldom recovers from rheumatic fever; as it was, it caused Dorathy years of suffering.

Today, infections such as Dorathy's can be fairly well controlled by products developed in the laboratories of bacteriologists and biochemists.[28] When I went to Ames, Iowa, to work on my Ph.D. in the 1940s, my major professor was doing research on ways to mass-produce penicillin, as were researchers at many other institutions around the country. I joined in that effort. The diseases conquered in my lifetime, along with their blinding, crippling, and debilitating effects, include lockjaw (tetanus), choking disease (diphtheria), typhoid, infantile paralysis, hepatized lung (pneumonia), wooden tongue, anthrax, rheumatic fever, and blood poisoning. What changes we have seen!

William Fowler emigrated from England to Canada at about the time this photograph was taken in 1900. Eric Fowler collection

Jane ("Jennie") Pickersgill came from England to the United States in 1906 to marry William Fowler. Eric Fowler collection

Annis Fowler Kaden, Dorathy Fowler, and Eric Fowler stand behind their mother, Jennie Pickersgill Fowler, in this family portrait. Eric Fowler collection

Although not related, the Fowlers all referred to Emma Ackerman as "Grandma." Eric Fowler collection

Owned by the Ackermans, a two-story cottage at Chautauqua Park on Big Stone Lake was a favorite summer destination for the Fowlers. Eric Fowler collection

Jennie Fowler, left, and Bertha Knipple enjoy the cool water at Big Stone Lake, while Eric Fowler stands on the dock. Eric Fowler collection

Eliza Rawson (seated, left), J. Charles Rawson, and their daughters Bernice (standing, left), and Ada helped the Fowler family, providing jobs and gifts of food. Eric Fowler collection

The door to the shed attached to the Fowler house, viewed from the south, stands open with the washing machine outside next to the shed. Eric Fowler collection

Before he left Milbank, Eric Fowler replaced the siding, roof, and wiring of the house and dug a new well, which also provided cold storage for food. Eric Fowler collection

Irving Patridge operated this ham radio and frequently invited Fowler to listen to conversations from around the world. Eric Fowler collection

*The Eric Fowler family, from left, Mary, Eric, Dorcile,
William, and Ruth Ann.* Eric Fowler collection

*T*he social environment of the Fowler family was meager. Politeness and appreciation we learned, the social graces we did not. There were few parties and formal occasions, and we had few friends or visitors. We did have playmates in the yard in summer, but we seldom had time for that. We celebrated Christmas and the New Year, participated in big community events on Memorial Day and the Fourth of July, and went to the County Fair. We went on picnics and day outings. Birthdays were noted, though not celebrated with big parties. Religious services and Sunday School provided important social outlets, and touring live bands and radio programming were central to the social environment of the time.

We did not look upon ourselves as "deprived" or different; that was just the way life was. You must understand that serving a cup of tea in Mother's real china tea cups (she had three of them) when the minister called was a social event to the Fowlers. The minister did call in those days, and if he found no one home, he would call again. Mother's English training relative to "station" did not encourage us to move beyond these bounds. In those early years, a large fraction of the sparse population in Grant County was pioneer settler stock and their progeny. Self-help and concern for others were the stuff of life. Certainly, many acts of kindness toward the Fowlers were important to our daily existence.

Then, too, our community was rural in the extreme. Milbank was and is the county seat of Grant County. It was a railroad center and boasted a granite works, a couple of automobile garages, a blacksmith shop, cafés, a meat market, grocery stores, and other businesses. In later years, two Swiss boys from Wisconsin opened a cheese factory, and the Flanerys opened a "sausage" factory.[29] Lawyers, bankers, businessmen, elected officials, and others lived in town, as well. Retired farmers, the original homesteaders, were beginning to partake of the "comforts of city living," and social life among the families of rural and labor background were similar to our own. The upper level of society lived differently, but we did not know how they lived. The latter group did have a country club, where they played golf, held formal dances, and did some "drinking" (prohibition was in force but did not stop those who wished to imbibe). We heard about these things but never saw them.

For the "lower social level," there were barn dances and house dances. The orchestras were from radio stations WNAX of Yankton, South Dakota, or from WDAY of Fargo, North Dakota. Lawrence Welk with his five-piece band visited Milbank on some occasions, as did the Sodbusters, who, like Welk, came from North Dakota. Johnny Wilfahrt and his band from Minnesota also played at times. I did not dance. We did not dance, although Mother was a good dancer. She used to tell about dancing in the streets of Leeds as a child. To put one's arm around a girl in public—never! I did try to dance years later when we had summer camps at Lake Campbell near Brookings. Lawrence Welk was there often.

Religion involved a good deal of socializing, important to the community and the Fowler family. My father was a just and upright man. Rev. Carl P. Bast, who preached his funeral sermon, told me this years later. I do not recall Dad's attendance at church. Early in life, he had worked in the Oxford Place Chapel in England, and, according to Mother, he received Communion before his death and said that he was ready to go "to his Maker." We three children were baptized by Rev. Bast shortly after Dad died. I do not know whether it was Dad's, Mother's, or Annis's idea. I do recall the three of us standing before the Communion table at the front of the church. Mother was not there. Mother attended church with us regularly until the time of Dad's death; after that, it was too painful, although she did attend on occasion.

We attended Sunday School and were active in the YCO—Youth Christian Organization. Sunday School was a quiet hour in which we were taught "Bible." I do not recall attempts to preach; the lessons related to reading and understanding. There were a number of Sunday School teachers, but the person most prevalent in my memory is Helen Mesmer. She was a maiden lady and a Bible scholar. She taught "her boys" the value of good thoughts and a good life and how both could be built on the teachings in the Old and New Testament.

She liked her boys and they liked her. As young people, we took over the Sunday service at times. On one occasion, Dorathy, Ruth Hunter, and I had the service. Ruth preached the sermon.

In the early days, the sermons often contained some exhortation concerning "hell fire and brimstone," but that gradually gave way to a social religious approach. I attended the Methodist church and the Episcopal church, but the Congregational church was our church home. When Rev. Bast left, the pulpit was filled by a new reverend and his family They had one daughter. When the boys began to attach the phrase "two-bit" to her last name, the implications were too much, and the family left Milbank. I had often thought of the ministry as an occupation, and thought seriously, but after observing the actions of the "good people of the church," I placed that occupation at the bottom of the list.

Religious influence, however, is a part of everyone's life, whether he wishes it or not. Many facets of life can and do become a religion, but I am thinking of religion in the Christian sense—man's need to believe in and to live on a higher plane. A scientist seeks truth and proof of truth; I classify myself as a scientist, but science and the Bible have never been at odds for me. Religion is life, what life is all about, what we do with it and for it. We do not need to discuss the universal solvent or the hopping flea on the table. Rather, we should set before ourselves the edict, "Leave the world a little better than you found it." To me, religion is not one church or one creed. Religion is an attitude toward fellow man that works for society's betterment. When religious questions cannot be proved or disproved, but are accepted as truth, I call it faith. As a scientist, I call tentative answers to big questions working hypotheses or "gut feelings." It is my belief that both religion and science have helped me understand life.

Holidays were just another day; Christmas was an exception. The first Christmas I remember was some years before Dad's death. I was asleep on the daybed in the living room, and the Christmas tree was in the northwest corner by the front door. Early in the evening, we had decorated the tree with loops of colored paper (the loops were fastened together with flour paste), a few glass balls, candles, and a string of small glass silver bells strung on tarnished tinsel. I woke up to the tinkle of those tiny bells. I did not look—I knew that Santa was busy; besides, the large hard-coal heater was between me and the tree, and it was pitch black in the room.

In the morning, behold, we had received a phonograph—an Edison—with diamond-point needle and some cylindrical records. Red Martin and his brother Clayton came in and listened to "Uncle Josh and His Rheumatism" and to "Cohen on the Telephone." Red's laughter never ceased as he looked into the grilled horn to "see the man." We would wind and play and wind and replay, and Dad and Mother would sit and smile; they had hit the jackpot. It was not stereo, of course; it was not even clear, but what a wonderful gift![30]

We always had a Christmas tree—almost always—and gifts, and usually the gifts were clothes. There was a year when the fifty cents for a tree was too much for Mother's funds, but Bertha Knipple begged a "demonstrator" tree from Lloyd Thirsk's grocery store and brought it to us. It was a most thoughtful present. And then there was the year that Bertha gave us two kittens, white and orange-tan, each with a big red bow. And one year as we came home from church on Christmas Eve in a beautiful Christmas snow, we four had to stop outside and look through the window. Wonder of wonders! The tree was lit by electric lights. Mother had bought the series string complete with Japanese bulbs, and Harry Boerger had placed them on the tree while we were in church. The Japanese bulbs did not last long—they never did—but we had electric lights on the tree, replacing the candles that Mother feared. We had gone "modern." Another Christmas, I received a coping saw, and I recall cutting designs from orange-crate wood. I occupied the middle of the kitchen floor as Mother tried to cook Christmas dinner. I still have the saw.

There was the sociable Christmas when we were guests of Bill and Bertha Knipple; they had one daughter, Genevieve. Bill was partial to boys—but their twin boys had died within a few days of their birth. Bill had purchased a present for me; it was a movie projector. It had a kerosene lamp, a strip of film in a closed oval with perhaps twenty frames, and a crank to drive the strip—around, repeat, around, repeat. After a scrumptious Christmas chicken dinner, Bertha hung a sheet. A telephone call from a neighbor interrupted us—

the neighbor wondered if Bill's bull could "visit" his lady cow? Bill asked whether the "lady" could wait until tomorrow, and apparently she could. We returned to the projector. Bill placed it on the table, lit the lamp, and there was a white blur on the sheet. Bill turned the crank; Bertha turned the crank; I turned the crank—nothing but a white blur. There were no instructions "to focus," and finally we blew out the lamp, and Bill said he would return it to "Sears Sawbuck." We were driven home in his 1919 brass-bound Model T. We had visited for Christmas!

One year, "black smallpox" was rampant in nearby Minnesota. We were vaccinated on the last day of school before Christmas; if we were to be ill, it would be on vacation time. And we were! Those vaccines were potent.[31] A few nights before Christmas, I turned, and mumbled, and tossed, and then, from nowhere, the bed was filled with frogs. Now I had no fear of such animals, but those frogs were everywhere. I remember waking up screaming, and Mother sitting on the bed trying to convince me that there were no frogs, and I remember being sick in the "slop pail."

Annis was to help Mrs. Jones prepare and serve Christmas dinner, and though not well, she went over to their place. "Keeping up with the Joneses" in our town was more fact than fiction—that is, until lawyer Jones was accused of embezzling one thousand dollars of Red Cross money. Annis returned late in the afternoon, after cooking, serving, and washing dishes. She was ill, and the fifty cents she had received for all-Christmas-day work could not help that. She came into the house and tried to sit in Mother's rocking chair—face first. Annis did not bend that way, and it was some time before Mother and I could get her turned around and stretched out on the floor. The rest of that Christmas is—and probably was—a blank.

In the early 1930s, I saved a few dollars and bought a Christmas present for the family. Mother and I went to Minneapolis, where I bought a Majestic radio for twenty dollars. It was a six-tube, line-operated mantle radio—Gothic style. That radio became the center of our entertainment. Many years later, after I was married, I brought that radio to our home, painted it ivory, and used it for several years. At the height of the Great Depression, my Christmas gift to Mother,

Dorathy, and Annis was a five-dollar bill each, wrapped in much paper. I had saved for weeks to buy presents and did not know what to purchase. I took the easy way out.

During the depression, President Franklin Delano Roosevelt used radio to talk to the nation; everyone listened to his "fireside chats" about his "New Deal" economic policies. But I recall best a different address he gave prior to Pearl Harbor when he spoke about world events and his disgust for war. "I hate waa; Eleanor hates waa; and Fella hates waa" (Fala was his dog), he said in his eastern accent.[32] His declaration of war speech to Congress after Pearl Harbor received worldwide attention. Everyone quit work to listen. It was probably the first time that radio had been used to broadcast such a declaration. It also signaled the end of uncontrolled radio operation; not until after war's end would the airways be free again.

Radio was good, clean family entertainment. Ten thousand-watt radio stations with huge "bottles," or vacuum tubes, at the transmitter drawing multi-amp currents were developed. Stations were few and far between, and the airways were uncluttered. Some of the stations heard in the Midwest were WNAX, Yankton; WCCO, Minneapolis; KSTP, Saint Paul; KFYR, Bismarck; WSM, Nashville; KDKA, Pittsburgh; KOA, Denver; WW-L, Washington, D.C.; WDAY, Fargo; KFI, Los Angeles; KMA, Shenandoah; WJR, Detroit; WLS, Chicago; XERA, Mexico; XELO, Mexico; WJN, Chicago; CBC, Canada.[33]

One- or two-hour programs of music featuring the big bands of the era were common; half-hour programs of comedy or story gave variety. In the earliest years, there were no "taped" programs; all were live. The programs included Ben Bernie (band), Lawrence Welk (band), Bob Burns (band and bazooka), Paul Whiteman (band), *Myrt and Marge* (detective-romance), Riders of the Purple Sage (western), *Fibber McGee and Molly* (comedy), George and Gracie (comedy), the Sodbusters (western band), *The Grand Old Opry* (western band), *Ramona* (organ), *The Street Singer* (vocal), *Amos and Andy* (comedy), *Sunday Evening at Seth Parker's* (church services), and, of course, news, football, and baseball.[34]

I recall a program called *The 64-Dollar Question*. "What was the first thing you said to your husband on your wedding night?" the announcer asked. After some thought, the woman said, "Boy, you gave me a hard one there." The MC said, "Give that lady 64 dollars." The statement was an innocent searching of the memory, but the program was taken off the air.[35]

About 1935, we had another hard Christmas. Dorathy was working for Dr. Flett, both at his home and in the office. Just before Christmas, she came home with a diagnosed case of scarlet fever. I went to Mrs. Swanson's (another Swanson just across the alley), and our house was essentially sealed; the red square in the window said "scarlet fever." The afternoon before Christmas, I walked home from the courthouse and asked Mother (through the window) whether she wanted a Christmas tree. She was angry—NO! She did not, and I should get back to work before I got fired! I do not recall what happened that Christmas Day, but the Fowlers had their first treeless Christmas.

Although Christmas was usually a social occasion, with a "drop in" neighbor now and then saying a quick "God bless you," we did not repay the calls. I was too bashful to go anywhere, especially alone, and Mother had few, if any, "visiting clothes." Ours was a closed world, and it would be years before I realized that other worlds might exist. For me, Christmas has always had a sweet sadness associated with it. I am not sure why because, in general, it was a happy occasion. Mother used to say after Christmas grace, "I wish everyone had as much and was able to eat it," and after a pause, "God help the poor wee ones wherever." The season would conjure up stories of "The Little Match Girl" and Tiny Tim and his twisted leg, and it did not take much to moisten the eyes.[36] I recall one Christmas when I was courting Dorcile that we were in her church, Swede Creek in Kansas. I believe the hymn was "Silent Night," and the tears came. Rev. Werner must have seen; his prayer was for peace of mind, and when we left, he squeezed my hand a little harder and whispered, "God bless you." Some years later, he was part of our marriage ceremony. Yes, Christmas will always be a sweet sad occasion.

As Christmas was *the* English holiday, New Year's was *the* Scotch holiday. According to Mother, it began on "last day" afternoon with much "Scotch" and continued for one week. (It was on that last day that Mother would tell us to look for the man with as many noses as days in the year. Our search for a freak of nature was futile, of course, as there was only one day left in that year.) One year we spent New Year's Eve with the Hunter family. Bob Hunter was Scotch. His father had drowned in the Hudson River on Christmas Eve when Bob was five years old. Bob had gone to work selling papers on the streets of New York and now owned the Hunter Granite Works in Milbank. He was from the old school and knew all about work. He was not Scotch with his money or his time; he was merry, kind, and helpful.[37]

That New Year's Eve was really a special social occasion. We "best dressed," and I wore a tie. There were three Hunters and four Fowlers at dinner. Bob, a collector of different and interesting pieces from around the world, had assembled complete services of "Arizona Gold"—from knives, forks, and spoons through goblets. On a white tablecloth, the beautifully decorated metal was a sight to behold. After dinner Bob tried to teach me how to play cribbage—without success. At midnight we sang "Auld Lang Syne." For the Fowlers, it was a very formal evening.

When Hunter died several years later, the men in his shop gave their time to produce a unique monument. They built a bench, similar to a church pew, that would seat four to six people, and each piece of the bench was a solid block of Milbank mahogany granite. The wide face of each arm end had a carving on it, a Scotch thistle on one and the square and divider symbol of the Masons on the other. The workers cut a three-word sentence into the back of the stone, "Bide a Wee." Even in death, Bob Hunter provided for someone's comfort.

The three Fowlers and Annis and her husband enjoyed one other formal social occasion. When J. Charles and Eliza Rawson celebrated their fiftieth wedding anniversary, we all received an invitation. On a cold, cloudy winter day, we walked to the Rawsons', where we had punch and little cakes. I heard Mrs. Rawson whispering, "Buddy, I didn't bake a pie." We each received an imitation gold piece that had a large "50" stamped on it; they were a gift from one of Papa Rawson's coal wholesalers.

I do not recall parties at home. I do recall one birthday at home. Mother asked my schoolmate Clarence Rosenquist to stop after school. (His father Ben owned an icehouse and transport business.) We had strawberry shortcake and then took a walk to the dam to watch the spring birds. It was a beautiful May day. On another 4 May in 1935, Mrs. Rawson called me at home and asked me to repair a window. Mother was at the Rawsons' cleaning house. When I rapped at the back door, Mrs. Rawson said, "Come in, Buddy." (She was the only person, other than Mother, who called me Buddy; it made me feel very close.) "There is hot coffee and apple pie," she continued. The three of us ate pie and drank coffee, and I crossed that narrow line between twenty and twenty-one. I repaired the window—my first job as a man.

Community celebrations were also social events. The three main ones were Memorial Day, Fourth of July, and the County Fair. Each of those events was associated with a community social activity, and we took part—"Lord willing and the creeks don't rise." There was always a parade for Memorial Day and for the Fourth of July. The early parades organized on a dirt-packed main street. On Memorial Day, many, many flags fluttered as the "boys in blue" and the "boys in gray" rode past in cars; the men would have been in their late seventies or early eighties.[38] Band concerts and speeches followed. The theme was often sacrifice—a theme that has been lost over the years. The community often gathered for a picnic in the park, at a table if one were lucky or on the grass if not. I shook hands with those who came to chat with Mother. After Dad died, Mother and Annis would rise early on Memorial Day, pick flowers, and go to the cemetery to "decorate" Dad's grave. We also called the holiday Decoration Day.

The format for the Fourth of July was similar to that for Memorial Day. After the parade would come the community sociable—a picnic lunch followed by speeches and a band concert. On that day, the theme would be freedom. I recall Cash Amsden as one of the speakers—later he became Senator Amsden.[39] Fireworks finished the day. We could watch them from our backyard and did not go to the fairgrounds, which was about three blocks northeast, down Linder's hill and over Whetstone Creek.

I have an especially happy memory of one Fourth of July. Father's job was ten hours a day and six days a week, standard at the time. It was a rare occasion when Father had a "day off," but such did happen once when I might have been six years old. It was the Fourth of July. I had found a skein of green-colored braided fish line and talked constantly about fishing. Dad took me to the railroad dam on the Fourth even though Mother thought he should rest. We went out just as it was getting light—early morning in July in eastern South Dakota. I had the green line, for which Dad had provided a hook, and Dad also had a line. There must have been bait, but I do not recall the nature of it. We sat on the railroad bridge. I dropped my line in without a float and tied the end to a nail. We did not catch fish, but something did break my line, which was not in good condition and had probably been discarded for that reason. I do not remember any conversation; I do recall the sky, the water, the birds, and the trees. But I had been fishing with Dad—the one and only time—and he had foregone much-needed rest because I had found a fishing line. Dad prepared a fireworks display for that evening. It was simple, with pinwheels, crackers, and skyrockets. Dad had become a naturalized citizen, and the message was freedom. He was an enthusiastic adopted American.

August was County Fair time. The fair was the culmination of the year's work and the last community sociable of the year. There were three ways to enter the fairgrounds—pay the admission, work for about two hours, or sneak in. Once, Mother gave Dorathy and me twenty cents to go through the gate with a ticket, but sneaking in was not difficult. The grounds occupied about one-half section of land, and the perimeters were lightly patrolled. Bill Lewis was usually one of the guards, and Pauline Lewis (his daughter) knew how much fence line her dad had to patrol; she and Annis had no trouble timing their entry to take advantage of that unorthodox doorway. At the fair, social life centered around group picnics. Groups of friends or neighbors enjoyed a light sack lunch and talked about crops, prices, weather, and the community. They covered topics in depth, for it would be late the next May before they had another opportunity.

Other, less formal social occasions included picnics and small gatherings. The annual Sunday School picnic of the Congregational church was held at Big Stone Lake and usually at Hartford Beach. The picnic was an all-day family affair. We would be driven to the lake by friends—often Bob Hunter in his Studebaker (President Series). It was polite to prepare lunch and eat with your transportation, and the two trios were Dorathy, Ruth Hunter, and me, and Bob and Mary Hunter and Mother. Annis would ride with or join other friends. We would stay through prayers and the evening campfire. On the way home to Milbank, we would sing songs. "Let Me Call You Sweetheart" was a favorite. Bertha Knipple also took us to the lake for a "small gathering"—just the Fowlers and the Knipples. Bertha's favorite spot was Eternal Springs on the Minnesota side. Once Mother and Bertha donned swimsuits and played in the water with us, a memorable occasion.

Other guests sometimes joined us on these outdoor adventures. Shikepokes are huge, slow birds, and as fish-eating waders, their long legs trail behind as they fly.[40] Traveling between water and land, they deposit a white feces over the landscape beneath. As we sat at the table on one of our gatherings, one spread feces over some plates. "Oh, it's that big bird," someone said. "Yes," I said, "It's a cream shitter." I stopped short and waited for a tongue lashing, but everyone was laughing, and it did not happen. No more mistakes like that! Mother might not laugh next time. Genevieve Knipple reminded Dorcile and me of the "cream birds" when we visited her fifty-five years later. Why do we remember what we do?

A "country bumpkin" social life? Maybe. I began by saying that the Fowler social life "was meager." I would now add, "but sufficient." As youngsters, we used these events to listen and learn; as we grew older, we attempted to pass on that learning.

7] Play and Recreation

In my youth, recreation was not a term in our vocabulary. We had an "off-day" or a "gathering" or a "visit." There were no formal recreational programs, except for Boy Scouts. We made our own fun in the house and outside; we played our own games; and we built many of our own toys. We went fishing for the day or to the river for a swim. We walked about town gathering bits and pieces that could be made into useful fun. We watched our neighbors and looked for anything unusual in town. A longer trip took us to nearby lakes. Occasionally, there was a trip to the city, and later on I went on what today would be called a "vacation."

On winter nights at home, we made spool tractors with a spool, a match, and a bit of Mother's elastic. The best tractor could climb the steepest grade. Spools and string were also used for spool gadgets. Spools were nailed to a board, connected with string belts, and the entire mass driven with Mother's sewing machine. We made roly-polys from oatmeal boxes, string, and a weight. The string was looped through the lids, tied, and a weight (usually a bolt) hung between the two parts of the loop. The string was wound tight by turning the box, and the gadget would roll over the floor as the string unwound. We made sand engines with paddle wheels; the wheel would turn as sand dribbled onto it from a hopper. Spinning tops were made from spools and a whittled peg and a piece of string.

Both girls had dolls. The heads were papier-mâché painted with enamel, and the cloth bodies were stuffed with sawdust or excelsior. Dorathy did have an exceptional doll: the head, hands, and feet were ceramic, and the body was soft leather. The doll's eyes closed under long dark lashes, and it had real human hair. The doll came from Aunt Annis in England and was dressed in red and white. Both Annis and Dorathy also cut paper dolls from discarded magazines—perhaps *Ladies' Home Journal* or the *American*. The popular doll at the time was the Kewpie doll.[41] I was the paper-doll fixer because I reattached the flaps or repaired tears. A piece of butcher paper and flour paste did the trick.

Orange crates were also in demand for toymaking, and they were available at Thirsk's grocery. We made push carts out of them using baby-buggy wheels. I once made one that was driven with a starter motor; Mr. Casman at the local battery shop supplied the battery. I had collected a set of cast-iron gears, probably timing gears discarded by some garage. The garages were my favorite stopping places whenever time permitted. Fitting the gears to the baby-buggy wheel and the starter required some doing. I recall spending weeks cutting the hub from the larger gear. I used a worn and broken hacksaw blade; I did not have a saw frame. I have a deep respect for the patience of the beaver. After the spokes had been cut, the mutilated gear was attached to the wire spokes of the go-cart wheel with baling wire. The smaller gear was fitted to the starter motor shaft with wood and "tin" shims. Lipton tea cans were used for everything, and strips from them made excellent shims. I could "drive" the push cart around the block before the battery needed charging, a service that Mr. Casman also supplied. I recall that Ruth Hunter was "amazed"; I was pleased.

We made scooters from discarded roller skates obtained at the dump, two boards, and a piece of lath. They were good transportation. Stilts were pleasingly dangerous; the contest was to see who could make—*and* walk—on the highest pair. The hoop and "T" were for those who could run. I made them and used them but did not run. They were simple, two laths nailed together as a T and a discarded wagon-wheel rim. The hoop was started and guided with the T. Who could roll the hoop farthest?

We collected leaves and made plaster-of-paris casts that we painted—if we could find watercolors. We collected flowers, wood from trees, and insects and tried to name them. We checked out books from the library, and Miss Minnie Shannon, the librarian, would spend time helping me with pronunciation and spelling of scientific names. After I bought my first scout knife, I carved chains and "idols" from cottonwood; one idol I called Ogi-Ony-Yen, I do not know why. I gave them away, some to girls I wished to impress. They were brilliantly painted with crows' talons for horns.

We learned to swim by trial and error. Our first ventures were in Whetstone Creek, which we dammed to form a swimming hole.

The hole, frequented also by cows, was mud filled, but we learned. We soon went to the railroad dam, much to Mother's consternation. The water was cleaner, and we had room to paddle. The boys usually swam in groups, but on one occasion, I was alone at the dam and was swimming at the railroad bridge. The water there was over twelve feet deep, and the bridge was ten feet or so above the water, making it a good place to dive. Traffic on the Sisseton line (called Hay Line) of the Milwaukee Road was two runs a day—one to Sisseton Agency on the Indian reservation and one back. The steam locomotive pulled freight and passenger coaches. The engineer would clear the naked bodies from the bridge understructure with a stream of high-pressure steam from the boiler. The bare bodies would jump into the water, and the female passengers would not be scandalized. My solo swim did not involve the Hay Line, however. That day, muskrats were swimming peacefully, and redwing blackbirds and white clouds filled the sky in a perfect calm. I had jumped from the bridge before, but this time I decided to dive. I cut through the water, down and down; I could see the bottom. My hands reached the silt, and I wanted to breathe. Somehow I turned around and, with bursting lungs, made it to the surface. Fresh air and sunshine never tasted or looked so good. I wish I could have seen it; it must have been a perfect dive. I never swam alone again; as I struggled to the surface, I realized that no one knew where I had gone.

Dorathy and I were quite close, perhaps because we were less than two years apart in age, and perhaps because we had each other and no others. We were usually seen together and were referred to as the "young couple." Playtime, such as it was, involved both of us. One January, a thaw resulted in a lake in the garden, and the subsequent cold weather resulted in a large area of smooth ice. Dad, who was a collector of bits and pieces, had acquired a discarded insulated drinking-water tank. It was about twelve inches in diameter and twenty-four inches deep. Dorathy and I decided to push the tank over the ice pond. We laid the tank on its side, and Dorathy slid in feet first. I lifted the tank to an upright position and pushed it back and forth across the ice. When Dorathy got tired, she bent her knees and squatted down. But when she wanted out, her knees had locked against the wall, and she was stuck fast in the tank. I do not recall what happened next; perhaps I was hiding somewhere. When Dad came home for lunch that day, he considered cutting Dorathy out of the tank, but at last he worked her legs free with his hands. That was the first and last "tank ride" for either of us.

Years later, I used the tank for an aquarium, taking tadpoles and small bullheads from the creek. I did not realize that the water had to be changed, and in a few days, the smell was horrible. I buried the entire mess in the garden, getting my first lesson in anaerobic systems.

I also "went fishing" with "Great Grandfather" Roberts (Grandma Ackerman's father). Mr. Roberts lived in a house next to Grandma's, was a Civil War veteran, and was probably in his eighties or early nineties at the time. He lived to fish. Grandma did not want her ageing father to be alone at the dam, and I was sent along to "protect" him. I may have been as much as six at the time. Mr. Roberts was tall, thin, and straight as a ramrod; his hair was snow white. He may have caught some fish, but what I remember are the hours of his talking and my listening. He was a great storyteller, and his retelling of the battles of the Civil War—especially the charges and counter-charges at Gettysburg—became real to me. I would walk home with him, and Grandma would be happy to see the two of us come up the path. She usually had a cup of "fresh" milk waiting. She kept two cows in the barn out back and milked them herself. Grandma gave Great Grandpa Roberts's pre-Civil War cap-fired musket to me after his death.

By observing our neighbors, we learned many lessons. John Lewis owned the northwest quarter of the block on First Street, where there was a house and an icehouse. John's brother Bill worked for John, and in the summer Bill delivered ice. Home brew was available, and too often a cold bottle in the ice chest had a swig reserved for Bill. One of the delivery trucks was a Model T with a low-low gear in the rear end; the tires were solid rubber. The icehouse fronted two roads and an alley. A driveway passed through the property between the house and the icehouse. Summer days were hot; the brew was good and cold. Bill would come home at about 6:00 P.M. higher than a kite.

Bill's first wife had died, and his family was gone except for the youngest boy. When Cora Casman's mother came to Milbank to live with her daughter, she and Bill became acquainted. Mrs. Casman's mother was a genteel lady, but for some unknown reason, she and Bill were married. He was a model husband for a while, but those hot summer days of drinking caught up to him. He would arrive home in the old Model T, come up the driveway in low-low, shift into high, and with a "whoopee" that could be heard for blocks above the roar of the engine, he was off down the alley, down Diggs Avenue, up First Street, and then, with a crunch of gears, back up the driveway. With another "whoopee," he was off again around the circle. It appeared that he could not — or did not want to — stop. Mrs. Lewis would slam the doors shut; Bill would go round and round; and we would not see Cora Casman for days. Thus we observed the evils of alcohol first-hand.

Another experience I had as a youth I will never forget. One spring evening, I was walking home from a Boy Scout meeting. The air smelled warm, but the trees had no leaves. It would have been about 1928. I carried a short piece of rope and was practicing knot tying as I walked, so I may not have been a Tenderfoot.[42] I was on the sidewalk between Boerger's and our house — almost home. Dead ahead of me appeared a brilliant blue disk — larger than a wash tub. The blue was the color of a high-voltage arc. The trees and the house had a bluish tinge. I noticed an increase in size; there was no noise. I thought it might be a meteorite, but it had no trail and no apparent side movement — it just came toward me. The light disappeared as suddenly as it had appeared, and all was dark except for the residual blue image in my eye. I saw it for a total of less than a minute, but I have never questioned its reality. Mother was in bed, but I roused her and told her of the experience. She laughed and asked me whether I had really been at a Boy Scout meeting. Many years later, UFO sightings began to be reported.[43] I have often wondered — was it possible?

There were aeroplanes as I was growing up; in fact, they were used in World War I for reconnaissance and the dropping of grenades by hand. Later there were machine guns and aces. The first aeroplane that I saw was before the United States entered World War I. The year may have been 1916 or 1917. Dad carried me on his shoulders to A. C. Grams's pasture — about three blocks from home. It was evening, and the plane had landed there for some reason. Mr. Grams and the pilot were leaving the field as we crossed the creek and entered the pasture. The pilot wore a leather jacket and a leather helmet. The plane was a pusher type, open fuselage, and a chain drove the propeller. There was much bamboo and cloth. The seat was in the open and had a windscreen. The propeller made a deep impression on me; it was laminated, mahogany, and highly polished. As we looked and looked, the pilot returned and pulled cloth sacks over the propeller.[44]

Early in the 1930s, the Army Air Corps was attempting to sell an air arm to the military. In one promotional scheme, a demonstration flight of planes flew from somewhere in the East to the West Coast. Part of the fleet flew over Milbank; I was working on Mother's house at the time. I saw bi-wing fighters, observation Monocoupes, and hospital planes that had large red crosses painted on them. The hospital planes were Ford Trimotors, then in their heyday. There were more than thirty planes and I was impressed. In about fifty years, our technology developed from cloth-winged biplanes to supersonic jets and rockets that placed men on the moon.[45]

The first radio association I recall was a T-T antenna assembly at Franz Wendland's, about 1920. Wireless had been developed as a tuned spark gap by the Italian Guglielmo Marconi about the turn of the century and was used for emergency communication using Morse code, especially ship to ship and ship to shore. The crystal set followed, using crude crystals and a "cat's whisker," or wire, for tuning. The crystal set was an advancement; voice transmission was a fact. Wendland's two boys, Alvin and Harold, had a large array strung from two towers. The towers were about thirty feet high and forty feet apart. There were four acceptors and a feed-in harness. The set was a crystal receiver, and the boys could bring in stations three to four hundred miles distant. I would look at the antenna on the way to and from school and wonder.

When I was about fourteen, I started building radios. The American inventor Dr. Lee DeForest had developed the "valve"—a receiving tube. It was a three-element tube, a filament (6 volt), a grid, and a plate. The grid used a high resistance called "grid leak" and a negative 6-to-9-volt potential. We used a piece of paper saturated with ink for the resistor; resistance was never checked or calibrated. If one piece of paper did not work, we made another one. A 45-volt "B" battery was used as a plate supply. We used discarded "C" and "B" batteries and old 1½ volt "D" cells for filament operation.

In a one-tube set, the tube acted as detector and amplifier. In the two- tube set, one tube was the detector and the other the amplifier. Popular tubes were 301A and 199, called a peanut tube because of its size. Tuning was accomplished by a wire-wound variometer or a primitive variable capacitor; either was wired across a wire-wound tank. The tank wire was wound on any cardboard cylinder—small oatmeal boxes were most popular. The amplifier drove a set of head-phones. Everything was scrounged from scrap bits and pieces. The components were mounted on a wood base called a breadboard. The ends of orange crates made good breadboards.

Homemade sets were often called "bloopers"; as a station was tuned in, there would be a *bloop* descending in frequency as the sta-tion frequency was approached, then a clear signal followed by a *bloop* of ascending frequency as the tuning left the frequency of the station. Almost all of the early homemade sets were self-regenerating, i.e., they acted as transmitters as well as receivers. The *bloop* and high frequency squeal would be transmitted—much to the consternation of a neighbor's receiving. As commercial circuits developed, one of the popular ones, manufactured by Neutrowound, squelched the squeal, and the airways calmed down. The Kennelly-Heaviside layer of the ionosphere, about fifty miles above the earth, became impor-tant for reflecting medium-frequency radio waves.[46] When "skip dis-tance" was just right, South America, Germany, England, and other foreign stations would come in. Clear, cold nights at 3:00 to 4:00 o'clock in the morning gave the best conditions for listening.

Our first commercial set was an Atwater Kent, three-tube. All components were mounted in the open and in polished brass. The set, a discard, was given to me by the Berkner Garage, which sold radios as well as cars in those days. I made our first loudspeaker with a set of headphones and a dishpan; it rattled and sputtered, but we could all hear at the same time. I replaced it with a real horn speaker, but the used 45-volt "B" batteries did not have enough "soup" to drive it for any length of time. The next speaker was a cone type, requiring less "B" supply, and it lasted for several years.

Line-operated radios were also being developed. The transform-
ers and rectifiers were huge. The early rectifiers were composed of
several liquid cells that were later replaced with solid filters. Finally,
the in-chasis complete-unit power supply arrived. In Milbank, Irving
Patridge owned "ham" station W9TI, and Francis Beck owned W9DB.
I spent hours in their "shacks" listening to conversations from around
the world.[47] The transmitters were open-rack mounted. We listened
to the few stations available with a polite attitude; one would never
break in on a frequency that was being used. The last time I was in a
shack, in the 1960s, one could not retain a frequency because someone was always breaking in.

It was the summer of 1932 before I first took what is known today
as a vacation, but "visits" for "recreation" occurred from time to time.
When I was very young, we visited Minneapolis. We stayed in a hotel,
and I recall Mother prodding me to get out of bed and dress because
the maid would be in to make up the bed. But that was the reason I
did not want to get out of bed. What if the maid should come in and
see me in my long johns? (We wore them winter and summer, awake
or asleep.) I also recall Mother in her finery, complete with her small
lapel watch with gold numbers and a silver chain. Her long-skirted
dress covered her high-button shoes. The top of the dress fastened at
her throat, and it had leg-of-mutton sleeves. Dad wore a suit and a
celluloid collar fastened with a gold stud. He had a black mustache
and wavy black hair. Annis had a pink-and-white gingham dress and
long beautiful golden curls.

I must have gotten up and dressed because my next recollection is
a picnic with the Wendtys at Saint Anthony Falls on the Mississippi
River. The Wendtys had moved from Milbank to Minneapolis, where
Bill worked as a railroad-car inspector for one of the big packing
plants. Dad carried me on his shoulders and, with Bill, walked over
to a power-generating station near the falls. The water turbines, the
generators, and the hum are still vivid in my mind. We also saw Minnehaha Falls. Dad, who was a great reader, talked about Indians.[48] I
recall nothing else about that visit, but I suppose we must have been
"re-created."

Grandma Ackerman had a cottage at Chautauqua Park, where we
were re-created on several occasions.[49] The place was far from new

and no more modern than others, but it was a beautiful place with a little "ice box" creek flowing past. Once, we drove there in a horse and buggy with a cow tethered to the buggy. It was twelve miles, but we had time. The horse and cow were placed in a pasture on the hill behind the cottage. Milk and butter were cooled in the creek. We built dams on the lower part of the creek and sailed homemade sailboats behind them. Grant Thomas, the son of Grandma's daughter Nell, came with us on one trip. He had cut his toe while chopping wood barefoot, and he had it wrapped in a strip of cloth torn from a sheet and medicated it with horse liniment or turpentine. What a smell!

Memory can be trained to store facts, but I prefer another kind of memory, one that relates impressions gathered through observation. Observations relate to the new, the unusual, and produce impressions visually that can be recalled at will. William Wordsworth's poem "Daffodils" expresses the thought:

> For oft, when on my couch I lie
> In vacant or in pensive mood,
> They flash upon that inward eye
> Which is the bliss of solitude;
> And then my heart with pleasure fills,
> And dances with the daffodils.[50]

Many flashes upon my inward eye relate to Grandma's cottage.

The cottage had a rectangular first floor, with a six-sided tower as its second floor. A screen porch surrounded the first floor on three sides. The porch roof, accessible from the second-story windows, was almost flat, and we made our beds on it and slept under the stars. The front of the cottage faced the lake (east), and that was the favorite "bedroom." After the supper dishes were washed and the day's accumulation of sand swept through the back door, we climbed the steps to the tower and made our beds on the porch roof. Dusk would be falling, and the eastern sky would be a deep purple; a zone of dying twilight stretched toward the west. Land birds muttered their goodnights, and owls began to hoot in the trees. An occasional muffled *clack* of an oar in locks marked some tardy fisherman making his way back to dock.

We sat on our blankets and gazed steadily into the darkening east, looking for the first star. Dorathy and I had a game we played. We were sure that anyone who had died and gone to heaven became a star in the sky. We looked for the first star because that was Dad's star. As the sky darkened and the stars brightened, the world about us changed. An occasional firefly flashed his light; a fish jumped and broke the silence with a *plop*. On quiet nights, the stars glittered in the lake; the land birds were stilled; an occasional heron would *swish-swish* home, and the owls would *hoot-hoot* or skim past on silent wings. Then frogs tried to out-croak one another, and crickets fiddled up a storm. At times, one could see the reflection of distant summer lightening on the horizon. The lights in cottages across the lake would tire of shining and disappear one by one. All would be dark, and as the temperature dropped, the crickets ceased to fiddle, and the frogs surrendered to a winner. At last, the gentle lap of the waves sang us to sleep, as they licked a few atoms of material from the rocky shore.

Dawn was as beautiful as dusk but in reverse order. Alarm clocks were not necessary; a gray streak in the east and a cool morning breeze blowing off the lake brought us into a sitting position. The land birds took up their conversations from where they had dropped them the night before. Twitters became sleepy songs, and the woods swelled to melodious sound. Redwings squawked and grackles chattered. Robins sang and swallows glided; shikepokes and herons paraded through the air up and down the shore. Seagulls were in flight, and stormy petrels dived for unfortunate minnows. The shore birds ran excitedly and stopped suddenly, as if commanded to halt, and then ran again. As the sky lightened, ducks took to the air, circled, and landed with much splatter of water. Their heads would go down as they unashamedly displayed their tail parts; ducklings would imitate their parents. Geese flew by on their way to some farmer's field; mergansers and cormorants fished the shallow bottoms.

The sun was not to be outdone. The eastern sky turned blood red, faded to pink, and then orange, and with a burst almost of joy, the sun rose over the eastern hills. As if to show its authority, it splashed a trail of yellow-red-gold across the lake and painted each and every wavelet on the way. The air filled with melody and harmony, and light and sound reached a crescendo of noises, heralding the day. We dashed down the stairs in whatever was handy for swimming, tumbled down the banks, scattering squirrels and chipmunks, and dove into the lake. A few shivers later, we sat at the table. Before us, Grandma placed a glass of cold milk and a stack of pancakes with molasses to make them slide down easily. Another day of beauty was before us, and we had all day to enjoy it.

I went on one special lake trip with the Boy Scouts. I had joined the scouts at the age of twelve or thirteen at the urging of Scoutmaster H. C. Gilbert and my school chum Adzit Taholke. Mr. Gilbert was as fine a scoutmaster as one could find. My sister Annis, who had finished her first year of teaching and was renewing her certificate by attending Northern Normal at Aberdeen, sent Mother six dollars so that I could go to scout camp at Enemy Swim Lake. Yes, that was a one-week fee. I did not know about the camp or the six dollars until Annis wrote and asked me when I was going. When I asked Mother about it, she said that camp was not for us. I guessed that she had used the money to buy food. Annis was upset and sent another six dollars to me—six dollars that I am sure she could not afford.

That camp is vivid in my memory. My bedroll was many quilts rolled into a bundle. I was embarrassed when H. C. Gilbert asked me what I was going to do with the "watermelon" I was toting. My swimming suit had been given to me by someone. It had a shirt top with short sleeves and shorts with legs that stopped just above the knees. I must have been a sight, but I did complete first-class swimming and the swimming merit badge. A fourteen-mile hike was required, but I could not walk fourteen miles. The alternative was a fourteen-mile boat row. An Eagle Scout from Aberdeen by the name of Tiffany (I do not recall his first name) and I climbed into the boat and were off. I believe he did most of the rowing. We completed the trip around the lake by late afternoon, and I had completed another first-class requirement. I was so sunburned that I did not attend campfire—my favorite event—that evening. Campfires, with the songs, skits, and stories, still flash back to me today when the night descends and "the firmament showeth His handiwork" (Psalm 19). I received my first-class about one year later, but I was twenty years old before I received my Eagle, requiring twenty-one merit badges, and twenty-one years old when I completed a total of forty-two merit badges. As Bob Soule put it at the ceremony, I was a Double Eagle.

In 1932, the same month I turned eighteen, I took my first true vacation. I was working in the granite works, and Melvin Berkner was a stone cutter whose specialty was lettering. The shop always closed on Memorial Day for one month; that was vacation time. Melvin and his wife, Florence, were going to the Black Hills. Would I go along? I would if Mother said I could; she did. My equipment was a borrowed pup tent and some old quilts and changes of clothing. Melvin had a Model A Coupe, and he removed the trunk lid to install a homemade "kitchen." The three of us rode in the single seat. It was a long day's drive on a gravel road—the "Old Yellowstone Trail"—across South Dakota to Dark Canyon near Rapid City.[51]

In Dark Canyon and on Grace Coolidge Creek, we caught and ate fish—trout, no less. Florence pickled fish to take home for winter. I saw buffalo at the State Game Lodge in Custer State Park and the beautiful pheasant dining room where President and Mrs. Calvin Coolidge had dined in 1927. I saw ten moths as big as my hand. The smell of wild roses was everywhere. The museum at the South Dakota School of Mines in Rapid City featured dinosaur skeletons and a replica of the "Lucky Strike" (not cigarettes) gold nugget. Slabs of polished stone were from all over the world and as beautiful as anything I had ever seen. Near Keystone, the carving of Mount Rushmore was underway, and we watched chunks of granite as large as a house being blasted from Washington's nose. We talked to Gutzon Borglum in his studio.[52] Surely, if there were a paradise on earth, I had been there—and been re-created—this time by the Creator Himself.

The next summer I was working elsewhere, but Melvin and Florence again asked me to go, this time to Yellowstone with them. In the previous two years, I had helped Melvin build his cottage on the shore of Big Stone Lake, and we had become firm friends as we blasted black granite and drove nails together. The previous fall, I had helped Melvin overhaul the engine of his Model A. We scraped bearings by hand and used cigarette paper to determine clearances. We had built a canoe in his basement and had used it to fish and hunt ducks. We would hunt ducks from dawn to about ten o'clock, fish from then until noon, and hunt pheasants from noon until four or five o'clock.

Mother's winter larder was stocked with canned pheasant and duck. Melvin, a few years older than I, had become a big brother.

It was a three-day drive to Yellowstone on graveled roads much of the way. We drove through the Wyoming Big Horns and Wind River Canyon. We crossed Wyoming and late one afternoon crushed many rattlesnakes as we drove along one short stretch of warm pavement in the western part of the state. Late that day, we pitched camp on the shore of Lake Yellowstone a few hundred yards from "Fishing Bridge." Melvin caught large cutthroat there on a Colorado spinner, reeling them in as fast as he could and—later—turning them loose. I was using Melvin's spare fly rod (I did not have one of my own) and continued to catch rocks until Melvin pointed out that there were no rocks and that I was experiencing strikes. I learned to set the hook and began to catch cutthroat. Here was paradise again!

We moved camp to Madison Junction and fished for rainbow trout. We spent a week there and did not see another camper. At one point a fancy blue touring car pulled up, and the chauffeur leaned out the window to inquire in a British accent, "Do you know where the Master can get a hot steam bath?" It should have been obvious from looking at us that we had no idea at all.

I saw grizzly sows with cubs and also black bear. I followed one black bear, with me on one side of a row of bushes, the bear on the other. I wanted a picture on my small vest-pocket Kodak. He (she) surprised me by coming through the bushes about five feet in front of me. Somehow, I took the picture. Another black bear, a young one, visited our camp several times. Someone had apparently trained him to do a trick, for he would slide his bottom along the bench of the picnic table, fold his paws, and bow his head over the table as through saying a blessing. After this performance, he expected a treat. We found him entertaining for awhile, but eventually I got fed up with his begging. A well-aimed raw egg caught him in the eye. He wiped his paw across the injury, lumbered off, and did not come back again.

We saw Old Faithful, mud pots, and Morning Glory Pool, and Melvin burned his ankles when one pool overflowed on his foot. We fished Crater Lake, which had a steep sloping bottom, and I caught the biggest cutthroat of my life.[53] Melvin had a movie camera and was taking pictures. I tried to keep my balance on the sloping bottom, keep my line tight, and work backwards so that I could flip the fish onto the steep bank. As I brought the fish near shore, it splashed and was off the hook. Probably five minutes had passed since the strike, and the fish lay in the water exhausted. I threw the pole on shore, dove in head first, grabbed the fish, head and tail, and threw it up on the bank where Florence stepped on it. She had been sitting in the sunshine watching the entire event. From then on, I was known as Heron.

Those were golden days, and we arrived home after a heavy rain. The air was cool and damp, and Mother was working with her flowers in the front yard. The three of us took one other vacation to the West Coast. It was a beautiful trip—mountains, prairies, the ocean, and fruit. But Melvin was not well. We fished; we visited the "Nut Tree," which at that time was a small roadside stand.[54] Melvin died of leukemia about a year later, and those vacations came to an end. How wonderful those trips were. To see a great and beautiful country, to think on man's struggle to tame and yet preserve it, to enjoy the friendship and the learning were all great experiences.

. . . .

"*G*et an education; it is something that nobody can take away from you," Mother continually admonished us children, and our education began at an early age. Annis, five years my senior, had always wanted to be a teacher. At some time, the three of us received a "store-bought" school desk with a roll chart at the top. The chart offered lessons in arithmetic, writing, and spelling. There were also pictures of fruit and toys. The roll was black and the print was white. The front was wood painted black—a black board—and hinged to drop down for a desk surface. Behind the front were wooden pockets and trays for pencils, chalk, and paper. The entire piece was similar to an "A" frame pivoted at the top so that when the back legs were separated from the front legs, the desk stood on four feet. Dorathy and I spent hours in front of that desk. Annis would drill and drill—and grill and grill—so that when I went to school, I had been through the first grade.

I recall the first day of public school. I do not think that Mother went with me; I may have gone with Annis. I wore a Lord Fauntleroy pants and jacket complete with hat and large bow.[55] That was probably Mother's concept of what a boy wore at school. I never wore the suit again, and I have often wondered why. Did Annis tell Mother that boys did not dress that way in America? Our school clothing thereafter was utilitarian with no frills. Girls wore knee-length bloomers and gingham dresses, long stockings, and high shoes. Boys wore gray woolen shirts, knickers, long stockings, and high shoes. Mother knit the stockings, but sometimes we wore store bought. They were usually black. I still wonder at the black dye used in those days. When legs were in direct light, the black color became an iridescent green. We were always clean, changing our clothes once a week.

Milbank Independent No. 1 was a long, three-story brick building that housed all the grades from first through twelfth. The first floor was downstairs (a basement); I counted the twelve steps down to that level many times. The boys' room was in the east end, and the girls', the west end. Being found in the opposite sex's area resulted in a trip to the principal's office. A closed-tube fire escape was on the north side of the building, and third-floor students would slide down it during a fire drill. The boys would run around the building to see the girls come down the chute and to comment on the color of their bloomers. Some girls had a flair for display. The second floor was up a flight of stairs and served grades one through eight. Students climbed up two flights from the basement to the third floor to attend grades nine through twelve. The eighth grade was a point of departure; many students did not go on to high school. After all, at the age of fourteen, one was expected to do a man's or woman's work, and many did. The interior was finished with wood, and the floors were saturated with floor oil. When the building burned in 1943, it was a whee of a fire.

The three "Rs" were the basis of education; reading and "rithmetic" did not bother me, but I was still printing left-handed, and "riting" (penmanship) was a problem. First grade was at the top of the south stair and to the right; each student shared a double desk with another student. We stood in line to go in and out, to drink at the fountain, and to go to the bathroom. Jap (Jasper) Kibby stood in line in front of me. Aggressive and somewhat of a bully, he was a runner, and he chased a large number of girls. On one occasion, as we marched down the stairs, Jap drove his elbow into my solar plexus. I remember landing on my knees on the metal-grating foot scraper. My stockings were torn, and I had a deep cut in my right knee. I still have the scar and wonder whether my lousy stomach is the result of that jab. My start in school was not auspicious.

When I entered second grade, a part of the class was moved to the Odd Fellows Hall at the south end of Main Street; the teacher was Miss Shuck. We now had single desks, but I do not recall any other exciting events. At Christmas time I saw, for the first time, Christmas written as Xmas. I knew that was wrong because Annis had taught us to spell it *Christmas*—Christ's birth. On the last day of school, we went up Main Street chanting, "School's out, school's out; teacher let the monkeys out." Miss Shuck came to the door and said that she would put the monkeys back in if we were not quiet. We ran home.

Third and fourth grades were in one room. Miss Sedam was the teacher for both grades. I spent more time listening to the fourth-graders recite; their material was new—third grade was old stuff. I remember one recess when Miss Sedam put her arm around me and asked whether I was ill; I was embarrassed. I do not recall what I said, if anything. I did not like recess; all I did was stand in the cold until the bell rang. In fourth grade, Miss Edna Olson was the art and penmanship teacher. Art was sissy, and penmanship was still a problem (it always has been), but I can still see Miss Olson, a tall, maiden lady, walking around the room reciting "push pulls, push pulls," "ovals, ovals," with an interjected, "I hear two lips, I hear two lips," and never a break in stride, chalk, or utterance.

Fifth grade is a blank, but sixth, seventh, and eighth are vivid. The tall, red-haired, freckled Miss Ling was our sixth-grade teacher, who helped me with my writing. She placed pictures on the wall—*Stag at Bay*, *The Gleaners*, and *The Angelus*. The latter was most beautiful, and it would flash into my memory every time I heard the Angelus bell ring at the Catholic church.[56] I do not recall the name of the seventh-grade teacher, but she was a whiz at math, demonstrating the relationship among radius, diameter, and circumference with a piece of string. She left during the year but visited the class in the spring. I remember how she blushed. She may have been married, and that was forbidden for female teachers at the time.[57] Miss Ona Sanborn, the eighth-grade teacher, was a disciplinarian. One winter day, she kept the entire class in after 4:30 because a few had been making noise. It was dark and beginning to storm. Miss Sanborn was called to the telephone, and when she came back, she whispered to me that I had better leave for home. I had had surgery the past summer and was on crutches. Mother had called, and I do not know what she said, but her Irish must have been up.

High school consisted of classes in English, chemistry, physics, Latin, biology, Greek, algebra, advanced algebra, manual training, drafting, and orchestra. For extracurricular activities there were sports, band, and debate and declam; but they seemed secondary to the purpose of the classroom. A poor student (other things being equal) was encouraged, then prodded, and then dropped. The strap hung behind the principal's door, and it could be used and it was used. Each subject had a different teacher, and they were all dedicated to their profession and to the students. I did not take gym, but

I did play in the pep band, although I have no idea why. I never did learn how to play the clarinet, which one of the town's businessmen had given me as a gift. I still have it and still do not know how to play it.

In the spring of my senior year, Elfreda Kauers asked me to take her to a show. She was a pretty girl, an emigrant from Germany, my biology partner, and she had the tickets. I checked with Mother, and she said that I should decide; the next day I said yes. Mother had bought a suit for me for graduation—long pants, coat, and vest. When I dressed to go out, Mother said, "Your Dad would be so proud of you," and started to cry. It had been nine years since Dad had been killed. (I wore that suit, when needed, through three years of college seven years later.) Elfreda and I went to the show, and afterwards we walked and walked until I finally walked Elfreda home, where-upon she put her arms around me and kissed me. I was shocked and stopped at the school grounds on the way home to recover. I had never kissed a girl, but then I still had not—she had kissed me.

Soon after I had graduated from high school, I recall playing with the pep band at a banquet. Jack Manders, then playing for the Golden Gophers at University of Minnesota, was the speaker. (He would play for the Chicago Bears from 1933 to 1940.) As one of the six members of the high-school pep band, I had attended basketball and football games when Manders had been a football player on Milbank's winning team. Now Jack did not have money, but he was in college. I talked to him and asked him how he managed that; he said that he had a scholarship. So why not me?

It would be seven years before I returned to academia, however. I began by taking a few courses at South Dakota State College in the fall and winter of 1938. I was then working nights for the Civil Works Administration in Brookings, setting up recreation centers, and needed something to occupy my time during the day. I enrolled as a special student under unbelievable circumstances. I had no money, no books, and no transcript, but I was enrolled on a verbal promise to pay. It was "pay as you can." I did. An administrator telephoned the bookstore, and I was in college.

I was seven years out of high school and competing with fresh, young minds, but I wanted to know, so I worked hard. I enrolled in physics, chemistry, bacteriology, human physiology, human parasitology, and diagnostic bacteriology. Those were happy days; each day brought something new. Charles Stumbo, my bacteriology professor, became interested in me. My plan was to go to a teaching hospital and become a medical lab technician. He convinced me that I would always be competing for women's wages and that I should work instead for a B.S. degree. That summer, he wrote that he had a job for me at Kansas State, where he had relocated to complete his Ph.D. Would I come?

In September, I finished my last day of work for the CWA. I went home and packed. Bethine Brown (a girlfriend), Mother, and I set out in my Model A Ford. Bethine was driving through Nebraska when we had a blowout. Although we were not traveling fast, the car skidded and tipped over on the gravel road. Mother's back was injured, and we spent two days at the sheriff's house as guests. I went on to school, and Bethine took Mother home on the bus. I arrived sore and bruised, lost, and ill at ease in Manhattan, Kansas. Charles and his wife, Vi, took me in. I did not have enough money to pay the fifty dollars out-of-state tuition, but I borrowed that from the student loan office and enrolled. I also got a student job.

On the first day of work when I reported to the office of the Microbiology Department chairman, Dr. Leland Bushnell, a young lady named Dorcile Samuelson, dressed in a red-and-white gingham dress (although she says it was pink-and-white flowered) and looking for all the world like a blond goddess, took me down to P. L. Gainey's lab. Gainey taught microbiology and bacteriology. I spent three happy years in that lab at twenty-five cents per hour, one hundred hours per month. From that twenty-five dollars, I paid enrollment fees, board, and room, did laundry, and bought books. And I repaid my student loan. I gave my activity ticket away except for one time when I sold it for fifty cents. Who had time for activities? I graduated from Kansas State University with a Bachelors Degree in science in 1942, three and one-half years after I had first taken courses at South Dakota State College in Brookings.

Chemistry and physics were my majors, but after graduation I went into the Department of Agronomy, also at Kansas State, as a graduate student in soils. Dr. Clifford Hide was my major professor. His department was interested in some of the work I had done in bacteriology for its relevance to soil treatment, specifically, sub-surface tillage. The dust storms and widespread erosion problems of the preceding years had pushed soil-conservation work to the top of scientific research agendas. I spent two years researching stubble mulch in the field and laboratory. My work asked what effect tilling six inches below the surface had on bacteria in the soil. It was thought that the minimal disturbance of the soil, characteristic of subsurface tillage, might cut off the supply of nutrients necessary to sustain bac-teria in the soil. The bacterial population in the soil is quite impor-tant from the standpoint of solubilizing certain kinds of nutrients that plants need. We found that in fact the bacteria bloomed and grew like mad. When Dean ("Daddy") Ackert read my thesis, he sug-gested that I go to Columbia, Missouri, take some course work, and submit the thesis for a Ph.D. I enjoyed the soils work, but I was more interested in chemistry and bacteriology. So I sent applications to Cornell, the University of Wisconsin, and Iowa State University at Ames. Researchers from Iowa State had heard me deliver a paper at the scholarly annual meeting of my field, and they were interested in my work.

Dr. Charles Werkman, head of the Microbiology Department at Ames, called me and offered me eight hundred dollars per year to undertake graduate work in biochemical and biophysical microbiol-ogy. Would I come? Dorcile and I, who were married by that time, talked about the possible future and decided. I called Dr. Werkman and told him, *yes*, but I was getting nine hundred dollars per year and I needed that much to live. He met the salary, and in late August, I left for Milbank to see Mother. She and I enjoyed a few days together and then took the train to Minneapolis to Dorathy's home. World War II was on, and the train was filled with young men in uniform. I stood in the aisle part of the way. I returned to Ames by bus to take up the last leg of a twelve-year journey toward an education.

For six years, I lived chemistry and bacteriology, home remodeling, and teaching. At Iowa State I still did some work with soils, but my research was more laboratory based and not so much fieldwork. My research used carbon 14 as a tracer to follow chemical reactions. In a general way, my studies addressed nutrition and how bacteria cells worked: what they produced and how they produced it and whether it was useful for the cells or a waste product. In nonscientific terms, my work in part examined how food is digested and what parts of it are used to build new cells. I became an assistant professor when I graduated at Christmas time in 1950. At long last, I had a Ph.D. sash and diploma.

I was never a good student—fair perhaps, but not good. I would have liked to redo my education on a more relaxed basis and with sufficient money not to worry about tomorrow's breakfast. But it was all worthwhile, and I would do it again. We went to school because of Mother's admonition, "Get an education, it's something that nobody can take away from you," and because we learned from Mother's experience of what the lack of an education could mean. My mother also would often say, "We learn all our lives and die wanting." She was right, for although our sphere of the *known* expands, so does our contact with the *unknown*. We can never attain complete knowledge. Mother would say, "He who lives longest will see most—and know least." How true that is!

B y now, one might have the impression that the middle name of all Fowlers is "work." My father worked long and hard in England in order to survive and so did Mother. Dad worked long and hard in this country because his new home needed his work to grow and develop. Work from Father's time in early South Dakota calls to mind a story about the Swede who visited relatives in the United States. When he returned to Sweden, he was asked how the *arbeit* ("work") was in America. He answered that they did not have *arbeit* in America, but they had something they called work, and that was hell. No question about it, some phases of any work can be hell—even to the most dedicated.

The basic facts of economics were clear to Mother and Dad. Needs were obtained using a medium of exchange. Dad and Mother had labor (an ability *and* desire to do work) as a medium of exchange; for that, they obtained another medium of exchange, money, with which they could purchase something they needed. A minimum wage did not exist then, and a day's pay varied with the job; jobs were not paid for by the hour. Jobs were never "long" in supply, and money was always short. Mother expressed it well when she misquoted from 1 Timothy (as many do), "Money is the root of all evil,"[58] and then added "but I'd just as soon have a little more of the root and less of the leaves."

Dad passed on this edict about work: "Work a little longer and a little harder than the next fellow; do the best job you know how, and you'll always have a job." Mother did not pass on an edict, but she passed on an example. Anyone who did less than his best was slovenly and not to be trusted. Work was a continuing contest, man against man. Who could drive a spike fastest and squarest? Who could best shoe a horse? Or harness a horse, or mend a harness, or pitch bundles, or fire a boiler? Simply put, work was hard and long and often dirty (dirty in the 1920s sense of not clean). The work ethic was straight-forward: "Do the best damn job you can, but be sure that it is better than anyone else's." Add the words gas engine, auto-body, carpentry, electrical wiring, and plumbing to the contest for "best job" to account for changes during my lifetime, and what appears is the backdrop against which my work life was painted, from shoeing a horse to isolating a microbacterium.

When Dad went to Wisconsin, certain chores were assigned to me. The household needed input—wood and coal for the kitchen cook stove, hard coal for the heater, well water for drinking and cooking, and soft, or cistern, water for washing. Out of the house came ashes, slops, and more ashes. Wood came from several sources. One was a pile of cut ties, much of it oak, and I declared personal war on the woodpile at the young age of seven or eight. The single-bit ax had a large heavy head and a twisted handle, part of which was missing. That ax joined the war on the side of the woodpile. Dad had many good tools, but the ax must have been a reject from Alley Oop.[59] The cutting edge was at least one-fourth-inch wide, and any splitting was purely accidental. The battles continued every morning until time for school and every evening after school. One good point—I might have broken my leg by a miss, but I would never have cut off my foot. I made a solemn vow that one day I would heat that ax bit white hot, pound the hell out of it, grind and polish it, provide a new handle, and it would split wood whether it wanted to or not. When the tears of frustration would start to drop, I would remind myself of that vow. Then the dents in the blocks would be a bit deeper, and a few more splinters would be produced. Ten years later, when I went to work in the blacksmith shop, I looked for that ax bit. I never found it; it was hiding somewhere, no doubt in fear.

"Catywumpus" from us across a dry slough lived Horton and Lila Mills, who had retired from the farm and lived in a beautiful house on about five acres of land (now Second Street). They had invested money in old houses, and Mr. Mills spent his time rebuilding, fixing, and painting. Mrs. Mills cared for their two cows and many chickens. Her butter and eggs were in demand, and I often pulled a wagon full of her loaded butter crocks and egg crates up town to Thirsk's store, where they were exchanged for trading chips. Those aluminum disks or hexagons, each stamped with a value, were returned to Mrs. Mills, who placed them in a large crock with hundreds of others to await the day when their value would increase.[60] I received a nickel for my effort; the nickel went into Mother's apron pocket. I recall that Annis worked for Mrs. Mills one entire day at housecleaning. Perhaps ninety percent of the house was never used, but it was all cleaned once a year. Annis also received a nickel for her work; she "may need some school pencils," Mrs. Mills remarked.

My first "real job" was with Mr. Mills the summer I was nine years old. It was the first summer after Dad was killed. Mr. Mills was a craftsman's wonder. He could lay out and cut a jack rafter that fit like a cabinet joint; he could plumb a stud by eye, and it was a perfect vertical; he could lath as fast as the nail could leave his mouth and the lathing hatchet drive it home. I probably spent more time watching him lath than I did at work. His cheek bulging with lathing nails, he gave a *pftt*, a bang, and had another lath in his hand. In phase, but at greater lengths of time, his *tu-e-e* shot a stream of tobacco juice in a different direction. The tobacco was to neutralize the poison from the nails! In all probability, I contributed little, but I did learn to pull nails, to clean up, to use a square, to saw, and to drive nails. Together, we laid siding, sheeting, and shingles. I recall seeing acquaintances playing with their wagons in the street as I stood shaking on a scaffold, and I wondered, "How come?"

Mr. Mills was a kind gentleman, but he was also practical. As we quit work on the first Saturday evening, he asked me, "How much?" I did not know. He gave me $2.50 with the admonition, "Don't tell my wife; she's so tight she'd skin a louse for its hide and tallow." I was probably overpaid. When I got home, the money went into Mother's apron pocket as she stood discussing flower gardens with her dear friend Helen McGiven. Mr. Mills died that winter of leukemia (not called such at that time). Probably his death was hastened by his diet of fried potatoes and re-re-reboiled coffee.

In the years that followed, I mowed lawns, shoveled snow, gardened, did minor house repairs, and worked on screen and storm windows. I was never out of a job of some kind, and the nickels, dimes, and sometimes quarters went into the family fund. One summer, I worked for Bill Schmidt who lived across the alley and did custom threshing. I was "taken on" as his "grease monkey." I may have been twelve or fourteen years old. Steam supplied the power to the thresher via a Case single-cylinder reciprocating steam engine. It was belt driven. The driving wheels, perhaps two feet wide, were fitted with wedge-shaped lugs; the wheels were at least twice my height. A long and black fire-tube boiler generated the steam. The cylindrical boiler was full of water and twenty to thirty steel tubes carried the heat from the engine fire through the boiler. Cylinder exhaust was directed to the smoke stack to provide draft for the fire box. Coal and wood served as fuel. The thresher, clad in galvanized sheet metal, was also a Case.

There was much to do to keep the rig running. The long leather drive belt was frightening; I stayed clear. Several systems were driven by the engine: the threshing cylinder, the shakers for cleaning, the blowers, the elevators, and the bundle conveyers with the cutting knives. All were driven by leather belts and all required greasing by way of grease cups. There would be fifteen to twenty-five cups on a thresher to provide this lubrication. It was my job to keep the metal cups full of grease. Every once in a while during the runs, the steam would be shut off, and I would screw the cup cap down a little bit in order to squirt the grease. All this kind of equipment used grease for lubrication; there were varied combinations of greases depending upon what they were used for. Oil was not used for that kind of lubrication; it had to be something more stable than oil. Oil did have to be added to the boiler feed, and the steam engine required both oil and grease. A fire needed to be built each morning in the fire-box chamber, and the water wagon needed to be filled continually from a nearby slough or horse tank. A team of horses pulled the water wagon, and the hand-driven pump was pushed and pulled until the tank was filled. I serviced the water injector and pressure regulator continually.

At moving time, I would sometimes sit in the engineer's seat and guide the monster down the dirt road, pulling the thresher and water wagon behind. It was then that the whisper of steam and the feel of power at the throttle would cause such joy that I would pull the whistle cord and watch the nearby cows make a mad dash for distant parts. Bill would stand beside me and roll his cigarettes, Prince Albert tobacco in good times and Bull Durham in bad. We laid plank across the country bridges; I would walk across, and Bill would maneuver the multi-ton hulk over the often-rotting bridges. Being a grease monkey was my kind of life; steam was king and I was a prince.

No, I alone did not do all those jobs; I did some of them and helped with others. But I did learn, and it was exhilarating to watch the counter-balanced flywheel (to create uniformity of speed), to hear the *swoosh-swish* of the piston rod as steam leaked past the packing gland (an elastic sleeve that was *supposed* to prohibit such leaks), and to listen to the *pooh-pooh* of the black smoke in response to the cylinder exhaust. I would look to the sky and dream of the day when I would own my own rig; the ball weights that turned the steam valve on and off on the governor (the speed device) would have to be polished brass!

Another of my work experiences related to the Flett family. It was late fall, and I was out of school. The Great Depression was in full swing. Dr. Flett had returned to the barter system and was taking produce as pay for his services when necessary. He took in chickens, eggs, and sides of beef and pork. On some evenings, I would help him cut meat; we used the kitchen table as our operating table. Mrs. Flett and Dorathy would watch from the "theater"—Mrs. Flett from a wheel chair or her hospital bed. I was taught a fair amount of anatomy in those sessions.

Dr. Flett delivered many of the Grant County babies, and although he was lame and getting worse, he was available twenty-four hours a day for office or house calls—town or country. Our phone would ring at any hour of the night, and Dr. Flett would say: "These babies come at nine months to the minute, and you know how much night work that means for me. Will you drive?" In a short time, the old green Chevy would pull up, and we would be off, usually west to the hills. Dr. Flett always started the drive. The dirt roads would become ruttier and the snow deeper, and when he had the car completely stuck in the inevitable snow bank, he would say, "I have some things to prepare; perhaps you'd better drive." I would back out, take a run, back out, take another run, and finally we would be in the farmer's yard.

Doc would take his black bag and his worn "baby" bag, which contained the set of large "spoons" (forceps) and go to the house. He was usually back in a short time to say that it would not be long or that it would be long; in the latter case, I made myself comfortable and tried to keep warm. A lot of events occur in car seats; a restful night's sleep is not one of them. Some of those births were to unmarried girls, but as my Mother would say, "The first can come any time—the second takes a little longer." I became acquainted with a number of dogs and cats. I heard the absolute stillness of a country night in winter. When the sky was clear, I became acquainted with many constellations and with some of the planets. Venus was always most beautiful. If nature had been kind and the birth were easy, Doc would drive home. If the birth had been long and difficult, I would drive. I believe Doc averaged about three hundred babies a year, and over the years that was a lot of babies. I did learn a certain amount of patience, although I have never been a patient person.

Just before I was seventeen, I was offered a job in the blacksmith shop of Harry Fowler and Halen Knutson. Fowler was not a relative; he was a coincidence. After school in the spring, that summer, and after school in the fall, I would swallow the dust and dirt, be burned with hot sparks from the forge, manhandle hot iron, struggle with the front and rear of horses (and clean up after the rear), help rebuild wagon wheels and set the heated tires, grind and polish plow shares and cultivator shovels, and drop exhausted on the back step when I got home. I was too exhausted to eat and too dirty to go into the house. That summer the railroad dam was a godsend. I would take a bar of homemade soap, walk the two blocks to the dam, strip, and scrub and wash my hair. I wondered at the dirty soap suds. How could one collect so much dirt in a ten-hour period?

I often smile when I think of how things have changed. In those days, we case-hardened plow shares and cultivator shovels with sodium cyanide, sprinkling it on the cherry red steel in the forge. The share was then quenched in a large wooden tank; the water was soon saturated with sodium cyanide. One day a stray dog wandered through the shop, lapped from a puddle that leaked from the tank, and died before he reached the street. That quenched steel was later ground and buffed (by me), and the cloud of dust, with cyanide, that filled the grinding room was a nightmare. We were not provided with respirators—probably unknown at the time. Neither did we have protective eye wear. Sparks from the large carborundum wheel formed a hot stream directed on face, hands, and clothing. When I smelled "rag burn," I would stop grinding and beat out the smoldering spots on my overalls. The hot flesh on my hands would also cause me to stop and douse my hands in a bucket of water, which always brought a laugh when Frank or Harry saw it happen.

One day the inevitable happened. I received a piece of hot steel in the pupil of my right eye; I remember feeling it hit. Within a few days, the pain was so great that I wore an eye shield to keep out the light. A few mornings later, I could stand it no longer. I told Harry Fowler that I was going to the doctor. He suggested that I sharpen a horseshoe nail and that he would dig the piece out—that was standard operating procedure for the day. I did not take his advice and went to Dr. John W. Pay, who found the spot and removed the small piece with a sterile needle. That Saturday's paycheck was forty cents short; I had been docked for being absent. I still have a blind spot in my right eye.

The blacksmith shop was about one-half block long; the front faced Third Street and the rear faced the alley. The well pump was inside by the office, and under the spout was a gallon jug of buttermilk delivered on Thursday or Friday by some farmer friend of Harry Fowler's. The buttermilk was *real* buttermilk and was cooled by water from the pump; it contained small curds and small flakes of real butter. It might last as long as two days. Across the alley was an "eat shop," which served hamburgers and coffee and cold beer if one knew how to ask for it. Coffee (or beer) and hamburger were five cents—for both!

The combined telephone and power poles for the shop were located in the alley. Many stray dogs used the alley to scrounge food and the poles as a place to relieve themselves. The hangers-on at the eatery also used the poles as a relieving station. In the heat of summer, the stench of urine was powerful, and a west breeze carried it into the shop. We had sufficient horse urine in the shoeing stalls; we did not need further fragrance. A solution materialized in the form of several Model T Ford coils—a potent source of high voltage—that I owned. Frank Kransberry, a seasoned worker about twenty years my senior, and I wound fine wire around the favorite pole, brought the single lead wire into the back door, and attached it to the coil, a "hot shot" six-volt battery, *and,* finally, a push-button doorbell. We waited for the first customer; it was a male dog. We pushed the button as the dog lifted his leg and the stream began to flow. To see that dog hop on three legs, stop to lick, and then hop and lick as he dashed down the alley was funny. But the first human customer was more amusing. The air was blue with four-letter words. No more humans! After treating a few dogs, there were no more dogs either, and the smells in the shop returned to rag burn and the burned protein of horse hoof.

Overall, however, there was little "fun" in that shop. In the middle of a job, Harry, who was very sarcastic, would often say, "When you finish resting, go do . . . (this, that, or something else)." One time when I was under the floor boards in the coal hole pushing the then-being-delivered blacksmith coal into its place, Harry came up with his "when you finish resting" bit. I looked out of the hole and replied, "When you finish talking, why don't you go to hell." It was the only time in my life that I ever talked back to an employer, and I probably would have been fired on the spot, but Frank Kransberry laughed and said, "Good for you."

Frank was a person to be reckoned with. He did most of the horse-shoeing for the shop, and he knew how to handle a horse. Most horses withstood their shoeing calmly enough, but one old buggy horse had a habit of biting Frank in the backside when he turned and stooped to place the front hoof between his knees. One day Frank lost his patience. The horse bit; Frank whirled around and hit the animal squarely between the eyes with the shoeing hammer. The horse went down. It was some time before the beast staggered to its feet. It never bit Frank again.

Two experiences in the shop suggested that my guardian angel was still watching. I was grinding a piece of work on a high-speed, quarter-inch wheel mounted on a stand about chest high. I always wore bib overalls and carried a wallet in my chest watch pocket. I am not sure why I carried the wallet—it was always empty. I believe it was Dad's and probably it served as a status symbol. The wheel exploded, and one piece struck me in the chest, point inward. The point passed through the wallet and penetrated my sternum, where it drew much blood but caused no other damage. That piece could have gone through my throat or head. How lucky can one person be? The other incident also involved a grind wheel. I was told to finish-grind the inside of a yoke that had been welded; the space was a little larger than the wheel was wide, and I did not like the idea, but I had been told to do it. The yoke caught, followed the speeding wheel, flew loose, and hit the back of my arm. The yoke weighed about two pounds, but at that speed it was a lethal missile. Again, why not my head? I winced for weeks every time I picked up a hammer and struck a red-hot horseshoe or plow share.

As fall advanced, school and blacksmith shop became less and less compatible. I put in my last Saturday and drew my last check. "Work can be hell," the Swede had remarked, and that period of time surely was. I was never large or strong. I had gone through a siege of polio, and my leg, back, and arm were in constant pain. I was not "cut out" for heavy labor, but what else was there? Sometimes the pain and depression would get to me, and I would weep. There were occasions when I wondered why that yoke had not been allowed to hit me in the head. It was difficult to rationalize the need to do a job well, but it was also necessary to do so. The ten cents an hour, ten hours a day, six days a week, with time donated on Saturday nights—until the last farmer had collected his bits and pieces—was an experience that taught me a deep regard for the man who must earn his bread with his own two hands.

My next job was in the Hunter Granite Works. It was the spring of 1932. The depression had reached the Midwest, and *everything* was going to "hell in a handbasket." Again it was hard labor, but I jumped at the chance. The night before I started to work, I dreamed vividly of the tool room at the works, and I saw things I had never seen or even imagined before. The tool room in my dream contained a set of two immense sandstone wheels about five feet in diameter and five inches wide. They were driven by a belt from a jack shaft. The tool rest was a board with an angle iron protector. The boxes of tools contained three kinds of chisels—narrow, broad, and serrated, each with a cylindrical shaft of steel. There were chippers and handsets also. A metal powder can hung over each wheel. A nail hole at the bottom of each can was plugged with a whittled plug, and water dripped onto each wheel. I woke up shaking at the thought of those huge wheels exploding at high speed—for I had been there. The next morning, I walked into the tool room at about 7:15, and there it was, right down to the powder cans and the whittled plugs. I was told to grind tools; no one showed me how. The whistle blew at exactly 7:30, and the jack shaft turned and the wheels turned—but at a pleasingly slow speed. My fears vanished.

I ground tools as I thought they should be ground; the feel of the wheel on steel was pleasing. There were no sparks and no hot metal. The wheels cut fast, and I began to organize: to-be-sharpened, on the right; holder (a piece of pipe that fit the tool shaft), in my right hand; those sharpened, into the box on the left. Chippers and hand-sets were separate and required more detail. The sharpened tools were to be delivered to the cutters; the dull tools were picked up and taken to the tool room for sharpening. It was routine; it was eight hours a day, five and a half days a week; it was cleaner than black-smith work; and it paid twenty-five cents per hour. I had it made. I learned to use the popping Johnny and to split twenty-ton polished slabs into blocks for the cutters. I learned how to polish and help the cutters when they needed muscle to swing the ten-pound hammer against the bull set, which they always held.[61] Silicosis did not bother me; after all, I had been initiated on blacksmith coal.

Don Hunter was not too well liked, and on one occasion he "chewed me out"—everyone took his turn at that. But he was the boss, and he was the owner's son. Don had "laid out" a slab from the polishing bed. Gus Swanson ran the overhead crane, and he was to stand the slab on edge as I transferred the pattern to the polished side. As Gus brought the lift chain snug with the crane, I noted a gleam of parting metal in a chain link. Gus stopped the lift at my frantic waving. We backed off and Gus got Don. The slab was lowered without incident. But when Don asked Gus how he had found the breaking link, and Gus told him that I had seen it, Don turned on me and told me that I was there to work and not to be looking around. He used his goodly supply of four-letter words to emphasize the fact. That was more unreasonable than Harry Fowler had ever been, but it was not over.

I transferred the patterns; Gus turned the slab. I used the chipper along the lines, drilled the proper holes, set the feathers and wedges, and broke off the blocks in order. Don came out to check the work and mark the blocks for the cutters, and then, referring to his order box, he blew his stack. I had improperly transferred and ruined two blocks, he said. Sad experience had taught me that if I were not to be assumed guilty, I had to defend myself—something that I had not done previously because the boss "was always right." I pointed out that I had transferred the patterns exactly. Gus was called; the blocks were turned over, and, sure enough, Don's layout and the transfers were exact. Don never said that he was sorry; he walked off in a huff, but he did not chew on me again.

The granite works was shut down in the fall. For some time, the only orders had been for grave covers for rich people in the East. Such products were beautiful, with craftsmanship written all over them. To remove a lump of stone from a huge extrusion from the earth, to cut and polish it, to form it by hand with the aid of a few air-driven tools, and finally to produce a quietly beautiful monument to someone's life required real skill and attention to craft. That monument would stand through the ages of heat and cold, rain and snow, and define the resting place of a loved one because someone did "the best damn job" that he could. Today, computers have replaced the cutters. Hand-lettering has given way to sand blasting, and craftsmanship is rapidly disappearing. The cemetery is becoming a memorial garden with small bronze plaques, but yesterday's "rock of ages" stands as a memorial to a life and death. It is also a memorial to a dying craft.

The Great Depression had struck, and it struck hard. In November 1932, President Herbert Hoover lost the election for a second term; his plan for recovery went with him. In March, Franklin Delano Roosevelt came in with many of Hoover's plans, and the Democratic Congress rushed them through—the Bank Holiday, the Agricultural Adjustment Administration (AAA), the Works Progress Administration (WPA), the National Recovery Administration (NRA), the National Youth Administration (NYA), and the Civilian Conservation Corps (CCC). The PWA (Public Works Administration) funded construction projects similar to those in the Hoover Administration. The many programs were often referred to as alphabet soup. Social Security was born, and programs changed name and direction over time. The WPA, CWA (Civil Works Administration), and FERA (Federal Emergency Relief Administration) were similar programs, all with a similar goal.[62] Much was happening and fast. We were priming the pump, but if the foot valve of confidence were worn out, what good the prime?

I was out of high school, but there was no work anywhere—not in stores, not in banks, not on farms, not anywhere. The ultimate shame—I went to the courthouse and applied for relief and was assigned a street job through the WPA. Each worker was assigned a number of days of work as defined by need, on a pay-per-hour basis. I was back to the ten-cent pay level. The investigation of needs and skills came later, and after two days, I was reassigned to an office in the courthouse. I held many and various jobs in the next six years in Milbank, Grant County, and eastern South Dakota, but those two days on a street gang in the fall of 1932 were the last days of heavy labor for which I ever drew pay.

In the courthouse, I worked first in a section that received applications for relief work. In those days, there was one type of applicant— *he* was down and out, with a family, no food, no job; he had sold the last possessions he could afford to sell, and much of the time he was ill. Once-successful farmers sat at my desk and cried their hearts out in shame at having fallen so low, men in their fifties and sixties. An interview for surplus commodities might go this way:

> "Do you have a source of food?"
> "We do have some barley."
> "What can you use the barley for?"
> "We boil it and roast some of it for coffee."
> "Have you had other food?"
> "Not for a month and a half."
> "How long will the barley last?"
> "We boiled the last of it yesterday."

And who cried? Both of us. One man said, "God help us," and I replied, "Amen!"

One applicant, who wore neat but tattered clothes, was not a farmer. Could he find work? We filled out the application. For clothing, the family had received "the barrel" in the past but not in the last year and a half.[63] Did he have possessions that he could sell? He had sold all his books except one; he had sold his three-year-old car for thirty dollars several months ago; that money was gone. He had walked fifteen miles into town, but he was used to walking to visit his people. What people? He was a minister who had not had cash pay for over a year, and all he wanted was a few days work to support his family so that he could continue to serve *his* people. And then we wept. I could not write, and he squeezed my hand and said, "It could be worse." Good Lord, how much worse could it be?

There were the lighter sides. A farmer boy, Olson by name, who had graduated with me came in one day to apply. We chatted; I asked questions; he provided answers:

"What manual dexterities do you have?"

"What does that mean?"

"Well, what can you do—drive a team, be a catskinner (caterpillar operator)?"

"Don't know about cats, but I have skun skunks."

And then there was the time that Herman Wagner, who was an assigner of crews, chose to chew out the foreman over the telephone. The office staff heard only one side of the affair: "Hank, I put you out there to run things." Pause. "Hank, you got to beat some heads." Pause. "Hank, remember, next to me you are the *big cheese!*" We all nodded in agreement.

I moved into Surplus Commodities to manage food and clothing. Clothing was produced upstairs in the courthouse by widowed or deserted women. I do not recall that divorcees were included; they were still ostracized by the community and made themselves scarce. The sewing room produced clothing for men, women, and children. I was embarrassed by the women's underthings, but I had a female assistant at times and that helped. But one day I was on my own, and Mrs. Hans Hanson came to my window. She was large, toothless, and from the western county hills. "Pur 'leven byes over halls—here?" she said. I took out the book and saw that last week she had received size eleven boy's overalls, and the week before, and the week before that. "But Mrs. Hanson, you have had three pair of boys 11's in three weeks," I replied. Quick as a flash she said, "Yah—you vant 'im to go

shool dirr-ty?" It turned out that the woman had no water for washing; the well had gone dry, and the livestock, including horses for
hauling, had been sold.

Surplus food arrived by railroad car, and workers transported it to
the courthouse basement by truck. Because it was everybody's and
nobody's, the food was sampled along the route. Canned beef, flour,
sugar, butter, grapefruit, oranges, potatoes, bacon, ham—all were
surplus. All were purchased by Uncle Sam, and all were available
to relief clients. I learned early the value of the "two-lip" telegraph
and discontinued the posting of arrival notices. Food was distributed based on family size. We dispensed at the Grant County Courthouse and delivered to stores around the county. Twin Brooks, Marvin, Stockholm, Strandburg, LaBolt, Revillo were on the routes. Big
Stone City was a separate trip. Only county dump trucks, open to the
air, were available; in the winter, stores received frozen grapefruit,
and in the summer, they got melted butter.

The father of a farm-boy friend of mine called one day and asked
for food. "But Mr. Sanders, you are not a client," I said. "Well, I pay
taxes, and I help buy this stuff—and look here, Eric, it's only fair that I
get some," he replied. He left without food but noted that they "would
be back." Greed was about to raise its ugly head. Dugan Prevey called
me into his office shortly thereafter and said that Billy (Sheriff Wil-
son) had told him they were coming. "Don't try to stop them—and
get out the back way," Prevey said. He picked up a 45-automatic from
his desk and continued, "They may get a rope around my neck, but
I'll get some of them first." Dugan, the county director, had been
accused of favoritism. "They" were farmers from the hill country of
western Grant County, and they had always solved their own problems.[64] Dugan was big and Irish, and he solved his problems, too.

At one time, a group of WPA workers met to form a union to
demand better working conditions and more pay. Pay varied from
two dollars to six dollars per week—it sounds like an hourly wage
now, but remember that bread was five cents per loaf and milk five
cents per quart. Denim overalls *and* a chambray shirt cost ninety-
eight cents. The best calves liver (called cat' liver) was free for the
asking; soup bones—with some meat on them—were free; corn, used

for fuel, could be picked in the field for five cents per bushel. Wood from the dead and dying tree claims could be had for the cutting, but one-half had to be delivered to the owner, cut and split. Melvin Berkner, his brothers, and I cut many cords. Eggs were eleven cents per dozen. Prices made little difference—there was no money. In the end, the workers' union did not get off the ground.

Frustration did erupt—not on the WPA crews, but on the farms. Banks had encouraged farmers to borrow money and expand when times were good. The banks' wealth was in paper notes, and when the depression and drought struck, the return was zero and banks foreclosed on the mortgages. Farmer after farmer was sold out, and then on one of those rare occasions when farmers do cooperate with one another, everything changed. Farmers armed with shotguns appeared at the foreclosure sales; the only bidding they allowed was by neighbors and friends. Outsiders were invited to leave by some-one's shotgun. Cows sold for a nickel, machinery for fifteen cents, grain supplies at five cents per hundred bushels, and the land at one dollar per hundred acres. At the end of the sale, all was turned back to the original owner, and he was free of debt. Within weeks, the banks called off their sales. In related activities, farmers and others hungry for meat dug up tuberculin-reactive cattle that had been shot and buried, but that was also stopped—by federal marshals.[65]

I applied for the Civilian Conservation Corps, was accepted, but at the last minute decided not to go. Mother had said nothing, but I felt everything that she was thinking. I had been replaced at the courthouse, and I was out of a job. Two days after I passed up on the CCC, Hank Reeves, a friend who was a little older than me, came to the house and pleaded with me to take the timekeeper's job. He was fed up. I took the job at seven dollars a week—one dollar extra for all the nighttime book work—and thus began my stint of walking twenty miles per day. I visited all the WPA work crews during the daylight hours, noting attendance, and at night I filled in the time sheets. I became acquainted with the population of Grant County; the names are still familiar when I hear them. I was young, and I listened because it was not polite not to listen. I heard of family problems, relative problems—all kinds of problems, from a broken wagon to a broken hand to a pregnant wife or daughter (sometimes unmarried).

The relief projects varied from a football field at Milbank to a dam at LaBolt. All workers employed pick, shovel, wheelbarrow, team, and dump wagon; no heavy equipment was allowed. I saw the older men load, wheel, and dump wheelbarrows for eight hours a day, stopping only to clean mud off their shovels (with a "timekiller," or wooden paddle) or to wipe perspiration from their eyes. Only one worker was allowed per household. Young men would find a girl, any girl, and be married at the courthouse by the justice of the peace, Mr. Ligget, and apply for relief on the way out. The crude joke was, "Why apply— they just married it." I saw those young men report for work, work their tail off for the first week, and after that spend time asleep in a wheelbarrow under a tree. Martin Konstant was one of the outstanding older men. There were many of the younger, and their names are forgotten.

I once lost my way while returning from a crew west of town, probably in 1934. A "black blizzard" had descended. I bumped into a pole and sat down on the leeward side to wait out the dust storm. It was the middle of the afternoon. I did not know where I was, but I thought I was in town. When the storm began to clear, I discovered that I was in the lee of a light pole, and in my lee was a drift of red dust (Oklahoma?). The lights had been turned on but were invisible through the blackness. I was in Irving Patridge's backyard and was so covered with red dust that I did not go back to the courthouse. I walked home. Mother was removing the dust from window sills and floors. The storm was the worst of many we experienced.

Although there was no rain, there was plenty of cold and snow. After one blizzard, the neighbors had to dig us out; we could not open the doors from the inside. Dorathy and I walked to the dam later and saw the tops of telephone poles sticking out of the drifts. Trains were snowed in. Our crews tried to dig them out; it was hopeless. I saw inertia plows make flying switches and the multi-ton gondolas slide over the top of the solid drifts. A rotary plow from Montana finally released the two trains. It was horribly exciting. But with the dust and snow, walking for the timekeeper's job became almost impossible, and an old 1920 Overland did not help; it seldom ran—perhaps because I had overhauled the engine with screwdrivers, pliers, and a few broken wrenches.

I transferred to the State Recreation Program of the WPA and moved to Brookings, South Dakota. We held summer camps and taught swimming (I had a Red Cross lifesaver certificate from Boy Scout days), crafts, and nature study. We established recreation centers in Milbank, Elkton, Arlington, De Smet, Bruce, White, and Brookings, where I worked at the center from 6:00 P.M. till 11:00 P.M. From 12:00 MIDNIGHT to 6:00 A.M., I worked at Harry ("Hod") Spaulding's ice plant, learning much about diesel, compressors, and ammonia refrigeration. The days required a short nap; the rest of the day was free. To occupy my days, I enrolled at South Dakota State College (later University) as a special student. I continued to work at the recreation center and the ice plant. It was a happy time, and I was able to send some money home.

From 1933 through 1938, many of us lived with the aid of government programs. My family of four lived on six dollars per week. We were not proud of our dependence, but in retrospect, the central core of almost all programs was a paying job, or pay for work performed. In spite of various self-help efforts, by my estimate at one time about sixty-five percent of county inhabitants were dependent on federal, state, or local aid programs.[66]

Self-help took many forms. Individuals whose property was blessed with a functioning well raised small gardens of potatoes, beets, and carrots. Wild rabbits appeared from everywhere, and many blessed the stew pots of family and friends. Everyone shared. Fish from local lakes and creeks became an important part of a survival diet. Too much for one meal or two? No problem, housewives canned or dried the extras for future use. Hunting, like fishing, also provided food, not relaxation. Geese and ducks rested on, and pheasants beat a path to, those scattered bodies of water that remained. (The water level of one pair of large lakes in the area lost ten feet in two seasons. Smaller lakes became depressions of baked and cracked mud.) Shells for twelve- and twenty-gauge shotguns could be purchased at two cents each in batches of ten. Again, the women canned the surplus for winter consumption.

The months of no rain meant no greens—except for Russian

thistles. Before sunup, the women of most families were out picking thistles that had sprouted along the roadsides. Those and dandelion leaves provided a change from ground barley, corn, wheat, or oats—if and when those grains were available. Hay meadows in the low lands sometimes provided lambs quarters.[67]

As depressed as life and living were at times, people attempted to lighten the load with a laugh—and often they managed it. Fred Snyder was a county employee who worked at the treasurer's office in the courthouse. Each noon, six days a week, rain or shine, Fred closed the office at 12:00 sharp, walked the two blocks due north to Grams' Meat Market, greeted his life-long friend Ed Schliesman, the butcher, purchased meat for dinner, and walked home. One butchering day, another employee, Blackey (a dark Italian with a tongue-twister of a name), slaughtered, gutted, and skinned a dry cow. He cut the teats from the udder and wrapped them with one hind quarter. Ed then hung the quarters in the cooler, retrieved the teats, and hung one through his buttoned fly, dropping his apron back into place.

Bud Grams, the youngest son of A. C. (the owner) and a friend of mine from down the alley, and I were in the front of the market, I to pick up some free soup bones, and Bud waiting for a ride home with his dad. Fred Snyder entered at his usual time. Ed walked to the end of the refrigerated show case/counter, threw his apron over his left arm, and asked, as usual, "What's it to be today, Fred?" Fred took one look and said, "Good Lord, Ed, cover that thing up or put it back." Ed glanced down, "G____ D____, is that out again?" He then walked to the meat block, picked up a cleaver, laid "the thing" on the block, and—*wham*—neatly cut it off. Ed dropped the apron and said, "Now, what's wanted today?"

Fred, white as new fallen snow, hung onto the counter with both hands. The quiet was so complete it hurt. Then a mixture of laughter came from the men in the back room behind the swinging doors. Fred relaxed, fumbled his way to the bench provided for waiting customers, and flopped down on his backside. A grim silence, and then *he* laughed, and the day changed from gloomy to relaxed. Fred probably did not "chew" on farmer X that afternoon for his request to delay payment on his property tax. The humor was probably a bit off color, but such stunts did lighten many a person's desperate day.

Throughout the dry and dust-filled years, some people prayed, some wept, many worked, many more shared, and everyone learned lessons. Perhaps in those years lies a great truth: we all learned that our salvation lies within us—within ourselves—and that each of us must accept responsibility for himself first and for his neighbor next.

Not too many months after I began classes at South Dakota State College, Charles Stumbo, my bacteriology professor, encouraged me to go to Kansas State to complete my B.S. He obtained a job for me there in P. L. Gainey's laboratory. I enrolled. The job required one hundred hours per month and paid twenty-five cents per hour. Later I also obtained a breakfast-preparation and clean-up job at the college cafeteria that earned me my meals, Monday through Saturday noon. On Sundays, I had a cup of coffee and a doughnut for five cents. I took a third job in the statistics laboratory with H. C. Fryer and then I could pay all my bills and eat fresh grapes on Sunday evening. Some money went home.

Dorcile Samuelson worked as a group secretary in the Bacteriology Department; we were married on 27 May 1942. That was the most important event of my life—before or since. Her quiet and patient acceptance of each of my steps was what I desperately needed to build the confidence in myself so that I might be able to be someone and do something.

I graduated from Kansas State in 1942 with physics and chemistry majors. Soil conservation called at about graduation time, and I went to work on a master's degree in the agronomy department with a two-year grant. The job paid a princely nine hundred dollars per year. At last, I was doing research and was pretty much on my own. Circumstances, however, stepped in and opened new doors. World War II was on, and graduate students were in demand. Although I enjoyed the soils work, I was more interested in chemistry and bacteriology. I accepted Iowa State's offer to complete my graduate work in biochemical and biophysical microbiology and to work in the position of Instructor at a wage of nine hundred dollars per year. Dorcile worked in statistics. We moved to Ames in 1944.

In Ames, I rented a house that belonged to a staff member who had enlisted in the army. Dorcile worked until she became pregnant. Our daughter Mary was born a year later while we lived in that rented house, but the owner was returning from the war, and we had to move. There were no places to rent because the Army Specialized Training Programs were in full swing in Ames, and married student housing had not been invented.[68] We answered an advertisement in the local paper and bought a house and almost three acres of land for seven thousand five hundred dollars. We paid $45.00 per month at four percent interest. The property was located about three miles from the campus on Garfield Avenue. We did not have a car, so I walked, rode a bicycle, or rode with a friend. Our furniture consisted of a bedroom suite, a crib, a table and six chairs, and three orange crates nailed together. (We kept the orange crates as a reminder; they are still painted pink.) A trip to Des Moines secured the necessary appliances—refrigerator, stove, and washing machine bought on credit—not easy in wartime, but our guardian angel was watching. Shortly thereafter the ABC washer had to be returned—wartime model—and Dorcile washed the diapers by hand until we could secure a replacement. She also gardened, canned seemingly countless quarts of fruits and vegetables every year, and kept chickens and rabbits to help keep body and soul together on my meager salary. Ruth Ann was born while we lived on our acreage.

I graduated in 1950, twelve years after I first enrolled at South Dakota State College. I had three degrees. Mother and Dorathy had attended each graduation. I continued on at Iowa State with my research and working as an assistant professor, teaching courses in microbiology and agronomic bacteriology. My belief in the work ethic continued. Right or wrong, I have often wondered, but I worked twelve hours a day and often much longer. Research demanded it.

In 1955, C. W. Christenson called from Los Alamos, New Mexico. He had read some of my publications and talked to people who knew me. "Would I come to work for Los Alamos Scientific Laboratory?" We moved to Los Alamos in 1956, and I spent my career there, retiring in 1982.[69] I was in the health division's environmental group at Los Alamos, working on radioactive waste. We had our own treatment plant and our own laboratory to follow the treatments. We were interested in how various biological populations might affect, or be affected by, the disposal of waste. The work focused on various kinds of disposals that were being used or proposed for use and what effect they would have on the environment *if* they were introduced. We were also concerned with finding ways to hasten the decomposition of radioactive waste. As a radioactive substance decays, energy is lost, and eventually the substance becomes non-radioactive. However, this process takes an extremely long time. We worked with diluted radioactive waste, mostly low and some medium levels. The highly radioactive material is dangerous to have around, which is one reason there is not much work on that level.

The work at Los Alamos stayed consistent over my tenure there. Nuclear energy research poses big problems, and when I left we were still looking for the best ways to dispose of our radioactive waste. One especially memorable event occurred in the 1960s. At that time, the United States flew nuclear bombs around the world. The country was condemned for it at the time, but the United States viewed it as an attempt to try to enforce peace. If other countries knew we had a nuclear bomb readily available, the thinking at the time went, they would behave. A crisis in Spain occurred when one particular plane crashed. The atomic bomb did not explode, but it broke apart and exposed the countryside to radioactivity. My group at Los Alamos went over to Spain and picked up some of the soil to test it. We wanted to determine the strength of the radioactivity, to see if it might destroy the agriculture in the area. Fortunately, our tests revealed that most of the A-bomb had stayed together and what had leaked had been picked up and disposed of properly.[70] Eventually, the United States quit flying A-bombs around the world.

My mother was sure that "hard work never killed anyone." She was right. I have never regretted any of my days at labor—physical or mental—but I do regret that in some cases I did not work as hard as I might. I also regret that my wife had to work as hard as she did, often under adverse conditions. I would not wish my work life on anyone, but I would not trade it for anything. It taught me much.

Conclusion

. . . .

In these pages, I have shared some of what I remember of the past—some of it is sad. In truth, I have tried to document only events that I remember vividly enough to be sure of them, and, even so, some are but flashes of the bits and pieces of my life. The Fowlers did not have many of the "finer" *material* things of life, but we had a close-knit family, each member aware of the other's feelings and each member loving the others. Such finer things are impossible for me to set forth in the written word. And if I could set them all forth, I believe that I would not. They are too precious and must be lived; they cannot be discussed. In retrospect, I lived through a wonderful period—from horse and buggy to walking on the moon. I have seen many changes, the conquering of some diseases, improved transportation, and labor-saving devices, but all changes have not been for the better. Modern communications and better transportation have made us less interdependent.

In becoming more independent, perhaps we have tended to dissolve part of the cement that holds a society together. The demand for more and more while producing less and less has become a way of life. Modern advertising, it seems, throws out these thoughts of more each day: "Move up to Buick," "smell better," "live the elegant life." How long can our economy stand a better smell and a more elegant life? I also worry about the pollution of our environment; that is my forte. Still, I believe that society can work out its own salvation if people want to work it out, but people must be willing to accept responsibility.

So what is the "bottom line" of my past? In the United States, we are each only one of millions. We must first creep and then walk. If each of us will try to leave the world a little better, if we will try to teach, if we plant seeds, perhaps those seeds will grow and reproduce and be replanted. The harvest may be bountiful.

Notes

. . . .

1. Dr. David Livingstone, a British missionary-explorer, set out to find the source of the Nile in 1866 only to go missing. United States journalist Henry M. Stanley ventured to Africa to find him. The two are famous for Stanley's line when he finally found the explorer in 1871, "Dr. Livingstone, I presume." The 1939 movie *Stanley and Livingstone*, starring Spencer Tracy and Cedric Hardwicke, ensured that the phrase and the men became part of American popular culture. Martin Dugard, *Into Africa: The Epic Adventures of Stanley and Livingstone* (New York: Doubleday, 2003); "Stanley and Livingstone," *Internet Movie Database*, http://www.imdb.com.

2. Because there were few telephones in the 1920s, the company hired a young boy to carry messages telling employees when and where to appear for work. Interview with Eric B. Fowler, Albuquerque, N.Mex., by Molly Rozum, 27 Mar. 2009.

3. English author Charles Dickens (1812–1870) published *Oliver Twist* in 1838, hoping to expose the problems of England's institutions for the impoverished; the orphaned Twist worked in a poorhouse. John Kucich and Dianne F. Sadoff, "Charles Dickens," *The Oxford Encyclopedia of British Literature*, 5 vols., ed. David Scott Kastan (New York: Oxford University Press, 2006), 2:154–63.

4. William Fowler migrated to the Canadian West during the largest influx of immigrants from 1897 to 1913. British immigrants accounted for nearly twenty-five percent of the total, partly because Canadian and English officials encouraged the migration out of fear that farmers from the United States would move into and dominate the central part of Canada, creating "two Canadas, an East and West, with a U.S. in the middle" (interview with Eric B. Fowler, by Molly Rozum, 17 Mar. 2009). While there was a widespread assumption at the time that the United States desired to annex the Canadian West, the idea actually lacked support within both countries. The timber industry, which Will Fowler entered, offered immigrants a harsh introduction to western Canada. The work was physically demanding and dangerous, while living conditions were squalid amidst hordes of insects. In moving on to the United States, Fowler followed over two million other immigrants; only two of five remained on the Canadian prairies. John Herd Thompson and Stephen J. Randall, *Canada and the United States: Ambivalent Allies* (Athens: University of Georgia Press, 1994), pp. 41–44, 59–60; Gerald Friesen, *The Canadian Prairies* (Toronto: University of Toronto Press, 1987), pp. 245–56, 272, 292–95.

5. William G. Ackerman and his wife Emma were early settlers of Alban Town-

ship, Grant County, where Milbank was established in 1880. The original Homestead Act of 1862 allowed citizens a grant of 160 acres from the public domain of the United States, and the 1873 Timber Culture Act allowed homesteaders to claim an additional 160 acres on which they had to plant a set number of acres in trees. Will Fowler and his wife Jennie both worked for the Ackermans at various times before and after their marriage. Doris Louise Black, *History of Grant County, South Dakota, 1861–1937* (Milbank, S.Dak.: Milbank Herald Advance, 1939), p. 31; David J. Wishart, "Land Laws and Settlement," in *Encyclopedia of the Great Plains,* ed. Wishart (Lincoln: University of Nebraska Press, 2004), pp. 239–40; interview with Fowler, 17 Mar. 2009.

6. The Chicago, Milwaukee, & Saint Paul Railroad was known as the Milwaukee Road. Its Hastings & Dakota Division platted the town of Milbank in 1880 as it extended its line thirty miles northeast from Ortonville, Minnesota. The Fowlers lived in one of the houses originally built for railroad workers building the line. Herbert S. Schell, *History of South Dakota,* 4th ed., rev. John E. Miller (Pierre: South Dakota State Historical Society Press, 2004), pp. 161–65.

7. William Fowler survived the most serious pandemic of the last century. Over five hundred fifty thousand Americans died of influenza, known as Spanish flu, between 1918 and 1919, ten times the number of Americans who died in World War I. Half of those killed were young adults, rather than the elderly or young. Alfred W. Crosby, "Influenza," *The Oxford Companion to United States History,* ed. Paul S. Boyer (New York: Oxford University Press, 2001), p. 387.

8. The Fowlers had a long association with Dr. Charles Flett (1866–1948), a family doctor who lived in Milbank from 1910 until his death in 1948. After graduation from high school, Dorathy worked in the doctor's office in the afternoons and moved in with the Flett family to care for the doctor's bedridden wife, Adeline, in the mornings and evenings. Eric Fowler discusses his own work with Dr. Flett in Chapter 9. Interview with Eric B. Fowler, by Molly Rozum, 18 Mar. 2009; *100 Years in Grant County, South Dakota, 1878–1978* (Milbank, S.Dak.: Grant County Historical Society, 1979), pp. 314–15.

9. During the school year of 1927–1928, Annis Fowler taught in Marvin, South Dakota, at Mazeppa No. 1. In the early 1900s, public high schools frequently offered normal-school, or teacher training, as an option. Annis graduated from high school at the age of seventeen with a "Normal Certificate," probably an entry-level third-class certificate, and began teaching in the country school at Marvin, boarding with a local family, and returning to the Fowler home in Milbank on the weekends. Her high-school certificate also allowed her to take upper-level courses at summer Normal Institutes as she progressed to second- and first-

class certificates. Her career fits the pattern of most long-term teachers of the period, who eventually enrolled in nearby teachers' colleges. With the exception of the years she took off to raise her family of four children, Annis taught her entire life, sometimes riding horseback to country schools but eventually moving to town schools. She was fifty-two years old when she finished her bachelor's degree, and for the last ten years of her career, she worked with special needs children. Interview with Fowler, 18 Mar. 2009; A. James Dowd, comp., *The History of Grant County: Its Romantic Past, Its Progressing Present, Its Possibilities for the Future* (Milbank, S.Dak.: By the Compiler, 1928), p. 39; Mary Hurlbut Cordier, *Schoolwomen of the Prairies and Plains: Personal Narratives from Iowa, Kansas, and Nebraska, 1860s–1920s* (Albuquerque: University of New Mexico Press, 1992), pp. 48, 56–57, 59–68; interview with Fowler, 18 Mar. 2009.

10. Annis married Max Kaden, a farmhand, and the couple lived on his employer's land near Watertown; Annis commuted to teach. After working for the Flett family, Dorathy graduated from a business college in Minneapolis, Minnesota, and worked first as a secretary for a shoe company for many years, eventually becoming a buyer for the "jobber" Northwest Footwear. Later, she moved to her church's office, where she worked until she retired at about the age of seventy. Dorathy never married. Interview with Fowler, 18 Mar. 2009.

11. The Grolier Society first published the subscription-style *Book of Knowledge*, an encyclopedia set sold door-to-door, in the United States in 1911–1912. Written by English writer Arthur Mee (1875–1943) and originally published as *The Children's Encyclopedia* in 1908 in England, the collection of books included informational articles in a magazine format. "The Book of Knowledge," *Collectors' Quest*, www.collectorsquest.com; "Arthur Mee: The Children's Editor," *From Wonder . . . to Wisdom*, www.wonder.riverwillow.com. The World War I photograph that Fowler refers to can be found in *Collier's Photographic History of the European War* (New York: P. F. Collier & Co., 1916).

12. Sadirons, which were cast in one solid piece and heated on a stove, circumvented the dirt and inconvenience of earlier methods, which used iron boxes that held charcoal. "These were quickly named sadirons—not, as some have supposed, out of sympathy for the laundress," historian Earl Lifshey explains, "but because sad can mean compact or heavy" (Lifshey, *The Housewares Story* [Chicago: National Housewares Manufacturers Assoc., 1973], p. 227).

13. Most of the products on the Fowler medicine shelf were popularly used to salve wounds, relieve minor aches and pains, stop infections, and relieve itching, all situations likely to be familiar to an active boy. Boric acid has antiseptic properties; tincture of iodine is an antiseptic; and turpentine oil is used as

an ingredient in liniments and to relieve congestion. Arm and Hammer Baking Soda, a brand name since the 1850s, was widely used for cleansing and deodorizing. Vaseline, also a brand name, has been used since the 1870s for cuts, scrapes, burns, and even to prevent sunburns. Patented tonics, containing bitters, vitamins, minerals, iron, and often alcohol, aimed to soothe anxiety. Dr. Franklin L. Miles, an M.D., began his medical company in 1885 to sell his Nervine Tonic and Restorative Nerve and Liver Pills. *See* Martha M. Pickrell, *Dr. Miles: The Life of Dr. Franklin Lawrence Miles, 1845–1929* (Carmel: Guild Press of Indiana, 1997).

14. The 1870s Home Rule movement in Ireland attempted to provide more power to Ireland than that granted by the 1800 Act of Union, which had united Ireland and the United Kingdom. Home rulers wanted to establish an Irish parliament for domestic affairs, while keeping a connection to Westminster, the seat of the UK's government. From 1886 to 1920, four Home Rule acts were submitted to British Parliament; the fourth passed (1920) and was implemented, but it resulted in the partition of Ireland, which led to the Anglo-Irish War and an Irish Civil War. The nickname for Jennie Fowler's solid bread refers to the cry "home rulers for old Ireland" shouted by mobs as they threw bricks through windows during protests. James Loughlin, "Home Rule," Richard Vincent Comerford, "Land League," and S. J. Connolly, "Union, Act of," all in *The Oxford Companion to Irish History,* ed. S.J. Connolly, *Oxford Reference Online,* www.oxfordreference.com; Mary Fowler Worman to Patti Edman, 20 July 2009.

15. In the 1920s, Sears, Roebuck & Company and Montgomery Ward & Company, both based in Chicago, sent out mail-order catalogs annually to rural populations. In spite of the fact that non-glossy catalog pages often served as toilet paper, Montgomery Ward's sales totaled over $78,500,000 from January to May 1926, while Sears, Roebuck & Company's totaled over $108,300,000. "Rise in Mail Order Sales," *New York Times,* 2 June 1926, www.nytimes.com; Lori Liggett, "The Founders of Sears, Roebuck, & Company," www.bgsu.edu/departments/acs/1890/sears/sears.html.

16. Ed Johnson owned the pop-bottling factory in Milbank. Home well water, obtained by raising and lowering a bucket, was considered "sweet," that is, it did not have potassium or calcium or other minerals that gave metal tastes to many waters. Interviews with Fowler, 17, 27 Mar. 2009.

17. Silverleaf Brand Pure Lard came in half-pound boxes and was among the many products, including ham, bacon, and pork sausage, that meatpacker Gustavus Swift, of Swift & Company in Chicago, developed in order to make use of all the byproducts of his hog-packing plant. In addition to the Silverleaf Brand, the company sold Jewel Shortening, Premium Oleomargarine, and Pride

Washing Powder. "Everything But the Squeal: Swift's Wool Soap, et al," *The Chicago History Journal* (10 Sept. 2008): www.chicagohistoryjournal.com.

18. Retired farmers brought chickens, horses, and cows with them into town, creating what Fowler called "somewhat of a quasi-farm" from which townspeople obtained food, "in part because it was not available elsewhere" (interview of Fowler, 27 Mar. 2009).

19. Nominally, the Victorian Age encompassed the period from the succession of Queen Victoria to the British throne in 1837 until her death in 1901. During Fowler's childhood after World War I, the term "Victorian" was used to contrast unfavorably with "modern." Eventually, the Victorian Age acquired "derogatory connotations, from caricatured presentations of 'the Victorians' as blindly imperialistic, self-satisfied, humourlessly religiose, hypocritically sentimental, and above all sexually repressed" (Chris Baldick, "Victorian," in *Oxford Dictionary of Literary Terms* [Oxford University Press, 2008], in *Oxford Reference Online*).

20. Fowler knew, that is, that she could "produce a boy" (interview with Fowler, 27 Mar. 2009). Dorcile Fowler, on the other hand, was probably referring to the fact that she was forty-one years old when William was born and keenly felt her "advanced age," starting over with a baby when her girls were fifteen and thirteen (Worman to Edman, 20 July 2009).

21. The Hastings & Dakota Division of the Milwaukee Road had reached Ortonville, Minnesota, in 1879, moved west to Milbank in 1880, and on to Aberdeen, South Dakota, in 1881. Schell, *History of South Dakota*, p. 164; *100 Years in Grant County*, p. 5. Eric Fowler's father worked with the maintenance-repair team for the Milbank roundhouse, commonly known then as the "rip track." His father's unit ran the rip track, worked on locomotives, passenger cars, freight and box cars, and replaced ties and rails. The team did not build railroads but "did all kinds of odd jobs that demanded many hours of work" (interview of Fowler, 27 Mar. 2009). Newspapers reported considerable conflict and interruption of railroad service between 1919 and 1921. In the summer of 1919, railroad shopmen struck from Chicago all the way to Aberdeen, South Dakota, where three hundred to four hundred were "reported out," and to Milbank, where "some of the roundhouse workers have quit work." As a result, freight traffic was "badly hampered" (*Grant County Review*, 7 Aug. 1919). In 1921, an agricultural recession hit the state hard. By December of that year, the Milwaukee Road was "hard pressed in a financial way" and had begun layoffs of twelve thousand men, some of whom resumed work on a rotating basis. At Milbank, yard crews were asked to work every other day, section crews to shift to a three-day work week, and roundhouse workers to take a ten percent cut in wages. *Grant County Review*, 22 Dec. 1921.

22. William Fowler died either 21 or 24 April 1923 at the age of fifty. Funeral Service Records, Emanuel Patterson Funeral Home, Milbank, S.Dak.; *Milbank Herald Advance*, 2 May 1923.

23. Jane Pickersgill ("Jennie") Fowler, born 14 May 1880, died on 7 March 1965. Annis Fowler Kaden died 18 July 1973, and Max Kaden died 28 March 1993. Dorathy Fowler died 19 March 1996. Funeral Service Records, Emanuel Patterson Funeral Home, Milbank, S.Dak. Interview with Fowler, 17 Mar. 2009.

24. The condition called orchitis, in which mumps extended to the testes, made mumps especially painful for boys and was generally thought to cause sterility in men, although that was actually rare. "Orchitis," in *Dictionary of Nursing* (2008), *Oxford Reference Online*, and in *MayoClinic.com*. For a thorough discussion of health and sickness in the era before antibiotics, *see* Paula M. Nelson, "'In the Midst of Life We Are in Death': Medical Care in Early Canton," *South Dakota History* 33 (Fall 2003): 193–234.

25. When bacteria and related toxins enter the blood stream it is considered "poisoning." Many of the remedies also contained poisons. Salvarsan 606, for example, contained arsenic and was used to treat syphilis. Calomel, a purgative, was also called mercurous chloride. Mercury, which has antiseptic qualities, was used in various remedies, including Mercurochrome, before its debilitating effects were recognized. "Blood Poisoning," in *Dictionary of Nursing;* "Mercury in Medicine," *AccessWashington*, www.ecy.wa.gov/mercury/mercury_products_medicine.html.

26. The Spanish flu hit South Dakota quickly and hard. In September 1918, no cases were reported in the state, but by the end of October, over twenty thousand people had contracted the disease, and more than four hundred had died. The flu would claim over eighteen hundred lives in South Dakota by the end of the year. In Grant County from October to December 1918, 411 people contracted the disease and 3 died. South Dakota, Board of Health, *Fourth Biennial Report, 1 July 1918–30 June 1920*, pp. 148–67.

27. Although by the 1920s, it would have been unusual for a Mayo Clinic doctor to make a house call, in the early years it was common for local doctors to request a visit from one of the Mayo brothers. Drs. William J. and Charles H. Mayo began practicing in Rochester, Minnesota, in 1889, establishing their now famous clinic in 1914. An epidemic of poliomyelitis occurred in the United States in 1916, and occasional outbreaks, frequently in summers, continued in the 1920s and 1930s. It reached epidemic proportions again in the 1950s. A viral disease, polio attacks spinal nerves and interferes with impulses sent by the brain to the limbs, especially legs, causing muscles to shrivel. In 1953, trials began to test a vaccine that Dr. Jonas Salk had developed; the United States approved its use in 1955, effectively eradicating polio. Helen Clapesattle, *The Doctors Mayo* (Min-

neapolis: University of Minnesota Press, 1941), pp. 352, 534; W. F. Bynum, et al., *The Western Medical Tradition, 1800–2000* (New York: Cambridge University Press, 2006), pp. 250, 463; Mark Harrison, *Disease and the Modern World, 1500 to the Present Day* (Malden, Mass.: Polity Press, 2004), pp.167–68.

28. Rheumatic fever, which can come as a delayed response to an earlier respiratory infection or a bout of scarlet fever, is marked by arthritis and inflammation of the heart, which can leave scaring and life-long damage. As Fowler notes, vaccines, antibiotics (e.g., penicillin, tetracycline, sulfonamides), and other pain relievers have made his boyhood medical world largely obsolete.

29. Swiss immigrants Alfred ("Gonzie") Gonzenbach and Alfred ("Shorty") Nef opened the Valley Queen Cheese Factory in 1929 after some Milbank businessmen convinced them that the town was a more desirable spot for their company than Montana. The company remains in business today. George Flanery established the Flanery Sausage Company in 1946 to produce a wide variety of packaged meats. The company's products were sold throughout South Dakota until the business closed in the 1980s. *100 Years in Grant County*, pp. 141, 148–49; *Sioux Falls Argus Leader*, 10 Apr. 2005.

30. Thomas Edison invented the phonograph in 1877 and created a company to sell the machine, which played cylinder recordings made of durable celluloid. Sound issued from a horn, or cone-shaped speaker, attached to the machine. In the late 1890s, Edison hired Cal Stewart, known as "The Talking Machine Story Teller," to record comedy monologues on the cylinders—such as his popular "Uncle Josh Buys an Automobile" (1903). Joe Hayman used Yiddish humor to make fun of the telephone system on his million-seller tract "Cohen on the Telephone" (1914). "Cylinder Recordings," *Cylinder Preservations and Digitization Project*, Donald C. Davidson Library, University of California, Santa Barbara, www.cylinders.library.ucsb.edu/history.php; "Cal Stewart," *Wikipedia, the Free Encyclopedia*, en.wikipedia.org, accessed 7/10/09; "Cohen at the Telephone," www.raeproductions.com/music/cohen.html.

31. Hemorrhagic, or black, smallpox was a serious form of the disease characterized by bleeding under the skin, making it look black. It was usually fatal. Generally given in the upper arm, the smallpox vaccine, a live virus developed from cowpox skin disease, caused red, itchy bumps at the injection site, followed by a large, pus-filled blister that ultimately dried and fell off, leaving a scar. Most people receiving the vaccine also experienced a rash, fever, and body aches, although reactions could be more severe and were occasionally life threatening. Smallpox vaccinations were routine in the United States until 1972, when the disease was eradicated in this country. "Smallpox Fact Sheet," *Centers for Disease Control and Prevention*, www.bt.cdc.gov/agent/smallpox/vaccination/facts.asp.

32. Within the first week of taking office, Democrat Franklin D. Roosevelt,

elected in 1932, spoke to the American people over the radio about national banking policy. It was the first of what would become known as his "fireside chats," which he broadcast from 1933 to 1944. Roosevelt gave an "I Hate War" speech in Chautauqua, New York, on 14 August 1936, although it does not contain the quotation that Fowler remembers. *See* "I Hate War," in *The New Deal: A Documentary History*, ed. William Leutenburg (Columbia: University of South Carolina Press, 1968), pp. 221–24.

33. For a history of early radio and its impact on family and community in South Dakota, *see* Reynold M. Wik, "Radio in the 1920s: A Social Force in South Dakota," *South Dakota History* 11 (Spring 1981): 93–109.

34. Ben Bernie formed an orchestra that played from 1923 to 1929 at the Roosevelt Hotel in New York City and recorded extensively on several labels. Whiteman's orchestra played popular music to live audiences and issued records throughout the 1930s. *Myrt & Marge* was a radio soap opera delivered by a mother-daughter team and based loosely on Myrtle Vail's real vaudeville life. Buck Page formed the country and western band The Riders of the Purple Sage in 1936. The *Fibber McGee and Molly* comedy radio program (1935–1959) starred Jim and Marian Jordan, former vaudeville performers. George and Gracie, or the *Burns and Allen* radio show, derived its comedy from a "typical" marriage and its gendered dynamics. The Grand Old Opry, held at the Ryman Auditorium in Nashville, broadcast on WSM radio waves from 1925 to 1974. Dolores del Rio promoted the title song of the movie *Ramona* (1928) with cross-country tours. Arthur Tracy started performing on the radio as the Street Singer in 1931, appearing in a movie of the same name in 1937. The *Amos and Andy* radio show revolved around two black Alabama men—played by two white men in the tradition of black-face minstrel performers—who moved to Chicago to find jobs. The show had a national fan base in the 1930s. *Sunday Evening at Seth Parker's*, set in New England and created by the clergyman Phillips H. Lord, boasted "backwoods" humor, philosophy, and old songs, and in the mid-1930s had over twenty million fans. Peter Gammond, *The Oxford Companion to Popular Music* (New York: Oxford University Press, 1991), pp. 192, 239–40; *Old Time Radio*, www.otr. com; Dennis Pereyra, "Ben Bernie and All the Lads," *The Red Hot Jazz Archive*, www.redhotjazz.com; "Paul Whiteman," *Big Band, Lounge, Classic Jazz*; *Los Angeles Times*, 2 Sept. 2006, www.articles.latimes.com; *Internet Movie Database*, www.imdb.com.

35. The precursor of today's television quiz shows, the *$64 Question* began as the *Take It or Leave It* program on CBS radio in the 1940s. Host Phil Baker chose five people from the program's live audience. Each contestant had the opportunity to answer seven questions correctly for prize money, with the $64 question being the hardest and most rewarding,. The original show went off the

air in 1947, but it returned from 1950 to 1952 as the *$64 Question*. Eventually it transferred to television as the *$64,000 Question*. The title has become a cultural catch phrase for the unanswerable question. It is possible that local radio stations canceled the program after the incident that Fowler recounts. "$64 Question," 6 March 1944, *Time*, www.time.com; "The $64,000 Question," *Wikipedia*, en.wikipedia.org, accessed 7/3/09.

36. Hans Christian Andersen wrote "The Little Match Girl" in 1845, telling the story of a poor girl who lights all her matches to keep warm on a cold Christmas Eve instead of selling them for money, only to die in a doorway. *See The Stories of Hans Christian Andersen* (Durham: Duke University Press, 2005), pp. 215-219. "Tiny Tim" is a child who needs medical treatment in Charles Dickens's perennial favorite *A Christmas Carol* (1843).

37. Robert Hunter had been born in Greenoch, Scotland, in 1876 and he emigrated with his family to Troy, New York, at the age of four. In 1899, he moved to Minnesota and in 1920 to Milbank, where he founded the Robert Hunter Granite Works. The company quarried and finished outcroppings of Grant County's dark red or "mahogany" granite. Hunter also served as a state senator for Grant County from 1929 to 1932. Black, *History of Grant County*, pp. 67; South Dakota, Legislative Research Council, *Biographical Directory of the South Dakota Legislature, 1889-1989*, 2 vols. (Pierre: South Dakota Legislative Research Council, 1989), 1:518.

38. Most Civil War (1861-1864) veterans in Grant County—named after Union General Ulysses S. Grant—were Union men dressed in blue. They belonged to the early veteran's organization, the Grand Army of the Republic, and were honored every Memorial Day (a holiday that their organization had founded). By 1936, only one ninety-three-year-old veteran remained in Grant County. The organization built a soldier's monument, which was dedicated in 1904 on Milbank's courthouse lawn. Black, *History of Grant County*, p. 92.

39. Cassius Silas ("Cash") Amsden (1856-1943) grew up in Northfield, Minnesota, and was one of the earliest settlers in Grant County, arriving in 1878. He taught school and served fifteen sessions in the South Dakota State Legislature. He began his first term as a state senator in 1905, serving as president from 1915 to 1928 before moving to the house in 1929. While he lost in 1932, he returned to the house again in 1935. He became chairman of Milbank's New Deal National Recovery Administration board in 1934. He died in 1943. *100 Years in Grant County*, pp. 135-36, 249-51; *Biographical Directory of the South Dakota Legislature*, 1:26.

40. The "shikepoke" is the great blue heron. *See* Bernard Grzimek, *Grzimek's Animal Life Encyclopedia*, 2d ed, Vol. 8: *Birds I*, ed. Michael Hutchins et al. (Farmington Hills, Mich.: Gale Group, 2003), pp. 239-60.

41. *The American Magazine* circulated from 1906 to 1956. Both it and the *Ladies' Home Journal*, which first appeared in 1883 and is still published today, had over a million subscribers across the nation in this time period. The Kewpie, shortened from "Cupid," dolls were the creation of commercial illustrator Rose O'Neill (1874–1944). They first became popular in the 1910s in illustrated children's stories that appeared in mass-produced magazines such as *Ladies' Home Journal*; by 1913, toy makers began selling doll figurines as well. Helen Damon-Moore, "Magazines," in *Oxford Companion to United States History*, ed. Paul S. Boyer (New York: Oxford University Press, 2001), p. 468; "American Magazine, The," in *The Oxford Companion to American Literature*, ed. James D. Hard, ed., rev. Phillip W. Leininger (1995), *Oxford Reference Online*, www.oxfordreference. com. *See also* Shelley Armitage, *Kewpies and Beyond: The World of Rose O'Neill* (Jackson: University Press of Mississippi, 1994).

42. The Tenderfoot class is the first of three classes of Boy Scouts. To qualify, a boy had to be at least twelve years of age, be able to recite the Scout Oath and Law, to respect the American Flag, and to demonstrate knowledge "in full" of how to "tie the following knots: square or reef, sheet-bend, bow-line, fisherman's knot, sheepshank, slip, clove hitch, timber hitch and two half hitches" (*The Official Handbook for Boys* [New York: Boy Scouts of America, 1927], pp. 35–36).

43. So many people claimed to see Unidentified Flying Objects (UFOs), some type of light or object in the sky, that the United States military started investigating the issue in the late 1940s; a scientific report in 1968 concluded that no extraterrestrial cause existed for the phenomena, which typically turned out to be stars, planets, and known aircraft. Lawrence H. Larsen, "United States Air Force Efforts to Investigate UFOs: Great Plains Encounters," *South Dakota History* 12 (Spring 1982): 19–31.

44. This craft was probably a biplane. The propeller faced away from the plane and was behind the engine; it "pushed" the plane through the air from the rear as opposed to "pulling" it. For the most part, the pusher propeller design became obsolete after World War I. Wood and fabric dominated the construction of early planes; pilot seating was open to the air. Philip Jarrett, ed. *Biplane to Monoplane* (London: Putnam Aeronautical Books, 1997), pp. 15, 32.

45. Despite the Great Depression, advancements in aviation accelerated and influenced the growth of the military. In 1926, the United States Army began using air support and developing air corps units within its ranks, forming the Army Air Corps, a precursor of today's United States Air Force. The various Monocoupes, planes with distinctively curved fuselages, constructed of wood and steel and covered in fabric, were produced from 1927 to the 1940s. The all-metal Ford Tri-Motor (or "Tin Goose"), a monoplane covered in corrugated

metal with three engines and high wings, transported freight and passengers in the late 1920s and through the 1930s. The first transcontinental air service required passengers to take trains during the night. Neil Armstrong and *Apollo II* landed on the moon on 20 July 1969. Jarrett, *Biplane to Monoplane,* pp. 40–41, 61–62; "Roger D. Launis, "NASA," *Oxford Companion to United States History,* ed. Boyer pp. 532–33.

46. According to *Time* magazine, "To explain radio . . . physicists have imagined a stretchy blanket of ions encasing the Earth." This layer is named after Arthur Edwin Kennelly, a Harvard professor, and Oliver Heaviside, a "bookstore keeper who for amusement invented mathematical forms to describe the behavior of alternating currents" ("Kennelly-Heaviside Bulge," 27 Feb. 1933, *Time,* www.time.com).

47. The term "radio shack" derives from the slang phrase for the radio room on boats. To Fowler and his friends, a radio shack "was a group of individuals interested in radio who would meet some place, but they called themselves the radio shack." The phrase also applied to the "homes of men who ran amateur radio." A radio shack was thus both a place and "a group of people that discussed radio" (interview with Fowler, 18, 27 Mar. 2009). Irving Patridge secured one of the first amateur radio licenses in March 1916 in Saint Paul, where he took his federal examination. In 1945, he opened a radio and television business in Milbank. *100 Years in Grant County,* pp. 446–47.

48. Minnehaha Falls is located on Minnehaha Creek near its confluence with the Mississippi River. Its name, which derives from the Dakota Indian language, means "waterfall." The Falls became a popular spot to visit after American poet Henry Wadsworth Longfellow (1807–1882) featured them in his long poem *The Song of Hiawatha* (1855), which was based on Ojibway Indian legends. Today, Minnehaha Falls is the main attraction in a large Minneapolis/Saint Paul park. Saint Anthony Falls is located farther up the Mississippi and in Fowler's era featured sawmills, flourmills, and a hydroelectric plant. *City of Minneapolis,* www.ci.minneapolis.mn.us.

49. Chautauqua, or Simpson, Park is located a couple miles outside of Big Stone City, South Dakota, near Big Stone Lake, both of which are about thirteen miles northeast of Milbank on the Minnesota border. In 1899, the park became the home of the Big Stone Lake Assembly Association, which hosted speakers on the national Chautauqua circuit as well as summer teacher's institutes. By Fowler's time, however, the Chautauqua era was largely over, and the park served mainly as a recreational space. Black, *History of Grant County,* pp. 52–54; Michael R. Schliessmann, "Culture on the Prairie: The Big Stone Lake Chautauqua," *South Dakota History* 21 (Fall 1991): 248–49, 258–62.

50. Wordsworth (1770–1850) was a British prose and poetry writer. He composed "Daffodils," the final stanza of which is quoted here, in 1804 and published it in 1807. *The Complete Poetical Works of William Wordsworth* (Boston: Houghton Mifflin Co., 1904), p. 311.

51. The old Yellowstone Trail that passed through Milbank ran from the Twin Cities of Minneapolis/Saint Paul to Yellowstone National Park. Early roads were often the result of private efforts, and the Yellowstone Trail was the brainchild of South Dakotan Joseph W. Parmley, who founded the Yellowstone Trail Association in 1913 to finance and mark the road. The trail appears on the first state highway map in 1922 and ran from Big Stone City through Lemmon in South Dakota, from which point travelers would have to turn south to reach the Black Hills. Another route from Chicago to Yellowstone, known as the Black and Yellow Trail because it was marked with black and yellow signs, ran through the center of the state, passing through Brookings and leading to Rapid City. This route ultimately became United States Highway 14. By the 1920s, much of it was graveled or paved. Shebby Lee, "Traveling the Sunshine State: The Growth of Tourism in South Dakota, 1914–1939," *South Dakota History* 19 (Summer 1989): 204–5, 208; John E. Miller, *Looking for History on Highway 14* (Pierre: South Dakota State Historical Society Press, 2001), pp. 9–12.

52. From 1925 to 1941, sculptor Gutzon Borglum (1867–1941) led the carving of Mount Rushmore from his studio at the foot of the mountain. President Coolidge and his wife Grace spent the summer of 1927 in the Black Hills and brought attention to the project. The George Washington profile was dedicated in July 1930, but when Fowler visited the monument site, little carving was occurring because of lack of funds. In 1932, a federal Reconstruction Finance Corporation (RFC) loan to South Dakota netted the project fifty thousand dollars for continued work (see Chapter 9 for more on the RFC). Over one hundred eight thousand people visited Rushmore in 1932. Gilbert C. Fite, *Mount Rushmore* (Norman: University of Oklahoma Press, 1952), pp. 126–31. [Rex Myers], "Transportation and Tourism," in *A New South Dakota History*, ed. Harry F. Thompson (Sioux Falls, S.Dak.: Center for Western Studies, Augustana College, 2005), p. 490. For more on Custer State Park and tourism in the Black Hills in this era, *see* Suzanne Barta Julin, *A Marvelous Hundred Square Miles: Black Hills Tourism, 1880–1941* (Pierre: South Dakota State Historical Society Press, 2009).

53. All these sites can be found on the route to or within Yellowstone National Park. The Wind River Canyon and the Big Horn Mountains were on the way from Crawford, Nebraska, to Wyoming, on what the WPA Federal Writers' Project guide to Wyoming called the "Nebraska Line to Yellowstone National Park" route. A museum of park history could be found at Madison Junction, as well as

good trout fishing. The regularly exploding geyser that was called Old Faithful steamed, rumbled, and then jetted up over one hundred feet for tourists, who knew its name as well or better than the park's. Glaciers had gouged Yellowstone Lake to a depth of three hundred feet, and its one hundred miles of shore mixed sand, volcanic rock, and the odd forms of inactive geysers. Wyoming Federal Writers' Project, *Wyoming: A Guide to its History, Highways, and People*, American Guide Series (New York: Oxford University Press, 1941), pp. 323–38, 402–37.

54. Established in the shade of a black walnut tree planted along an immigrant route in 1859, the Nut Tree in Vacaville, California, began as a fruit stand along United States Highway 40. In 1921, the owners opened a small restaurant and gift shop that became nationally known after World War II. The entity closed in 1996, but a new one opened in 2006. Sam McManis, "Nut Tree Nostalgia," 25 Feb. 2000, *San Francisco Chronicle*, www.sfgate.com; "The Nut Tree, Vacaville, California," www.alamedainfo.com.

55. Frances H. Burnett wrote *Little Lord Fauntleroy* in 1886. The young hero wore fancy clothing of black velvet, a jacket, collar, cuffs, and a loose bow.

56. Sir Edward Landseer (1802–1873) of London created *The Stag at Bay*, and the French painter Jean-Francois Millet (1814–1875) painted *The Gleaners* (1857) and *The Angelus* (1859). Traditionally, Roman Catholic churches rang a bell three times a day to remind parishioners to recite the Angelus prayer in honor of the Annunciation.

57. Women teachers of the period who married were not universally required to retire, but local social and cultural expectations, or the desire to raise their own family for a time, often resulted in the resignations of newly married women. During the depression, however, individual school boards sometimes required women who married to resign so that the head of a family could have the job. Cordier, *Schoolwomen*, pp. 4, 88–91; Richard O. Davies, *Main Street Blues: The Decline of Small-Town America* (Columbus: Ohio State University Press, 1998), p. 92.

58. "For the love of money is the root of all evil." 1 Tim. 6.10, King James Version.

59. Created by Vincent T. Hamlin in 1932, Alley Oop is a long-running comic-strip character. A Neanderthal, Oop carries a stone club throughout his prehistoric adventures. "Hamlin," *Lambiek*, www.lambiek.net.

60. A few stores in town returned change in aluminum trading "chips," a form of money with the same value as United States dollar notes. Fowler recalls that many farmers took chips rather than money, but the practice ended with the depression. When businesses closed, the people with chips lost the money they represented. These chips may have been a system developed to help farmers do

their trading in town in hopes that the balance of accounts after harvest would turn out to be in their favor. Because most farmers did not receive much cash income until harvest time or when livestock was sold, country stores extended credit (without interest) until that time. Interview with Fowler, 17 Mar. 2009; Gary D. Olson, "Cities and Towns," in *New South Dakota History*, ed. Thompson, p. 178.

61. Hunter Granite Works, opened by Robert Hunter, was one of many quarries and finishing shops that mined and worked Grant County's bedrock outcroppings. Known as Mahogany Granite for its dark red color, the rock is composed of feldspar, quartz, and biolite mica. Robert Hunter started to quarry about 1909 and opened several finishing factories, one at Ortonville, Minnesota, and another in Milbank around 1920. The company shipped most of the granite to the East, and in the 1930s, employed about fifteen men at the quarries to saw thirty-five-ton blocks into eight-by-six-feet slabs, and another thirty employees at the factory in Milbank. Plant machinery included sandblasting letter carvers, a carborundum saw, and four polishing and two surfacing machines. The popping Johnny was a two-cylinder John Deere tractor, the exhaust of which made a popping sound. Black, *History of Grant County*, pp. 67–68; *100 Years in Grant County*, pp. 146–47; Tharran E. Gaines, *How To Restore Classic John Deere Tractors: The Ultimate Do-it-yourself Guide to Rebuilding and Restoring Deere Two-cylinder Tractors* (Stillwater, Minn.: Voyageur Press, 2003), p. 15.

62. In 1931, the Hoover Administration had created the Reconstruction Finance Corporation (RFC), which Roosevelt would modify and continue, and signed the Emergency Relief and Construction Act (ERCA). The RFC established $2 billion in credit to stimulate the economy and increase lending, and the ERCA provided loans for "direct relief" state programs, funding for construction projects, and also assisted states with processing failed banks. Generally, however, these measures were woefully inadequate, though they pointed to the path that FDR would eventually take. On 5 March 1933, the day after his inauguration, Roosevelt declared a national "banking holiday." A congressional act followed quickly, originally worked out by Hoover's Treasury office workers, some of whom continued to serve with Roosevelt; it allowed for the inspection, reorganization, and gradual reopening of sound banks. In May, the Agricultural Adjustment Act passed with core provisions that paid farmers for reduction in production acreage and taxed processors of agricultural commodities. In June, Congress also passed the National Industrial Recovery Act, which created the NRA to work out "fair practice" codes for industrial production and created the PWA to continue construction projects. FERA channeled relief money to state and local governments. Under the Civil Works Administration, the federal government hired workers at the minimum wage, only half of whom came from

those already enrolled for relief, with no "means testing" for the other half. CWA laborers worked on roads, schools, playgrounds, athletic fields, and airports. Also set up in 1933, the CCC was aimed at youth employment and at preserving the nation's parks and rural areas. The 1935 WPA continued construction projects and funded theatre, writers, and arts projects. The NYA, also established in 1935, provided jobs for college and high-school students and unemployed youths who were not in school. The 1935 Social Security Act organized "old-age insurance," unemployment compensation, disability coverage, and resources for dependent mothers and children. As the United States Supreme Court began to declare many of these relief and work programs unconstitutional, Congress passed similar measures under new names, which explains the proliferation and repetition of agencies noted by Fowler. Martin L. Fausold, *The Presidency of Herbert C. Hoover* (Lawrence: University Press of Kansas, 1985) pp. 162–66; William E. Leuchtenburg, *Franklin D. Roosevelt and the New Deal, 1932–1940* (New York: Harper & Row, 1963), pp. 38–43, 48–53, 64–65, 71–72, 121–32.

63. Religious and charitable organizations in large cities across the nation collected clothing and other relief goods and packed them in barrels, round metal-wrapped wooden containers, and shipped them out to places in need. They were often addressed to specific local churches or institutions. The severity of the Great Depression overwhelmed this form of private relief. Interview with Fowler, 18 Mar. 2009.

64. Generally the people of western Grant County "did not have the income that the people of the valley had." Agriculture thrived in the "low prairie, old lake area" of the eastern part of the county, and in the western part, "800 feet above the valley," the hills were "not desirable for trying to raise plants" and "became cattle country." Western Grant County was also "more sparsely populated" (interview with Fowler, 18 Mar. 2009).

65. In the summer of 1934, the AAA purchased 915,039 head, or nearly forty-two percent of South Dakota's cattle. About eighty-seven thousand head were destroyed as unfit; the rest were sent to canning factories to be distributed to the needy. Schell, *History of South Dakota*, p. 289.

66. Drought, dust storms, and land-use problems combined to make South Dakota one of the highest relief states. In December 1934, thirty-nine percent of the state's population was on relief, with over half of all farmers receiving some form of aid. Schell, *History of South Dakota*, p. 292.

67. The leaves, stalks, flowers, seeds, and roots of thistles are all edible. By the 1930s, overgrazing had turned Russian thistles into problem weeds, and the prevalence of these European transplants was another sign of a deteriorated environment. Ironically, the first report of Russian thistles in the United States came from South Dakota, where they had probably been transported in

seeds brought in by Ukranian farmers. American Indian tribes had traditionally gathered the early green leaves and later the seeds of lamb's quarters for use in meal preparation. Kelly Kindscher, *Edible Wild Plants of the Prairie* (Lawrence: University Press of Kansas, 1987), pp. 79–86; David B. Williams, "Tumbleweed," *Desert USA*, www.desertusa.com/mag01/may/papr/tweed.html.

68. During World War II, educational institutions contracted with the United States military to train soldiers in what were called Army Specialized Training Programs; the Navy had similar arrangements. The sudden influx of students strained the housing situation in university towns. Crystal J. Gamradt, "Adjusting to Serve: South Dakota State College Responds to World War II," *South Dakota History* 36 (Spring 2006): 66–87. *See also* James G. Schneider, *The Navy V-12 Program: Leadership for a Lifetime* (Boston: Houghton Mifflin Co., 1987).

69. C. W. Christenson headed the environmental contamination department of the Health Division, one of thirteen divisions, at the Los Alamos National Laboratory in New Mexico. The United States government established the laboratory as part of the highly secret "Manhattan Project" in 1943 to centralize research leading to the development of the atomic bomb. This research was considered vital during World War II. Interview with Fowler, 18 Mar. 2009; Lillian Hoddeson, "Manhattan Project," in *Oxford Companion to United States History*, ed. Boyer, p. 470. *See also* Eric B. Fowler and Wilfred L. Polzer, *A Review of Research Conducted by Los Alamos National Laboratory for the NRC with Emphasis on the Maxey Flats, KY, Shallow Land Burial Site*, U.S. Nuclear Regulatory Commission, Office of Nuclear Regulatory Research, 1988.

70. While the details vary slightly, the United States Defense Department reported that an accident occurred near Palomares, Spain, in January 1966, when two airplanes collided during refueling. The government transported around fourteen hundred tons of "slightly contaminated soil and vegetation" from the crash site back to the United States for long-term storage. U.S., Department of Defense, Los Alamos National Laboratory Archives, "Narrative Summaries of Accidents Involving U.S. Nuclear Weapons, 1950-1980," n.d, www.dod.gov/pubs/foi/reading_room/965.pdf.

Small-town Girl

"If There Is Trouble, Walk Right into It"

SHEILA DELANEY

Contents

Preface

. . . .

After retiring, I began writing my memoir with my granddaughters in mind because they think I sprang into being when they did. After two workshops on the subject, I began gathering and preparing materials for this little book, writing down some memorable scenes from my life.*

At the doorway of those recollections, someone so fine to look at, and so fine to know, suddenly became large to me, as in life. And, as in life, my father had such an easy way of taking over and overcoming everyone and every event by his sheer size and elegant style that I have willingly become an avid minor player in my own history. The result is a small remembrance of my father and his people. I was with him in life, from my birth to the end of his.

My father came to my mind strongly after 11 September 2001. The media released striking stories of the brave men who saved as many lives as they could out of the New York Twin Towers before being taken down themselves as they walked up the stairs looking for more survivors. These were heroes in the best sense. One who died saving others in the South Tower was a much honored, decorated Vietnam-War veteran. I read in the *New Yorker* six months later that he once told his wife, "The real heroes are dead!"[1]

Meet Spike.

---

*My gratitude and joy over the publication of this book requires the acknowledgement of several people whom I can never thank properly. Myra Ellen Jenkins, Patricia Clark Smith, and Eileen Stanton knew what I most wanted, believed in me, and went out of their way to help me begin my story. I give thanks to the wonderful editors at the South Dakota State Historical Society Press, Patti Edman and Nancy Tystad Koupal, who believed in my book and gave it their time and patience. Thank you to Molly Rozum for her insights and efforts. Most of all, my gratitude goes to Max Evans, who took time out of his busy life to read the entire manuscript and offer advice that did not spare the criticism, thereby helping to insure its publication. God bless all of you.

everal times in my life, I have heard or read an observation that women search for their fathers in other men. I am the youngest of his six offspring, a woman, and I have never searched for another father, ever. The original was grand enough for me, thank you. My tall father towered over most people and, when angered, could roar like a lion until your knees buckled. If he asked you to do something, a good plan was to do it right off. He would say, pointing his finger at me and cocking his thumb, "Sheila, take the instant way!"

I would.

"William Aloysious Delaney, Physician and Surgeon" was the sign on his office door. To his friends, his nickname was "Spike." To his patients and nurses, "Doctor," and to his family, "Dad," "Father," "Daddy Longlegs," and in certain times of duress, "Yes, sir." His own family called him Will.

As a young man, my father had red hair. He was a field surgeon behind the French lines in the First World War (1914–1918) and never talked about what he had observed, but, when he got back to his wife and son, his hair had turned pure white, of a good, strong coarseness. I have an infant memory of his face, with a white halo around it, looking closely into mine and laughing. I had no hair at all until I was three. Baby pictures show my head covered with a tam, or cap, or, my favorite, one of his old derby hats, stuffed to fit, in order to protect it from harsh South Dakota weather and overdue baldness in a little girl without her necessary curls.

My father is gone from us many years, and I think of him now as Spike. A good-looking, successful doctor; a surgeon who would never turn down a good brawl except to protect his hands; and a tough Irishman who loved his family, his patients, and the hospital. In that order.

As Will Delaney, a young redheaded athlete from Marcus, Iowa, he put himself through medical school playing professional baseball. He enjoyed boxing also, and old-timers remembered how Spike taught them the fundamentals. They all tried to dodge under his long arms for a "hit," but without success. The youngest of fourteen noisy, contentious Irish siblings, he would say laughing, "I had to box to survive."[2]

Before marriage, medical practice, and family, my bachelor father was looking for a place to settle after completing his internship. He got off the train at Mitchell, South Dakota, about 1911 to look around, and he liked what he saw. The town sits in one of the richest farming areas in the Midwest, the James River Valley. In those early days, the countryside teemed with pheasants and grouse, ducks and geese stopping by on their way south and north, and clouds of prairie chickens so numerous their flights blocked the sun. There were streams and rivers for good fishing, and he saw promise of a good medical practice taking care of the town people and the farmers who came to town to buy food and see their doctors.

Main Street runs north and south, and Mitchell has two water towers. In the countryside, which is mostly flat, amid bewildering rows and rows of section fences, one could see the towers a long way off. I remember a good lake to swim in and even a little golf course. When my father first appeared, Mitchell was well settled and wealthy for its size, with a small stable population of just under ten thousand. Many homes were handsome and large. The Davison County Courthouse and public buildings were solid, built for commerce and to endure midwestern extremes of weather.

I remember bitter winters and almost tropical heat in the summer. I think us kids carried temporary armor, for we endured being frozen and roasted in good spirits. Frostbite and sunburn, what the heck. Our reward was that sometimes the snow fell softly, silently, and our streets were candy pretty, each tree and house lavishly draped with the white stuff, chimneys puffing fragrant smoke into the still air. Good for snowballs, snow cream, and snow angels. Quiet, old-timey scenes tempered furious blizzards roaring through town on northern winds, rattling house windows, and throwing stinging ice pellets, knocking us around.

Between lightning storms and tornadoes, summers could be soft and quiet, golden still days and velvety nights. If there was not enough rain for the crops, everyone would worry. Celebration time was harvest time. Main Street was blocked off with carnival rides, and there was entertainment in the afternoon and evening at the World's Only Corn Palace. Father called it a "great blowout."

He married Miss Elizabeth Catherine McHenry ("our dearest Bessie") in September 1914 and began his family. When his sons were born, his plans for them began—they would be strong; he would teach them to hunt and fish and to practice medicine with him. I was the last, born in 1927. Already on the planet, and making plenty of noise about it, were siblings Bill, Mary, Bob, Patty, and Nan. In that order.

Father liked us all to be active. A prone body annoyed him. Summer mornings, he would come on the sleeping porch and tip our beds till we rolled out. "Wake!" he thundered one early morning: "For the Sun, who scattered into flight, / The Stars before him from the Field of Night."[3] Quoting from his current book, *The Rubaiyat of Omar Khayyam*, he growled in play and stirred us around on the floor with his foot. Departing, he announced: "I'm up now, so everyone is up!"

He did not walk or dawdle around but vigorously strode about his business in the hospital, at his office, or in the country hunting and fishing, which he also considered his serious business. He loved getting dirty and cold in the countryside and tramping around town in all weathers.

He loved beauty also, and if something moved him, he would cover his face with his hands to hide the tears. By any criteria, at any age, he was handsome, with a wonderful mane of coarse white hair. He was the tallest structure to me as a child, and I would hang on and climb up in times of "danger." If he was not busy, he would lift me "to safety," laughing.

Before my comprehension, my Roman Catholic family worried about the Ku Klux Klan in our town. Catholics were their primary target in Mitchell, especially the Irish Catholics. After assaulting and killing anyone else they did not like, the KKK's philosophy was "give the micks something to think about."[4] Some local merchants liked to get together, "hood up," and put on the white Klan robes. They would march bravely over in a group to our Catholic church and urinate on the front doors.

Father was a mick, almost six foot four inches with a chest like an icebox. He did "think about" what they had done to his church and worked up a grand head of steam. There was going to be a big state-wide KKK rally in the city auditorium, and beforehand Spike strode into the organization meeting alone, got up in front of them, and held up his fist. "Shut up and listen!" he thundered. They did. The meeting was being held in a local lumber store, and he backed up to a box of ax handles and took one in each fist. A family friend, John Hammer, was there and told my nephew Tim Delaney that Father bellowed and roared, "I'll fight every one of you sons a bitches!" He was a one-man war.

I know exactly the look on his face, grinning in anticipation. John said that he twirled the ax handles over his head and yelled: "Come on, come on, you little sissy girls. Put on your long dresses and hoods and step right up for it!" Nobody did. He would have fought hell that day, forgetting his surgeon's hands. They did not have a rally, nor march over to our church again. Ever. When I was older, I asked him for the story. He was modest. "I was not daunted," he said quietly. "If there is trouble, you must walk right into it."

In 1941, he wanted to get "right into it" when the Japanese bombed Pearl Harbor and World War II began. Father went right away that Sunday, 7 December, to the Naval Recruiting Office to enlist. They desperately needed doctors and medics; he was only fifty-six, but they told him he could serve better by staying home and taking care of local people. Along with his own sons, most doctors were gone to the war. He could not get anyone to help him with his large practice, so he went it alone. He worked seven days a week and many nights. My mother and I helped any way we could, but he was going it alone. Sometimes he was so tired he did not really know who I was, but I used to sit quietly and listen to him read Shakespeare and recite poetry. Hearing fine words rested him. "You can accomplish almost anything in life, if you have the right words, and they don't scare the horses," he said.

For all his size and toughness, my father had an easy elegance. He wore tweeds, the older the better, made to fit his long legs and expansive chest. He cherished his old beloved army pants, remnants from World War I. We called them his TOAPs, Terrible Old Army Pants.

He wore them hunting until they fell apart, literally, and my mother claimed she "had to take them out and shoot them."

If he was tired from a long day at the office and hospital, Mother would shush us, and in those early days, we would eat our dinner quietly with him. His cigar box of polished wood sat on a chest behind him, and often after dinner, Father would take out his key chain and unlock the box, lift the top, and take out a cigar. He would run it under his nose, say "AHHHH," and take a small scissors, also on his key chain, snip the end off the cigar, and light it. We would watch this ritual quietly, and he would finally sit down, exhale a long cloud of fragrant smoke, and ask gently, "And, how are you good people tonight?" Boy, I could not wait to have my own cigar box, in my own house, take one out, say ahhh, light it, smile, and ask too.

Norman Rockwell could have illustrated stories about Father: the kindly country doctor.[5] He *was* kind. He told me once, "God made me strong and tough so I could take care of those who aren't." He had a large following of patients, nuns, and nurses until his death. I remember every Sunday night he would take Mother to the Lawler Hotel for dinner and then to a movie. If the weather was fair, I could see them walking home holding hands together. On those fine nights, our dog Captain would wait outside the theater and, with his funny sideways trot, escort them home, circling back and forth to sniff and observe.

But Father was more complex than such nice little stories might suggest. I can tell you that sometimes it was not quite safe to be around him. If I said or did something that angered him, he could cleave the air with his powerful arms and hands, his deep voice a Roman battering ram. It was good theater, but one was never sure of *that* until the last fatal second. The noise alone was enough to alarm the neighbors. His sons and his work were his interest. Mother was there for everything else.

I knew that he had to be tough, but he loved things of the spirit. In Chicago where he was attending a seminar, I met him on my way home from college. He took me to my first art museum, and I saw so much beauty there. I sat down stunned, while he went along the galleries, holding his hat behind him, looking at the paintings. I did not know there was such a place on earth and shall never forget it. Before

I got on the train for home, he bought me a flower for my coat and a book on painting. I rode all the way with the book open, seeing beautiful images, and the new knowledge that I could go to a museum anytime and see wonderful things.

Working hard, sometimes twenty-four hours a day, Father loved intellectual conversations to test his mind. When I was quite young, his hunger for this converse drove him to find me when there was no adult around to "spark the mind." Once, he reached up with his powerful hands and plucked me out of my apple tree, my preschool residence in warm weather. He looked at me fiercely and shouted about the wonderful Roman aqueducts, showing me pictures in the *Encyclopedia Britannica*. Waxing so eloquently loud that the neighbors looked over the back wall, he shouted, "What a piece of work is a man!"[6] Hitting the air with his fist, he walked away with his book, leaving my five-year-old brain puzzling over those roaming akey ducks.

He was iron to my mother's softness. When I was older, I would sometimes clerk for him when he made rounds with his students, nurses, and his young sons. His deep voice echoed along the hospital walls as he strode along. We had to hurry to keep up. Once, I saw him go through his medical books and throw them on the floor. If there was nothing effective in his training or books, it did not stop him. After exhausting every effort, he once handed a seriously ill patient two fifths of bonded whisky. "I can't do anything more for you, Tom, it is up to a Higher Power," he said, "but drink these down and you'll feel better." Tom outlived my father to tell the story to my nephew. "Your grandfather is my hero," Tom said. "A man can die anytime, but how many times do you get to drink two bottles of bonded whisky!"

"Doctor Senior," as he was called to distinguish him from his sons, treated a nurse for a severe infection in one eye. In the era before antibiotics, she was at risk of losing her sight. However, there had been speculative literature about the powers of penicillin and other molds. Doctor Senior cultured something and administered it over a period of days. The treatment worked, and her eye was saved.

He carried large sums of unpaid bills on his books. If patients did not have the money to pay, he would not dun them. During the bitter days of the Great Depression and afterwards, he carried them. "I have enough," he would say.

Few people went to hospitals in the early twentieth century, so most care was given in their homes, including surgery, and Spike would go out to the farms every day, treating and observing patients. He would sometimes ride the freight to spots near farms or to the surrounding small towns, catch one back into Mitchell, and ride back again the next day. What a great sight he must have been then. Old-timers remembered a giant in a big fur coat, buckle overshoes, and gloves that went to his elbows. Sometimes riding a cutter to reach his patients, he would get out and run behind the cutter for miles to keep warm. Of the twenty or so degrees below-zero cold, he would say, "I was never cold." Later, his car, an American Motor Car Company Underslung, was a familiar sight on the country roads.

He encouraged his patients to come into town where he could better care for them, and they began to go into Saint Joseph's Hospital and the Methodist Hospital in Mitchell. Some days in deepest winter, the prairie air was crackling cold, cars would not run, schools closed, and people kept to their warm houses. Father would walk to Saint Joseph's Hospital, which was on Fifth Avenue about six blocks from our house, to see his patients. If I begged and made enough nuisance whining sounds, he would take me along. At age six and seven, I would hurry along to keep up with his big strides. He might take me on his shoulder to get over the snow drifts, but mostly I walked very fast beside him.

We must have been a strange sight, his tall silhouette and my short one with my buckle overshoes going around like pinwheels, our breaths puffing clouds of freezing mist. We did not care, "Rend us, We care not!" was our motto. Besides, I knew the nuns would warm me up with hot chocolate and something good to eat in the hospital kitchen. They would ask me about my prayers while Father made rounds. If Father's good friend and surgical nurse Sister Dechantel Duffy was not busy, she would sit a while and tell me stories in her thick Irish brogue about the "little paple, in Ireland hidin' under the shamrocks."[7]

Father liked to reminisce about one walk he took alone on a bitter cold day. A hungry creature was prowling about, looking for food or someone to bite into. Father heard a growl, looked back, and saw a mangy old mongrel following him. It snarled and bared its teeth, ran up and bit into his pant leg. Caught in the folds of material, it stuck there long enough for Father to reach down and grasp its muzzle in his strong pitching hand. Without breaking his stride, he pitched the dog up, up, whirling over the trees. He listened for a thump. None came. Father said he laughed so hard he fell down into a snow drift. He dusted himself off and walked the rest of the way, laughing. I sometimes wonder what that mean old dog thought, whirling away over Mitchell and maybe Sioux Falls, too.

In the 1940s during the war, the Ringling Brothers and Barnum and Bailey Circus train came to Mitchell, making an unplanned stop in the middle of the night. Henry Ringling North was riding the circus train that season, with special cars for all the animals, the calliope, and the circus performers and roustabouts.[8] Even the big top was on the train. After the unscheduled halt, Henry was taken off, writhing in pain, to the hospital's emergency ward, and my father was called. Henry's companions worried about the quality of doctors in our "podunk" town. Henry's family called from Florida and asked my father if they should send in specialists. "Not unless they want to learn something," said Spike.

Whatever Henry had, my father fixed it and cared for him there until he was well enough to travel. He and my father visited a lot and talked about France and England and the food in Paris. Henry promised to come back for a game dinner at our house. When Henry went home to Sarasota, Florida, to recuperate, he sent back a photograph of himself, signed "to Dr. Delaney, a Prince of Doctors."

The next season the train came to Mitchell again. This time it stopped in the daytime. In the circus tradition, they had a parade through town. The big cats were in their rolling cages; the calliope played; the circus elephants, horses, and all the performers in their costumes threaded through Main Street to the circus grounds. Henry, who was again with the train, came to our house for dinner before the show. Father wanted everything perfect, and we put together a pheasant with wild rice and champagne dinner worthy of the Prince of Doctors and his Excellent Friend.

Ordinarily, we had to wear shoes to the table, even in the summer, but there was not much occasion to dress for dinner. For this special dinner, I got silk stockings, pumps with a heel, and a nice black dress-up dress. I said to myself, looking in the mirror, "Wow, cute!" Maybe I would marry Henry and travel with him on the circus train. At the table, Henry told us stories about circus life, which he clearly loved. He said he was establishing a circus museum in Sarasota.[9] He said circus people had a language of their own. Merry-go-rounds were "simp twirlers," and Ferris wheels, "simp histers."

The famous clown Emmett Kelly, the tramp clown who had become popular during the Great Depression, was with the circus and would be there for the show, he said. I had never been to a circus. My parents, Bob, Pat, Nan, and I went to the show as a proud family, and Henry sat with us as our host. Everything was exciting. Father grinned and grinned. I loved it all until the elephants and lions. I saw that they were being hurt and frightened to do things they did not want to do. I cried for them. Emmett Kelly came to our seats and sat on my brother Bob's lap. A big spotlight shone on them, and he stroked my brother's balding head. Everyone laughed, so I did, too, but I never went to another circus.

Henry's love for France ignited my father to begin planning to take Bessie there. I could hear him rumbling away with a French diction-ary as he walked around the house. When he was a field surgeon during World War I, he was better able to tolerate the horrors of the battlefield after he discovered the French and their civilization, their restaurants, their arts and entertainments. They discovered *le doc-teur* also and gave him polish.

Polish was something I lacked at the time. During World War II, my adolescence began with a crash. I dropped the water pitcher and followed up with more spillage/breakage events. I tripped over every-thing, dropped everything, and blurted out disgusting jokes while wearing outfits that upset the nuns at school, and I scared the boys. My favorite headgear then was a sash from my father's old dressing gown that I would wind around my head like a turban.

I was a late bloomer. First my legs and then the rest of me shot up and out in different places. I slouched bent over so I would not tower over my friends. I found a black coat that buttoned to my chin while all that construction was going on underneath. I wore it in all weather and everywhere. Father reviewed my posture and advised me to stand straight and proud. I ignored this advice and slouched around like a black question mark.

Father was a big man, but he moved quick and silent. One day he came up behind me and, without a word, pulled my long hair up so that I had to straighten. Holding my hair up in a gentle clasp, he started walking, slowly propelling me in front of him with his other hand on my back. "Sheila," he said in a kindly voice, "a tall, red-headed girl is like a flame. If the flame is not upright, it will go out," and he gave my hair a little tug. "Remember that." I do. Other fathers might cajole or offer money to "please straighten up, Honey"; he took *the instant way*. I straighten when I think of him.

Father worked with the Presentation nuns at Saint Joseph's Hospital and loved to work with large groups. When he retired (although he never really retired), the nuns commissioned a large, full-length oil of their Doctor Senior. They planned to honor him with a public reception when the painting was finished. I told Sister Dechantel Duffy that his favorite maxim, "Take the instant way," should be inscribed beneath the portrait.

The instant way was not remembered with happy nostalgia by my sisters Nan and Pat. One night when they were sixteen and seventeen years old, he lifted both of them, each by their upper arm, either side of him, and holding them up with their feet grazing the carpet, took them up the stairs to the bedroom where I was sleeping in one of the twin beds. The room was my sister Mary's room, and I was allowed to sleep there the last weeks before her marriage. I was eleven years old and it was a special honor. Mary had a key and locked the door when she was gone to keep my sisters out. She decorated it with her personal things: pictures, pennants, plants, books, and nice bed coverings for the twin beds. She had fastened a large fraternity pledge paddle on the wall: a real paddle, not the little fraternity paddles coeds used then for decoration, but one large enough to hit two pledges at once. The pledges had made the paddle for "Lord-Active" Bob Dunham, Mary's fiancé. Their engagement had been a big event at the University of South Dakota in Vermillion.

Father gently laid my sisters face down across the empty bed, lined up their behinds, exactly parallel, ripped the paddle off the wall, and hit them repeatedly till it split into pieces. I looked, squinched my eyes shut, and pretended a deep sleep. A dead person could not have slept through that noise. *Whoom! Whack! Whoom! Whack!*, "My patient was dying! You _____, _____, _____. Let this be a lesson." *Whack! Whack! Whack!!!* It certainly was a lesson to me. I could see the stairs from my bed, and while my stunned sisters were still lying on the bed like caught fish on a bank, I saw him go down to the living room with the split paddle fragments. He said to his future son-in-law in his booming voice, "Here's your paddle, Bob, sorry for breaking it." I saw Father come up the stairs again and go to his bedroom. He was smiling.

Pat and Nan had committed the cardinal family sin: sneaking his car late at night and driving around the city. Taking his car and/or taking things out of his doctor bag before he made a house call were heinous crimes punishable any way he saw fit. "These ##*! kids get into everything!" I heard him complaining to Mother, shaking his gas mask at her. (He had brought home mementos from *his* war, and until caught, I wore the gas mask to school to impress my friends.)

The Night of Pat and Nan, Father had had an emergency call from the hospital; one of his patients had suddenly gotten worse and appeared near death. Father had to run to the hospital because there was only one car in the family and Pat and Nan were out "noodling" around town with it. When he got back, he sat in the living room calmly chatting with Mary and his future son-in-law until my sisters came tiptoeing in. Boy, were they surprised! After their spanking, Nan and Pat stood up to eat for a few days and limped around the house. They wore the shortest of shorts so that their bruises would show. Patty colored hers every day with a crayon. Some people in my house said they had not been hit hard enough! I thought so, too, but I did not say it. Father went to the jewelers and bought them both wristwatches. They had miraculous recoveries.

Bob Dunham had had earlier shocks from his new family. The first time he pulled up to our house and got out of his car to meet all of us gathered on the front porch, he was wearing a straw boater with a striped ribbon band. I said, "Wow!" From the metropolis of Sioux Falls, city-slick, handsome, wavy-haired Bob was president of his college fraternity at the University of South Dakota. A big man on campus, he sported a natty blue seersucker suit with a Clark Gable action back, a bow tie, and two-tone shoes.[10] Not waiting to meet their future brother-in-law, my brothers nipped the boater off his head and began playing keep-away with it. He made several efforts to retrieve it but finally gave up when my brothers waved the hat to our two family dogs and yelled, "Sick-em!" Cap and Jiggs galloped in and tore Bob's nifty hat into pieces, shredding it until it was hanging in long strings. Father retrieved it, but it was unrecognizable. He handed the dangling remains to Bob, bowed deeply, and said, "Welcome to our family, Bob. I'm terribly sorry about your hat." I did not think he was, though. A little Delaney humor, heh heh.

Three years after Mary and Bob's wedding, World War II was declared. Father was alone, and to save the practice for his sons serving in the war, he worked seven days a week and many nights. He would come home for dinner, his face white with fatigue. Sometimes, he was so tired that Mother would fix him warm milk toast and, while he was sitting in the den, massage his head until he could eat. Finishing surgery one night, he had a heart attack. They put him to bed in the hospital, but he got up and drove home. He was felled again, and yet he worked, holding the practice together for his sons. He was only fifty-nine when Bill and Bob got home, but his health was damaged.

When the war ended in 1945, and his sons were back to relieve him, he took Mother to France. They went in 1948 because he was afraid he would not live to see France again if they waited. The International College of Surgeons was meeting there, and he took Bessie to meet "my other lady," Paris. Some said the trip was too soon after the war for a visit, but the French were more than ready for them. They had a rollicking good time in Paris and in London, where my father made acquaintances with doctors he had corresponded with for many years. Mother kept a diary of their trip. Dad added comments, practicing his French. "Bessie," he wrote, "*J'ai faim, J'ai soif*" (I am hungry, I am thirsty). In her warm and funny way, Mother wrote in her journal: "All we do is drink, eat, drink, drink, drink, eat, drink, drink, and sleep. Expecting to see snakes any day now!"

Coming back, Spike realized his lifetime goal; he was practicing medicine with his sons at the clinic. He could finally relax a bit, but he did not know how to be idle, and many patients would see only him. If Doctor Senior could not see them, they would go elsewhere. So he took care of them, but he was wearing out like a smooth-running machine gradually running down. He had a small stroke. He was angry with himself for failing. "I have to take care of these people," he said when Mother begged him to rest. He would get up at all hours for his patients, "my dear friends." He had another stroke, and he walked with a limp.

Suddenly, my father went away to Chicago alone, where he had another heart attack. We did not know where he was until the doctor called. He died there in Saint Vincent's Hospital. The attending doctor told my mother that he tried to save him by cutting open his chest to resuscitate him, but his heart had broken into pieces. We were all huddled in a hotel, taking turns staying with him at the hospital, but he died at night there among strangers. It was 8 March 1955, just a few weeks after his seventieth birthday. I am sure he preferred to end his life in this manner. He had provided everything for us, working so hard and for so long that his great heart wore out. He had said many times, "I'll never be a burden to anyone!"

Over the years, I have thought about his life and death. I did not know him in his prime, but what I recall, and stories I heard, helped me in my own difficulties. "If there is trouble," he said often, "walk right into it."

ather loved his house. "My home is my castle," he would announce in his booming voice, welcoming friends in with arms outspread and sometimes thundering the words while helping the unwelcome out with his foot. And, castle-like, the house was strong-built to withstand South Dakota blizzards and summer tornados. Built in the Prairie style, it was masculine and heavy, with brick pilasters holding up the low-pitched roof shading the front and side of the lower floor. I cannot imagine my father living in any other house in Mitchell, for, like him, everything in it was big and generous. The rooms were finely laid out and lovingly kept by my mother. The house had large bedrooms and living areas. Set on two city lots on the northwest corner of Sixth Avenue and Burr Street, it wandered all over, extruding porches, terraces, and patios—plenty of outdoor spaces to play or entertain friends in. In the yard, elm, apple, and oak trees offered shade and adventurous climbing.

In summer, my mother, Bess, dressed the outside with large beds of roses, annual and perennial flowers. In the garden, Mother's favorite annuals, and ours too, were the colorful zinnias blooming among conservative pansies and lilies like dabs of red and orange exclamation marks. A tall line of fine white lilac bushes separated the front lawn from the back. They bloomed like no other lilacs in town, and Mother cut generous swags of them for neighbors and visitors. My father liked to go into the gardens before heading to the hospital for surgery or to his medical office. He would pick a rose for his lapel. He was not a sissy; his nickname Spike befit him as a big, hearty man.

I was born into those riches in June 1927 on the cusp of the Jazz Age, but the grim depression and drought were coming up the walk. So, although I was not welcomed as a visiting dignitary, my Catholic father put on a good face and dug deep into his pocket for Sheila Joan Colette Delaney. Five siblings were ahead of me. Nan and Patty were five and six years older than I. Bob, Mary, and Bill were nine, ten, and eleven. Father expected my brothers to be doctors and work with him. My three sisters would marry, be wives, and get off "the dole." I watched them to learn how to be something, too.

At dinner when Father was absent, Mary or my brothers would tell a joke and everyone would laugh, including me, although sometimes I did not get it. Mary was the family comic. If we had string beans or asparagus, she would stick one up her nostril and say, "I have a cold." Boy, that brought down the house! Everyone laughed and laughed, except my mother. I tried a joke, the old chicken crossing the road one. Nobody laughed. The family was a corporation. All positions, including chicken jokers and bean danglers, were filled. Nyah.

Ignoring this snubbery, I happily played around the house, sometimes in the attic or in the sand pile, where my friend Joe McMahon and I liked to dig around. For July Fourth, we would make big tall sand castles, and my brothers would put tin soldiers on them and blow everything up with firecrackers and cherry bombs. My father, anticipating more sons, saved in the attic the books, magazines, and toys he had bought for Bill and Bob. So, Joe and I had a treasure trove to read and play with. We read scary stories about ghosts and hauntings. We laughed, we would not be afraid. We would just say, "Scat!" And they would.

Father had many friends, nurses and doctors and nuns and priests at the hospital and school, his numerous patients, and members of the business community. After strenuous Jazz Age partying in the house, he did not want anyone "ratting around here" for awhile. But one family was always welcomed anytime: the McMahons. There was Mac, the father, for my father. They liked to hunt together and talk about their World War I. His son Bob was for my brothers and my sisters, and the best one ever was Joe.

Joe, the youngest of the McMahons, was for me. Two years older, he was the finest friend to grow up with, the finest friend I ever had. He heard all my worries and hopes, and he was around our house most of the time before World War II. Joe was neat looking in person, round headed with blonde hair and regular features. His shirt was always tucked in, and his pants had a crease. His sense of self was strong and carried him all through his life. One believed that whatever he did or said was the best possible. One night my nephew was fighting furiously in an alley with a large bully. They were tearing each other's clothes and getting in some good socks. Joe flung himself between them and stopped the fight. Joe was slight in build, younger and shorter than either of them, but he did not think they should fight. Period.

Joe told me he was going to be an architect like his grandfather, and I said I would have a big house with "a little face in every corner" (like my mother's). I used to practice kissing on him, and he would submit, laughing. He showed me how to draw and taught me to read before first grade began. We started with the alphabet and the Big Little Books, and then we read my brother's old adventure books in the attic. We would sit on an old couch up there and spend hours reading out loud to each other. Stacked away in a big bathtub with ball and claw feet were old *National Geographics*.[11] Boy, some pictures! Native women with nothing on their fronts. Native men without their pants! Joe frowned and said, "These pictures are no good; you shouldn't be looking at them." I did though.

Swimming together in the lake, going on picnics and dances together and apart, we enjoyed each other's company the best. Joe had a good laugh, a really infectious howl if something tickled him, and he was easily tickled. We grew up together. We had our own bench in my apple tree. We would sit on a board nailed to a branch to read, draw, or imagine we were in the jungle, away from Mitchell. We would watch for Indians or Cannibals and talk about how to protect our families. We believed ourselves. Being shorter people then, we could sit there in the tree and look down on everyone. We would not be afraid.

In 1938, when I was eleven years old, everything changed. I experienced real fear. Two spirits roamed our house, and I grew into womanhood knowing them. The Catholic church was stern about trafficking with otherworldly matters, so no one, including Father, talked about an angry spirit or an old woman spirit, and I said nothing to anyone. One night I saw the old woman. She opened a doorway in my bedroom wall where there had never been a door and quickstepped to my bed. Still awake, I looked up at a fully realized, thin old woman hovering over me. Her gray hair was pulled severely back into a bun, and she was wearing a long black dress. She appeared agitated but silent. Her hands shook in front of her as though beseeching me. I sat up, and she backed into the door, still trembling, closed it, and there was no door. I was eleven years old.

I went downstairs and told Mary and her fiancé, Bob, that I could not sleep. They came up with me and tucked me into bed and sat with me a while. But, I did not tell them about my visitor and pretended to be asleep so they would leave. I never doubted what I had seen, and after they left, I stared at the dark window a long time, wondering why the woman came to me, the most insignificant member of the family. I was not afraid of her, but was her visit a warning of my future life? Would I see her again? Who was she?

The other spirit was an angry, frightening spirit whom nobody saw, but whose presence was heavily felt and could raise the fear hackles on our dogs and neck prickles on us. The house was not a comfortable place to be alone at night anymore, or even in the daytime. There were stair creaks, doors opened and shut, and eventually footsteps came down the hall or stairs or through a darkened room. Always, it seemed to be looking for something. I was a light sleeper, and when everything was still, I heard closet doors opening and drawers clicking open and shut in wardrobes. At night, above our bedrooms in the attic, I could hear mice skittering and something moving heavy old discarded furniture around. My sisters told me a gorilla lived up there. Nearly asleep, I could hear footsteps coming down the attic stairs, shuffling down the hall, and stopping by my room. I dreamed it came in and sat by me. At dawn it would shuffle back up to the attic. The real thing came down later.

My same eleventh year, I was reading in the den on a warm sultry summer evening. The family had all gone to a movie, and I was alone in the house. Except for a reading light beside me, the house was dark. I was wearing shorts, my legs stuck to the leather cushion on the couch, but I was into my reading world. Two of our dogs were on the floor sleeping and twitching their feet ("runnin' rabbits," my brothers would say). Suddenly, there was a heavy presence in the adjoining living room. There was no sound, no doors opened or closed, but where there had been a darkened, empty room, something was *there*, moving in the shadows toward me.

The dogs came to me, pawing and whining to go out, their neck and back hairs standing straight up. They were great fighters and would not hesitate to attack an intruder. (The mailman would throw our mail on the porch and run.) I tried to rise, and my bare legs stuck to the couch. Stiff with fear, I slowly unpeeled from the cushion, rose, and opened the side door to the backyard. The dogs clawed up the back of my legs to get out and then ran around barking fearlessly on the lawn. I stayed outside on the front porch waiting for the family to come home. There were few cars then, and I could see our car's lights.

I did not say anything to them, fearing ridicule. But a little while later, the family began whispering among themselves of "someone or something" coming into their bedrooms and twitching the covers off their feet, or suddenly sitting on the bed beside the sleeper, who would wake with a start and find no one. I told them of my two experiences. They ignored me, silently looking up at the ceiling. I looked up, too, saw nothing, and wished a tub full of mother's cold oatmeal would fall on their heads. Pecksniffers!

I did not want to be alone in the house anymore or to be up in the attic or basement. There were noises and movement in the big rooms, even in daylight. Things moved in the shadows. Brother Bill told everyone about a night when the house was quiet and everyone was out; he chased some "thing" all over the house from attic to basement. For a sensible normal person, he surprised us by saying, "If you keep the lights on, it won't bother you."

Exasperated, Father called a priest in to bless all the rooms and put the spirits to rest. "And quiet your ###***!! nattering!" he said, looking grim and hitting one fist on the palm of the other hand as though it was our heads. The blessing effort failed. I never saw the old woman again, but cover-twitching, noises in the attic, footsteps, door and drawer openings continued. Apparently, the two only roamed the house when it was quiet. Or maybe they were all the time present, unobserved because of all the noise the family made. Then, Mother had an old picture of her grandmother, dead many years, and gave it to me. I recognized the old woman I had seen. My great grandmother Nell Crandall.

In town, our attic had a reputation. Some carpenters had worked up there, putting up more bookshelves in the main room, and said they were scared by "spooks." They talked to Father about it, and he teased them a little. But they would only come to work in pairs.

When I turned twelve and was allowed out Friday evenings until nine, a school friend asked me to a movie. He had been after me to go out with him for a long time, but Father kept saying "no." So now, a big grown-up twelve, I primped and wore a pretty dress. After the movie, he walked me home. At the front door, he took my hand and said: "I've been wanting to ask you this for a long time. Please, please, please, can I see your attic?" Heck. I thought he was going to ask me to marry him!

Anyway, I led him up the flights of stairs to the attic and switched on the lights. He stood there looking all around with his hands on his hips, and then he walked around and around, saying: "There's nothing here. I don't believe it!" Under the lights the attic was well illuminated. Suddenly, there was a crash in a far corner that was clearly empty. Another crash came along a vacant wall near us. He was a plump kid, but he took the stairs down three and four steps at a time like Jesse Owens soaring over the hurdles.[12] I yelled, following him out: "Believe it, Bubber!"

It is hard to believe now, but those old house spirits became almost acceptable to us, like our other ordinary irritating friends and visitors. Other family members began to talk about experiences, too, and the spirits were there with us while we went on with our lives: a tweak of the covers here, footsteps and a crash in the attic there. While our father and mother accommodated family and visitors for many occasions, we endured and carried on. Wedding receptions and Irish wakes were held in the house, and it was with us in our sorrow over our war dead, for the carrying out of the old, and the carrying in of new babies. And, for the clamorous hunting breakfasts for Father's hunting cronies. Almost everything we did, summer and winter was in and around the house.

The house was also a bulwark against the blows and banshee screams the Dakota wind dealt it in winter, as it whirled snow hundreds of feet up in the air, trying to get in at us. But, we were snug and safe at the hearth behind sets of sliding pocket doors that closed us in like a Chinese puzzle.

On those nights, Father sent us to the dark basement to bring up kindling and wood. We stood by like his assistants in surgery, handing him wadded newspaper, kindling, logs, matches for the grand lighting, and finally the poker. There were family gatherings during those blizzards and a fire every night after dinner. Everyone would sit around the hearth with the lights off, and the men would talk about hunting and fishing and bravery in war. Friends of my brothers and my father would mush over to our house in the worst weather just to gather around the fire. I would sit on the floor behind them and listen and doze, dreaming of taking that canoe trip with them up the Missouri. I would be quiet, so as not to be sent to bed, and stare into the shapes in the hearth and flickering on the walls and ceiling while the blitzkrieg tuned up outside. It was like being in a great warm cave, and I felt safe with my family, just like some earlier tribes, our ancestors, held together against the dangers roaming and growling outside in the winter dark.

In summer, noise was a constant. Father and Mother treated friends outside with ice cream and games. A favored place was the big cool porch that covered the front and side of the house. The porch had a smooth cement floor, and some summer afternoons, it was a skate palace. Mother would bring out a big box of skates that the family had outgrown for any visitor to try on a pair. The big porch amplified the sounds of caroming skates, and some afternoons it seemed everyone in town was there, whirling around and around. Mother kept the lemonade and cookies coming, and my dignified father would sometimes crank up his skate key and take a turn or two himself.

There was a slight slope in the floor, and a sudden sharp turn came up when the skater was going fast and had to put all body English into a half brake to make it around. I fell down a lot but never missed the turn. Occasionally, someone *would* miss it, zip down the front steps, and crash onto the lawn or, worse, skid onto the cement sidewalk. They would be examined for broken crockery, pasted up, dusted off, and set in motion again by those future doctors, my big brothers Bill and Bob.

My brothers were tall shadows, little known to me then because of our eleven- and nine-years age difference. A chasm. I knew Bill had dark hair, was the oldest, heaviest, and wore glasses. He would bend down and say "hi" once in a while, but skinny, redheaded Bob never did. He wore glasses, too. Thick ones. Maybe he did not see me.

But we all slept together in the summer on a big indoor porch. Our beds were in a big room at the end of the bedroom hallway. There were windows on three sides, and when they were open on warm nights, bedding down was exciting fun because we were up in the trees. Their branches scratched softly against the window screens, and in the morning, the birds woke us. There were lots of beds on the porch, lots of company to giggle with or be scared with.

Early mornings, Father liked to come into the porch and shake and tip our beds until we rolled out. He would quote poetry to us and order us to be down for breakfast. "The quality of Mercy is not strained," he would recite from *The Merchant of Venice*,[13] adding: "But don't bet on it. Now get up and get right down and help Mother in the kitchen!" One early summer morning on the porch, Patty shook me and told me to listen to her dream. "I have to talk about it right away, before it dissolves!" Patty snored loud like Captain, our bulldog, only with her mouth wide open. The noise was terrible. She dreamed, she said, that a moth flew into her mouth and she bit it in two and put the pieces under the rug. I pulled up the rug, and there was half a moth. She pinched me. Hard. "Shut up," she said. I did.

Patty was six years older than me, and I always minded her. To cross her resulted in pain. She was different, the only family member who got out of work. She was good at not working at anything. I asked her how she did it, for Father liked everyone busy. She said: "Genius people don't work. We think!"

I had been working since age ten, so that should indicate *my* intelligence. Father gave me a key to his office, and I began going to the Delaney Medical Offices in the Western Building on Main Street every Saturday afternoon. I rode my bike downtown, took it up in the elevator, and unlocked the office door. Having had prior instructions from Mrs. Nolt, the office manager, I straightened the lobby, dusted, stacked the magazines, assembled the instruments and rubber gloves into the sterilizer, turned it on, and swept the floors. Then I would turn the sterilizer off, take out the trash, and lock up.

The first two Saturdays went swimmingly, I thought, except that the rubber gloves burned in the sterilizer. The janitor managed to air out the building, but the third Saturday he gave me such a baleful look that I wrote everything out first, proceeded carefully, and made a success of it. I got my social security number then and got paid. I went out and bought candy for the family. And for the janitor. I began to enjoy Saturday afternoons working for my father.

On weekends, family members were awarded drinks after the weekly "grind." Before dinner, the living room was an oasis where everyone refreshed themselves and told about their week. Father had my brothers working with a highway crew building roads. Bill was sporting a nice tan from the sun, but Bob was burned and cranky. I had my cream soda, and laughter reverberated in the rooms and the house glowed with life.

Holidays and birthdays were observed with ceremony. Everyone dressed up for the events. On Christmas Day, Father carved the turkey at a separate table assisted by his sons, who listened to his surgical comments on the bird's anatomy. The pope's nose (the tail) was carefully excised and presented on a plate to any honored guest with great laughter. The house dogs sat against the wall, shivering in anticipation of their good dinner later in the kitchen and on the back porch. Father sat in his special chair by the tree to give out the Christmas gifts for all of us before Midnight Mass. But the phone always rang, and he always left for the hospital, a perfect record for every Christmas Eve.

In the kitchen, except for Father's clamorous hunting breakfasts, our mother Bess was the majordomo. The big room was full of interesting goings on. There was something cooking on the big stove, or roasting in the oven, or bread and cinnamon rolls rising on the steam radiator. There was room to cook everything: a little lunch or a sit-down dinner for a multitude. A big pine table in the middle of the room served informal meals, and on the porch rumbled a big commercial ice box, regularly tended by the ice man. Coming from school or upstairs, we would hang around there on Baking Day until Mother would give us some warm bread with butter or a fresh cinnamon roll and shoo us out with her apron.

My oldest sister Mary came to visit from her urbane marriage in Saint Louis. Looking around the kitchen, she shrieked out, "Oh my God! is this old junk still here?" She meant the big kitchen table with its generations of gum and suspect detritus stuck underneath, Bessie's big pullout drawer full of flour and visiting mice, and the big ice box. "Everything," she said, "out, out, out!"

I watched the kitchen transform into what Mary called Early American Decor. There were beams in the turkey-red ceiling, knotty pine everywhere, and a wagon wheel for a light fixture. There was an old-timey trestle table with its legs crossed. There were captain's chairs dressed with quaint ruffled cushions and American Eagle light fixtures. To show off her artistic efforts, Mary gave tours to curious visitors before going back to Saint Louis.

"A genuine wagon wheel," she would say in a solemn voice, pointing to the ceiling light. "And while you're looking up there, folks, notice the *real* railroad beams in the ceiling!

"Knotty pine all around!" waving to an endless sea of the wood on the walls and cupboards.

"Trestle table for casual dining," she continued.

Finally, "Little puffy cushions on the *real* Captain's chairs, and brass American Eagles with wings spread as light fixtures."

But Bessie's fried chicken did not taste the same without the big pine table. I could sit down there and really flex my elbows and jaws over my plate. Nanny said maybe it would taste better if a *real* captain sat with us and if we wore Pilgrim hats while sitting on the "little puffy cushions." Later, I learned new words for this kind of decorative cuteness, "ostentatious and silly." Sorry, Mary. That was the 1940s. If a war had come to our town or a tornado destroyed everything standing except the kitchen, imagine some future archaeologist trying to date our civilization from that room!

But, ordinarily, we gathered for lively evening meals in the dining room. Everyone chattered away over their food. My brothers had food fights, and the dogs fought for the scraps under the table. As everyone got older, and noisier, my father had his dinner in the den, away from the noise, but if there was an interesting guest, he would come in, sit a while, and visit. He would sometimes lecture on military maneuvers using the salt and pepper shakers, with silverware as Kaiser Bill's dead soldiers.[14]

His sons would be corrected often. One evening while we were all at the table, Bill was talking excitedly and waving his arms around like propellers. Father leaned forward and snapped him several times on the head. The propellers continued. Finally, Father leaned forward and poured a pitcher of ice water on Bill's head. I sat dead still. So did everyone. Bill excused himself, changed his shirt, and sat back down. He never waved his arms again — *the* "instant way" had worked.

Mother presided at the head of the table, and in the summer she kept a rubber fly swatter handy, not only for hitting flies, but sometimes "accidentally" hitting someone with it. It really hurt. The rubber fringe could wipe out the fastest fly and/or make one's head ring. We called it Mother's Revenge. Woe to the head that a fly used for a landing field. There would be a good *whack*, and Mother would say, "Oh, excuse the accident. I hope that didn't hurt!" Mother was sweet and loving, but, considering what she had to go through with raising us, I thought some times she hoped it did.

After dinner we would sit in the living room and share letters and other news. During World War II, Joe McMahon was a soldier, and I would read his latest letter to everyone. And, we would share grief for many young men of our town and farms who died or were wounded and languished in places so far and strange from us. I learned to spell their names. Nan's husband Vince was killed when his bomber went down over Ploesti.[15] Many friends came to see my father when they were on leave; some would never return. When the victory days began, week-long celebrations took place in the house, renewed each time a favorite son came home.

After my father died in 1955, Mother moved out of the house, and my brother Bill and his wife, Agnes, and family moved into it. They were generous with their hospitality. But I grieved for our house. It was never the same without my parents, and its elegant years were gone. I always knew our house was different, and some years ago, I came across a book that discussed Frank Lloyd Wright's designs and saw it, my house: the oriental cast of the facade and roofs.[16] Wright got many ideas while he was living and designing buildings in Japan. I wished I had the house. I was far away when our dining room, fireplace, library, attic, and special rooms and haunts went to others. Before Bill sold it, I flew there from Santa Fe for my mother's funeral. There were so many people in the house, so much noise and confusion. I could not look around to see where we had all been together as a family so many years before.

Some years after that, I went back to have a quiet look. I drove over and parked across the street. I surveyed it from the front and then parked on the side and looked some more. The tall white lilac hedge my mother had planted, and so lovingly tended that it bloomed like no other lilac hedge in town, had been torn out, leaving an ugly gap in the lawn. And the trees my father had planted and named for his children (including the Sheila apple tree) had been cut down. Mother's gardens had been covered up with ugly river stones, but I saw some of her flowers peeping up from them. The house looked old and slumped down. From the car, I raised my arm to it, and its old windows glittered in the afternoon sun.

I wished I had not done it, for then I wanted to go and touch my house, go round and pat each remembered place, each brick and door. See my sweet hiding place by the porch where I would crouch, heart thudding, waiting for "Ollie Ox in Free." Peer in the front door glass, remembering everyone rushing outside for a shivering minute to look back in the glass at the twenty-foot Christmas tree on its first lighting, ablaze in the front hall, its star up to the second floor of the stairwell. But it was not Christmas, and I did not live there. I drove away slowly, the house getting smaller and smaller in my rear-view mirror. I pulled over and, to the amazement of a little boy on his tricycle, wept and wept for the old house, for my youth, my parents, and for all of Spike's people.

essie could play a ricky-tic piano in our house. She could play "March of the Gladiators" when things were serious and "Bessie Couldn't Help It" when the guests were trying the latest jazz steps. There was a big piano in the living room, painted white with a Spanish shawl draped over it. The fringe fell nearly to the floor, and I liked to stretch out under there and imagine I was in a tent, in Araby maybe.[17] She could sing, play the piano, whistle and dance, by herself if necessary. In a moment she could play suitable music on the piano for a funeral, fox trot, or an Irish jig and get up and demonstrate the buckin' wing.

My father survived a noisy clamorous home life as a youth, where fistfights were often the day's entertainment. He vowed to establish a refined environment in his own fine home. He was looking forward to evenings listening to his wife and children playing the piano and singing softly together, with each child virtuoso in musical instruments to soothe him after a hard day's work. My musical mother Bessie bought each child a violin. She would be a good teacher, she thought, and set them all to practice together after school. She sat down in the living room with Bill, Mary, Bob, Pat, and Nan, and they sawed up some fine, earsplitting cacophony for Father's arrival home. Except for one "accidentally" stepped upon, the violins went back to the store.

That was before my time in the family, but I heard often enough about the violins that I do not doubt it. That was our Bessie, pleasing her husband and family. Anything within the law that we wanted, she would set herself to do it, right away. If that did not work, she would do something else, until it did work. The only thing that completely defeated her was my brother Bill's singing. I can remember her working and working with Bill to teach him to sing, starting with "doh." And "dooh," and "dooooh." And our dogs would howl along, "woo, wooo," and "wooooo!" until finally Father told them all, dogs and singers, to stop that damn ruckus. Blessed be silence!

Often we did not even ask for help. When I spent summers roosting in the apple tree, sitting on a perch that Joe and I had nailed up, reading and drawing, she would come out with lunch in a basket, tie it on the handle with a rope I would let down, and I would pull it up. She would come out again after a while, and I would lower the empty basket. Holding it out in front of her with both hands, like a holy relic, Mother would solemnly, silently, march into the house.

One summer day when she was dressed up "in her finery" to visit some friends, she stopped on her way to the car and got down on her heels to teach me to play "migs" (a game of marbles). Beyond good sense, she loved us, as she loved the big sprawling house, keeping it in tune for everyone. She would run up and down the flights of stairs from attic to basement many times a day to see that everything worked, was picked up, cleaned up, and shined up, including me. One night I went to the hospital with Father very late. We saw the lights in the kitchen when we were coming home. Father said: "There's Bessie waiting for us to see if there is anything we want. She's our light."

Our Light came to Mitchell from Dennison, Iowa, with her mother, Nellie, her two sisters, Ethel and Helen, and a brother, Vince, after her father Charles had died. They were the McHenrys, Scotch-Irish and English in origin. My mother, Bess, or Bessie, or Elizabeth, was the oldest, Elizabeth Catherine. Ethel and Helen were real beauties, but while they were posing in their hammocks fanning themselves, my mother charmed the socks off their suitors. She wore glasses and had lost the sight in one eye, but she was little, cute, and vivacious. She must have been a noisy little person.

McHenry men had a distinguished military background. They were on British rosters for the French and Indian War and served in every American war. They were patriots in the Revolutionary War and the War of 1812 and with the Union in the Civil War. Uncle Vince McHenry was a pilot in World War I. He was full of fun, and before he left for California to live, he taught me the right way to spell "hammer." I was studying for the school spelling bee to go to the finals in Sioux Falls. Thanks to his coaching, I recited, standing in front of Sister Joan and my class, "hammer: f-a-r-t, hammer." I did not go to Sioux Falls, but to the principal's office. She said, with a red face, "Sheila, never, *ever* spell that word in my school again!"

The McHenrys were warm and funny and hardworking, and they

established a popular boardinghouse on West Second Avenue in Mitchell. But the scoldy old matrons of our town viewed the McHenrys as if they were uncouth Iowa Huns invading their genteel civilization. An excommunicated member of their matronly teas relayed their sour comments on Mother's people.

"Who do they think they are coming in here like this?" she heard them say.

"The oldest girl whistles," she heard another one say often, as though condemning the whistler to Mitchell social hell. They frowned over their tea cups.

"Ladies don't work for heaven's sake. Sniff."

"Thank God for us. Sniff."

Mother could imitate them perfectly, sniffs and all, curling her little finger as she sipped imaginary tea. When they saw Bess out walking, the matrons would walk toward her smiling and, just before they met, would turn their backs on her and walk away. This behavior made her cry, and Uncle Vince told his sister, "Bessie, those old farts could be out tea'd and out dressed anytime by you."

In fact, those tea ladies nearly fell off their rocking chairs when Bess McHenry married that "nice doctor Delaney" in 1914. "What kind of background do those McHenry people have?" one asked, while another forecast grimly, "There will be whisky and dancing and what not in that house." And what not, indeed, ladies. And the Charleston, the turkey trot, and the shimmy, too!

Bessie, who was family caretaker for her mother, sisters, and brother, also helped out with the McHenry boardinghouse. I heard from father's friend John Hammer that word got around town that her cooking was worth looking into. One bachelor eating there regularly was my father, Spike Delaney. He was new in town and getting his medical practice established.

Matrons set their daughter's caps for the young redheaded doctor who roared around town in an open roadster, accompanied by a big meaty bulldog who gave townspeople aloof snorts, barks, and other bulldog comments. Before Bessie was acquainted with my father, she was out walking one warm afternoon with some town boys. They came across the roadster parked on the road with the bulldog in the back seat. The keys were in the ignition, and they took off in it, revving the motor and dashing it around the country roads outside Mitchell. My mother was driving when it veered into a shallow creek and stuck. No one was hurt, so they left the car, with the bulldog still in the back seat, and walked back to town. Meantime, a farmer noticed my father's car and dog stuck in the creek and got a tractor and pulled them out. The incident made an impression on Spike, and he began to keep company with Bess McHenry. "To keep an eye on my car," he said.

But it was other things, too. He was a serious man and she could make him laugh. And her cooking was sovereign, the best in town. Everyone loved her fried chicken, and as many times as I watched her prepare it, I never got the hang of it. Nor did anyone else. Bess had a secret ingredient.

Love, I think, was the main ingredient in everything she did for us in unlimited measure. She was a vital, energetic force in our family. Many nights she would sit up in the kitchen waiting for my father to come home after a late surgery to see if he wanted anything to eat. Bess had help who stayed in the house to assist her, but she loved to do the cooking and gardening and anything for her family. We were too much work for her to have a real social life, but she made time for dressing well for my father. I, a kid in "tennies" and overalls, liked to linger in her closet, put my arms around her dresses, sway with them, and breathe the perfume. Ahhh.

After our dinner, we would all gather together in the living room as a family. Bess could never relax or sit still. She would be in the kitchen, or dusting around us, or having us lift our feet for the carpet sweeper. Woe to dirt anywhere; she had declared war and filled her days sweeping, washing, vacuuming, scrubbing, and obliterating the enemy in every possible way, including those pesky corners.

I was fifteen and feeling pretty one day while we were sitting in the car outside Father's office waiting for him to come out. Down the street I spied a cute boy from my class and got ready to wave coyly at him. Mother suddenly reached out, got my head in a hammer-lock, and, pulling out one of her pretty handkerchiefs, spit on it and began scrubbing my ears. "Sheila," she said loud enough for him to hear, "you always forget your ears!" Oh, the horror!

When not chasing dirt, or us, or taking care of the house, Mother loved to play the piano. I had heard Bessie's piano was a great gathering place for young couples during the Roaring Twenties. Parties went on through the night, and sometimes the entire weekend, and sometimes "through the roof!" Our house was commodious; and its big outside porch accommodated any overflow of guests in the summer. Someone was always dancing to the Victrola on the porch or to Bessie's piano in the living room. The Charleston and the turkey trot dances were hot stuff for the "flappers." My father wrote in his journal when he was eighteen and still in Marcus, Iowa: "There is nothing I like better than a house full of friends. . . . I vow that if I ever have a house of my own and the necessary, I shall be cramming it full of guests from one end of the year to the other."

The "cramming" ended about when I could grasp events; the twenties had almost roared themselves out. I heard that my mother had been a flapper, too, but it must have been hard to flap much with six hungry children and a hardworking doctor husband. In our attic clothes racks were her old dresses and satin shoes with pointy toes. You could really stick somebody with those shoes. Sometimes when Joe McMahon and I were playing up there, she would put on a pair of those shoes and do a Charleston for us. She would give us "the word" to go with the shoes. "I'm a candy kid with a gum leg!" she would say kicking her heels up, or, "Kiss me, kid, I'm chocolate!"

Once, peering through the banister in the front hall with my sister Nanny, we watched my mother play a jazzy tune while a woman, who was usually reserved and polite, burst into the living room wearing long red underwear. She capered around the living room and made a flying leap through the air singing out, "TAAA DAAA!" From our catbird seat, we watched her soar toward the arms of a young man, also in long red underwear. He missed her, and she crashed into the fireplace, which was unlit. Everyone laughed. Father helped her out and declared her fit to continue. Someone handed her a drink. Then she and her underwear-clad partner did a shaking dance together. Nanny said it was the "shimmy." They linked arms for a "Shuffle Off to Buffalo" dance in their bare feet, out the front door. And then came back in for another drink. Was that ever spiffy, I thought. I could not wait to do those dances and wear long underwear.

I got to do both. After school, when I was a little older, Mother registered me at Miss Sandra's dance studio. AND, I wore great long underwear when it was cold, the era before snow suits. I learned the "Shuffle Off to Buffalo" and one she called "Hop, Shuffle, Ball Change." But Miss Sandra said the shimmy was "yesterday's mashed potatoes." Miss Sandra got a red face when she first saw me pull up the back seat on my underwear and button it after I used the commode there. And then pull up my long stockings over the underwear legs, hook them to a garter belt, and pull up my underpants to secure everything. And finally pull my dress skirt down. Whew! Getting the stockings smooth so my legs were not covered with wrinkles from the underwear was beyond me. I knew Miss Sandra was laughing at me, but what the heck. I never did get the hang of it. One had to be careful, remembering to button up the back seat, and pull the underpants over it to keep it in place, or it could hang down from under your dress and cause everyone much merriment. Especially at school. "Hey, Hey, Missus Brown, your old trap door's a hangin' down!!"

During this time period, the Dancing O'Connors were at the Corn Palace, and after their matinee, they all came to the studio.[18] The O'Connor mother asked her son Donald if he would dance with me a little. He looked spiffy in his black suit and necktie, with his hair slicked back with real plugmuckum. I thought of marriage. The future dazzling movie star gave my wrinkled stockings over my wrinkled underwear legs a good look and said he was tired. But I knew why.

Later, Miss Sandra coached me for a solo appearance at her Corn Palace Kiddy Revue; no long underwear this time, but black sateen trousers, a red jacket, and tap-dance shoes: a China doll. I tapped hop, shuffle, ball change, and sang, "All I want is a Bowl of Chop Suey and Youey." I threw kisses to the audience and shuffled off the stage to thunderous applause from my mother.

Father loved great food, and Mother was a great cook. We would eat anything she turned out with gratitude. A peanut-butter sandwich was better if she made it. We said her fried chicken was world-famous, along with her "biskits" and cream gravy. She made for our pleasure a procession of rich, exotic desserts. And, almost always, a choice of two: pie or cake and/or floating island, apricot whip, icebox cookies, chocolate cookies with homemade ice cream, puddings with mountains of real whipped cream, cream puffs, strawberry shortcake, peach pie, blueberry pie, lemon pie with a towering cap of meringue, coconut cake, or chocolate bars. Everything was made with cream, butter, and eggs "right off the farm." In the kitchen, Mother reigned. Sometimes, I helped, too. Her big room was full of good-sniffing fragrances of something cooking on the big stove or roasting in the oven.

Eating events for the different hunting seasons originated in the kitchen. With Father, Mother organized the huge breakfasts for visiting hunters like an impresario, producing with flourishes platters of eggs, sausages, rashers of bacon, ham, and fried potatoes, caldrons of coffee and tea, and toast, "biskits," and pancakes with syrup, honey, and crocks of country butter. "Here," she would say to the guests, "try these on your whiskers."

The kitchen was where we headed after school, looking for her and for something to eat. On Baking Wednesdays, the smell of breads and rolls rising in the kitchen drew us from the front door after school or from our rooms. She would shoo us out snapping her apron, and we would drift back again. We would hang around, pull in our cheeks, and act palsied and starved until she fixed us each a warm treat.

But, like all great chefs, she could misfire, and then we were afraid to even drink the water. Once, there was a near destruction with creamed lima beans. Lima beans! Ick!!! An unnatural sprightly green, floating around in cream sauce, the limas looked exactly like a picture of something I had seen in one of my father's medical books. There were moans of despair. "Glands!" Brother Bob said, shuddering away from his plate.

Father stood up. "Well," he said, glaring at us six cowardly, ingrate children. "You are all going to eat these lovely beans Mother has prepared for you, and thank God you have them. Those starving Armenians would have given anything to have a swell dish like this.[19] I want to see a big smile from each of you while you are eating." We dug in and chewed, smiling like corpses at our own funeral, except Bob, who did neither. In the mouth, the beans seemed to multiply and grow larger. We took big gulps of water to tamp down. Bob was left sitting alone at the table, contemplating the cold green things lying in a gelatinous sea of curdled cream.

The next morning, the cold beans were served to him for breakfast, and for lunch and dinner also, and he sat in the dark of the dining room with them until bedtime. Finally, Bob got real food after he showed his father the smears on his smiling face and the empty dish. Father pounded him on the back and said: "That wasn't so bad now, was it? You have to learn to do things you don't want to do." Bob was in high school then, and after he graduated from medical school and joined the airborne troops for World War II, someone found a napkin at the bottom of the umbrella stand in the front hall. Rolled in it were the petrified lima beans. We had a good laugh, and Mother said she might save them for him until he returned from France. "They age everything there," she said.

I thought she would never leave us. If love could save, she would still be feeding us, clothing us, waiting for us to come home, taking care of her grandchildren, and laughing at our dim jokes. She said we were wonderful. And when we were around her, we *were* wonderful. No matter how old we got, we were always her kids. "Oh, Kids," she would say after grace and before her fried chicken and 'biskits', "eat slow so you can eat more!"

Aside from taking care of us, little babies were her specialty. Her smiling face, her dark springy hair, and her mellow voice got their attention. She would lean over and talk to them in their language, and the tiniest "just hatched out" babies would almost leap out of their diapers for joy. Their little legs would go around and around. At last, someone who understood them! The sourest baby would laugh and coo in her arms. She had the kind of hands to caress a baby, smooth my father's tiredness, tend a garden, and "slap up a pie." When new mothers called at our house for help, Mother would give them her advice on their newborns before she turned them over to Father. He said, jokingly, she was practicing medicine without a license. Good medicine.

Bessie was a terrible disciplinarian. Her heart was not in it. Once she sent me to bed without dinner for starting a fire in the backyard. I had not done it, but I figured I had earned it because of what I had not been caught doing. First came the spatula, her favorite disciplinary weapon, and mine, too, for it did not hurt. "This will teach you!" she shouted in her mean voice, about as mean as her strawberry shortcake. Then she sent me to bed without my dinner. Reading in bed on a nice summer evening on the sleeping porch was punishment to be cherished. Especially when I heard the back stairs squeak. Mother was bringing up a tray of food, tears streaking down her face. On the tray was creamed chicken and little carrot sticks fixed the way I liked them. And the best ever! Floating island dessert. Softhearted lady, my mother.

Usually, she did not discipline her children. My father took care of the boys, and my sisters were so smart and good they did not need any. Ha, Ha. She could bootleg it, though. Once when Father was not around, Bill burst into the kitchen and shouted a new word he had picked up in high school: "Crap!" I was sitting on the kitchen counter, watching her make a pie, and I laughed because my big brother said it, so the word must be something wonderful. But she took his arm and marched him over to the sink. "Open your mouth," she commanded in her mean voice, and he did. She scrubbed around in it with a wet bar of yellow laundry soap. Some bubbles came out: an interesting event for a five-year-old to see. There were family rituals and protocols, and I thought this was one I should know about, but Bill would not talk about it.

Bess was not a saint, either. She was a demon with the enema can. The equipment had a tin bowl and some kind of evil plunger. They made a clanking noise when she came down the hall toward the sick room, causing the sick one to shiver with dread. After the position was assumed, she clanked the plunger up and down. Patty said the Inquisition used it to make people talk. If you told her you were sick, you had better be good and sick because here comes Mrs. Frankenstein, *clank, clank, clank!*

Bessie was a great, natural gardener and knew the names of every plant and weed in South Dakota. She belonged to a premier garden club in Mitchell, and once a year they all came over to her home to see and admire her flowers and have lunch among the blooms. She loved wearing a pretty dress and showing her gardens and home to visitors. All of us had been warned to stay away from her party, "or else!" I forgot.

The discriminating tomboy could find wonderful treasures in summer. On Mother's special garden day, while inspecting our backyard that fine morning, I found my old teddy bear under some bushes.

He had been mauled about and chewed by our dogs. He looked sad. Mister Delaney had enjoyed a distinguished life with me until first grade at school made me more sophisticated about my playmates. Then, I tossed him away or kicked him under my bed until somebody put him in the trash.

Seeing him lying on the ground in his shocking condition, I remembered how grand it was to dress him in my old baby clothes and stroll around the neighborhood pushing him in an old buggy. I sat down and hugged and squeezed him carefully now because something might fall off, remembering how I feverishly squeezed him when I could not sleep because there might be a gorilla around. I thought about what I could do to honor my old friend. Apparently, my previous hugging and squeezing wore on his appearance. And, clearly, he had been taken out of the trash and chewed and dragged around for some time, one furry leg hung down about a half foot below the other. The stuffing was mostly gone from that leg, and I tried to repair it with some cotton and safety pins from mother's sewing basket.

But, he was beyond any serious repair, one glass eye was gone, and the other one turned toward his dented nose. Half of his red felt tongue had disappeared, but the remainder still stuck out valiantly as if to defy the world. I tied a rope around his neck and shimmied up the big oak tree above the gardens with him and thought about what I would do with my old friend. I let Mister Delaney hang down from a branch by his neck, and in my opinion he looked excellent like that with his tongue sticking out. I let out more slack, secured it so he could swing back and forth in the breeze, and went somewhere else, and did something else, and forgot.

I did notice some tables out on the back lawn under the tree with white cloths on them. Later I remembered my mother was preparing for her garden club luncheon that day so that they could admire her roses, perennials, and annuals. The guests arrived in their frilly dresses soon after I left my "decorating," and my mother was enjoying their admiration of her garden on that unusually fine summer day. Mr. Ryan, the gardener, came over from across the street to share her pleasure, and they both looked up smiling as though, on this excellent day, there was "all this and heaven too." The garden was blooming gloriously, the women looked like flowers themselves, and over all the pretty tables, lazily drifting back and forth, swung old Mister Delaney, his leg snowing stuffing and his tattered old tongue sticking out.

I do not know what my mother said. I found out about the luncheon from my sisters, who rejoiced when I had done something wrong. Mr. Ryan got his long ladder, climbed up and disconnected Mister Delaney, and Mother probably carried off the luncheon as though the poor old thing was some charming outdoor chandelier—and then went inside and laughed and cried over her fate in life.

Like daughters in biblical times, I left my husband's house and visited my mother when I was expecting my daughter, Katy. My father had died some two years before my visit, and Bess was still in the house, alone. I slept in my old bedroom, and she made my favorite food. It was a quiet visit. Her sons had told her she must move out of her beloved house into an apartment. She did not complain and prepared to obey, but a sadness was in her manner as she moved around her house, pausing to look in at the rooms and going in and touching the furniture. Agnes and Bill were going to take most of the furniture when they moved in, and I saw her pick up a pillow on one of the beds and hold it to her for a moment, as though holding a precious baby. In the tradition, as she had done for my sisters, she made her prediction. "You will have," she said gravely, "a hard labor and a pretty, dark-haired girl." And so I did. Now I look at her namesake, Elizabeth Kathryn ("Katy"), and my granddaughters, a bouquet of lovely flowers. How she would have loved them. Does love them.

My mother died in 1966. The family and friends gathered at her old house before and after the service. Arriving from New Mexico for that sad day, I sat quietly, listening to my brothers and sisters in the living room. My brother Bob announced, "As her executor, I have prepared a wonderful funeral for Mother." Agnes, practical sister-in-law, and her husband Bill, my practical brother, told us that when Mother died the place erupted with noise. They heard furniture moving around upstairs when everyone was downstairs.

We went to Mother's service in the Holy Family Catholic Church where she had married my father. We were all seated there, family and friends, with the big church doors closed against the November cold. When the pallbearers brought my mother's coffin to the outside, one of them rapped loudly on the door. The priest, wearing his finest vestments, walked up the aisle from the altar to the front door carrying a staff. He knocked sharply with it, three times, and said loudly, "Come in, Elizabeth." And they carried the coffin in, placed it by the altar, and opened it so that we could say goodbye to our mother. My sister Mary knelt at the casket and laid her arms out in her flowing mink coat, fingers of one jeweled hand tinkling her silver rosary. I thought of mother rising out of the coffin and saying to us, as she had so many times when she left us to go to church or the store or on a trip with my father, "You are on your own, kids."

I went up last, afraid I might cry, knelt and looked down trembling. I thought, whoa, wait a minute, who is this? I covered my mouth with my hand. This was not our Bessie. She would never have allowed that ugly colored shroud, her most unfavorite color. Or lain so quietly. Or allowed her springy hair to be disciplined into dignified waves. I thought of her great mellow voice that none of us inherited, singing, and imitating fools, and laughing, stilled now and away from us. And those warm hands, always so lively and so slacking on the spankings, resting in a pose crossed on her breast that she would never have assumed, except in mime. I remembered reading that the spirit leaves the body, and somewhere else, indeed, had gone Mother's warm and loving spirit, her fried chicken and "biskits," and her "horrible" punishments with the spatula. Nobody in that coffin prayed eighteen rosaries every day for us.

The solemn burial, then, was on one of those iron-cold, colorless November days in South Dakota that took the heart out of a person. At the cemetery, everyone stood shivering in little clumps, looking gray as the day. We went back to her old house and tried to be cheery with coffee or tea and some dim jokes, but the light and warmth was gone. We were on our own.

Our house took the knocks and blows of the family's activities, including a solid blast into the living room wall by my brother Bob while sighting-in an "empty" shotgun. I was sitting watching him do interesting things with the gun, when suddenly it banged and something *whooshed* over my head. I jumped up scared, ran outside, and hid. There were good hiding places all over the house and outside, too. If I was quiet, nobody could find me. At eight years old, my favorite was a sweet summer place by the front porch under the spiraea bushes, a cool and dark secret spot where a small, still girl could look out through the branches and keep watch. I was good at hiding and drifted through childhood mostly unrecorded and unbothered. I spent hours in the attic alone, sitting in the apple tree, or playing with my friend Joe McMahon.

The kids I walked to school with were nice, and I liked them a lot, but my father and brothers were simply "sockdolagers." I hurried home to be around them. They knew everything. I sat with them and listened and learned. They laughed a lot about things that happened *before* I was there. Like the time Bob fell in the lake. Oh boy! Or the duck that got under someone's feet. That was a good one! I loved to sit and laugh with them about those stories.

Family roles were understood. My brothers were going to be doctors. My sisters would marry important men. I never heard what I was supposed to be. I guessed I could be something really amazing by myself. I could not wait to find out. My exploration then was in the world of books. Prowling around in the attic, I discovered the cache of old books my father had bought for Bill and Bob. They were kept in the tall bookshelves that spanned the wide main room. Full of mouse tracks and dust, an ancient rump-sprung couch sat next to the shelves. I sat down and began reading of giants and castles and splendid wars with knights sticking bad men with swords and pikes. There were martyrs and adventures up the Missouri River with the Indians.

Along with those riches was a book about Tarzan, who lived in jungle trees in Africa.²⁰ When he had to travel around, he swung from one branch to another like his relatives the apes. If those leopards or lions got funny with him, he beat them up and made pants out of their skins. Pictures showed him looking nifty in the jungle. Before Tarzan and those nifty pants, my friend Joe helped me read the Big Little Books and comics. Then, I went on to first grade. In our reading class at school, I would humbly go through the abc's, again, and Dick and Jane's old stuff. Then, I would go home and read the real stuff. When everyone was through with the daily newspaper, I took it to the attic to read. And in the attic, I read how Tarzan got out of tight fixes from those cannibals, lions, and leopards with bravery and skill. Just like me. Ha ha.

But reading Tarzan got me into a fix myself when Father caught me. Mostly my activities were ignored; the family was busy, busy. But someone may have questioned what I was doing up there alone so much. Father moved silent and fast. Before I knew he was there, he had palmed my book. He looked at Tarzan's near-naked picture, opened the window, and cast out the book. I saw it hit the lily pond and sink—like my heart. Father took my arm in an iron grip, and we went down to his study. He handed me two heavy books, *Shakespeare* and the King James Bible. He pronounced The Rule: "One stanza from Shakespeare and one verse from the Bible memorized every day and recited to me after dinner. For one month." He said, "Sheila, you have the gift of early reading, like me. You mustn't spoil it with junk. It will rot your mind like candy does to your teeth."

It was summer, and every afternoon I opened the heavy books and chose a different stanza and verse to memorize. "The Quality of mercy is not strained," I began the stanza from the *Merchant of Venice*, one foot over the other, reciting while he listened. I yearned to be outside with the others on such a fine evening. "The Lord is my Shepherd, I shall not want," I recited from Psalm 23. "He maketh me to lie down in green pastures." Boy, I wished. Father let me off after two weeks, saying I was doing a pretty good job with the punishment. But the memorizing and reciting stayed with me. I would steal into the study alone and open the heavy books again. I did not take them to the attic but sat there reading aloud, relishing the curious tempo of the words.

I may have been the only kid in grade school who sat down and read *Shakespeare* and the King James Bible for pleasure. Plenty of stabbings, crookery, and nobility going on in both of those to keep me reading for years. In a bicycle ride with some school friends, my bike's tire got a flat. "My kingdom for a horse!"[21] I shouted, wheeling the crippled bike home by the handlebars. Out of the corner of my eye, I saw two friends tapping their foreheads. They considered me nice but well, . . . you know. I kept on reading. My English teacher, Sister Grace, finally explained the addiction. "Those books have the rhythms of iambic pentameter," she said, "like your heartbeat." But, along with Macbeth, Hamlet, and King David, my heart belonged to Tarzan. I fished him out of the pond, dried him out, and ironed the pages. And included him with those grand saints and knights.

Like the people in them, houses in our town were well kept and serious. But, as I read about Tarzan, Mitchell became a steamy jungle, crawling and creeping with lions, and cannibals with bones stuck through their noses, and big gorillas lurking in the grass and trees everywhere. Elephants stood around quietly, fanning their big ears, while crocodiles lurked in the goldfish pond under the lily pads. There were some big snakes winding around the oak tree; they could snap you up whole and it was over for you. In the midst of this peril, calmly gardening by herself, was my mother. I got a big stick and held it behind me, staying casually around her during her gardening in case one of them charged. I kept it under my bed at night so that it would be handy to protect my family.

That was summer. In winter, of course, we had the Indians. I could hear their drums at night and them creeping up to the house. I would go out and smoke the peace pipe with the Mighty Sioux and save my family. I read that Tarzan lived mostly in Africa and drove around the country on elephants. But he went home to England sometimes to visit his father, Lord Greystoke, and have tea. South Dakota would be a good place for Tarzan to summer, I thought. Mitchell was quite a bit like Africa. Maybe we would get married. There were plenty of dresses around the house and hanging on a rack in the attic. I could tuck one up for a wedding dress.

I addressed an envelope to "Tarzan care of Africa." Everyone there knew him. I consulted with my friend Joe McMahon about what I should write in a letter.

"Dear Tarzan, how are those apes?" I shouted.

"Sounds O.K.," Joe said, his face in a book about castles.

"Please come here in Mitchell South Dakota this summer. I invite you. You wood like our house. Our trees are big. I'll wait in the third elm tree from 6th street. Love, Sheila Delaney"

I sealed it up and put it in the mailbox on the front porch and prepared for the event.

I found an old raccoon coat on a rack in the attic, cut it up, and secretly hand-sewed a jungle dress out of it. It went over one shoulder. I put it on, looked in the mirror, and, oh, it was really perfect. I modeled it for Joe: "TAAAA DAAA, here's Sheila Joan Colette of the Apes!" He frowned and said, "Cover up more." What did he know, he never read Tarzan.

My plan was to wait in the elm tree. The month of June in South Dakota could sometimes bring on frostbite, but every day in my outfit and bare feet, I climbed into the elm tree and waited and waited, and shivered and shivered. He never showed up. Someone complained. Maybe the neighbors in the next block. They were always complaining. No matter how the news about my tree-sitting got to them, my parents were raising five noisy and rambunctious children and the complaint was the last straw from me, the silent sixth.

After waiting in the tree one chilly afternoon, I gave up and went to my room to go through my Tarzan book. Maybe I had missed something. My mother was sitting on my bed waiting for me. Patty and Nanny were sitting beside her, smiling wide, showing their assorted teeth. Mother, who always had difficulty looking grim, managed a frown. "What in the world were you doing sitting outside in a tree wearing a get-up like that so the neighborhood can see you?" she asked. The Cheshire cats on each side of her rolled their eyes up and nodded to each other, pursing their lips.

"I'm waiting for Tarzan!" I said. Surely anyone could see that.

"Give me the dress," Mother said, holding out her hand. I took it off and gave it to her.

"People must think we keep you chained in the basement like the

Wild Man of Borneo," Patty said, "and once in a while you escape and scare everybody on the block because you don't have any real clothes to wear! Sniff."

Mother reached in the closet for a dress. I put it on. Nanny offered to take me shopping for clothes. "So's not to scare the neighbors," she said. I never saw my beloved dress again. I should forget Tarzan, Patty said. I never did, though.

"Tarzan care of Africa" never got out of the mailbox. I did not know about postage. The letter was read aloud at dinner with lots of flourishes in front of my red face. They laughed, so I laughed. They smiled and I smiled. But I wanted our guard dog Captain to give them all a good bite. Or, to have them in a row of coffins I could tap dance on. Or, I could fall down dead myself, and then they would cry!

A t age five, I thought the Great Depression and drought were events like Corn Palace Week, Mitchell's annual harvest celebration, and that everything else went about its business. Growing older in the late 1930s, I read about the stock market crash and crops failing all over the Midwest, people losing their jobs and jumping out of windows. On Main Street on Saturdays or in Father's medical office, I heard farmers talking about "the drot." At the Paramount Theater, newsreels showed the "Okies," dispossessed Oklahoma farmers, driving to California. Their old cars were heaped up with everything they owned. No rain to speak of fell spring or summer. The sky was molten or dense with dust, and the farmer's topsoil was blowing away. Banks were foreclosing on our South Dakota farmers because they could not grow enough crops to pay their mortgages.

Father took care of them for nothing. "I have enough," he would say. Those who could paid him with dressed chickens, eggs, and crocks of churned butter left on our back porch. They would not stay to visit, only say, "For Doctor." Sometimes Father got tears in his eyes over those gestures from "the best people in the world!" I listened to the talk at our table. Father pounded the table hard. *Wham, wham, sock!*

"Our farmers have to have rain, our parched countryside is blowing away in the hot winds!" He stood and threw his hands up. "The whole Jim River Valley could blow away now, and I ask you, how will we eat?" Mother's brother, Uncle Vince, said, "Well, now, Spike, we'll just get us each a tin beak, follow the horses, and pick corn with the sparrows!"

The barren sky filled with grasshoppers. Grasshoppers! Ugh! They flew in swarms and landed on the farmers' fields devouring what little the farmers could plant. They were everywhere. One hopper taking residence under a person's shirt or pants could guarantee the most clumsy dancer at least one flying leap into the air and a spin like

Nijinsky.[22] These days, when I see dancers on television spinning on their head with their body in the air, I think "hoppers!" The insects had sticky feet and big googley eyes and spit a brown substance. We called it tobacco juice. When they were killed, everything inside them splattered, including the tobacco juice. They had no respect; once one landed on my father's breakfast eggs with a *plop*. He stabbed it with a fork and scraped the whole mess into the garbage. "Our family is a lot of hungry mouths to feed, and these ##**!!! grasshoppers are eating up our breakfast, lunch and dinner!" Personally, I never saw a grasshopper I liked.

Well, one exception. Two actually. A sculptor was commissioned to create two huge granite grasshoppers to guard the entrance to the county courthouse. Like the lions guarding the New York Public Library, grasshoppers appeared to the selection committee as a South Dakota cultural item. I loved to feel their smooth backs. Some of the town fathers had them removed because they were not appropriate. But what could have been more appropriate!

While the countryside was crackling dry, we would pray and pray at Mass and in school for rain. At home after dinner, we would get on our knees and pray. The drought went on and on. No rain, not a drop fell. It was too hot to play. The sidewalks were so hot us kids had to do the unspeakable—wear shoes! Shrill witch winds blew constantly, burning everything they touched. In the house, Mother kept the rooms dark and cool with floor fans blowing over cakes of ice. Sometimes we moved to the basement to eat and sleep on cots in the main room. The merciless sun dried up the lake so much that we could not go swimming. My friend Joe McMahon could not come over and play because his mother said he might get sunstroke. We kept on praying.

One summer night, my father came onto the sleeping porch and shook us all awake. He turned on the light and rolled his eyes. His white hair stuck straight out, and he looked like a madman from the movies. "Listen!" he hissed, holding his hand behind his ear. We listened. We could hear little drops of rain pattering on the tree leaves. A coolness breezed through the porch. The drops became big drops and then gushing torrents. Thunder and lightning ripped the skies. The trees swayed madly in the wind. Father led us all downstairs and outside into the sandpit and made us stand in the rain in our pajamas and bare feet. Father grinned and grinned and put his arms and his face up and yelled to the heavens.

Mother did not join us, and she was mad at my father. She made us come in the house the back way, down the basement stairs, and stand in the shower there. First the boys and then the girls together to wash the mud off, and she handed us dry pajamas. It was swell, us being all together in this. Waiting for his turn, Father strode around in his bare muddy feet, his pajamas sopping, hitting his palm with his other fist, and grinning. But the blessed rain did not fall long enough. Depression and drought continued.

Despite everything, we had a wedding in the fall of 1938. We stood stiffly for a formal wedding portrait. Everyone in the family posed in our living room, except my parents. As the proud originators of the bride, their portraits were separate. My oldest sister Mary was regal, her long satin train carefully spread out before her. As flower girl, I had just sprinkled rose petals on it at her request and looked exactly what I was, a small insignificant member of the wedding party. There was some discussion about taking me out of the picture. I spoiled the symmetry, they said. The bride, my protectress, said firmly, "Sheila stays in the picture!" Behind me stood the groomsmen, including my brother Bob, and next to him the best man, my brother Bill, strangely without his glasses. He must have lost them, and I knew he was blind as a deep-cavern bat. My sister Patty was next to the maid of honor, and Nan, in her light peach dress, surprised everyone. At sixteen, she was suddenly gorgeous. Everyone noticed. She was old Nanny goat to me, though. My friend. It was 1938, September third. I was eleven years old.

After the wedding, Mary had gone away and my father had something to announce to the rest of us. Mother made sure everyone was home, lining us up in the living room in our birth order, Bill, Bob, Pat, Nan, and me, and Father rushed in. He did not tolerate debate, he gave The Rule.

"In case you forgot, the depression and drought are still with us," he said grimly, striding up and down. "And we are headed for WAR!" While we were digesting that rocky news, he roared: "How would you like to pay for Mary's wedding? Would you? Or you?" He went down the line stabbing a finger at each of us. Everyone croaked out a scared, "nnno."

"I'll be in debt a long time paying for those #$%!!** caterers, photographs, ice cream favors shaped like little slippers, cake boxes, flowers, dances, gowns, monkey suits and tuxedos, portraits, teas, invitations, presents, announcements, lunches, dinners, and cocktails, for God's sake! What does any of that have to do with two people who want to be with each other for the rest of their lives?" We shook our heads and shrugged our shoulders. We did not know. He was full throttle, roaring and shaking his fist: "Marriage is a serious business! I didn't have a wedding like that, didn't expect to. I have you two boys to educate in medical school, and all of you must never, never, *ever*, *ever* plan to have anything to do with a big commercial, barn-burner wedding like Mary's!" Finished, he walked swiftly out the front door and slammed it so hard the windows rattled.

With regard to barn burners, we never, never, *ever*, *ever* had one. We all had weddings, some of us had several, but never barn burners. There are sitcoms on television and movies about people driving and flying and hitchhiking furiously from all points of the world to a family wedding, and everything is wonderful when they get there with heart-warming scenes of laughing and crying and hugging. I sometimes have a comic book picture in my mind of my brothers and sisters driving or flying or hitchhiking furiously in the opposite direction from a barn burner, pursued by those ice cream slippers, little cake boxes, luncheons, dinners, and cocktails, etc., etc., etc., "for God's sake!"

Mary was gone, my brothers were at medical school, and I gloomed around the house like Marley's ghost from Dickens's *Christmas Carol*. Patty and Nanny were always fixing each other's hair, trying lipsticks, and talking about boys. They were sixteen and seventeen years old to my eleven, and I thought I would learn something from them, but they did not want me around. Patty said: "We are teenagers, call us Pat and Nan, and you are just a baby. Go away and play with your dolls!" They hurt my feelings, and I began to write about them and draw their pictures. I wrote that Patty was a maggoty, snaggely-tooth old witch, whose breath smelled like a bucket of horse apples and scared all the boys away. I drew pictures of her riding a broomstick with big halitosis fumes coming out of her mouth. I wrote that Nanny was a beautiful fairy lady, who always saved me from the witch. I drew her as she took her wand and really cold-cocked her sister.

Alone, I spent time in our attic reading. Among the scads of good books up there was one called *The Lives of the Saints*. It was about the holy martyrs who died for their faith. Pictures showed them being roasted in red-hot chairs or like hot dogs over a grill, their arms and legs pulled off by horses, and other parts of them chopped up by axes. But, while all this was going on, they never stopped praying to God. There were pictures of them smiling and having a good time with their torturers. The nuns said that, if we kept holy, we would laugh and smile, too.

I was being as holy as possible. I went to Sunday Mass, Holy Communion, and Confession on Fridays. I made many visits to the church and said hundreds of aspirations (little prayers). I memorized all the prayers I could find and recited them to myself before I went to bed. Saturday night was the time to get ready for Sunday Mass. My sisters and I washed our hair and laid out our Sunday clothes. Sunday morning, when there were just the three of us at home, we all piled into one car with Mother, and my father drove. Sunday after Mass was the time for visitors.

On special occasions, the nuns at the hospital would invite us to Mass in their chapel. These special invitations were for Christmas Midnight Mass and Easter Sunday. With Bill and Bob home for the Christmas holiday from college and medical school, we all sat in one pew that was reserved for us. First to go in was Mother, followed by Bill and Bob, Pat and Nan and me next to my father, who sat last in case he had to leave to see a patient.

One of my brothers had a bad cold one memorable Christmas Eve and during Mass coughed and sneezed a lot. Mother nudged and whispered to him to use a handkerchief. In taking it out of his pocket, he accidentally got his necktie tangled up with it and blew into it with a loud *honk!* My father, seeing the possibilities of this event, whispered to me that he had to see a patient right away, hurriedly genuflected, and left, leaving my mother to deal with the situation. She calmly took a little pair of scissors from her purse, snipped the tie off Bob's neck, and stuffed it and the hanky into her purse. Alleluia.

One Sunday morning, Pat and Nan got permission to drive Father's car to Mass, taking me. Pat was driving, and the minute we left the driveway, they pulled out cigarettes and started to smoke. They turned the radio music up loud. I was in the back seat, and when I realized we were not going to church, boy, I felt really smooth. I would get a cigarette from them and light up, too! Then I had second thoughts. Terrible thoughts! Missing Mass was a mortal sin, enough to send us to Hell. Hell, my readings showed me, was even worse than the martyrs' fix, at least martyrs finally went to heaven and got some rest, while sinners burned forever in Hell.

Pat and Nan did not care which way they went. I tried to listen to the radio while the car filled up with smoke, but all I could really think of was Satan putting his mark on us. He would climb in and scar us with his claws so he would know us when we got to Hell and have us burn forever in the various fires he kept going. I started sweating at the thought of it. I got sick from the smoke and rolled down the back window and threw up. "You baby! You can't come with us anymore!" Pat yelled. They took me home, dumped me out of the car, and drove away, screeching the tires.

I told Mother I had gotten sick at church. Lying was a venial sin, unless you killed somebody and said you did not. This event was my first really good sin. I did not feel possessed with evil, like the nuns told us we would, just gray and dirty, like dishwater. Anyway, it filled the bill for Friday Confession. Kneeling in the confessional, I told Father Tom, and he said I should have made my sisters go to Mass. I said they were bigger than me and would hit me. "Offer it up like the martyrs!" he said. I was not holy enough for that yet. He gave me five Hail Marys and five Our Fathers for penance. That was a relief; I said them right away. Everybody heard about the kid who had to wear beans in his shoes for a week for penance. I thought, boy, what in the world did *he* do? My brother Bob said they were baked beans.

Before World War II, no kid I knew had any money for candy or movies. To overcome this depression-era cash-flow problem, Mac McMahon built an amazing Ferris wheel in his backyard. A spectacular looking creation, the wheel had one seat only for one passenger. Any more would have been impossible weight for the operator, Mac, to make the wheel go around. Ten turns for a penny seemed about

right because he had to push and pull hard for the complete revolution. The contraption would pay, he told my brother Bob, for the
candy, the movies, and, he grinned, "the girls."

I went over to see it with Bob. I wanted to ride in it. I did not have
a penny and whined for a free ride, but Mac said, "This is business."
His first customer, Bob, royally seated himself and slowly unfolded a
dollar bill. He may have been the only kid in town then with a dollar.
I watched my brother majestically rise and descend in his chair one
thousand times, while below, bathed in sweat and wearing a hole in
the lawn, labored Mac, the creator, his arms blurring like pistons.
That was before World War II. Afterwards, Mac was a handsome
decorated fighter pilot with ribbons and medals, and the girls, ah, the
girls . . . they gave *him* candy.²³

With no pennies for the Ferris wheel, or candy, we depression kids
were experts at free entertainment. At twelve and thirteen years old,
I belonged to a neighborhood group like "Our Gang" in the movies;
it was young and sexless.²⁴ After dinner on warm summer nights, my
parents would say, "Now Sheila, go and play with your little friends."
So until nine o'clock, my friends and I roamed the streets like bandits,
threw rocks at the street lights and passing cars, peeked in windows,
and jumped out at kids, scaring them. The boys peed in the bushes,
too, but I did not. Shorty was the leader, and anything he did was
good. He was an excellent rock thrower, and one dark night scored
a direct hit on a streetlight. It swung around wildly and smashed to
the street. The lone city police car sputtered out of a nearby alley with
its siren blaring, and we took off in all directions, laughing. On those
rare soft summer nights, we ran and ran, hearts pounding, feeling
light as a feather, as though we could run forever, away from the vil-
lains, leap over houses, spread our arms, and float. Anything could
happen on such a night. My brothers and sisters "ganged" at my age,
too. But, later, they became too dignified to admit it was fun.

I was the only girl in the gang, and only Mother could have sorted
me out from the boys. My hair was cut short for speed, and I wore
good pickings from the rack in our attic. My best gang outfit was a
pair of bib overalls and tennis shoes that laced up high. "Tennies"
were decidedly nifty and geared to run. They had an honorable past
in high-school basketball with brother Bob, and I wore them with

respect and three pairs of socks so they would fit. Depending on the weather, I wore a sweatshirt or nothing under the overalls. Nothing to hide. Yet.

Before we entered ninth grade, on our last summer as a gang together, we decided to "do it" together. Namely, we would tip over the Koop sisters' outhouse. "Doing it" was big time. Years before, my dignified sister Mary had done it, and Father thought it was funny. So I was ready and fearless, in spite of the story that the sisters, Annie and Rose, were witches and ate kids when they caught them. "That's perfectly true," my good friend and advisor Joe McMahon told me. The Koops lived near Joe, and he said he was walking around the neighborhood one day when their garbage was out for pickup, and he saw some big gnawed-up bones and some teeth. Joe's face was grave. "Human," he said. I shivered with dread; this was getting spiffy.

We had gone to the Koop house many nights to stand in front of their house and yell our brilliant battle cries: "Hey, dumb old Koops. Hey, old chicken Koop poops." The Koops's house was a decrepit Victorian with rotting boards, peeling paint, and a widow's walk around the sagging top story. We would stand there, holding hands, and yell until one of them opened the second-floor window and threw boiling water down at us. They always missed, and that was the end of our contract with them. We ran somewhere else and did something else.

But for this expedition, we made a serious daytime reconnaissance of the Koop outhouse, mapped it out, and figured where we would stand for the charge forward. We would link arms and run together and push. It was a big outhouse, and we would have to give it everything we had to get it over. We rehearsed on our front lawn. Night came and we ducked out of our houses and met down the street. We trotted over to the Koop house, walked to our places quietly, and linked arms. Shorty said, "Go!" and we raced toward our target, dimly ahead of us, its door with the half-moon crescent standing ajar. Just before we got to it, we all slid into the big pit.

Splash!! The "house" had been pushed behind its pit, instead of above it, and we were *in it*. It was full and nasty. "Dire crooks!" yelled Shorty. We helped each other out and squished and sloshed our separate ways home. We NEVER talked about it to each other or to anyone. I went home and bathed and bathed and threw my clothes into the trash. My mother said that was the first time I had taken a bath and washed my hair without being told. Father appeared pleased as their cleansed and shiny-haired daughter appeared the next morning. He said to Mother: "Well, would you look at Sheila. She is finally getting to be quite the little lady."

But leaving childhood was hard. The departure started in earnest in the fall, and I would sink into spells of deep sadness. Someone lovable was leaving me. Someone in bib overalls and tennies. There would be times when I flirted and giggled and went to parties and wore lipstick and dresses. But then I would go home and withdraw, see no one, and sit quietly or find a good place to write or draw. Or play furiously with dolls. I worried and worried, what was going to happen to me? I was fourteen, not getting any younger. I wanted to be married, but who, or what, was coming around this fading year of 1941, besides Christmas?

December seventh came around. Pearl Harbor and the Japanese came around and finished the doll-playing, finished the depression, and ended our tranquil, pastoral life. And took from us, forever, some of the best people in the world.

Both Eric Fowler and Sheila Delaney remember the dust storms of the 1930s. One such "black blizzard" buried machinery on this farm in southeastern South Dakota in 1936. South Dakota State Historical Society

As a bachelor, Dr. William Delaney made his rounds in this 1913 American Car Company Uunderslung. Sheila Delaney collection

Substantial brick buildings lined Mitchell's Main Street in the 1930s. Mitchell Area Historical Society

Joe McMahon, left, and Sheila Delaney joined their families on a duck hunt around 1930. Sheila Delaney collection

William A. Delaney holds Sheila in the backyard of the family home in about 1928. Sheila Delaney collection

Hunting was a passion for William Delaney, right, shown here wearing his favorite World War I army pants. Theodore Roosevelt, Jr. (left), and an assistant hunted with him in about 1919. Sheila Delaney collection

Sheila Delaney, front left, was the flower girl for her sister Mary's wedding to Bob Dunham in 1938. Bob Delaney is fourth from the left, and Bill Delaney, as best man, stands directly behind Sheila. Patty Delaney is fourth from the right, and Nan Delaney is second from the right. Sheila Delaney collection

The World's Only Corn Palace was located about five blocks from the Delaney home. Shown here in 1941, the facility hosted many famous entertainers and politicians. South Dakota State Historical Society

The Delaney home, shown here in a modern photograph, was the center of family life. The wide eaves, brick porch supports, and hipped roof are typical of the Prairie style of architecture. South Dakota State Historical Society (photograph by Jason Biggins).

Sheila Delaney relaxes at an apple orchard in New Mexico in 1977.
Sheila Delaney collection

uring the first months of the war, a decorated fighter pilot and family friend sent my father a picture of him in his plane with the name "Spike's Butcher Shop" painted on the fuselage. My father was pleased with that kind of tough tribute. But the young pilot was killed by the Japanese, and the war engulfed us like a bad dream, always with us as we went about daily routines. Joe McMahon and his brother Mac went away to be soldiers. Many schoolmates were already in the army or navy or in training. Families were allowed to serve together, and a family of Mitchell sons and their father were on the Battleship *Arizona* (one son lied about his age). The Japanese sank the *Arizona* that terrible day at Pearl Harbor, Sunday, 7 December 1941. "A date which will live in infamy," President Franklin D. Roosevelt said.²⁵ I thought my heart could not bear it, but there was more tragedy to come.

We read about the places where our people were killed. Places we had never learned of in school. My sister Nan's husband, a bomber pilot, went down in flames over Ploesti. She said he used to wake in a sweat, dreaming his death. "Shorty," the destroyer of streetlights in my gang, was killed in the Pacific Theater. Mac McMahon became a fighter pilot and was immediately in combat over Australia and then in Europe. Dear friends were lost forever. My brothers were hurried through medical school. Bill was stationed on the destroyer USS *Stephen Potter* as medical officer, and Bob became a medical officer with the Eighteenth Airborne in England, France, and Germany. Both would come home highly decorated.

Everything and everyone was changing. I put my dolls away in the attic and got a permanent wave. I wanted to be a woman soldier, but I was only fourteen. I wanted to be in the war somehow. Life's tempo grew. Even the music. The jitterbug was a fast couple dance, the male dancers throwing their partners in the air and spinning them on the floor and all around their bodies. And there were great movements of people swarming over America, some to defense factories. A small air base was opened in Mitchell, and Nan met her next husband,

Clint McCain of Shreveport, Louisiana, there; he was the commanding officer.[26] Everyone entertained the soldiers.

I kept clippings and stories about the battles. I read everything I could find and waxed knowledgeable about the war to anyone I could capture. I sat down with Father and some men who were talking in the den about the corn crop. I said, "Say, did you folks know those *Stuka* dive bombers release their bombs while they are still in their dive and pull up sharply to avoid the explosion?"[27] There was silence, and Father told me to go and help Mother. Later, I was told by Mother, "You shouldn't be talking like that to the men." Who then?

Well, apparently not in Current Events at school either. Standing in front of the class, I found no one wanted to hear a fourteen-year-old female discuss bombs, explosions, and enemy dive bombers. I guessed the nun complained to Father. He called me into the den and said: "Sheila, your mother and I think you are getting very pretty, and in six years or so, some nice man will want to marry you. But you must stop reading and talking about the war. We men will take care of that." I nodded in agreement. I stopped talking about the war, but I did not stop thinking about it or reading about it. I could not. Reading was my life. My oxygen. Things were going on!

During wartime, crops were abundant again, although farmers were hard put to find anyone to help them. We prayed hard for our soldiers to come home. Friends and schoolmates turned up on leave, handsome and serious in their uniforms. We went to the train station when they left and cried together over our cokes at Nickel's Drugstore. Everything we could think of was done to help the "war effort." Mother planted a victory garden and attended to the rationing of cigarettes, butter, meat, and gasoline. Everyone had to have stamps to buy anything.[28]

New German words entered our vocabulary. *Ersatz* meant to replace with inferior material. Our dress shoes were *ersatz* leather; Nan said they were cardboard. If wet, the dye got on your feet. We had meatless meals. One night a week after dinner, we sat around the dining-room table and wrote to everyone.

At my school, Notre Dame Academy, the altar boys were gone to the war, and the nuns taught us schoolgirls Latin responses to help the priest at Mass. "*Introibo ad altare Dei,*" the priest would intone.

"I will go unto the altar of God." We would pipe in our girlish voices, *"ad Deum qui laetificat juventutem meam"* ("to God who gives joy to my youth"). But none of us were joyful. Newsreel pictures of Japanese committing atrocities in Nanking were shown at the Paramount Theater, and after the newsreel there was weeping in the audience.[29] A woman cried out, "Oh, our young men!" My father, proud of being tough, walked with me out of the theater, tears streaming down his face.

We still found laughter whenever we could. Even from the air-raid wardens, who were serious older town men with helmets and flashlights. Regulations for blackouts were printed in the newspaper. When the sirens blew, we closed special blackout shades and the curtains, too. The slightest crack of light from our windows could bring a warden banging on the door. House doors were never locked, and the air-raid warden would come into the front hallway, shine his flashlight around, and shout: "They can see you. They can see you from the air!" And we would hurry to find the crack of light and shut the curtain or pull the shade. But who was up in the air? No one had an answer for me. Father said: "You ask too many questions. Just shut the curtain, and your mouth, please!"

While Bill served in the navy, Agnes, his wife, stayed with us. One night Mother and I were sitting in an upstairs bedroom with her as she was changing the diapers of Bill's little first-born son, officially baptized William Aloysious Delaney III. Just then the siren sounded, and Agnes closed the curtains and left a little light on in the room because changing Bill's diapers took dangerous maneuvering. The warden pounded on the door, charged into the front hallway, and shouted up the stairs: "They can see you. They can see you from the air!" I leaned over the upstairs banister: "Who can see us? Who's in the air?" I wanted to settle this. "Why," he said in an amazed voice at my ignorance, "the Germans and Japs, that's who." I persisted, "What in the world would the Japs and Germans want with Mitchell?"

He hit his forehead with the heel of his hand so hard I could hear the smack. Clearly, he was dealing with an idiot. "What would they want, young lady? What would they want? I'll tell you what they would want. They would bomb the Corn Palace! That's what they would want!!!" He shone the flashlight on his face to show me the biggest frown humanly possible, laughed a sour laugh, and left, slamming the front door. At night, the noise of planes flying in and out of the small air base at Mitchell were part of my dreams. As result of a low-flying squadron from the air base, I dreamed German *Stuka* dive bombers were roaring toward the Corn Palace to begin their bombing run.

The Corn Palace was just a few blocks from our house, and I still think of it in amazement. Such an exotic flowering in the seat of Davison County. Dive bombing the building from the air, even at night, would have been easy. It is there foursquare for anyone to see. There could have been problems, however, for the *Stukas* roaring in on their bombing run. Before they released their bombs, they might have spun out of control and crashed on Main Street at the sight of the large, exotic structure, topped with big colored onion-shaped domes and minarets resembling those on an oriental palace, a veritable love child of the Taj Mahal.[30] Before they crashed, the bomber pilots might have been close enough to see the building's huge panels, front and side, covered with pastoral scenes made of different colors of corn. The panels are corned-up with new pictures every harvest and illuminated with floodlights at night during events. Making fun of the building was something our group, the local smart set, chose to do. Surviving adolescence and nearing adulthood, showing our sophistication despite having to live in dreadful "Corn Pone City," we would say, hurrying by the building, "Ahhh," as vapidly as possible, dragging smoke through rationed cigarettes, "the Palazzo di Korno."

No one has come forward about those wartime cigarettes, but I can confirm they kicked like an army mule. One seductive advertisement proclaimed, "So round, so firm, so fully packed." And they were indeed round, firm, and fully packed, but with what? Slitting one carefully with a razor blade, an autopsy revealed what appeared to be old wood scraps, ground up tires, and dried cow dung. On inhale, they could generate sweating and near blackouts. Thinking of them today makes me dizzy. We smoked and coughed away valiantly, observing the eternal occupation of young people defying death in the most unpleasant ways possible. Joe McMahon would say, offering me one, "Care for a coffin nail?"

The Corn Palace might have seemed an anomaly to the *Stuka* pilots, but it is there yet. With a battered dignity, the building, a sports arena on the inside, has stood solid in various forms for more than a century and has continually hosted without a blush such things as donkey ball, mud wrestling, basketball games, dances, concerts, meetings, prize fights, and war-bond drives. In the days of big bands, the palace was right on the circuit, and we grew up dancing to Stan Kenton, Woody Herman and his Woodchoppers, the Dorsey Brothers, Count Basie, and Duke Ellington. The big bands liked playing there during harvest week so they could get off the road for a while.

Before those big bands, there was Paul Whiteman and his orchestra from Denver. When I was too little to go anywhere except to bed, he played the Corn Palace and came to our house for dinner. After the matinee, he walked the few blocks to our house with some of the singers. Mr. Whiteman was tall and fat. He had an amazingly big head with shiny black hair and a teeny black mustache. He wore a long white overcoat that came down to his two-tone suede shoes. Black and white they were. Father welcomed the party at the door; Mother took their coats and sat them at the table. Being close to the ground then, I crawled under the table to those shoes. My little eyes had never seen shoes like his before. Mother was calling for me, so I stayed quiet under there with the shoes. I patted them gently; they were like big puppies. I kissed them a little. He put his big head under the table and said, "Oh, what a cute little kid!" I was hauled out and put to bed. Years later my mother said she heard him talking to one of the singers who was also a guest that evening. He said, "Good eats, but I wanted to kick that ##** kid over the moon!"

Besides Whiteman and his orchestra, the old palace gleamed and glimmered with celebrities each fall. After harvest the town had a week-long celebration with a midway and rides. The farmers came in with their families; there were always dances after the show. Lawrence Welk was one of the favored performers, and the promoters tried to book him for Corn Palace Week as often as possible, but there were other entertainers, too. Jack Benny came as a headliner one harvest week and laid an egg bigger than any dinosaur could. I did not think he was funny, and neither did anyone else. During his act, he would put his hands on his hips, glare at the audience, and say, "Well!" Nobody laughed. Someone yelled, "Well what?!" Benny never forgave us. He made remarks on his television show about the Corn Palace and about chickens clucking around the stage with him and laying eggs. Father directed me to write to him that *he* had laid the eggs! He did not answer. Only *we* could make fun of the Palace of Corn; it was ours.

During the war, we were supposed to hate the Germans and Japanese. We did not know any Japs, except in the newsreels, where they were called "the yellow peril," and our neighbors and friends were German. They were the farmers and businessman, our schoolmates, and the majority of my father's patients. Father said they were the best people in the world. And they made sovereign pastry. There was a German pastry shop downtown, and anytime I had money, I would take a "pastry ride" on my bike.

My father's medical practice was large, and during wartime, he was busy keeping it together for his sons. He managed war-bond drives and sent Mother on expeditions to family members scattered far from home. Mother was the wizard of wartime train schedules, making amazing connections with them at any time. Traveling with her was a rich adventure. One Christmas, by various trains, she and I went to New Jersey, where Pat and her husband, Yale, were stationed. Mother had accumulated a good supply of scarce items, nylons, scotch, and cigarettes, to take to them. I was fifteen, gangly, and knew it. Everything I had was growing and changing. Under my clothes, busy construction went on day and night. I wanted it all done fast so that I could get married.

Going out, a troop train was hooked onto our Pullman car. After we had had our dinner, the soldiers passed our Pullman on their way to the diner. I was sitting up reading in bed, when one of the soldiers leaned into my curtained berth and tried to kiss me. The sergeant pulled him out by his tie and said, "Are you nuts; she's still got her baby teeth!" I tapped my teeth with my fingers and said, "*Au contraire!* These are my grown up teeth!" but they hustled away.

My sister Nan spent part of the war dating a government agent from Washington. She stayed with us briefly. One night, before going to sleep, she said he had told her that America had a terrible weapon that would end the war.

"Really? What could do that?" I asked.

She whispered softly, "An atom bomb!"

"Really? Like Adam and Eve?"

"No, no!" She spelled out, "A-t-o-m, atom, atom bomb! Everything will be destroyed, people and buildings. Everything!!"[31]

I shivered. A wisp of cold air snaked through our cozy bedroom.

y first awareness of existence was falling about a foot and a half with the baby jumper under the doorway into our kitchen: a cartwheel fall and then a kaleidoscope of my mother's face, her soothing voice calling my name, and pain around my head. The jumper was hung from a hook under the doorway so that she could watch me while she and the hired girls ironed the mountains of sheets, shirts, dresses, diapers, etc., on Ironing Day, which was every Tuesday. Before the ironing brigade set up their boards, and I was strapped into the jumper, Patty on her way to school that morning carefully scissored almost through the strap that held the jumper on the hook. She was well into the first period Our Father and Hail Marys when the crash came. "My timing was perfect," she told me with relish years later. Patty was smart; everyone said so.

Growing up, I did not have much luck being friends with my sisters and/or my brothers. Bill and Bob were years older than me, but they were around with all of us, except when father took them away on hunting and fishing trips. They were going to be doctors, and he wanted them to be strong and tempered them to pain and discomfort. And somewhere on those trips they grew ideas about themselves as inhabiters of "the kingdom" (their words) and also about women. "You," Bob said, pointing to us sisters, "will have to go away. Except for Mother, the two of us and Dad will be the only ones here. In the kingdom." We thought that was funny. They held themselves apart from us "wimmin" and displayed a quiet contempt for us. Nan said once in exasperation, "They think Dad had 'em."

All my siblings together, Bill, Mary, Bob, Pat, and Nan, were a beehive, always in a buzz, going somewhere, fighting each other, or suddenly zooming at me for fun. In first grade, I was best reader, and when my family hurt my feelings (which they often took a spell of doing), I found in my mother's Missal the Psalms of King David. Of his enemies, God promises to "break them with a rod of iron . . . dash them in pieces" (Psalm 2), and David recognizes this as no idle promise, for "thou hast smitten all mine enemies upon the cheek bone, . . . broken the teeth of the ungodly!" (Psalm 3). "Boy!" I said out loud to myself, "King David said it! Ha ha!" Some people I know could be walking around in pieces and gumming up their dinners!

But in my heart, my brothers were IT. They would not have disagreed. I loved them. I was honored to sit with them, shivering in a goose pit for hours in the winter dark waiting for dawn, or to freeze my toes in a pair of borrowed waders in a duck blind waiting for ducks to answer their imitation quacks. Everything humanly possible that they did, I did. I imitated their language and read what they read. I shadowed them whenever possible, gathering wisdom. I listened to how they would defend themselves from a big bully trying to scare them. "Let him have it in the crotch," Bob said. Bill agreed. "That'll take the starch out." They were not talking to me, but I was hanging around picking up wisdom.

The next time that big kid came by my yard and pushed me out of my swing and took it over, I would let him have it. I knew where that "crotch" was, I thought. He came over soon after and knocked me out of my swing. My usual brave defense was to run into the house crying. But that time I pulled him out of the swing by his big feet. He fell flat on his back, and I kicked him where I thought that place was. He gave me a funny look, got up, and walked slowly away. I could not wait to see my brothers. "I took the starch out," I would tell them. They would wildly approve.

Nobody approved. The boy's indignant parents came to the front door with him in tow, and Father examined him. He told them that except for a little bruise, he was okay. Then my father talked to me in the den three times with the door closed. It was worse than anything. The first talk was reasonable. I understood I must not do things like that because someone could get hurt. The second talk was a lot of shouting, "Don't *ever* do things like that again, or we could be sued!" And the third time was reasonable again. Father actually smiled a wintery smile when it was over. Later, I heard him laughing with Mother. I wanted to forget it, but no one else around the house forgot. My sisters really loved that one. I felt terrible for a long time. I saw him at school and told him I would give him some cookies if he wanted to come and swing again, but he never did.

The swing was cut down anyway, so that was that. Keeping busy, I created a pair of wings from crepe paper and coat hangers and showed them to my brothers. I said they were for flying. They laughed, winked at each other, and said, "Sure they are." I showed them to the little boy from next door. He thought he could fly with them, and I thought he could, too. He seemed to me aerodynamically perfect with his round little body and slightly oval head. He told me his parents never took him anywhere, and it would be a treat to flap around the neighborhood with those wings, peeking into people's windows. We climbed up on the garage roof. I fastened the wings and told him to jump off and fly. He did and did not, and his mother would not let him play with me anymore. My brothers quit talking in front of me. I missed them.

Of the two, Bill would not want anything written about him, good or otherwise. He took care of his family, his medical business in Mitchell, and his wives. And after Mother scrubbed out his mouth with laundry soap, never said another swear word. Bob, the younger, grew up tall, graceful, and warmly funny. Like me, he sometimes committed amazing gaffes; unlike me, he could generally charm his way out. He had dimples, a cleft chin, and white teeth, requisites for a dashing young man. When he smiled, he could get almost anything, or anyone—especially women. Even little "wimmin" like me adored him.

When he was punished, Bob displayed a sort of genteel contempt for the whole business and endured it. His reddish hair began to recede in high school and was in full retreat by the time he began medical school. Semi-baldness did not detract from his attention to women and vice versa. After a few squeaks and squawks, his voice dropped to a smooth baritone like Father's. He grew tall as his father and had his long-legged stride. Bob loved nice clothes and the social amenities and dressing up for events. There were proms in high school, fraternity parties and tea dances in college. Around the service people, the gas station attendants, the sales women, the waitresses, the nurses, *and* his sisters, he would pull himself up, peer down at them, and frown like a gourmet viewing a plate of spoiled oysters. This silliness was forgiven. He had scads of friends, enjoyed a full life practicing medicine in Mitchell, and was generally courteous and one of God's warmest, funniest men.

Bob was so eager to join the paratroopers and see action in World War II that he feared the war might end before he graduated from medical school and served. Coming home from the war, he quietly arranged for a trip to Africa to work with the White Fathers and, incidentally, do some hunting.[32] Those were the days when the wild animals might come out of a shooting engagement on top of the hunters and eat them. He fell in love with the country's dangerous wild beauty and wanted to live and farm there. But he came back to practice medicine with his father and brother and raise a family. In his graceful years, I remember shivering with Bob in a duck blind in South Dakota during a blizzard, with icy water up to the top of our waders. He began to reminisce about the plains of Serengeti and the wonderful animals there, and we were warmed by the thought. I still shiver a little today when I read of Africa, the hot sun on those plains, so beloved by my brother.

My oldest sister, Mary impressed us all with her grandness. If she had been a pizza, she would have been a supreme, deluxe, gigantic, table-sized special with ten toppings and ten kinds of cheese. As an adult, she weighed in at about eighty-five pounds, but there was plenty of her to go around. She had curly reddish hair, dressed "to the nines," married well, and was a world traveler. She had great courage, dared much, and accomplished much. She was not a beauty, but she had something much better. Mary had presence. When she would show up for a visit, jewels sparkling on her fingers, ears, and everywhere, her mink coats flowing, and her red hair shining, her voice a distinctive contralto, she commanded attention. She expected it.

Of all her accomplishments, all the glitterati famous people she socialized with, Mary cared most deeply about us and assisted in my delivery from adolescence to womanhood. A long labor. My mother was busy with Father and the rest of the family, and I mostly grew up alone, with one disaster after another. Mary took over and saw that I was dressed appropriately for school and had a bath, when she could catch me. She gave me advice on handling events. "These," she said, "will get you through things you can't understand now:

"Always wear clean underwear (in case of accidents);

"Chew your food thirty times;

"Brush your hair one hundred strokes a day;

"Don't kiss boys."

"Well who in the world would want to?" I asked.

Grim answer, "Just you wait."

She took me to her college for a week and to art class, where I drew and painted along with her. At home in Mitchell, she had a special bedroom; she let me sleep in the other twin bed. She showed me how to layout my homework. She collared me to go to Mass with her every Sunday. She showed me how to read a Missal and bought me one. Finally, I thought, there might be something to this religion. Friends called her "Pinkie" because of her hair, and she called me "Little Pink" because mine matched. When she went away to be a wife, I missed her and grieved for a long time.

Before her marriage, Mary planned to study sciences and become a surgeon. The Delaney men were shocked, and my father scolded her. Bob called her, "My sister with balls." She obediently studied the fine arts. But her hands were surgeon's hands, strong and dexterous. She could carry, take apart, and put together large items that men usually worked on. And could she ever pinch! Mary would have been a fine doctor. She had a surgeon's daring and strength.

And great heart. As a child, she had had rickets, a vitamin D deficiency that causes misformed bones, and was bowlegged from the disease. She learned to walk and stand so you would not notice. Other childhood sicknesses also weakened her. My father called her his "little cricket," and she was like one, jumping around and making noise, perhaps to show him she was alive, though there were times then when she barely was. But Mary did not want to be sickly. Through pure grit, she transformed herself into an athlete, a good tennis player, skier, swimmer, and golfer. She played bridge like a shark. I never thanked her for the good things she had done for all of us. She did not expect thanks. Like my mother, Mary was a caretaker and a giver.

For years, she had a successful life. Married to a Ford Motor Company executive, her homes were forever open to us, and we could stay with her as long as we wanted. She shared her homes, her food, and her friends. Once, I stayed with her for an entire year when my father commanded me to, "Pick up on her life." I did not, could not. Mary was the grand one.

So I looked to my two remaining sisters to find someone to emulate. I had mixed results. Five and six years older than me, they were like twins together through their marriages and children and comforting each other during their bad times. Nan had a flurry of marriages, children, and divorces, but she always came home. Pat lived in a small town close to Mitchell. She married a doctor, had a big house like Mother, and filled it with children. Like Mother.

Nan could attract people like bears after sweets. She radiated charm and life's energy, and in a room with her, one sensed she would make something happen. She had dimples and a cleft chin and dazzling white teeth. Men talked about her big dark eyes. They grew darker when she was angry. In the summer, her skin turned golden and her brown hair sun-streaked blonde. She was beautiful and kind. My friend.

With her looks, Nan did not have to be funny, but she was a real, red-nose clown. One summer day when I was thirteen, she walked with me downtown to a dark, dank bar on Main Street. Once inside, she sat me in a booth with a Shirley Temple and went to work organizing the men who spent their afternoons drinking there with their girlfriends and fighting in the alley. She told them she was casting director for a movie, and if they would stand in a row on the dance floor, she would "cast" them. They left their girlfriends and obediently lined up in front of her, and she went down the line giving some thumbs up and discarding others with thumbs down. She gave them each a line to say. "Frankly, Madam, I don't give a damn!" or, while walking on their tiptoes and waggling their hips, "I am Tondelayo."[33]

A battered-looking man, who seemed to have gone through life on his face, she ordered to go home and wash and change his shirt. "And smile!" Nan ordered, stamping her little foot. He ran home, washed, changed his shirt, and hurried back, smiling and grinning, showing gaps in his front teeth. Such was her charm that all of them were completely quiet and obedient to her. I sat, drinking my Shirley Temple, amazed at my sister standing by herself on the dance floor ordering them around. After awhile, Nan took me by the arm and quietly led me out the back door. As we ran home, she said, "Don't ever be like me!" I wanted to be like her all my young life. But Nan had a darkness. I felt it sometimes. She seemed to know a secret thing and must hurry, hurry to get everything done. Now, I think of her as running alone at dusk, up our street, trying to get home before night.

When my brother Bill, looking handsome in his navy officer's uniform, was preparing to marry Agnes Gilmore in Omaha, as many of us as possible went there as a family. World War II was on, and Father was "holding down the fort" at home. Nan and Pat were already in Omaha. Earlier that year, Pat had decided they should situate themselves next to Creighton Medical School there in order to attract some interns. (Pat met and married Yale Charbonneau, a nice future doctor from Boston and the father of her children.) Pat stayed with my mother, and I went with Nan to Pat and Nan's apartment.

The night before the wedding, I was asleep in the apartment alone. There was a rehearsal party going on, and Pat was at the hotel with Mother. I heard the front door click, and Nan leaned over and gave me a kiss, patting my face. She went into the kitchen, turned on the stove gas, and put her head in the oven. I dozed, but the gas odor woke me. It was sickening. I got up, went into the kitchen, turned the stove off, and pulled her head out of the oven. She slumped to the floor. As near as I could tell, she was not breathing, her chest was not moving up and down. I opened the kitchen window and dragged and rolled her into the living room away from the gas. I tried kneeling over her and pushing her chest, matching my breath, a resuscitation I had seen in a movie. After a while, she took some deep breaths and sat up.

I started to pat her face, but she smiled and stood up. She said not a word to me, went into the bathroom, put on some lipstick, and left the apartment. On the stove I found a note. It read, "I can't go on, my life is over." I tore it up and flushed it down the toilet. I do not know why I did any of those things. I had felt calm and purposeful while she was there, but now I began to cry. I was afraid Nan would go somewhere alone and die. I called for Mother and Pat, but they were at the party. I called the bride's sister, who was mystified but no help. I prayed and prayed and made a deal with myself. If she came back,

I would not tell the family. After a while, she slipped in and quietly went to sleep in the other bed.[34]

I kept the deal. And Bill and Agnes married with all but Father present. The wedding was a small, elegant service followed by a catered brunch. It was 13 June 1942. Nan was twenty. I was almost fifteen.

8] Hunting and Eating

y father hunted until the year he died. Hunting was a constant activity of his sons, also. They all worked hard, and they hunted hard. Observing the ordinary social amenities of successful men, they golfed and drank, but mostly they hunted. And when they were not hunting, they were talking about hunting. They went after pheasants, ducks, geese, quail, rabbits, and prairie chickens when they were abundant. They hunted varmints and fished all the streams and lakes. When old men, my brothers still plotted in vain to catch "Old Charlie," a big clever trout. They also stalked big game. My father went into the grizzly bear country and brought home a huge bear carcass, cured into a rug. It hung over the banister in our front hallway, its mouth in a snarl showing teeth and claws to everyone. We called him "Old Griz," and he stayed up there, scaring little kids, until the moths got him.

Opening Day weather for the pheasant hunt was usually kind, sunny and warm with a tang of fall. Before the hunt, the driveway of our house was alive with cars, hunters coming from all over to participate in "the drive."[35] Father ran everything and helped Mother in the kitchen dish out a huge breakfast for everyone. Caldrons of coffee were poured into Thermos bottles, and the all-important lunch to be served from the back of the station wagons was loaded in. Upstairs, my brothers prepared themselves like warriors for the hunt. We were not to disturb them while they were making serious choices on each opening day. The right guns had been oiled and cleaned; the right breakfast would be eaten; a specific lunch and dinner would follow. They dressed carefully in the right clothes and carried the boots, guns, shells, etc., downstairs to eat breakfast.

Personally, when I was too little to do anything except get in everyone's way, I commemorated the opening day of pheasant hunting by standing at the back stairway hoping to see Brother Bill emerge slowly, tentatively, his stocking feet first, then, Zoom!!! rocket down the stairs on his back with guns and shell boxes and hunting boots and hats flying everywhere. Alarmed hunting dogs barked hysterically. I only observed this cavalcade a couple of times, but it was enough to whet my appetite for more. Bill finally realized that if he put his boots on before he took to the stairs, he could descend with dignity. But his unscheduled flights in his stocking feet were the memorable ones for me. He did not ever think it was funny, but once in a while, the image comes back to me and makes me laugh out loud. The center of all the noise and confusion, Bill had a deadpan, untroubled look, just like the calm face of the great comic Buster Keaton as he hurtled terbuckety down the skids in his new boat and sank.[36]

Mother treacherously said once, as we were plucking an endless mound of duck cadavers on the back porch, that the only reason men really liked hunting were the breakfasts, lunches, and dinners. Myself, I did not think my father got enough to eat when he was growing up youngest in a big Irish family of fourteen siblings. He ordered and supervised the hunt breakfasts at our house, and there were staggering platters of sausage; rashers of bacon; ham; eggs cooked to order; flagons of coffee; and fried potatoes. Pancakes, oatmeal, toast, muffins, and "biskits" we also served with jam, jellies, syrup, honey, and crocks of country butter. A guest who managed to clean his plate found it swiftly heaped up again.

And then there was Lunch! On a pheasant drive, the women followed the men in their station wagons from field to field, and when the hunt ended at noon, the tailgates were let down, the guns unloaded, and lunch was served. The hunters ate sandwiches and cold meats heaped on platters, hot soup, potato salad, hot breads, cheeses, cakes and pies, fudge and cookies. For their dry throats, there was beer, wines, and whisky. After the hunt and lunch in the field, everyone admired the birds stacked up for the camera. The men stood around in their hunting clothes and posed for pictures with the colorful trophies. Father served drinks, and much bragging and laughing ensued.

The mighty hunters and their guests then went to rest and clean up for a hunt dinner, with wives vying with each other to cook the best game dishes at the house of one or another. They were sure to serve platters of pheasants, duck, geese, and quail with more rich desserts. Whisky and wine followed, as the hunters indulged in much bragging and the annual hunting jokes. Cigars and brandy came next and then out to the local club for an evening of hunter hilarity, dancing, drinking, and more snacks. If you were a guest and survived the eating events without a coronary, another day might find you there again beginning with . . . "Ahhhh, Breakfast!"

One hunting season when my brothers and father entertained visitors from out of state, I saw two of the guests sitting at a counter at a local drugstore quietly eating shredded wheat. I asked them why they were not at our house for breakfast, and one of them said, in a rather desperate way, "We just couldn't take it anymore!" A family friend sent me an ancient picture of a duck hunt with everyone posed for the camera holding up some duck cadavers. He wrote on it, "And, here comes Bessie with the slumgullion. UMMMM!"

Observing the different hunting events while helping my mother stoke the hunters' breakfasts and clean up after they left, I concluded that goose hunting was a special, family thing. Sometimes just my father and my brothers hunted the geese, and sometimes they went out to them with a few close Mitchell friends. I begged and begged to go with them. I was twelve years old, and I promised over and over not to cry or anything.

One bitter cold morning, Father snapped on the lights in my bedroom and pulled me out of my warm bed. The window was still dark, and he said, grinning, "Well, Sheila, how do you like the goose hunt so far?" "Wonderful!" I said, "Wonderful!" I danced around in my pajamas and bare feet to show him I was alive and kicking. I really was going on the hunt! Mother, up at four A.M. to give us breakfast, looked at me and sighed. She helped me into a suit of father's big long underwear and folded the legs up for extra warmth, adding layers of stout clothing. Staggering into the dining room, my clothes were so thick I could barely sit. But I packed in breakfast with the men, and soon, after some masculine swearing while arranging and rearranging guns, shells, cameras, and the coffee, everyone settled into the car.

Father drove us a long way in the dark and cut the lights as we approached the Missouri River. He gave orders to everyone before we got out. I hunched over, head down the way they did, and trod softly toward the river bank and the shelters. I slid quietly into one with Bob, and Bill was with Father in the other one. There were mobs of

Canadian geese on the river, honking softly to each other. We could barely see them in the dark, and we did not want them to see us. A bitter cold prairie wind was blowing from the north as we shivered, waiting for the sunrise.

Back then, my family shot geese with great enjoyment, and we ate them with great enjoyment. I loved to be in Mother's warm kitchen while geese were roasting in the oven, stuffed with her savory dressing and ravishing our noses with their popping fat odors. They were not just roasting for dinner, they were roasting for a feast. All the best table linens and silver were laid out. Sometimes, there were guests. But guests or not, we dressed up for the Canadian visitors. "Ahhh!" Father would say, piling up his fork, "You have to suffer to have this!"

Whoever has hunted geese in South Dakota winter knows the suffering. Crouching immobile in a cold-as-the-grave earthen dugout, your hands, feet, top, and bottom freeze from the north wind blowing up your knickers. And eyeglasses, too. As it began to get light, I carefully rolled my eyes sideways to look at my unmoving brother Bob, crouching beside me, his thick glasses frosted over like ice cubes. A few geese "scouts" slowly flew around reconnoitering the place for enemies. Geese had to be got on the fly, by daylight, either coming or going, so we remained still and kept our faces down until faint light.

Suddenly, my father stood up and slid the bolt on his shotgun. The patrols veered off in fright. Their honking alarms went off above us. "Danger, danger, danger!" they honked, and the whole flock began to rise and veer up to get away from us. There was a confusion of swirling, wing flapping, and honking, and then they regrouped and rose in their orderly way. That close, I could hear and feel their wings surging the air. The bucking sounds of shotguns commenced. *Ka-boom, ka-boom.* I watched them fall. They were big; their bodies hit the river with a splash or the ground beside us with a thump. Everyone had their limit in a few minutes, and the shooting stopped.

Accompanying this hunt, as most hunts, were some of the dogs of our lives. Captain, a handsome Boston bulldog, was dearest to me. Of the generations of hunting dogs roaming around our house he was my father's favorite, too, along with Jiggs, a fox terrier. My mother hated so many dogs underfoot, but Father tolerated and fed them all. During the depression, drought, and World War II, there were spaniels, retrievers, Labradors, and Irish setters. But Jiggs and Captain were my father's best hunting dogs. He had trained them to hunt together on signal. They worked as a team in the country and in the farmer's field retrieving any game that had been shot and lost. An illogical looking pair, Jiggs and Cap were lightweight unmatched house dogs bred to be snoring by the fire and bringing my father's slippers. Now they tracked down and retrieved the dead and wounded geese, laying the huge carcasses respectfully at my father's feet.

My brothers carefully arranged the bodies for a photograph. The smooth gray shapes with their black feet and bills had a banker's elegance. Their powerful wings were still; their bodies were large and aerodynamic. I sat beside them and smoothed their still-warm feathers. Cold tears slid down my face. I hid them from the men. I helped load the geese into the trunk, and Father drove us to a little café in Chamberlain to refresh ourselves. When the waitress brought coffee, I wrapped my hands around my steaming cup to warm them. Cold to the core, I could not stop shuddering. Father pulled a flask of whisky out of his pocket and poured some into my cup. I drank it down and felt its trickling, thawing warmth.

The drive home was quiet. The hunt was done. I was dirty and tired, but I had been miles away in another country and seen the frozen winter countryside at dawn's first light. I had felt real pain from the cold, seen the big Canadians up close, felt their wings thrumming the air around me, and seen them rising. I had seen death administered.

My glamorous sisters were amused at my appearance, and I never talked to them about the hunt. I had stepped over to a place they would never go. Or ever imagine. Somewhere I read that if you eat something a lot, you can become that something. So I would be going South with the geese, looking down at the big Missouri, talking to my friends flying beside me, and cleaving the air around us with our great wings. Maybe I would see our house.

9] Education

Sister Jacob taught ninth grade at Notre Dame Academy.[37] Her classroom was downstairs, across from the girls' bathroom. The ninth grade was beyond my imagination, ninth graders were royalty, large and omnipotent. They had their own playground with the other highschoolers, and if a younger student ventured there, they pointed at her, jeering, "First Grade Baby, Sittin' in the Gravy." One fine morning at recess, I whistled myself down the stairs and into the girls' bathroom. I had a good whistle going and continued a few more bars as I washed my hands. Suddenly the door slammed open, and Sister Jacob's voice, which was a match for my father's baritone, roared, "Who's whistling in here?"

I was paralyzed with fear; I had never seen her up close before. She was not much taller than me and was very, very round. She stood there, arms akimbo, fists on her hips, and bellowed, "Whistling girls and crowing hens, always come to bad ends." And slammed her way out of the room and back to her class. I crept up the stairs in silence. I supposed those crowing hens did unspeakable things in the chicken coop. As for those whistling girls, well, the Lord only knew.

Patty said Sister Jacob kept a steel ruler on her desk and used it for concentrating the mind. I was not in any hurry to get to *that* classroom. Any spanking on me was done by Mother, who was too soft hearted to do much, except once for something I did not do. So it was a surprise to find, the first day of school, that the nuns freely gave the children spankings, and there was a strap hanging in the principal's office where we could see it. The bigger boys were disciplined by the priests, who did not spare the punishments either. My brothers said they were getting "holey socks." The priests came to class on our first day and told that us the nuns had dedicated their lives to educate us and that it was a blessing. We should be thankful, and we should always mind them.

I was hardly ever touched. I was not all that good; the omission was due to my father, who doctored many of the priests and nuns for nothing. Once, in exasperation, one of the oldest, most respected teachers, the school's principal, Sister James, gave me a light slap. She was going down the girl's line in church slapping faces and mine got one, too. She stopped her momentum when she saw me, and her hand barely grazed my cheek. I was glad for the slap to be included with the rest of the kids. We stopped what we were doing, namely giggling. I did think enough of it, though, to tell my mother that I had gotten a little slap from Sister James for giggling. "I won't do it again," I started to say, but she put her hand on my mouth. She phoned Sister James. "No one," she said in a voice I had never heard before, "no one at that school shall lay a finger on any of my children. The next time you feel like beating one of my children, let me know, and I'll come right over and you can try it first with me!"

The little slap was hardly a beating, but my mother's attitude required some serious thought. We were supposed to obey the nuns no matter what. If we got in trouble with them, we were in trouble with the world and with God. But apparently not with my mother. For a while I had grand thoughts of Mother putting on boxing gloves and getting into the ring with Sister James. That was sinful, so I stopped thinking about it. Mother was a great whistler. She could whistle on key, and after Sister Jacob's rule about whistling girls and crowing hens, I began looking at her with disapproval. After one particular heavy frown from me, she gave me a light slap, not unlike Sister James's. Life was confusing.

But mostly us school kids had the attention span of gnats and went on talking and giggling. Wonderful things were going to happen as soon as we grew up. We knew it. In the meantime, we did our best to respect the nuns, who seemed to know our thoughts, even if we were a long way off. So we tried always to have good thoughts. Even about those boys who went around the playground beating everyone up.

We liked it best when one of the priests visited our classroom. We needed a lot of help about the Holy Ghost. He just confused us terribly. We could not make head nor tail of Him. Father Jim came in to give us a chalk talk about the Trinity. That included the Holy Ghost. We were third-graders then, and he said we were ready for it. We sat up to take it in. "The Trinity is the Father, the Son, and the Holy Ghost," Father Jim said. He told us that the Ghost lived in the tabernacle on the altar and came out during the Mass. The Ghost was like the gas that makes a car go, he said. He drew a picture of the engine of a car and explained when the foot was on the pedal, the accelerator shot raw gas into the carburetor. He said that was like the Holy Ghost shooting into our bodies and minds. He drew little arrows to show the gas shooting into the engine. We listened gravely and nodded knowingly.

At the next Mass, I sat up close to the altar to see the event. But, except for the priest taking the chalice out and putting it back, nothing came out of the tabernacle. No gas, nothing. I asked Mother about this. She laughed and told me to go play. I went to my sister Nan. She was a big eighth-grader. She had never heard the gas lecture and did not know anything about the engine. But she said she had to stay after school because she asked her teacher about the Holy Ghost. "Who is this Holy Ghost, anyway, Sister?" she had asked. "Just what the heck does He do? Jump out of the tabernacle and turn summersaults?" My father laughed when he heard that. He said when he was a little boy, he asked the nun at his school to explain the Circumcision. Did he ever have to stay after school! I am surprised he is not still there covered in cobwebs, his long legs sticking out under his little desk.

Nan said maybe there was something to the Holy Ghost business. When the church was empty, we walked onto the altar and looked at the little door on the tabernacle. It was locked. We decided the Holy Ghost had to be really little to fit in there. Maybe he shot out when the priest put his foot on the gas. I asked Nan if she thought the Holy Ghost did anything special on Halloween, his saint's day. Nan said, "Well, probably he comes out on a broomstick and zooms around the people!" We went home and told our mother. She laughed again, this time really hard, and slapped her arms. Nan told me privately that my mother was a convert to Catholicism so she did not understand holy mysteries. Anyway, there were plenty of other mysteries around our house all the time.

In the 1930s, the papers had been full of the Charles Lindbergh baby kidnapping and bank robberies and shootings by Chicago gangsters, especially John Dillinger and Baby Face Nelson. These men were hotly pursued by the FBI. I read the *Chicago Tribune* every day in the attic, after everyone else had finished with it. Since the men in my family walked around full of secrets and untold truths, I read to

get at the truth of things. There were stories about gangsters and feature stories on Ma Barker and Bonnie and Clyde. And the Lindbergh
baby kidnapping.[38]

In the winter of 1934, when I was seven years old, Bill suddenly
came home from college and drove me to school and picked me
up when school was out. I was used to walking the six blocks in all
weather with friends, and seeing my big brother pull up in my father's
car was a surprise. But I had to leave the kids I walked with because,
Bill said, opening the car door, "Only Sheila, kids, sorry!" Bill held a
pistol in one hand while he drove. I asked to hold it, but he said, "No,
it's loaded." I thought, boy! was that ever nifty! "What are you carrying that for?" I asked. Bill said sternly, "Never mind!" And added
before letting me out of the car at Notre Dame: "Don't talk about this
at school! Or to anyone!" I did not.

When Bill went back to college, someone always picked me up and
delivered me to school and back home again. I would either be driven
home for lunch or to a soda fountain downtown, where I would sit at
the counter and eat hamburgers and drink big malts. Mother would
greet me after I got delivered from school as if she had not seen me
for years. She would give me a feet-off-the-floor hug and a plate of
warm cookies, hot chocolate, or a fresh-baked roll with butter. I was
getting fat.

Everyone was so nice to me then, and all that attention made
me nervous. I concluded I was dying from something, and nobody
wanted to tell me. That did not surprise me because they never told
me anything. I learned by reading and listening. Standing quietly in
the hall outside the den, I learned that my father had gotten a kidnap
threat in the mail, the kind that was pasted up with cut-out letters
and words. The letter ordered him to leave one thousand dollars at
a certain place at a certain time, or, "You will never see your baby
Sheila again." He was to put the money in a paper bag and leave it at
the designated time at a train depot. The train only slowed down at
that stop, and the pickup man would jump off the train to grab the
paper bag and jump back on. The letter was signed John Dillinger,
Pretty Boy Floyd, and Baby Face Nelson.

I overheard that they were hiding out on some farm near us. Things
were going on! A lot of whispering and talking on the phone. Two

nice men in suits came by and talked to me a little. And then they had a meeting with everyone else behind closed doors. My family must have thought I was deaf. And pretty dumb. I learned from the whisperings and phone calls that the men were FBI agents. I heard conversations about me through the door. I told Patty, and she said: "Pooh, nobody would want you. It's Bill they're after." Finally, she did believe me. And I understood the pistol and my privileged rides while my friends walked. "You are not to tell anyone about this business," Patty said, "You mustn't talk about this at school!" Boy! Was I excited! I looked in the closet and packed some clothes for when they came to kidnap me. I packed in a lot of candy for them. I supposed they would climb a ladder to my window as they had with the Lindbergh baby, and away I would go. This was getting good! Maybe I would get married. I would make them go to church every Sunday.

Then I heard that at the time for the money pickup, my father and his friend, Mac McMahon Senior, drove to the depot and, after putting the bag down where they were told, hid and waited. They had shotguns and were going to use them. The train slowed down and then left the station. The pickup man never showed, and after waiting a while, Mac and my father retrieved the bag and drove home. Father then gave the *Chicago Tribune* a statement that he would give the kidnappers "plenty of lead" but no money. It made the front section, and I cut it out and saved it. No one talked about it.[39]

Further *Tribune* reading showed that summary execution of gangsters was the style then. No one said, "Well, hi there, Mr. Dillinger, how are your folks? Kindly put your hands up, please." In Chicago, Dillinger was shot mortally coming out of a movie. Another gangster, Pretty Boy Floyd, was chased and killed in a cornfield after having lunch at an Iowa farm house. Father said, "Bullets for dessert!" Our kidnap situation was over when I heard that the FBI stopped and boarded the train before it got to the depot where my father and Mac were waiting. They arrested the man. And I had to walk to and from school again, and there were some hugs but no cookies.

I stayed at the Catholic school for eleven years. After my junior year, Pat decided I should leave Notre Dame and attend Mitchell High School for my senior year. She said I was too shy and that it would do me good. She and Nan had gone to Mitchell High, and it had done wonders for them. "You will love it," Pat promised. Did I ever love it. I met boys and dated them. Went to dances and formals. Some of the kids had cars, and we rode around and puffed on terrible cigarettes (we called them Hack 'n' Coughs). We went to the Mitchell Recreation Center (the REC) after school and danced to a nickelodeon. We formed little groups to do things. We had a debate society, and our art class had real oils and charcoals. We drew posters to help the war-bond drives.

My father was against everything, so I kept my good times to myself. At the recreation center, I met Buster Hanson. He lived on a farm around Mitchell, but he did not look like any farm kid I ever knew. He was tall and handsome. His thick hair was wavy black, and the pupils of his eyes were black, the blackest and biggest ever. His skin was whitest white. His hands had never done farm work; they were long fingered and unblemished. He told me his father lived in Chicago and sent him clothes from Marshall Field's.

Buster wore a thin leather jacket in the bitterest cold. No gloves or hat. I used to take his cold hands and warm them between mine. We spent time together after school. He told me he was not a Hanson, that he was Italian and his real first name was Nicholas. When he graduated from Mitchell High in the spring, he was going to join his father in Chicago and go into business with him. He said his mother was a show girl who boarded on a farm in South Dakota until she had a baby and could go back to work. His father paid the farmer to raise the baby. "And that baby was me!" he said, raising his arms. He said his father was a wise guy. "A wise guy?" I knew about the Wise Men who visited Jesus in his crib in Bethlehem, but I never heard of a wise guy. I could not find a definition in the dictionary. We would go to matinee movies on Saturday and sit in the balcony with our arms around each other.

The Catholic high school had frozen out any hugging and such, but he gave me ideas of thawing possibilities. I thought I would go through life with Nick. We would always be together. He liked to hold me close, and sometimes I would move away. He would shake his finger at me and twist my arm lightly and laugh. Once I had to leave early, and his eyes got black and he twisted my arm and would not let go. It hurt. He said, "Everybody leaves me!" I was scared and ran home. I told Pat, and she said I should not see him anymore, and she told Father, who was then in a towering rage and threatened to place me in a convent school for college. "I don't ever want to hear about any damned boyfriends again, ever!" he thundered. I was very innocent and wondered what Pat actually told him. Father would give me terrible looks. Nick was quiet when I told him I could not see him anymore. Later he fought another boy in school and was expelled. I never saw him again, except in my art-history book years later when I returned to get my degree. I found an artwork captioned, "Portrait of a Roman Youth, Second Century A.D." Nick, I thought. Hey, Nick.

College, at nineteen, was not a good investment. My busy father tried to do right by all his children, but the two years of college, which he chose and paid for me after my graduation from high school in 1946, were a waste of his hard-earned money. For my freshman year, he chose a convent school for young ladies, Saint Mary-of-the-Woods in Terre Haute, Indiana. One wag told me before I was packed off that the college was a holding pen for young virgins. It was a nice school, and the students were nice, too, and the subjects I learned were really nice and quiet. But all seemed to me not to relate to the actual life I was seeking. My English teacher at the college asked us what books we had read recently so that we could have discussions. I said proudly *Brideshead Revisited* by Evelyn Waugh. She looked at me like the hunter Frank Buck confronting a dangerous carnivore. She swirled around and wrote on the blackboard, "Nancy Boys!" I stayed after class to ask her what "Nancy Boys" meant, and she said grimly, "Never mind!"[40] There were other indicators that I did not fit into the milieu there.

For one thing, I missed the intellectual give and take at the dinner table of our house. *Whack, bam! wham*, "You're wrong! ##**!!! it! I know what I'm talking about!" Pound, pound! "Read this and learn something," etc., etc.! I was only an observer of these battles, but I could not wait to grow up, "read and learn something," and have some fun at my own table in my own house. Reading was a major occupation in my father's house. He loved books and created a rich literary environment for us. The shelves in his den were filled with classics and a large collection of books on President Abraham Lincoln. We could sit on the floor or on comfortable chairs, put our feet up, and read and read. Ditto the attic, where there were more shelves filled with books.

I finished out the academic year and went home to beg off any more time at that convent college. A family conference *without me* was called, and my sister Mary Dunham came home to Mitchell to advise them all. The decision was for her to "plant" me personally in her old sorority at the University of South Dakota (USD). I raved and shouted and stamped my little flat foot: "I don't want to go to college anymore! I'll run away." I wanted to go to a big city like Chicago, get a job, and have a place to live. "And see what's going on! And that's final!" Well, it appeared the word "final" did not last as long as it used to. Sister Mary was firm. My father was firm. "Sheila, academics will enrich your life far beyond your mere discomfort now of fitting into yet another school," he said. "You have to try again." I felt like a prisoner. But, I promised.

Mary drove me to USD at Vermillion and used her position as a former sorority active to get me in as a sophomore pledge. So, there I was again, "placed" in yet another house of women, a sorority. "I'm going to live it all again through you," Mary said, patting me, before leaving. "Wonderful things will happen, you'll see!"

I did see. At USD more alcohol than ever before appeared in various forms for every occasion. I had an English professor who had read and loved *Brideshead Revisited*. Sorority pledges were not supposed to drink; on occasion, most of us did. Otherwise we obeyed the sorority actives in the house. We had to clean up the place every week and run errands for our big sisters. We had to entertain them, too, one night a week, and they never laughed, no matter how funny we were. Sometimes we were very funny. I wrote and produced a skit, and all of us pretty pledges put on long underwear and pranced out with our trap doors hanging down. "Oh, la," we sang, kicking our legs up like the Rockettes. "The life of a sorority girl. We're the very dickens! We will stay virgins so we can marry surgeons!" Creating the little skit was fun, but the rest of it had nothing for me. I did not understand sorority life. I did not fit in. It was not that I was ahead of them intellectually, or behind them. I was just not with them.

However, there was Charley's, a decrepit old house on campus where students congregated, drank beer, smoked, ate, played cards, and occasionally studied. I met new people there. The place was old and dirty and smelled of urine and burnt grease. It was always crowded and noisy. It was The Place. That academic year, 1947–1948, new students could be found in Charley's. They were the change agents. World War II was over, and veterans were coming to the university under the GI Bill. The fraternities had to make fast adjustments because many freshmen pledges were hardened battle vets, and they did not in the least feel like bending over for the traditional paddling from the lord active, who was still wet behind his high-school ears. Colleges all over America had to scurry and make way for them.[41]

The veterans changed the universities and our culture forever. They were not progeny of wealthy benefactors of the university come to play Joe College. They were mature men, like my brothers and Joe and Mac McMahon, and like them, many had endured horrifying experiences in the war. Some had been wounded. They were serious about their studies and anxious to get on with their lives. Some wanted to start families while they were studying and married quarters were hastily put up for them. Rarely would they talk about their war experiences, except to joke with one another. One had been with the One Hundred First Airborne in Normandy and was dropped wrongly into German lines during the D-DAY invasion. Another was blasted off his ship in the Pacific by a Kamikaze hit and spent weeks alone, floating around the ocean. We were engaged and, after I took him home for the weekend family treatment, un-engaged. When the year was up, I left the world of college.

After college, I made several stops before I went home to work at the Delaney Medical Office in Mitchell in the early 1950s. The first stop was Scottsdale, Arizona, where my sister Nan owned a western-wear shop, and I wrote local-interest stories for the village newspaper. I followed her and her son to Shreveport, Louisiana, at her request; she wanted family nearby. Nan married a commanding officer from the airbase at Mitchell, whom she had dated during the war. I wanted to work and did so briefly, but I was told by a frosty relative of Nan's husband, "Ladies do not work." So I went home where ladies did work.

But first, I spent a year with my sister Mary in Dearborn, Michigan. Her husband worked for Ford Motor Company. I went to a business school, where I learned shorthand and other administrative skills. Back in Mitchell, after previous years of helping out on weekends and holidays, I was happy to fit into the familiar Delaney office again, full time. Postwar, my two brothers, Bill and Bob, were in practice with my father. And soon—in 1953—the Delaneys opened a new clinic on Fifth Avenue across from Saint Joseph's Hospital.

I knew Gregg Shorthand well, and my father loved to dictate.[42] He was a stickler for his letters to his patients, and I found medical terminology had a beauty of its own. He would go over the letters before he signed them and give me some advice, too, as he was signing. "You see," he said once, "I write carefully in a letter because the written word has some impact on a patient. And it is permanent. Never write, 'We think you have cancer.' Write, 'It would appear that within parameters of this condition, you may have a malignancy, and we would like follow up with you until we are sure.'" Father would sign off his letters, "Be assured of my continued interest in your welfare." It was true. Sometimes I thought my father loved his patients better than us. My father died in 1955. I stayed at the Delaney Clinic until 1956, when I met and married Paul Evans. I suppose I was an old maid.

Paul Evans came into my life to fix that. I met him in a cornfield.

We were having a family pheasant hunt, and some people from Rapid City were invited. Paul was handsome, with dark hair and eyes, and had a great sense of humor. We had a lot of fun dating and getting serious. He would barrel up to Mitchell for an evening dinner and barrel back the three hundred miles to Rapid City to open the office in the morning. Paul and his father ran the Evans Equipment Company. One thing led to another, and we were married and had a daughter. Katy had her father's good looks, three grandparents, a nice house, and plenty of playmates. We had a good marriage, many friends, and belonged to the country club. But, in the end, we divorced in late 1962—a sad, unwanted event. I thought marriage lasted forever. "Until death do us part" had been part of our ceremony.

Accepting divorce took me a long time. I took Katy to Santa Fe to live, and we both struggled in that new environment. Except for my mother sending us seventy-five dollars a month, we had little family support; our home and friends were absent. Our hearts were almost broken. I stayed home with her for a year, but there was little money. Eventually, I took a part-time job at the Laboratory of Anthropology, assisting the editor of *El Palacio* to prepare anthropological papers for publication.[43] The laboratory was the beginning of my continuing education in southwestern prehistory. I made good friends there and stayed for some years.

In 1966, when I was still at the anthropology lab, I read about the newly elected Republican governor David Cargo. A political naïf, I went to his office with my résumé, had an interview, and was hired. My knowledge of politics was dim, but his secretary, Ramona, said they needed someone in the office who actually worked and was not a political appointee. I thought I could learn something there. And indeed I did. The press wire services were in the administrative building called "The Round House." The governor called many press conferences on issues and events statewide and national, anything that affected New Mexico. I learned to write simple press releases and better letters. The United States was in a new war, the Cold War, and it was playing out in Vietnam. The War Department issued monthly lists of New Mexico men killed in combat in Vietnam. There were so many of them! The governor asked me to write personal letters for his signature, instead of using the machine in the back room that cranked out multiple letters; they looked too much like machine letters.

It was the middle of the Sixties; reporters were around most of the time. I recall, in particular, that New Mexico experienced its own civil rights movement. In 1967, from April to June, representatives of Alianza Federal de Mercedes ("Federal Alliance of Land Grants") protested at the capital with speeches and signs that said *"Nuestra Tierra!"* ("Our Land"). The organization voiced grievances that dated to Spanish colonial times and to the Mexican-American War.[44] Some people with the Alianza thundered into the Round House, up into to Governor Cargo's offices and the press office. The media and television news focused on my small reception room, filled with the governor, protestors, and reporters. By June, the state National Guard had been called out to quell the violence. I received threatening phone calls and sent my daughter to South Dakota to stay with my brother for a time. The experience changed my life, and I realized that, despite the violence and anger, the Alianza people were right about their land.

I left the governor's office after Cargo was re-elected. I needed to rest and spend some time at home with my daughter. I worked in a series of quiet, nonthreatening work positions, but I also took a class at the College of Santa Fe on primary research. Professor Myra Ellen Jenkins, a state historian and archivist, was a well-known scholar. She sharpened my desire both to write well and to study more.

When my daughter Katy married in 1975, I sold our house and moved to Albuquerque, where I hoped to finish a double major in art history and English at the University of New Mexico (UNM). I found the language and methods of art history to be similar to the medical language of diagnosis, with which I was so familiar. My courses in the English Department brought me back home around a dining-room table once again! English professors love words, and talk, and arguments. They could be genuinely moved to tears with a fine poem or some words. I studied poetry with them and began to write poems. Then, I could not stop; it became an obsession. Poems poured out day and night. I showered friends with them. They took to avoiding me: "Hide! Shhh! Get down!! Here she comes with more of those ##!* poems!" The poem spigot finally ran dry, and I applied myself to narrative writing. I wrote some things that on later inspection made me blink with dismay. Then the written words flowed again, only this time I was handing out great "Sheila prose treasures" saying, "Read this!"

While taking courses, I was working full time at the College of Education and trying to keep up with my writing. After about a year, I met Arthur Greenfield, a good-looking attorney from New York who had moved into my building. He had come to lecture at the UNM Law School. Both of us were divorced and one thing led to another. We shared interests in fine arts, good books, good talk, and good food. Arthur was full of the energy and intellect I craved, and we planned to marry, but at the age of forty-nine, my tough heart gave out. I had a heart attack, and Arthur took care of me better than any doctor or nurse. We eventually married on 20 August 1976, but we divorced three years later. I simply could not keep up.

I am immensely grateful to Arthur for the time he spent showing me his life in New York, Chicago, San Francisco, and most of France. On our honeymoon in Paris, we had a *pension* from which I walked across the Seine to savor the marvelous Louvre treasures while Arthur was doing business. We flew to Cap Ferrat and then to Normandy, but I ended up in the American Hospital in Paris for severe chest pain. On weekends to New York, we saw Baryshnikov dance, visited the great Metropolitan Museum of Art, went to Shakespeare in the Park with Meryl Streep performing, and attended any number of plays and restaurants in the city with his family and friends. He enriched my life.

After we divorced, we remained friends, and I found starting over in Albuquerque hard but not impossible. I needed work. I did not think that my over-fifty age was a detriment, but some employers did. After a year, a position finally opened to me at University of New Mexico Hospital in the neurosurgery department. The salary was minute, but I liked the work. I liked the doctors, and I stayed for two and a half years in administrative work. One of the doctors was a writer, and I helped with his manuscripts.

Soon I found a better paying position in the office of the president of the University of New Mexico in Scholes Hall. I answered an advertisement in the *Albuquerque Journal* for an executive secretary. The position required Gregg Shorthand! I dusted it off and applied. I had taken many UNM administration workshops and budget classes, and I was confident that my experiences would pay off. They did. I hung on to my studies, so precious to me, serving several presidents' administrations, and, finally, I worked in the Provost's Office, also there in Scholes Hall. That office oversaw university budgets, academic tenure, faculty contracts, student issues, and the Dean's Council. We worked there almost 24/7. I was fascinated to learn how those matters were administered, and my studies fell by the wayside. Again.

I eventually retired from the University of New Mexico, having learned so much about the Southwest, language, art, and myself. In New Mexico, I had raised a daughter and built a life for us—with its sorrows and joys. I had found friends and had meaningful work experiences.

A Personal Epilogue

. . . .

My later life may seem to some readers like a travelogue of different work places and what I learned from them. And it is the story of working in New Mexico for many years and as a girl for my father in Mitchell at his office on Main Street and clerking for him on hospital rounds and later at the Delaney Medical Clinic. All these experiences gave me the finest education with the finest teachers anywhere on earth.

When I was growing up, women were taught to expect a husband, a home, children, and a place in the community. When those things were taken away, sometimes abruptly, women such as myself and my sisters were cast out of our comfortable lives. Many women I knew saw psychiatrists, traveled, and joined groups of like victims. They drank to excess, took too many pills and too many lovers, and, in the case of four I knew, committed suicide. Many years ago, my father gave good advice to his youngest daughter, sobbing in bed over some minor upset. Many times it has saved me from the fate of too many women I have known. "Sheila, you must get up and go to school," he said. "You must study hard there, and you must keep up with your reading and learning. You'll forget your troubles!" These words were the greatest healing medicine of all from my father. He bestowed a love of words and literature upon me. Go out and work, inquire, read, and learn. Find joy in life. Find wonderful new things to learn and people to know and love. And I did.

But I can never say goodbye to those years at home without embracing in my mind my dear parents, both gone now, as are my siblings. It does not seem so long ago that all of this happened. My parents held us together like a fort in that house of my youth, helping us through the depression, drought, and World War II. They fed us, clothed us, paid for our education, and nursed us. They never gave up on our struggles to overcome adversity, constantly applauding all our little victories.

While I was writing these recollections, I dreamed during an afternoon nap that I was in the family house, reading in the attic on my favorite old couch. My father appeared, so clear and close that I could see the pattern on his tie; I could smell his after-shave lotion. The years of sickness were gone, and he walked arrow straight to the bookshelves and picked out a book of poems. He sat beside me on the couch and put his arm out for me as he read. As I leaned against him, I began coming out of the dream. I did not want to leave him. He said, "Remember me," and I woke in tears.

Rising, I thought again of one of our walks together, my father slowing down his momentum to take a good look at my adolescent-skinny legs. My high-school name was "Storkey." I do not know how he did it so fast, but soon my father had me wearing a uniform with a short skirt and boots and carrying a baton on Flag Day in front of our American Legion Drum and Bugle Corps. As we walked along, ready to march whenever the band began to play, I remembered my father saying, "If there is trouble, walk right into it," and again he had shown me how. We passed by Father standing on the sidewalk, smiling and holding his hat over his heart.

. . . .

1. Quoted in James B. Stewart, "The Real Heroes Are Dead," *The New Yorker* (11 Feb. 2002): 60.

2. Quoted in *Mitchell Daily Republic*, 3 Feb. 1954. Delaney was born in 1885 on a farm near Cherokee, Iowa. Both of his parents were Irish, his father, Thomas Joseph Delaney, from County Clare, Ireland, and his mother, Bridgette Foley Delaney, from Elmira, New York. Six of the fourteen Delaney children were taken in after being orphaned when scarlet fever killed their parents. Delaney graduated from Creighton University Medical School in Omaha and also attended Saint Mary's College in Kansas and Saint Thomas College in Minneapolis.

3. *The Rubaiyat of Omar Khayyam*, trans. Edward Fitzgerald, in *The Norton Anthology of Poetry*, ed. Alexander W. Allison et al. (New York: W.W. Norton, 1970), p. 738.

4. Frederick M. Binder and David M. Reimers, *The Way We Live: Essays and Documents in American Social History, Vol. 2: 1865–present* (Boston: Houghton Mifflin, 1999), p. 169. In 1921, a KKK organizer visited Sioux Falls, South Dakota, and the organization spread across the state from 1922 to 1928. Mass rallies were common, and up to eight thousand people might attend one. *See* Charles Rambow, "The Ku Klux Klan in the 1920s: A Concentration in the Black Hills," *South Dakota History* 4 (Winter 1973): 71, 73–74, and Betti VanEpps-Taylor, *Forgotten Lives: African Americans in South Dakota* (Pierre: South Dakota State Historical Society Press, 2008), pp. 160–62.

5. From 1916 to 1963, Norman Rockwell painted over three hundred covers for *The Saturday Evening Post*, depicting typical American scenes based on the themes of family, work, children, pets, the seasons, and patriotism. "Norman Rockwell's 323 *Saturday Evening Post* Covers," *Norman Rockwell Museum*, www.nrm.org/page 60.

6. The line is from William Shakespeare's *Hamlet*, Act 2, Scene 2, in *William Shakespeare: The Complete Works*, ed. Peter Alexander (London: Collins, 1951), p. 1043.

7. The first Saint Joseph's Hospital was constructed in 1906 through the efforts of local physicians and the Sisters of the Presentation of the Blessed Virgin Mary, an Irish order with a motherhouse in Aberdeen, South Dakota. By 1922, the growing city of Mitchell required a larger hospital, and a new eighty-five-bed facility opened that September. The Presentation Sisters provided both financial assistance and nursing staff for the hospital. *Mitchell Re-Discovered: A Centennial History* (Mitchell, S.Dak.; Mitchell Centennial History Committee, 1981),

pp. 72–73; Susan Peterson, "From Paradise to Prairie. The Presentation Sisters in Dakota, 1880–1896," *South Dakota History* 10 (Summer 1980): 211, 218–21.

8. Henry Ringling North was a nephew of Albert, Otto, Alfred, Charles, and John Ringling, five brothers of German descent who began the Ringling Brothers Circus in Baraboo, Wisconsin, in 1884. Soon, the successful brothers began buying out other circuses, including the Barnum and Bailey Circus in 1907. Henry North and his brother John ran the company from the middle of the 1930s until 1967. The early circus trains traveled with up to ninety-two cars. "Ringling Brothers," *Topics in Wisconsin History*, www.wisconsinhistory.org/topics/ringlingbros/; "Henry Ringling North, 83, Dies," *New York Times*, 3 Oct. 1993, www.nytimes.com.

9. North established The Ringling Museum of the American Circus in Sarasota, Florida, in 1948. "Circus Museum History," *The John and Mable Ringling Museum of Art*, www.ringling.org/CircusMuseum2.aspx?id=622.

10. Movie star Clark Gable (1901–1960), whose career took off in the 1930s, often wore a jacket with a half-belt sewn on the middle in the back, with pleats above the belt. It became known as an "action back."

11. Big Little Books were "fat books," three inches thick or more. Inexpensive, the books were based on comic strips and movie characters. Whitman Publishing Company of Racine, Wisconsin, published the first chunk book in 1932, *The Adventures of Dick Tracy*. The heyday of publication lasted until 1938. Titles published included *Tarzan of the Apes* (1933), *Ella Cinders and the Mysterious House* (1934), *The Laughing Dragon of Oz* (1934), *Danger Trails in Africa* (1935), *The Arizona Kid on the Bandit Trail* (1936), and *Alley Oop and Dinny in the Jungles of Moo* (1938). More were issued in series featuring Tom Mix, Buck Rodgers, Buffalo Bill, Mickey Mouse, and Little Orphan Annie. The *National Geographic* magazine had a circulation of over seven hundred thousand in 1920 and used black and white photographs, color tinting, and paintings to convey content. During the 1930s, developments in color photography and reports of wide-ranging explorations helped readers "visit" the world. "Learning about Big Little Books," www.biglittlebooks.com; "Evolution of National Geographic Magazine," *National Geographic*, press.nationalgeographic.com.

12. James Cleveland ("Jesse") Owens (1913–1980) was *the* track-and-field star of the 1930s. This African-American from Alabama reached his pinnacle in 1936, when he won four gold medals at the Berlin Olympics. David Wiggins, "Jesse Owens," in *Oxford Companion to United States History*, ed. Paul S. Boyer (New York: Oxford University Press, 2001), p. 574.

13. Quoted from Act 4, Scene 1, which can be found in *William Shakespeare*, p. 246.

14. Kaiser Bill was Emperor Wilhelm II (1859–1941), king of Prussia and the German Empire from 1888 until 9 November 1918, two days before the end of World War I.

15. Nan Delaney had married Vince Taylor of Mitchell before World War II. He died in one of the United States bombing raids that targeted the Romanian city of Ploesti, which supplied a significant share of the crude and refined oil that Germany needed to wage war. At different times, the Soviet and United States militaries raided the tightly guarded city. The North African-based United States Army Air Force conducted the most famous raid in August of 1943, suffering 532 casualties and losing 54 bombers. "Ploesti," in *The Oxford Companion to World War II*, ed. I. C. B. Dear and M. R. D. Foot, *Oxford Reference Online*, www. oxford-reference.com.

16. *See* Virginia and Lee McAlester, *A Field Guide to American Houses* (New York: Alfred A. Knopf, 2000), pp. 438–41. Based in Chicago, the architect Frank Lloyd Wright (1867–1959) established the Prairie style around 1900. Houses in this style are usually two-story, with a low-pitched roof, wide eaves, and, frequently, massive porch supports. Constructed in 1910 by W. S. Hill, the Delaney house contained the features that constitute a Prairie-style home. Mike Vogel, "National Register of Historic Places Registration Form: Hill, W. S., House," 11 Feb. 2009, pt. 8, State Historic Preservation Office Collection, South Dakota State Historical Society, Pierre; Robert McCarter, "Frank Lloyd Wright," in *Oxford Companion to United States History*, ed. Boyer, p. 851.

17. Many Jazz Age musicians recorded "The Sheik of Araby." The song took advantage of the popularity of the silent movie *The Sheik* (1921), starring Rudolph Valentino, in which an Arab sheik captures an independent British woman, taking her to his grand tent in the desert, where he eventually wins her affections. "*The Sheik*," *Internet Movie Database*, www.imdb.com; "Sheik of Araby," *Jazz-Standards.Com*, www.jazzstandards.com.

18. Lawrence O. Gale, Louis Beckwith, and other businessmen of the Corn Belt Real Estate Association conceived of the first Mitchell Corn Palace celebration as a type of "grain expedition" or "fall harvest festival." The building itself was first constructed in 1892, eleven years after the town's founding. Each fall, residents celebrated the harvest with the festival of Corn Palace Week, just as the founders had conceived, with a midway on Main Street and popular entertainers such as Bob Hope, Red Skelton, and the Three Stooges, performing on the Corn Palace stage. Subsequent to his visit in Mitchell, Donald O'Conner became a movie star, most famous for his dancing in *Singin' in the Rain* (1952). His parents were from the vaudeville and circus tradition and worked for the Ringling Brothers. Bob Karolevitz, *An Historic Sampler of Davison County* (Virginia

Beach, Va.: Donning Co., 1993), pp. 57–77; *Mitchell Re-Discovered*, pp. 8–9; "Donald O'Connor," *Internet Movie Database*, www.imdb.com.

19. During World War I, suspecting its Armenian population of treason, the government of Turkey force-marched them to remote areas away from military intelligence. Over one million died of exposure and starvation. *Harper Encyclopedia of the Modern World: A Concise Reference History from 1760 to the Present* (New York: Harper & Row, 1970), p. 389

20. Edgar Rice Burroughs's character Tarzan of the Apes first appeared in the *All-Story* magazine in 1912. Burroughs went on to write twenty-four books about Tarzan. The Big Little Books had an entire series, which in addition to *Tarzan of the Apes* (1933), included *Tarzan Escapes* (1936), *The New Adventures of Tarzan* (1934), *The Return of Tarzan* (1936), *The Son of Tarzan* (1939), *Tarzan the Fearless* (1934), and *Tarzan Twins* (1934). John F. Kasson, *Houdini, Tarzan, and the Perfect Man: The White Male Body and the Challenge of Modernity in America* (New York: Hill & Wang, 2001), pp. 6–7; "Learning about Big Little Books," www.biglittlebooks.com.

21. *King Richard the Third*, Act 5, Scene 4, in *Shakespeare*, p. 746.

22. Vaslav Nijinsky (1889–1950) was a famous Russian ballet dancer known for the versatility, elevation, and complexity of his dancing.

23. Robert F. ("Mac") McMahon, an Army Air Corps pilot, earned many medals for his actions in the Pacific Theater during World War II. He downed three Japanese planes near Darwin, Australia, and survived a bailout from his own fatally damaged plane. Karolevitz, *Historic Sampler of Davison County*, pp. 143–44.

24. "Our Gang" was the general name for a series of twenty-minute films directed by Robert F. McGowan. Based on neighborhood children banding together for adventure, the series began in the silent era in 1922 and lasted into the 1940s. Later, television packaged the gang under the title *The Little Rascals*."Our Gang" and *"The Little Rascals," Internet Movie Database*, ww.imdb.com. G. D. ("Don") Lillibridge also writes of such neighborhood "gangs" in Mitchell a few years earlier. *See* his "Small-Town Boys: Growing Up in Mitchell in the 1920s and 1930s," *South Dakota History* 25 (Spring 1995): 22–23.

25. On 8 December 1941, President Roosevelt used these words to begin his address to Congress, asking members to declare war on Japan. Japanese admiral Isoroku Yamamoto had ordered two waves of air attack, 183 and then 167 planes, against the United States fleet stationed at Pearl Harbor in Oahu, Hawai'i, on 7 December, killing 2,403 United States military personnel and wounding another 1,178. Of those killed, 1,103 were stationed on the USS *Arizona*, now submerged as a memorial with and to the sailors below deck who did not have time to escape

as the ship sank. James C. Bradford, "Attack on Pearl Harbor," in *Oxford Companion to United States History,* ed. Boyer, p. 585.

26. The Mitchell air base was a subbase of the Sioux City Army Air Base and ran a Civilian Pilot Training Program to plan for emergencies. The base became the city's general public airport after the war. Herbert S. Schell, *History of South Dakota,* 4th ed., rev. John E. Miller (Pierre: South Dakota State Historical Society Press, 2004), p. 317; *Mitchell Re-Discovered,* p. 16.

27. Germany used the Junkers Ju. 87 *Stuka* in the invasion of Poland, France, and the Soviet Union. As these Junkers dived, high, piercing sirens frightened populations psychologically while highly accurate machine-guns killed and destroyed property. Douglas Rolfe and Alexis Dawydoff, *Airplanes of the World, 1490–1976,* rev. ed. (New York: Simon & Schuster, 1978), pp. 214, 221.

28. Even though private gardens were common sources of food for many people during this period, the government encouraged women, communities, and even school children to plant fruits and vegetables as a patriotic duty to aid the war effort. These so-called victory gardens provided forty percent of the nation's vegetables. Local boards also issued ration books full of stamps, or coupons, for gas and various foodstuffs such as meat and sugar. Cooperation with rationing also communicated patriotism. R. Douglas Hurt, *The Great Plains during World War II* (Lincoln: University of Nebraska Press, 2008), pp. 99–101, 120–46.

29. The Japanese captured Nanking, China, in 1937; soldiers ravaged the city, destroying property and raping and murdering citizens. Hundreds of thousands of civilians were killed and/or abused. The officers in charge of the occupation were executed after the war, but the Japanese attempt to "forget" Nanking in its official history has extended this World War II conflict to the present. Stephen Turnbull, "Nanking, rape of," in *The Oxford Companion to Military History,* ed. Richard Holmes, *Oxford Reference Online,* www.oxfordreference.com.

30. In 1920–1921, the Corn Palace had been rebuilt and located on the corner of Sixth and Main streets, five blocks straight west of the Delaney home. In 1937, new towers and Islamic-Moorish minarets, or "onion domes," were added to the structure, inviting the comparison to the Taj Mahal of India. Karolevitz, *Davison County,* pp. 67–68, 73–75; *Mitchell Re-Discovered,* pp. 8–9.

31. World War II essentially ended when President Harry S. Truman authorized the United States military to drop nuclear weapons on Hiroshima, Japan, on 6 August 1945 and three days later on the city of Nagasaki. Over two hundred thousand Japanese children, women, and men died or suffered from radiation sickness. Prior to these events, the general public knew little if anything about the government's "A-bomb." As a senator, Truman himself had known only about massive congressional spending for a secret military project, and he learned

about the new bomb only after Franklin D. Roosevelt died. In other words, Nan Delaney was sharing top-secret information. *See* Robert H. Ferrell, ed., *Harry S. Truman and the Bomb: A Documentary History* (Worland, Wyo.: High Plains Publishing Co., 1996), pp. 8–10.

32. Catholic Archbishop Charles Lavigerie founded the Society of Missionaries of Africa in 1868 in Algiers to provide service and work for the conversion of Africa. The order of men was known as the White Fathers because of the distinctive white robes they wore during the society's foundation period. John Forbes, "White Fathers," in *The Catholic Encyclopedia,* vol. 15 (New York: Robert Appleton Co., 1912), www.newadvent.org.; *Missionaries of Africa in Britain,* www.thewhitefathers.org.uk.

33. These lines are from the movies *Gone with the Wind* (1939) and *White Cargo* (1942), respectively. The phrase, "I am Tondelayo," marked Hedy Lamar's grand entrance dressed in a sarong. *White Cargo* was set in the Congo, and Lamar played a mixed-race character named Tondelayo. "White Cargo," *Internet Movie Database,* www.imdb.com.

34. After several attempts, Nan Delaney ended her own life in Michigan in 1966 at age forty-two.

35. The "drive" distinguishes the group nature of the pheasant-hunting experience. A large group of people walk slowly from one end of a field to the other, causing pheasants to fly, while another group serves as blockers at the other end of the field. This group will do most of the shooting. Strict "rules" choreograph the hunt to ensure safety. For more on pheasant hunting, *see* James Martin, "'We Always Looked Forward to the Hunters Coming': The Culture of Pheasant Hunting in South Dakota," *South Dakota History* 29 (Summer 1999): 87–112.

36. Buster Keaton (1895–1966), who starred in vaudeville and both silent and sound films, is often remembered as "The Great Stone Face" for the refusal of his on-screen character to smile. "Buster Keaton," *Bio.True Story,* www.biography. com.

37. Notre Dame Academy, located next to Holy Family Catholic Church, at 200 North Kimball Street, included a grade school (1886–2000s), a high school (1912–1968), and a junior college (1922–1950). The Presentation Sisters of Aberdeen staffed the school. The building was razed in the early 2000s. *Mitchell Re-Discovered,* pp. 68-69.

38. John Dillinger (1903–1934), Lester ("Baby Face Nelson") Gillis (1908–1934), Charles ("Pretty Boy") Floyd (1904–1934), and Bonnie Parker (1910–1934) and Clyde Barrow (1909–1934) were all notorious gangsters. They bootlegged alcohol during the Prohibition Era, robbed banks, cafes, and grocery stores, and murdered FBI agents and others. Constantly in the news, they became celebrities. Kate ("Ma") Barker was "mother" to the "Barker-Karpis Gang," made up

mostly of her sons, whose exploits also involved kidnapping. In 1934, Dillinger and Baby Face Nelson robbed close to fifty thousand dollars from a bank in Sioux Falls, South Dakota. In the end, FBI agents gunned down most of these criminals. In contrast, Charles Lindbergh (1902–1974), world-famous for his solo flight across the Atlantic Ocean in the *Spirit of St. Louis* in 1927, was a victim of crime. His toddler son, Charles, Jr., was kidnapped from his home in New Jersey in March 1932. The boy's body was found in May after numerous ransom notes had been exchanged, the FBI had been called in, and the Lindberghs had paid fifty thousand dollars in ransom. Robert L. Gale, "John Dillinger," Frank R. Prassel, "Charles Arthur Floyd," and David E. Ruther, "Clyde Chestnut Barrow and Bonnie Parker," *American National Biography Online* (American Council of Learned Societies and Oxford University Press, 2000), www.anb.org; Richard Brow, "Ma Barker," *Crime and Investigation Network*, www.crimeandinvestigation.co.uk; "Charles A. Lindbergh Jr. Kidnapping, March 1, 1932," *Charles Lindbergh, An American Aviator*, www.charles.lindbergh.com.

39. Dr. Delaney told the press to tell the kidnappers, "that I'm off the gold and on the lead standard, and if they want lead, they will get plenty of it" (quoted in *Chicago Daily Tribune*, 11 Feb. 1934). In mid-February 1934, numerous kidnapping episodes and ransom notes filled the front pages of both national and local newspapers, and some details that the seven-year-old Delaney overheard outside her father's door may have related to these episodes, as well. *See Mitchell Evening Republican*, 9–16 Feb. 1934.

40. Taking as his subject an aristocratic Roman Catholic family, Evelyn Waugh (1903–1966) explored both religion and sexuality in his novel *Brideshead Revisited*, published in 1945. "Nancy Boys" was a mid-twentieth-century phrase that meant homosexuals. Frank Buck (1884–1950) originally published his best-selling book *Bring 'Em Back Alive* in 1930 about his adventures in South America and Africa collecting animals for zoos and circuses in the United States. The book became a movie of the same name in 1932, with Buck as its star. Buck visited Mitchell during this period to see a caged African lion that he had captured on exhibit in the lobby of the Roxy Theater. "History," *Frank Buck Zoo*, www.frankbuckzoo.com/History.html; Karolevitz, *Davison County*, p. 139.

41. The United States Congress passed the "GI Bill of Rights," or the Service Men's Readjustment Act, in 1944. Sixteen million veterans took advantage of mandated special-rate home loans, educational benefits, job-hiring preferences, and unemployment provisions. J. Garry Clifford, "World War II," *Oxford Companion to United States History*, ed. Boyer, p. 850. For more on the adjustments in colleges, *see* Robert G. Duffett, "South Dakota and the GI Bill of Rights: Opportunities for Institutions and Individuals," *South Dakota History* 36 (Spring 2006): 88–118.

42. John Robert Gregg, an English immigrant to the United States, published the first American edition of *Gregg Shorthand* in 1893, and his stenographic system for rapid note-taking soon dominated the field.

43. *El Palacio* magazine, first published in 1913, focuses on scholarly research in archaeology, anthropology, and history and is still in publication. It was associated with the founding of the Museum of New Mexico in 1909 in Santa Fe. John D. Rockefeller, Jr., funded the Laboratory of Anthropology in 1927 for the purpose of fieldwork in archaeology, ethnology, linguistics, and physical anthropology. The museum and laboratory merged in 1947. The combined institution helped set standards for investigation and preservation of archeological sites. In the 1960s, the laboratory focused on salvage archeological projects related to dam-construction and highway projects. *El Palacio*, www.elpalacio.org; Timothy D. Maxwell, "Archeology at the Museum of New Mexico," *New Mexico Office of Archeological Studies*, www.nmarchaeology.org.

44. The University of New Mexico now houses the Alianza Federal de Pueblos Libres Collection, 1963–1997 (the name of the organization changed over time), in the archives of its Center for Southwest Research. *Rocky Mountain Online Archive,* rmoa.unm.edu.

Index

. . . .

THE COMPLETE GUIDE TO WRITING

SUCCESSFUL FUNDRAISING LETTERS

FOR YOUR NONPROFIT ORGANIZATION

By Charlotte Rains Dixon

THE COMPLETE GUIDE TO WRITING SUCCESSFUL FUNDRAISING LETTERS FOR YOUR NONPROFIT ORGANIZATION

Copyright © 2008 by Atlantic Publishing Group, Inc.
1405 SW 6th Ave. • Ocala, Florida 34471 • 800-814-1132 • 352-622-1875–Fax
Web site: www.atlantic-pub.com • E-mail: sales@atlantic-pub.com
SAN Number: 268-1250

ISBN-13: 978-1-60138-247-4   ISBN-10: 1-60138-247-2

Library of Congress Cataloging-in-Publication Data

Dixon, Charlotte Rains, 1954-
  The complete guide to writing successful fundraising letters for your nonprofit organization : with companion cd-rom / by Charlotte Rains Dixon.
     p. cm.
  Includes bibliographical references and index.
  ISBN-13: 978-1-60138-247-4 (alk. paper)
  ISBN-10: 1-60138-247-2 (alk. paper)
  1. Fund raising. 2. Nonprofit organizations--Finance. 3. Fund raising--Case studies. I. Title.

  HG177.D59 2008
  808'.066658--dc22
                                   2008028303

Printed on Recycled Paper

INTERIOR LAYOUT DESIGN: Nicole Deck ndeck@atlantic-pub.com

Printed in the United States

We recently lost our beloved pet "Bear," who was not only our best and dearest friend but also the "Vice President of Sunshine" here at Atlantic Publishing. He did not receive a salary but worked tirelessly 24 hours a day to please his parents. Bear was a rescue dog that turned around and showered myself, my wife Sherri, his grandparents Jean, Bob and Nancy and every person and animal he met (maybe not rabbits) with friendship and love. He made a lot of people smile every day.

We wanted you to know that a portion of the profits of this book will be donated to The Humane Society of the United States.

–Douglas & Sherri Brown

THE HUMANE SOCIETY
OF THE UNITED STATES ©

The human-animal bond is as old as human history. We cherish our animal companions for their unconditional affection and acceptance. We feel a thrill when we glimpse wild creatures in their natural habitat or in our own backyard.

Unfortunately, the human-animal bond has at times been weakened. Humans have exploited some animal species to the point of extinction.

The Humane Society of the United States makes a difference in the lives of animals here at home and worldwide. The HSUS is dedicated to creating a world where our relationship with animals is guided by compassion. We seek a truly humane society in which animals are respected for their intrinsic value, and where the human-animal bond is strong.

Want to help animals? We have plenty of suggestions. Adopt a pet from a local shelter, join The Humane Society and be a part of our work to help companion animals and wildlife. You will be funding our educational, legislative, investigative and outreach projects in the U.S. and across the globe.

Or perhaps you'd like to make a memorial donation in honor of a pet, friend or relative? You can through our Kindred Spirits program. And if you'd like to contribute in a more structured way, our Planned Giving Office has suggestions about estate planning, annuities, and even gifts of stock that avoid capital gains taxes.

Maybe you have land that you would like to preserve as a lasting habitat for wildlife. Our Wildlife Land Trust can help you. Perhaps the land you want to share is a backyard—that's enough. Our Urban Wildlife Sanctuary Program will show you how to create a habitat for your wild neighbors.

So you see, it's easy to help animals. And The HSUS is here to help.

The Humane Society of the United States
2100 L Street NW
Washington, DC 20037
202-452-1100
www.hsus.org

Dedication

To all the passionate, dedicated people who work tirelessly in the world of philanthropy and the non-profit.

Table of Contents

CHAPTER 4: GETTING STARTED — WHAT YOU NEED TO DO BEFORE WRITING 73

CHAPTER 5: KEY ELEMENTS OF THE SUCCESSFUL FUNDRAISING PACKAGE 83

CHAPTER 6: CONTENT OF FUNDRAISING LETTERS..................................... 107

CHAPTER 7: TYPES OF FUNDRAISING LETTERS . 173

Foreword

By Karen Ashmore

Fundraising from individuals is more competitive than ever and the myriad of available media contributes to the growth and the need for specialization of skills. At the same time, it also means that people are being bombarded with more and more messages so it is important that your message stands out.

Charitable giving in the U.S. was $306 billion in 2007, exceeding $300 billion for the first time in history. Individual giving, the stronghold of fundraising, reached $229 billion, or 74% of total giving in 2007.

The Complete Guide to Writing Successful Fundraising Letters for Nonprofits shares great insights into the many different aspects of raising funds from individuals in a straightforward and proven approach that includes case studies of real-life situations.

As the Executive Director of a growing international foundation that works in one of the poorest countries in the world, I know that fundraising letters are the bread and butter of revenue generation. One of the unique aspects of this book is that it takes a holistic approach and prepares the reader for all the steps for a successful letter writing campaign. That means covering all the preparatory steps before you even write the letter – setting a fundraising strategy and goals, knowing your donor, branding, defining fundable themes, and understanding the value of each component in a fundraising package.

With these important preliminary steps, you are then ready to write the letter. This book does a thorough job of presenting techniques and sample letters for many types of fundraising needs. Using a practical approach with actual examples and case studies, you see what has worked for other non-profits. One of the most important rules to remember is to keep it personal and use story telling to reach your goal – which is to motivate the reader to send a donation.

Whether you are using direct mail, e-mail, or other media, this book covers all the angles for a successful letter writing fundraising campaign. I cannot guarantee how much money you will raise, but I can guarantee that you will raise money if you follow the steps in this book.

Good Luck on your fundraising endeavors!

Karen Ashmore
Executive Director
Lambi Fund of Haiti
Supporting economic justice, democracy
 and sustainable development in Haiti
Washington DC
www.lambifund.org

Karen Ashmore is the Executive Director of the Lambi Fund of Haiti, whose mission is to assist the popular, democratic movement in Haiti by supporting grassroots organizations that work for economic justice, democracy and alternative sustainable development. She has over 20 years experience in social change philanthropy and has won awards for her activism in human rights, racial justice and women's issues. She and her husband are the parents of five children, including two sisters adopted from Haiti. She also serves as the Board President of Grantmakers without Borders.

Introduction

DO YOU NEED TO READ THIS BOOK?

I f you work for a nonprofit organization or deal with one in any capacity, the answer is yes. Let us borrow a writing technique you will learn later in this book to expand on the answer to this question: the famous five Ws and one H.

- **Why** should you read this book?

- **Who** can benefit from reading this book?

- **How** can you best use this book?

- **Where** can this book best be put to use?

- **When** should you read this book?

- **What** does this book cover?

WHY SHOULD YOU READ THIS BOOK?

You should read this book because recent surveys estimate there are over 1.4 million nonprofits in the United States today, all of them doing good in the world and deserving of support. And let us not forget that every one of those 1.4 million nonprofits needs the same thing — money. To that end, these nonprofits send an estimated 100 million fundraising letters every year. With this kind of competition, you must learn how to set your nonprofit apart. You must be able to explain why the donor should choose you over other nonprofits.

There was a time when nonprofits could rely on quaint grassroots efforts to get the word out about their services and to find the money to provide those services. No more. Fundraising is big business, and like all businesses there are techniques you can learn and guidelines you can follow to create the most success.

In *The Complete Guide to Writing Successful Fundraising Letters for Nonprofits*, we will not only teach you strategies to share your message effectively, but we will also present underlying theories of marketing on which to base your letters. And do not worry — we know the words "business" and "marketing" may make you cringe. That is probably why you work in a nonprofit, because you have a passion to serve. You will now learn how to turn that passion into a marketing concept that will make the community just as passionate about your services as you are.

WHO CAN BENEFIT FROM READING THIS BOOK?

Anybody who needs to learn to write fundraising letters, or knows a little about the subject but would like fresh tips and techniques, can benefit from reading this book. Because developing fundraising packages and writing fundraising letters needs to be an integral part of every nonprofit's mission, every person involved with a nonprofit can also benefit from the information in this book. This includes:

- The executive director

- The development director and his or her staff

- The marketing director and marketing staff

- Public relations and advertising staff

- The board of directors and advisory council, if one exists

- All staff in support positions

- Volunteers

- Consultants to nonprofit organizations

HOW CAN YOU BEST USE THIS BOOK?

The best way to use this book is to read it carefully to absorb all the information, do the writing exercises, study the sample letters, and follow the step-by-step directions for drafting a fundraising letter. To learn a new skill, you need to use it. This book will make learning the craft of writing successful fundraising letters as delightful and pleasurable as possible.

WHERE CAN THIS BOOK BE PUT TO USE?

This book can be used in any nonprofit organization or

nongovernmental organization (NGO), as well as in the offices of anyone who deals with fundraising in any way —consultants, volunteers groups, and advertising agencies that create campaigns for nonprofits.

WHEN SHOULD YOU READ THIS BOOK?

Now is the time to read this book. Never before have so many people been so interested in giving. Suddenly, it is hip to give. Former president Clinton has written a best-selling book about it. Bono has teamed with the organization One to encourage people to give of their time and money. Celebrities need to give back to gain the approval of their fans. This is because individuals are beginning to understand that they need to show gratitude for what they have by giving back.

With the ascendancy of the Internet, everyone is connected globally, and people are beginning to understand that what affects one affects all. President Clinton, in his book, *Giving, How Each of Us Can Change the World*, points out several reasons for the advent of this atmosphere of giving, including more people living under elected governments, more millionaires and billionaires, and more people in general donating to nonprofits and charities..

It is an exciting time to be involved in the world of nonprofits, and organizations can capitalize on this by learning solid techniques of creating fundraising packages.

WHAT DOES THIS BOOK COVER?

While you will get the most benefit from this book by reading it all the way through, completing the writing exercises, and studying the sample letters, it is a fact that many people who work for nonprofits are overworked and unpaid. Thus, you might be eager to get to a specific part of the book without reading the whole thing. If you need to write a fundraising letter now, for instance, you might want to find the chapter that provides step-by-step directions for completing a letter. This will work best if you go back and read the rest of the material when you have time. Here is a chapter-by-chapter summary.

Chapter 2 will offer pertinent information for your organization and its goals. This chapter will offer a definition of nonprofits and reveal how they relate to the community, pointing out that nonprofits exist to fill a need outside the organization itself. It is vitally important for the nonprofit to answer the question, "Why do we exist?" To sell itself and its story through fundraising letters, a nonprofit must know itself and its mission thoroughly. After doing a thorough evaluation of the nonprofit's services, the next step is to define its current needs and forecast its needs for the future. The most successful fundraisers are those who completely understand the mission of their nonprofit and are clear about its goals for the present and the future. To this end, a good starting point for a fundraising campaign is to write a strategic fundraising plan, or review it, if it already exists. This chapter will present a list of questions and considerations nonprofits need to have pondered about their overall fundraising plan. This will cover such areas as setting fundraising goals, creating a budget for development, developing income projections, and identifying assets and weaknesses.

After a deep inquiry into the goals of the organization, it is important to understand the donors. Chapter 3, will address this in detail. Fundraisers must grasp the psychology of giving. What drives people to get involved or give money? And how can the fundraiser utilize this understanding to write successful fundraising letters? This chapter will address the emotional aspect of people giving money, and you will learn how to tap into that emotion. Find out about what motivates people to remain unmoved by an appeal for money or help and look at the mental-sorting process that people go through when reading a fundraising letter. Chapter 3 will present a template for better understanding the donor, through questions such as, what is he passionate about? What is her association with the nonprofit? After reading this chapter and completing the exercises, the nonprofit should have an excellent idea of the profile of its target donor.

Chapter 4 seems a bit distasteful for fundraisers. You as a fundraiser need to look at marketing, because fundraising is, at its heart, marketing the services of what a nonprofit does. Nonprofits may resist marketing, but to create a successful fundraising campaign and accomplish the organization's goals, fundraisers need to understand the basics of marketing. The good news is that marketing can actually be authentic and joyful. This is especially true of nonprofits, since they exist to create change, help others, or solve social problems. It is important to learn how to tell the story of what the nonprofit is doing and get others to support it. That is the essence of marketing. Once comfortable with the concept of marketing, you will work on the marketing concept of the fundraising campaign. In this chapter, you will learn about the importance of giving each campaign a unique theme look. It will address how to find ideas for the marketing concept by looking to the problems and challenges of the organization and by quizzing the frontline staff.

Before beginning work on the fundraising letter, you will need to do some prep work, which is the focus on Chapter 5. Using the work that has already been accomplished —the thorough look at the organization, the donors, and the marketing — this chapter will focus on preparations specific to the fundraising letter package. Fundraising expert Alan Sharpe says, "The most important part of any direct fundraising appeal is what you do before you write a word of the package." This chapter will focus on those things you need to be clear on before writing. This will include a list of questions about whom you are writing to, why now, and what you want them to do.

In Chapter 6, you will learn how to take all this information and hard work, and put it into a fundraising package. Some fundraising experts argue that other aspects of the package, besides the fundraising letter, are the most important elements of the package. Take the envelope, for instance. If donors are not compelled to open the envelope in the first place, they will never read the fundraising letter. In this chapter, you will learn about the four crucial parts of a fundraising letter package: the outer envelope, the letter itself, the reply device, and the reply envelope. You will also learn about optional enclosures, such as the buckslip, the freebie offer, and the premium offer, and find out when it is appropriate to use these tactics.

In Chapter 7, you will look at the content of the letter package. You will learn about the characteristics of effective fundraising letters, and you will see how to get those onto the page in a compelling style. We will cover how to format and structure a letter, when to use the word "you," how to phrase appeals, and how to utilize emotional triggers. We will also dissect the writing of a fundraising package, step by step, including what to write on the envelope and reply form, the greeting, the opening lines, how to phrase the ask line, and how to close the letter.

In Chapter 8, you will learn about all the different types of fundraising letters, defining each, explaining when each type of letter should be used, and offering a sample letter. Types of letters covered include the follow-up, thank-you, front-end premium, back-end premium, survey, special event, petition and protest, special appeal, renewal series, major donor, sustainer, lapsed donor, recruiting new donors, and straight contribution letter.

Chapter 9 covers writing tips. Writing for fundraising is about writing for results. To that end, many tips and techniques can be utilized to make the letter accessible and even enjoyable to read. You will learn how to use the techniques of storytelling (the most important skill to master), how to be personal, what techniques to use to generate the best response, how to write with a sense of urgency, and many more tips. The writing exercises in this chapter will teach how to transform prose into results-oriented copy.

Chapter 10, the conclusion, will consist of a review of everything the book has covered, from the essence of the nonprofit's mission, through looking at the organization's reason for being, its donors, and the fundraising goals.

You will review the most important aspects of writing a fundraising letter, and you will see what kind of results can be expected.

The appendices are where all the forms and exercises are included in one handy place. You will find a bibliography, a glossary, and writing exercises here. Let us start by discussing the essential qualities of the nonprofit organization.

CASE STUDY: ARIANE C. DIXON

Ariane C. Dixon- Development Associate, Special Events

Oregon College of Art and Craft

8245 SW Barnes Road

Portland, OR 97225

I write fundraising letters on a daily basis, including cash and in-kind donation letters, sponsorship proposal letters, community partnership proposals, follow-up thank you letters, and acknowledgment letters.

The most successful fundraising letters are tightly written, well composed, strategically researched, well presented, enthusiastic, and persuasive. Failed letters are too cut and dried and don't successfully dictate the appropriate benefits that a donor would receive. They also don't strike that certain persuasive chord with the recipient.

As far as pre-planning goes, I look at our history with each and every donor before I compose a letter and if applicable, I speak with a member of our Board of Trustees for any insider information they may have. You must make sure that the recipient is a good fit with your organization or you will look silly and naïve.

It is so important to know your constituents. Who are they? What do they hold as important? What types of organizations do they care about and fund? What other organizations are they involved in? Research your donors and businesses and listen to want they want. Make sure that each situation is mutually beneficial.

CASE STUDY: ARIANE C. DIXON

Do not assume anything—just because someone donated last year certainly does not mean they will again. Even if they told you they will donate again, they may not. Never let your guard down or write in a way that may appear nonchalant or unprofessional. Never disrespect your constituent's time. They have very little of it and will only be frustrated if you send them a letter wasting their time.

To come up with ideas for a fundraising package, I ask, does it make sense for my organization? Would someone expect, and be excited about this theme when participating in my organization's event? Continuity is also important.

When writing fundraising letters, everything should be tight and well thought out. Neatness counts, as does spelling. It should all make sense to the recipient when they receive it. Don't write for academia, but don't dumb down your writing either. You must strike a balance. Most important, know your audience and appeal to them.

To get ideas for fundraising letters, we pull from blurbs that have been written by our grants manager and other promotional materials. It is important, regardless of what department of your organization is writing a letter, that the mission is universally accepted, agreed upon by everyone in the organization. Make certain that every department is saying the same thing so that your organization as a whole is getting the same, cohesive message out.

Be sure to write about the thing that sets your organization apart from the rest—and play it up. Don't rest on your laurels and assume that your organization is the only one out there that needs funding, because it most certainly is not!

Your Organization and Its Goals

You might not want to read about the nonprofit organization and why it exists. And you probably know everything there is to know about your own nonprofit. You might not need to work on defining the work of the organization because you know it through and through. After all, you have sat through many meetings in which your nonprofit's goals have been defined and debated. You probably want to get on to the good stuff — the writing of the fundraising package.

But wait a minute. If you are bored with the mission and goals of your nonprofit, your community will feel the same way. If you take the services of your nonprofit for granted when you sit down to work on your fundraising letter, so might those who read it. The letter will be dull, flat, and unconvincing. Conversely, you might be a brand new foundation or organization, just bursting at the seams with excitement about your mission. If this is the case, make certain you know yourself as thorough as you should. Be sure you have defined every aspect of what you plan to do for the community.

Whether you are a brand-new organization bursting to share what you do, or you have been in it for years, take the time to read this section thoroughly. Answer the questions in writing or in a group setting (you can make it fun, serving pizza and drinks, or having a dessert party, for instance). You might be surprised at the renewed fervor you feel for your organization or the new things you learn after going back to review its basics.

In these chapters you will be uncovering strategic information about your organization, its clients and donors, the perception of it in the community, and much more. You will be pondering branding, positioning, and other marketing standards. All of this information is incredibly useful for writing fundraising letters.

Before going any further, get a file folder, a legal pad, or a notebook, whichever you prefer, and use it to corral notes specific to the letters you will soon be writing. As you gather all this information about your nonprofit, you will be sparking ideas for your fundraising letters. If you continually make notes as you move through the exercises, you will find the fundraising letters have practically written themselves, because you will have all the information readily at hand.

A DEFINITION OF NONPROFITS

Your nonprofit organization exists to fill a need outside itself — to address something that is lacking in the community or to solve a problem for the world you live in. It is not a corporation, designed to make money for itself. The nonprofit is based on need and service, and it is formed specifically for performing a public benefit. While a nonprofit corporation can make money, it is not allowed to have moneymaking as its primary goal. Of course, gaining nonprofit status has the immense benefit of making the organization exempt from state, local, and other taxes. Look at some of the types of nonprofits in existence:

- **Charities.** Examples of these would be the Red Cross or the Salvation Army. Charities have helping people in need as their mission.

- **Religious organizations.** Churches and organizations devoted to worship fall into this category.

- **Foundations.** These are private in origin and begun by an individual or family to direct their wealth or resources toward a specific community benefit. Examples would be the Ford Foundation or the Kellogg Foundation.

- **Social-welfare organizations.** These nonprofits devote their resources to improving the social fabric of lives, focusing on one specific segment of the population. They are engaged in advocacy for the rights of this group. Examples are the American Civil Liberties Union (ACLU) or the National Association for the Advancement of Colored People (NAACP).

- **Trade organizations.** Members of the same profession or occupation band together to promote knowledge and awareness of their profession. In some cases, these nonprofits also establish and govern professional standards and practices. Examples include the

American Medical Association, local Chambers of Commerce, and the American Bar Association.

Additionally, nonprofit organizations fall into one of the following categories: arts, culture and humanities, education, environment and animals, health, human services, international and foreign affairs, public societal benefit, religion, and mutual or membership benefit.

All of these categories and types of nonprofits have one thing in common: they serve a perceived need in society. There are a variety of reasons why nonprofits have come into existence. An economist might tell you that it is a simple matter of the demand of the marketplace, that there is not a big enough need for the service to attract a for-profit corporation. Similarly, from a governmental standpoint, if there are not enough constituents loudly clamoring for certain services, the government will leave it up to the private sector to fill the need. Rather than attempt to convince a majority of citizens to come to their side, concerned activists can simply create an organization themselves. Plus, many have an inherent distrust of "big" government and would rather receive needed services from a smaller organization. Bear in mind that, historically, many communities existed before formal governments, and thus people banded together themselves to solve problems together. This has had the additional benefit of fostering civic pride and participation.

WHY DO WE EXIST?

Although it is important for you to understand where your nonprofit group fits within the larger picture of the nonprofit world, the most vital thing for you to understand is why your organization exists.

"To help people," while a nice answer, is not nearly specific enough. It is a good idea to review this question and your answers to it periodically. The introduction referenced one good exercise to be used in writing fundraisers - the Five Ws and One H. So, apply that here, and see what you come up with.

For starters, whom exactly are you going to help? And what, exactly are you going to help these people with? This second question may result in a long list of needs that the people in your population require. So you must ask yourself which of these services you will offer? Why is one more important than the other? How will you offer these services and solve these problems? Finally, where and when will you offer your services?

Here is an example. Say that the group of people you want to serve is those who are HIV positive. What kinds of issues does this group face? Perhaps you have identified a long list of the needs of HIV-positive people, but the number one issue facing them, you feel, is the high cost of medication. This is the most important issue to tackle because the medication is lifesaving, but is so expensive that many cannot afford it. Now you need to identify how, precisely, your group will mitigate this problem. Will you dispense medicine or money for medicine? Will you provide vouchers to medical clinics or provide stopgap insurance coverage? Finally, decide where and when you will offer help. Are you going to provide ongoing assistance or emergency, temporary support? Will clients come to a clinic you have funded, or will you handle their needs from an office location?

In the world of for-profit businesses, one of the current favorite buzzwords is "niche." Every entrepreneur, large and small, is encouraged to develop a niche. Trying to be all things to all people simply does not work in this global, information-driven world any longer. In business, it is considered more efficient and more profitable to do one thing well than to do many things halfway. The same is true for nonprofits, as you can see from the above example. It is vitally important for a nonprofit to look carefully at the niche it serves and find the best ways to work for that niche.

Clearly, this question of why your organization exists is much more complex than it first appears, and it is vital to spend time answering it in a detailed fashion. The good news is that in taking time to answer this question, whether for the first time or the 20th, new ideas will arise. Out of the need to constantly define your organization's mission can come effective brainstorming sessions that will produce new programs and new directions for your organization.

THE STRATEGIC FUNDRAISING PLAN

Now that you have accomplished the difficult work of defining your mission, it is time to strategize how best to raise the money to support these services. But in order to raise money, you need to know how much money you need. That is where your nonprofit fundraising plan comes in. You must thoroughly know your mission and everything that supports that mission, such as operating expenses.

If you were a for-profit business while you were in the planning stages of creating your business, you would write a business plan. As a businessperson, you would sit down and figure out what, exactly, you were going to sell and for how much. You would also plan for how many of your product you thought you could sell, where, and how. You would then revisit, review, and revise this business plan as needed, at least once a year.

Many people working in the nonprofit sector do not like the word "business." After all, you probably joined the nonprofit world because you have a passion for helping people, and now you are being asked to write a business plan.

For nonprofits, the business plan translates to a strategic fundraising plan — a vital part of the planning process. Businesses use business plans to protect their fiscal health, and nonprofits need to also. Maintaining a strong financial base is what enables you to go forth and serve. You cannot share food with the needy if the food shelves are bare. It is also true that many nonprofits have grown from the ground up, without much formal planning at the outset, because they were formed to respond to an immediate need. This sometimes forces them into a reactive mode, responding to a crisis here, throwing resources at each need as it pops up. Writing a strategic plan can help you to even your resources and responses. Having a clear idea of your current and future budget needs is the starting point of writing a successful fundraising package. Once you have written it, you will know what you have and what you need, and you can go forth and fill those needs. But before you go into the specifics of a fundraising plan, you will also want to look at broad planning issues for your nonprofit. These issues include:

- The needs of the community you serve

- Whether your organization's mission still contributes to those needs

- Whether your programs are still vital and useful

- Whether the community you seek to serve is aware of you and your services

- Whether the community at large is aware of you and willing to support you

- Whether it is time to take your programs in a different direction to better serve the need

- Whether it is time to expand or contract a program

- Whether you have been nurturing your own organizational needs or ignoring them for the sake of your clients

- What the best uses of your organization's time and energy are now

- What the best uses of your organization's time and energy will be in the future

While you might not want to hash out such a lengthy overall plan, the truth is that many nonprofits find strategic planning an energizing, exciting activity. It reconnects them with the initial vision that started the nonprofit, and it often generates new ideas for programs and events. Approach the planning process as a way to rejuvenate your organization and your mission, and you will find it a pleasurable activity. You might also find the perfect marketing concept for your fundraising campaign because understanding the needs of your organization, inside and out, is where the best ideas are germinated. This subject will be addressed in a future chapter. For now, look at what you will want to include in your fundraising plan.

COMPONENTS OF THE STRATEGIC FUNDRAISING PLAN

To begin writing a fundraising plan, you must figure out where you are starting. You will need to examine where you are, where you want to be, and what the steps are in between — in other words, how much money you are going to need to raise to accomplish your goals and how you are going to do it. Take a look at the component of the strategic fundraising plan, and then each of them will be addressed in detail.

- Perform an external analysis of issues affecting the organization.

- Review the information you have already collected about your organization and make certain it is an accurate internal analysis.

- Write or review mission, values, and vision statements.

- Identify strategic issues.

- Identify strategic goals.

- Identify strategies to reach goals and action steps.

- Set a fundraising goal. This will include creating a budget for development and checking income projections, overhead, and so on.

- Evaluate your assets. You should have an excellent head start on this if you have been following what we have talked about already in this chapter.

- Develop your strategy. Brainstorm what sorts of goals and activities you want to focus your fundraising on.

- Create your final plan by making your final decisions. The impetus and material for your fundraising letters will come from this plan.

PERFORM AN EXTERNAL ANALYSIS

The importance of looking carefully at every aspect of your nonprofit organization has been addressed, but it is also important to look at external factors that might have an impact on your work. Are there societal, technological, political, or economic trends that might affect your work? You will want to look at economic trends such as legislation, federal funding, demographic trends, and issues with labor. You should also investigate what your stakeholders' views of the organization are and whether they have changed in any way. This includes the following groups:

- Community leaders

- Donors (This is covered extensively in the next chapter)

- Volunteers

- Clients

- Other outsiders who might have an impact or influence on your group

REVIEW INFORMATION

This is your chance to review, revise, and commit everything you have learned about your organization to paper. By the end of this step, you should be ready to:

- **Write mission, value, and vision statements.** Your mission statement explains why your organization exists. This is your chance to hone it into a neat, concise description, and commit it to paper. The vision statement explains what you hope to do for your clients. The vision statement is traditionally written in a compelling style. Spend some time with this and ponder it deeply, as it will be especially valuable in creating your fundraising letters. You might end up using whole chunks of it in your letters, as it lays out the case for your existence. Finally, write your value statement, explaining the values your organization is based upon.

- **Identify strategic issues.** What are the immediate and long-term issues that your organization faces? It could be that your employees are chronically underpaid, that you have a difficult time attracting board members, or that you have such a low profile in the community that nobody has ever heard of you — making it hard to raise money. Also, determine what your weaknesses are, both inside and outside the organization.

- **Identify strategic goals.** Consider the above issues and weaknesses and start to develop goals around them. It is vitally important in this step to note immediate needs and long-term goals. Make sure that they align with your mission, vision, and value statements. Many management experts also recommend SMART goals:

- Specific

- Measurable

- Agreeable to all parties

- Realistic

- Time-based

Verify that all your goals are SMART goals, and you will be on your way to achieving them.

- **Identify strategies to reach goals.** What are your plans for reaching the above-named goals? What are actions steps you might take? For instance, the nonprofit with the low profile might design action steps such as inviting the community to an open house or creating a series of informational evenings to explain what they do. Brainstorm and toss around ideas. Have fun with it. Let the wildest and craziest visions come out, then weed out the impractical ones, and write down the practical goals. It is important to define them clearly, as these goals may end up being part of your eventual fundraising letter.

SET A FUNDRAISING GOAL

Now that you have all the information you need, you can begin designing a fundraising goal. Your goal can be based, in part, on how much you raised last year. Can you expect to raise more this year, or will the economy or other external forces prevent that? Determine the minimum, bare-bones amount that your organization needs to operate. Other things to consider are creating a budget for development activities, administrative overhead, and non-cash contributions. All of this will impact how you structure your fundraising package, and the amounts you ask for in your fundraising letters.

EVALUATE YOUR ASSETS AND WEAKNESSES

When you thoroughly understand the strengths and weaknesses of your organization, it is time to look at them from a fundraising and economics perspective. Besides financial assets, what other pluses can your organization boast that will assist you in your fundraising goals? Do you have several loyal, hard-working volunteers you can call upon to handle specific tasks? Perhaps you have a high profile in the community or dedicated board members. Note all of these. Not only will you want to use them to implement your fundraising action plan, but also you would be surprised how often you can use information like this in your fundraising letters.

While looking at your assets, it is also a good time to review the issues your organization faces, also known as weaknesses. Viewed through the lens of fundraising, you might want to consider whether you have a person with writing skills on staff or as a volunteer, or whether you will need to assign someone to develop these skills. If that person will need to take a course, you will need to build in time for the learning curve. If everyone on your staff is too busy to take on writing a fundraising package, you will want to look into hiring an outside consultant, or freelancer writer. That will take prep work — part of which you are doing by reading this book and completing the exercises.

DEVELOP YOUR STRATEGY

By now, you should know every aspect of your organization, down to the smallest detail, including strengths, weaknesses, and financial needs. Now you will learn how to raise the money. Writing a fundraising letter may be only a small part of your overall fundraising plan. You might also be planning special events such as auctions, wine tastings, or parties. You must then determine whether all of these will be linked by a theme or be separate elements. An underlying marketing concept for your fundraising will be addressed in detail in a future chapter, but for now, it is important to realize that strategy and marketing are two different elements. Strategy can be thought of as how you plan to achieve your needs, whereas marketing is the specific way you are going to present those needs to the community. To write the story, you first need to know the specifics.

When strategizing how to raise money, it is important to refer back often to your mission, values, and vision statement and stay true to all of them. For instance, an organization devoted to ending drunken driving is not going to want to host a wine tasting. Likewise, a group whose goals include ending childhood obesity is probably going to shy away from a dessert offering. These underlying considerations will also guide the writing of your fundraising letters.

It is also important to develop a strategy that has a diversity of activities and appeals for money. You do not want to rely solely on the income from one big event each year, because that might not be as successful as you anticipate. Likewise, you will want to have a mix of potential donors identified in case one group does not come through. A source of government funding may suddenly dry up, or an anticipated grant might fall through. Chapter 3 will address the subject of donors in more detail. For now, just be aware that a nonprofit should never place all its eggs in one basket. The main goal should be stability in your finances, and that is going to come from a variety of sources.

CREATE YOUR FINAL PLAN

Those who create goals and write them down are he most successful. Having a plan committed to paper in a final form gives you a basis that will guide your efforts in the short and long term, and it gives you something to refer back to when questions or problems arise. Having a fundraising strategy committed to paper is also vital when writing fundraising letters and packages. The plan, in its written form, should include the following:

- **A schedule.** What time span does the plan cover? You should plan to commit to paper detailed goals and strategies for the next year, and more general ideas for at least two to five years out.

- **Description of your goals.** Write this in detail. It will be the meat of your fundraising strategy, and you will refer to it repeatedly in creating your fundraising packages.

- **Calendar of events.**

- **Delegation of duties.** Who is responsible for what? What will his or her specific tasks be? Who will be writing the fundraising letters? Who will edit them? Who will have the final power of approval on them? If hiring an outside consultant for the job, who will choose the person?

- **Backup plans.** It is always good to have a Plan B. What if the auction does not raise the money you hoped? What if the fundraising letter you send out does not net you the number of new members you had forecast?

Now that you have gone through the rigorous process of looking deeply into your organization, identifying strengths and weaknesses, and strategizing to create a fundraising plan, you should be feeling good about your nonprofit and your role in the community. That brings up our final point — having confidence in your organization, what you stand for, and the value you bring to the community.

JETTISON THE CHARITY MENTALITY

Because nonprofits have solving the ills of the world as their goal, it is easy for them to fall into the charity mentality when it comes to fundraising. Bear in mind that you, as the nonprofit, must take care of your own needs first to serve others. It is a little like the instructions you receive when boarding an airplane. The attendant is always careful to explain that, should there be a change in air pressure, masks will fall from the ceiling. Then they emphasize that those passengers traveling with small children or others in need of help should put their own mask on first. This is because they will not be able to help their child if they have passed out from the lack of oxygen. This same principle holds true for nonprofits. You need to put your own mask on first.

Some nonprofits may also cringe at the whole idea of asking for money, shuddering at the thought of a begging mentality. But bear in mind that no less a luminary than wealthy philanthropist John D. Rockefeller considered that "begging" or asking for money was a perfectly acceptable, enjoyable thing to do.

Sometimes, because nonprofits have to ask for money and employees in this field traditionally earn less than their private-sector counterparts, a sense of inferiority can develop. Unfortunately, this society bases its assessments of worth solely on money, but, in the case of nonprofits, this is not always an accurate assessment.

In a perfect world, all organizations and corporations would be judged by their contributions to the common good.

Even though that is not the case, nonprofit organizations can take pride in the good they do and the services they provide. After thoroughly reviewing your organization, you should be even more proud of it and of how hard you work. Consider that not only do you, as a nonprofit, have to figure out how to do this good work; you have to figure out how to raise the money for it. Corporations do not have to take time and energy to deal with raising money. So be confident and proud of the work you do, and carry that attitude over to the next chapter as you delve deeply into the minds and hearts of your donors.

Your Donors

The largest source of income for most nonprofits is from selling goods, establishing fees for certain services, or interest from investments. The next highest source of income is governmental grants. Surprisingly, private donations to nonprofits are actually a relatively small portion of their income. Estimates say that nonprofits get approximately 10 percent of their income from private donations.

However, there is good news. As noted in the introduction, more and more people the world over are currently concerned with giving, whether it is a lot or a little. In America, an estimated 70 percent of households give some portion of their income to charity. In a climate where giving is considered hip, you probably will not have to work as hard to convince donors to part with their money. Take a look at the various sources you can expect will donate money.

- **Traditional Funders.** These are groups such as private foundations and other community grant-giving operations.

- **Board of Directors.** Your board is traditionally responsible for the health of your nonprofit's finances. If your board members also help with fundraising and contribute generously themselves, it establishes credibility for your organization.

- **Governmental Grants.** Some government grants are available to aid nonprofit organizations; these require specific and rigorous application processes.

- **Private Individuals.** It is interesting to note that in the United States, the typical donor is lower to middle income.

- **Midsize and Major Donors**

Since the purpose of this book is to discuss fundraising letters, the bulk of our discussion of donors will focus on the private sector. Most governmental donations and foundation requests require the specific expertise of a grant writer, and that subject is best left for another book. Let us start by looking at the individual donor.

According to many fundraising experts, the motivation of the individual donor is quickly changing. We have noted the renewed vigor with which individuals are channeling their energy to nonprofits, but what motivates them to give? They see problems in the world and feel like it is their duty to contribute in some way. They probably are not able to take a year off to help impoverished children at an African school — but they can contribute money to that school, perhaps "adopting" a child to sponsor. But what motivates a donor to open her checkbook for one nonprofit and not another?

Every fundraiser would love a specific answer to that question, but it is as elusive as the question of what makes a book a bestseller or a movie a huge hit. It all has to do with human psychology, and, as much as we have learned about how the brain operates, there is still a vast amount we do not know. However, this issue has been extensively researched, and studies of fundraising through the years can give us some ideas. We have learned that successful fundraising appeals tend to run their course. What works one year might not work the next, perhaps because familiarity breeds contempt, or the human mind simply becomes impervious to a certain kind of appeal. We are beginning to understand a little bit about our instinct to give.

Many believe that the impulse to help others is hard-wired into our basic personalities. Sociologists and psychologists posit that this impulse has been necessary, historically, to ensure group survival. While survival of the fittest rules in the jungle, among humans group survival depends on care and concern for the weakest members of our society. Beyond that, most potential donors will consider a few common things.

The more you can understand potential cues that spur your donor to give, the more you can incorporate those cues into your fundraising letters, and the more successful your appeals will be. Some of these cues may be:

- The donor feeling good about himself/herself

- The donor needing a tax deduction

- Supporting a certain politician or political point of view

- Supporting a certain strong belief

- Supporting an agency or nonprofit that has helped him or her or someone he or she knew in the past

- Supporting a charity that addresses a medical issue they have struggled with

- The donor feeling strongly about a certain social or environmental problem

- Influence of friends or family

It is also important to note that several of these motivators may play in the mind of your donor at once. For instance, he or she may be looking for a tax donation, ask friends for recommendations, and then choose according to his or her familiarity with the topic. Or perhaps one of your fundraising letters landed in his or her mailbox just as he or she was looking for a place to donate.

YOUR TARGET DONOR

Your task is to figure out whom your target donor is, how to reach him or her, and what emotional cues might trigger him or her to give. Begin by looking for the obvious groups. You will want to include those who have donated in the past, of course, and anyone who has been helped by your organization, as appropriate. You can then start to amass information about your target donor with a little market research. While you might feel that you already know this information thoroughly, take some time to ponder it again. As previously noted, things change quickly in the public psyche. For instance, a few years ago most people thought global warming was the message of a few rabid scientists calling wolf. Now, many are concerned with the problem and looking for ways to conserve and go green. What you learn might surprise you, and it might be the perfect detail for the fundraising letter. The more details you can learn about your target donor, the better chance you have of convincing him or her to write a check.

Here are some things to consider. As you compile this information look for aspects of his or her personality and life style that might cause the potential donor to align himself or herself with your cause.

- Neighborhood or zip code.

- Household income

- Profession

- Education level

- Family status

- Hobbies

- Preferred recreational activities

You will also want to investigate, whenever possible, what sorts of social, political, or medical issues your target donor has experience with. A good place to start searching for this information is with your existing donors. You can call them or send them a thank-you letter (more on thank-yous in a future chapter), and ask them questions about their preferences and habits. Another excellent strategy is to contact lapsed donors and ask them why they quit donating. You may be able to convince them to donate again in the process. Do not forget the power of the Internet, either. You can use your Web site for surveys of potential donors, and you can track pages that people visit with ease. Some organizations with larger budgets go so far as to conduct focus groups within the community, but this takes time, money, and energy that are beyond the realm of most nonprofit groups.

WHAT YOUR DONOR GAINS

Previously, it was mentioned how your donor might be motivated by feeling good about himself or herself, but it is also important to look at the specific material gains a donor receives. First, of course, is the tax deduction. Not everyone who donates to your organization will care about this, because it only applies to those who itemize their deductions. For many, however, it is a powerful motivator, because they are constantly looking for deductions and other ways to reduce their tax bill.

You might also want to consider offering an incentive to donate in the form of a freebie. This is important to have decided before you begin writing your fundraising letter because you will need to incorporate it into your letter. Organizations such as the Public Broadcasting System (PBS) have perfected the art of offering incentives. Televised PBS fundraising drives often compel people to contribute by offering a free DVD to donors. Freebies can also be used to motivate people to donate at a higher level.

Most nonprofits that use freebies structure them to various levels of donation. The lowest amount will receive some simple promotional item, with higher amounts garnering more and more elaborate gifts, which can include T-shirts, coffee mugs, DVDs, tickets to events, or packages that include all the freebie items at the highest levels. As with your events, plan your freebies to coincide with the mission and values of your organization.

WHAT MAKES YOUR DONOR PICK UP HIS OR HER PEN?

Examine what makes a person respond. You have looked at the motivation of a donor, but people can have the best intentions to give in mind, yet never feel compelled to actually pick up the pen or visit a Web site to give money.

Many professional fundraisers have studied what motivates a donor to respond to a plea for donations. After all, it is what their success depends on. Studies have noted that people respond for diverse and sometimes surprising reasons. Most often it is for the simplest reason — because they are asked. Other motivations include everything from liking the celebrity who signed the letter to perceiving an urgent need. For the most part, the reasons people send money center around their own wants and needs, not the wants and needs of the organization. Bear this in mind as you plan your letters, and tap into the donor's desires, fears, and guilt.

MIDSIZE AND MAJOR DONORS

Midsize and major donors require a bit of special handling and TLC that you probably will not lavish on smaller, individual supporters. When you write most fundraising letters, it is not the larger donors you are going after. It is far more common for a fundraiser to approach a big donor on a one-on-one basis. You will probably approach existing donors to massage them into giving again, or be looking at getting to know a completely new set of major donors. Some organizations even assign donors to staff members by the amount of money they make. However, it is still vitally important for the fundraising letter-writer to understand the special needs of the larger donor. This is because you will no doubt be writing special letters with these donors in mind, including invitations to special events, requests for annual renewals, and quality thank-you letters after they have made their donations.

To handle the larger donors, you will need to do some special research to identify them; it will then be important to get to know them. Most nonprofits maintain careful records of information about their donors; these files should be your first stop. But bear in mind that the information might need updating. Perhaps the major donor has changed jobs or spouses or decided to throw his or her support to a different organization. It is vital to keep your information about major donors up to date, because when approaching donors individually and writing letters to them, you will need to know as much as possible. With luck, you will also have some new donors you hope to wrangle into the fold. In both these cases, you are going to need to do research.

You will be looking for much the same information that you collected for individual donors, but on a more personal basis. When approaching the wealthy for money, you want to feel confident that the person shares your organization's values, and it helps if he or she has a special, personal concern for the work you do. For instance, your potential donor might be a self-made man who was once homeless and thus has a natural inclination to give to homeless shelters. Or perhaps that same self-made millionaire might now have a passion for art and thus be interested in supporting scholarships for the underprivileged at a small private art college. Through research, you might also learn of special connections this donor might have to your organization or board or staff members. This is all information you are going to want when you walk into a meeting with the potential donor.

You might also want to look into the donor's cultural background. In a world of diversity, the standard approach used for prospects of European descent simply may not be effective for people of other cultural backgrounds. Different cultures have different approaches to all sorts of things, including fundraising. What is considered polite in one culture can often be rude in another.

Start close to home, by talking to people in your office. You have already combed the files for any information you might be able to find, and you have a good starting point. Ask other staff members for information on donors you have identified as prospects. They might be able to steer you in a direction you had not thought of, or give you a tip about the donor that will help add to your picture of them. Then, it is a good idea to speak to board members, who often have amazing networks of connections among the movers and shakers of any community.

Finally, you will need to head to the Internet to fill in

the cracks. Start with Google. It is amazing how much information putting a name into Google can turn up. Be sure to put in variations on the name, such as a middle name that is sometimes included and sometimes not. Often, the slightest difference in search engine keywords can open up a completely new avenue of research. You can visit sites such as **www.forbes.com** and **www.fortune. com** to find information about your prospective donor's business background. At **www.imdb.com**, you will find extensive listings of people in the entertainment industry. For information on doctors, try **www.ama-assn.org**, and to learn about architects, visit **www.firstsourceonl.com**. If you know your donor has books in print, go to **www.amazon. com**. If none of these pan out, and you are unsure where to find more information, ask your local librarian for help. They have always been whizzes at handling information in books, and now they are quite good at whipping about the Internet.

While it is one thing to legitimately collect information about a prospective donor, it is yet another to invade the privacy of that donor. Be careful not to intrude into a person's private life. This will anger the donor and guarantee you will not get a donation. A good guideline is to confine your search for information to anything that is relevant to your fundraising effort. For instance, earlier it was mentioned that your donor might have changed spouses. This falls into the category of private information that is most likely not relevant to your fundraising efforts. However, when you want to invite this prospective donor and her new husband to a special fundraising event, then it is important to be able to use the spouse's name, and therefore, not an invasion of privacy. Use reliable sources, and do not pretend to be someone other than yourself. There have been some high-profile cases of this happening lately in the corporate world, and these instances have led to the public downfall of the people who did the investigating.

CULTIVATING RELATIONSHIPS, OR KEEPING YOUR DONORS DONATING

Bear in mind as you plan your fundraising letter writing that you are going to need to stay current with your donors. Part of your fundraising activities will include writing thank you letters and special appeal letters to your best donors. We will look at the specifics of those letters in detail in a future chapter. For now, just remember that this is something you will need to be aware of constantly. It is vitally important to cultivate your relationship with your donors, keeping them interested and aware of events and activities that you are sponsoring. This strengthens your relationship with the donor, and the stronger your relationship, the more likely the donor is to keep giving. It is especially important to consider this after instituting a successful new fundraising campaign that might bring in new donors. Merkle is a direct response agency that also specializes in donor management. They recommend the following measures:

- Empower Donors

- Serve Your Donors

- Respect Your Donors

Merkle emphasizes that nonprofits need to start viewing

donors for what they are — the lifeblood of the organization - without donors the nonprofit would not exist. They advocate a donor-centered approach that might not sit well with all nonprofits. However, it is useful to take some of their ideas into consideration when pondering your donors.

Some ways to keep donors happy are to thank them quickly, keep them informed through newsletters and longer fundraising letters, and invite them to your site, office, or operation headquarters to see behind the scenes. The idea is to keep your name in front of the donor as often as possible through mailings or other activities.

By now, you should have full pictures of your individual, midsize, and major donors. You should also have an understanding of how to keep them happy and donating. Be sure to keep good records as you complete all this research, as you will be referring back to it repeatedly when you compose your fundraising letters, as well as other specialty letters, such as thank-you notes.

Chapter 3

The Dreaded M Word — Marketing and the Marketing Concept

Marketing is a vitally important aspect of fundraising. While marketing is what businesses do, it is what you, as a nonprofit, do every time you create a fundraising campaign. To "sell" the services of your organization to prospective donors, you need to know how to market. Not only that, the next step in creating a campaign is to develop a marketing concept for it.

Because many nonprofits have a natural aversion to the concept of marketing, they tend to ignore it. Also, with resources and staffs stretched thin, many feel they have no time to spend on marketing. In truth, you will save time in the end by making time for marketing in the beginning. Having a solid grasp of marketing and the marketing concept for your fundraising letter campaign will help you to make it as successful as possible. The good news is that marketing can be an activity that is authentic and joyful.

Marketing is about expressing the essence of who you are, whether that is a business or a nonprofit, and sharing that story with the world to convince them to support you. It is about making sure that your clients' expectations match your services, and tweaking one or the other if not. If your constituents expect one service, but you are providing them with another, your organization will not last long. Your services must be well understood in the community. You know there is a need, but does the community grasp it? Marketing may uncover the need for more of an educational component to your fundraising letters.

All the hard work you have done in defining your organization, its strengths and its weaknesses, will be a good starting point for your marketing plan. The essence of being able to communicate your own wonderful uniqueness starts with knowing who you are. And since you have been taken through an exhaustive process of uncovering just that, you should be in good shape to start pondering marketing.

First, work on some definitions and historical backdrop. Most nonprofits held the idea of marketing at arm's length and resisted anything that smacked of marketing until around 1975, when Philip Kotler wrote his seminal book, Marketing for Nonprofits. Kotler's book was instrumental in breaking down the resistance of many charities to marketing. Many have embraced the concepts and put them into play in their organizations with great success.

At its simplest, marketing is about selling stuff, which is why nonprofits have traditionally veered away from it. However, in truth, it is much more complicated than that. From a business point of view, marketing looks at a potential customer base and targets how to sell products to that customer. For nonprofits, marketing is a bit different because you need to satisfy not only your "customer" (your client) but your donor as well.

Here is a good, basic definition of marketing. Marketing is what you do to meet the needs of your customers while receiving something such as sales in return. Most marketing is product-specific, meaning that for every product or service a company or organization offers, a separate marketing plan will be needed. Marketing can be broken down into two areas. "Inbound marketing" involves learning what the customer base is and what their needs are, and how you, as a company, can meet those needs. This aspect of marketing includes analyzing competition and pricing products. "Outbound marketing" encompasses such areas as advertising, public relations, and sales.

The essence of marketing is making sure that you are meeting the needs of your customers and providing them with service. In the case of nonprofits, your "customers" are two-fold: your clients — or the population you serve — and your donors. Many experts make a distinction between inbound marketing and outbound marketing. Here is what is included in each:

INBOUND MARKETING

- Marketing Research

- Branding

- Competitive Analysis

- Positioning

OUTBOUND MARKETING

- Advertising and Publicity

- Customer Service and Customer Satisfaction

Not all of these categories are going to be applicable to nonprofit marketing. However, it will serve you well in your efforts to write successful fundraising letters to consider a few of the most important categories. Look at how nonprofits can utilize traditional market research, branding, and competitive analysis.

MARKETING RESEARCH

How is your nonprofit doing? Are you still serving the population you set out to serve? Are you meeting the needs of the community? You have looked at the organization from the other point of view, gathering an extensive picture that you have drawn up. Now it is time to get a picture from an external focus. Start by asking those on the front lines — staff that works directly with you clientele and volunteers, and the clients themselves, if possible. This is an excellent way to find out whether they have needs that are not being met. It might also yield you some excellent material for your fundraising letters. You exist to fulfill the client's need, and making sure you are filling that need is vital.

BRANDING

While you probably are not going to want to go through the hassle of changing your name, you will want to look at the issue of branding. Your brand can be your greatest asset.

Think about the Red Cross, and what comes to mind? Help in a crisis or disaster. How about MADD? Campaign to eradicate drunken driving. Doctors Without Borders? Medical care for blighted areas.

All of these nonprofits have readily identifiable brands. You might not have thought about it in exactly that way, but each one of them has a mission that is synonymous with their name. In business, think of companies like Nike or Apple. You do not have to explain what any of these companies or nonprofits do because they have a readily identifiable brand established. Branding is about presenting a consistent message about who you are to the world. When people see your name, you want them to think of what you do immediately.

Begin by finding out what the current perception of your brand is. This process began with the recommendation that you do some market research and ask clients and volunteers what they perceive the goals of your organization to be. A good source of valuable feedback is also your donors. Ask them what they perceive to be the most important goals of your organization. Combining this with the market research you did, and you should have a good picture of how the community thinks of you. Does it match your own goals and perceptions? If not, you either have some tweaking to do in branding, which will be reflected in all of your fundraising letters, or you might want to look at the services you provide and consider whether they are still relevant.

For instance, if your soup kitchen provides a hearty breakfast once a week in an outdoor location, but the community's perception is that you provide only holiday dinners, you will want to tweak your message. But this is also good feedback about your services: does the community idea about holiday dinners indicate a need that is going unfilled? Are people not getting the message about your breakfasts because of lack of publicity or has the need for your service shifted from a once a week meal to a more elaborate, and less regular, holiday preparation?

In this way, branding and marketing becomes a valuable tool for nonprofits, showing you not only how you are perceived, but also how to stay relevant and vital as an organization.

After uncovering this information, you can ask yourself what the one thing is that you do better than anyone else does. There may be many soup kitchens, but yours is the only one that provides a nourishing hot breakfast. Just as a for-profit business would, you need to focus on what sets you apart from the others — the reason for you existence.

Next, you need to create a plan to implement your branding message. Determine how you are going to get the word out that you are the only organization in town that serves hot breakfasts. Understanding the branding message you want to show is important to writing fundraising letters because you are going to want to focus those letters around your brand.

It is important to make certain that all staffers and volunteers understand the new branding message so that they can participate in presenting a united image to the community, so make certain to spread the word internally as well.

COMPETITIVE ANALYSIS

Competition is best left to the commercial world, where businesses vie with each other to sell more to the consumer. Nonprofits traditionally do not have a commercial focus on selling a product or service. That is why many of them got started in the first place — to provide a service the business world considered unviable, and therefore, unprofitable. Examine why a nonprofit should have to do a competitive analysis and how it applies to fundraising letters.

Consider this scenario: your soup kitchen has decided to go from serving a once-a-week breakfast to providing a daily morning meal to the needy. However, due to this, you need to raise more money. Therefore, you write a fundraising letter, evoking the needs for the homeless to eat a healthy breakfast, only to learn that the soup kitchen down the street has beat you to it. Not only are they serving a daily breakfast, they also serve lunch and dinner, and their fundraising letter eloquently evokes what it feels like to be hungry and homeless, and it has even you, their chief competitor, reaching for your wallet.

A little competitive analysis can go a long way. In the current business climate, both donors and clients are demanding more accountability of nonprofits. For instance, look at the outcry that followed the Red Cross's admission that some of the funds collected for the victims of September 11th actually went to other needs. With the economy tightening, nonprofits also face a shrinking pool of available resources, and non-duplication of effort is important. If your competition, the neighboring soup kitchen, already has the leg up on serving breakfasts and finding funding for those meals, you may find it difficult to get a response to the fundraising letter you send out. Take the time to answer a few simple questions and you can avoid this problem.

- Are we the best organization to offer this service?

- Are we spreading ourselves too thin?

- Is there another organization offering similar services more effectively?

- Is competition good for our clients, or should we pair with a similar organization to better serve them?

By looking at some of these issues of competition, an organization can make crucial decisions that will influence the success or failure of fundraising-letter campaigns.

POSITIONING

The buzzword in marketing circles these days is niche marketing. Your niche is your unique market position. In the business world, success comes from finding a niche that is not filled by others. It is not enough to operate a catering business; you must run one that fulfills a special niche. A niche might be a vegetarian catering business, but even that may not be specific enough. So you narrow it further and decide to run a raw foods catering business, and in that small, narrow niche, you suddenly find yourself positioned as the go-to business for anything raw. The caterer next door does not know how to prepare raw food, so she sends the business your way.

Now return to the soup kitchen example to explore how this relates to the world of nonprofits. You are serving one breakfast a week, but you have learned that the soup kitchen down the street is serving breakfast every morning. In doing your market research, you learn that your competitor's breakfast is little more than an offering of a highly processed, packaged muffins donated by a local bakery because they are past their sell date. Better than nothing, but hardly the makings of a nutritious breakfast. You, on the other hand, serve a hot meal cooked by volunteers that features all of the vital food groups.

So there is your niche: not just any breakfast, but a hot, nutritious breakfast, cooked from scratch. Because of the time and energy your volunteers and staff put into meal preparation, it is not something that you can do every day, but your clients can go down the street for their muffin at the other soup kitchen on weekdays. You each have your niche; you are each vital to your constituents.

The world needs you and your nearest soup-kitchen competitor. Your clients know that; you see them lining up for the hot, nutritious breakfast you serve every Sunday. But you need to convince your donors and your community of this fact. Using marketing techniques allows your nonprofit to do this — to find the way to communicate your value to the community.

You have already done the hard work of market research and analysis, so if you feel your positioning needs tweaking, it should be an easy adjustment, as you have all the information you need to accomplish it.

Now let us move on to look at how outbound marketing affects writing fundraising letters. To refresh your memory, outbound marketing includes advertising, public relations, sales, customer service, and customer satisfaction. Advertising and publicity will be addressed first.

ADVERTISING AND PUBLICITY

Advertising and publicity complement your fundraising letters, and they have something in common — they are based on written communication. If you work at a small nonprofit agency, you may wear many hats, and be responsible for writing ads, press releases, and fundraising letters. At a larger organization, your domain will be letter-writing, while someone else heads up advertising and yet another person deals with publicity. However, all three of these areas, since they are based on written communication, need to be coordinated, with the same marketing concept underlying each. For example, if your ads focus on the value of one aspect of your program while your publicity and fundraising letters deal with another, you are not going to have much luck with the public and donors. They will become confused. So even if you will not have anything to do with the actual ads, you will want to know what they look like and what the advertising copy covers.

CUSTOMER SERVICE AND CUSTOMER SATISFACTION

Your "customer" is your client, the person your agency serves — the homeless person to whom you offer dinner and warm bed at night, the AIDS patient whose medication bills you cover, the artist whom you offer a grant to cover art supplies for an upcoming show. In some cases, it is an easy task to assess customer satisfaction, but in others, such as for those nonprofits serving a fluctuating population, this may be more difficult. In the latter case, you may well need to depend upon reports from the field — front-line staffers and volunteers, and perhaps even board members and donors. Earlier, it was mentioned how important it is to uncover the community's perception of you and your services and "customer" satisfaction falls into this category.

THE MARKETING

Now all of your hard work will come to fruition as you take all the work you have done so far and review it to come up with a marketing strategy or marketing concept. In the next chapter, you will systematically go through all the things you need to do before actually writing a fundraising letter. The basis of that is identifying the marketing concept. Some people may call this the "copy platform." It is the details about your organization that you have selected to feature in your fundraising material — the underlying marketing concept, which will identify the purpose of the fundraising letter, the person you are asking for money, and the benefit that person will derive from donating to you.

You will need to ask for a specific amount of money in your fundraising letter. Will you have different levels of donation on your reply cards? Will you call your donation a membership? Are you offering freebies for donations? All of these questions need to be answered. Next, you need to identify the person you are asking for money. You have done your research on donors and potential donors, so you probably already have ideas on this, but be specific here. Are you writing to new donors? People who are long-time members? Finally, what is the benefit that your donor will receive? Will he or she get a tangible benefit or just the pleasure of knowing he or she has done well in the world? Are you offering various freebies or services that might come with a membership?

According to many experts in the field, a useful marketing concept needs to be clear, complete, and organized. It should also be authentic and appropriate to your organization and its constituents. Finally, it should be appealing.

Keep it Clear. This means that your potential reader gets the message loud and clear. It is simple, and by the time your potential donor finishes reading it, he knows exactly what you are asking for and why.

Keep it Organized. Make certain that the fundraising letter and package works together to create one seamless whole. Your reply card does not compete with your letter, and you are not dangling one benefit in front of the donor in the lead, and then displaying another near the end. It also means that you do not send mixed messages. For instance, when you send a fundraising letter, that is all you send. You do not include it with your monthly newsletter or an invitation to a special event.

Keep it Authentic. Check to be sure that everything

in the letter rings true and reflects the nature of your nonprofit. This means that whoever signs your letter (and fundraising letters are best written from one individual to another — more on that in an upcoming chapter) is appropriate to your organization. For instance, you might not choose a famous sports figure as a figurehead for a homeless shelter — unless it is well known that he was once homeless. On the other hand, a sports figure would be the perfect signer for a campaign against childhood obesity.

Be Appropriate. This admonishment to children also applies to your marketing concept. You will not address an appeal for arts funding to a group you have identified as outdoor enthusiasts. And you might not want to send an appeal for a senior center to new college graduates.

Be Appealing. A pox on writing boring letters! Do not write dry, dull copy. We have many ideas and tips on writing that will help with this in future chapters.

We have a few last tips and techniques to cover under marketing. Take a glance through them and make a note to come back later if need be. The next chapter will start to put everything we have been talking about to use as we begin the last step before actually writing fundraising letters — preparing to write.

Final Marketing Tips

Here are some key tips for marketing nonprofits, gleaned from a variety of experts. Bear in mind that you will need to translate these concepts to your fundraising letters.

First, remember that you are marketing your mission. Now all that hard work of defining or re-defining your mission and values and vision come in handy. What you need to market is your vision for service, not the service itself. As a soup kitchen, for example, you may serve nightly dinners, weekly breakfasts, and occasional special meals on holidays. Attempting to market all of those different services to your donors is just going to cause confusion, so return to the bottom line of·your mission: feeding the hungry.

Next, remember to communicate your successes. Potential donors want to feel they are contributing to a cause that makes a difference. Remember, they want to feel good about themselves. It is also important to remember that your target market is probably not aware of your successes — it is your job to tell them!

When marketing, show not only your successes, but your strengths as well. Show the world what you do well and allow them to join in and be a part of it.

Do a little market research with your constituents. What is their view of what you do? Do they have a positive or negative idea of your nonprofit? Are they able to articulate, precisely, what it is that you do, the needs you serve? Or do they have a vague answer about all the different services you provide, some accurate, and some not? If the latter is true, then you might need to return to your mission statement and make certain that your organization has not become too diversified. Perhaps you have strayed from your original focus and intent. Marketing research can help you identify problems such as these by first identifying the public's idea of what you do or do not do. Then you can look at how closely their perceptions match the truth, and whether you need to consolidate and return to your core mission.

Chapter 4

Getting Started — What You Need to Do Before Writing

While you may be wearying of the focus on the organization and wonder when we will get to the actual letter, all fundraising experts agree that the preparation for writing is at least as important as the writing. Many argue that it is even more important, and that should make you feel better. After all, we have been focusing so much on preparation work that you might wonder when we will ever get to the actual letter writing. The answer is, just as soon as you answer a few questions about the letter itself.

Answering questions about your organization helps to put you on solid ground before you start asking others for money. These questions will cover whom you are writing to, why you are writing to them, and what you want them to do. Of course, it is not quite so easy as to answer three questions and then be on your way to copywriting. We need to go through each question in depth. Remember, by doing all this prep work, you are improving the odds of your letter's success.

WHERE TO LOOK FOR IDEAS

As you go through this chapter and answer the questions, you will also want to be thinking about the overall theme for your fundraising letter. Are you going to feature a story? Which one? Do you need a catchy headline to snag attention? What is the hook that will capture your readers' attention? You do not have to figure this all out now, but it helps to have it in mind as you do this prep work. If you are new to fundraising, you might not know how to come up with a creative approach. Conversely, if you have been doing this for many years, you might need some tips on how to write with a fresh angle. Here are several places to look for them:

- **Staff or Volunteers in the Field.** Talk to employees working on the frontlines with clients. They are in the trenches on a daily basis, witnessing the work your organization does. You might glean a story or even a whole approach from them. Be especially alert for any mention of challenges they might face. Writing about conflicts your clients face or problems in the field can translate into compelling letters.

- **Previous Letters.** You do not want to duplicate what has been done before, but reading through previous fundraising campaigns, combined with your knowledge of the organization's status, can be a good way to come up with new ideas.

- **Anniversaries or other Milestones.** There is no better hook for a fundraising campaign than a recent anniversary. It is effective to use in fundraising because you can emphasize how long your nonprofit has been in operation, how much good it has done, and how much more there is to do.

- **Recent Successes or Goals Met.** Donors love to feel that they are part of a successful team. Think about sharing some recent successes or goals met. In addition, go another step further and ponder whether there are ways to personalize these successes through storytelling.

WHY ARE YOU WRITING THIS LETTER AND WHY NOW?

It is important to identify why you are sending out the fundraising letter at this precise moment. Needing money is not reason enough. Every nonprofit organization needs money. You need a specific reason. You may need to write a letter to solicit new members, or perhaps write an appeal letter. Maybe this letter will be seeking donations for a specific cause, or appealing to lapsed members. Maybe you need more volunteers, and thus need to recruit them in your letter. Perhaps you are writing a planned giving letter? Ask yourself what the specific goal of this letter is, specific being the most important word. How does this request fit with your annual program? Will you be asking this group for help again? Be certain that you can state exactly what you will do with the money you are expecting to raise. Finally, it is important to note why you are asking for the money now, and why you think the potential donor will respond now. For instance, have they responded to requests for emergency help in the past?

WHO ARE YOU WRITING TO?

You have already done a lot of hard work toward defining your target donor. Now look at those donors specifically through the lens of writing a fundraising letter to them, which is a subtle difference. Look at some of the things you will want to consider.

- **What is their common passion?** What sets your potential donor apart from all the other people in the world? Do all of your readers have something in common with each other? Are they all veterans, for example, who have fervor for a political cause or social issue, or do they share the same profession? Do your potential donors all belong to a certain age demographic or live in one area of the country? Identifying their passion will help you focus your letter.

- **What is their relationship to your organization?** You need to identify to whom you are writing this letter. Are you writing to a stranger? Someone who has donated before? Board members? Major donors? Volunteers? Current or former clients? Understanding the reader's relationship to your organization will dictate what kind of letter you'll be writing—and there is a big difference between a major donor letter and a straight contribution letter.

- **What do they already know about your nonprofit?**

Do your potential donors understand your cause or service? Will you need to educate them about what you do, or can you assume a high degree of familiarity already? What else do they want to know about you? Answering this question will help guide you to decide how much information about your cause to include. If in doubt, write more. Don't assume that everyone knows about you.

- **How loyal are they to your cause?** How long have they supported your organization or been a member? Are they committed enough to volunteer for you? People who have donated in the past are far more likely to donate again.

- **Do you understand the typical feelings of the people you are writing to?** Are they angry about your cause? Do they feel compassion for the people you serve? Are they upset about problems in their personal lives, like family or economic issues? Knowing this will help you strike the right tone in your appeal.

- **What experiences and ideas will your potential donor have that will help him grasp the issue?** For instance, a potential donor in an urban area might have a great deal of experience with homelessness, but a reader in a rural area might not. Conversely, a rural woman might have little experience with traditional art, whereas a young woman living in New York City might visit art galleries regularly.

- **What do they respond to?** Which appeals and themes

will your audience respond to best? Will evoking an emergency (disaster, impending legislation, or change in funding) motivate them to give or turn them off? What will make them open their checkbook?

- **Why do you think this person will respond favorably?** Has he been a member for years? Has she inquired about volunteering? Do they have a personal connection with your organization? Answering this question will also help you decide what category to put the potential donor in.

- **What do you want your letter readers to do?** You can write the most stylish, beautiful fundraising letter in the world, but if you do not understand exactly what you want your readers to do, you will not be able to ask them to do it. You want to move them to action, not admire your beautiful prose.

- **What exact actions do you want your readers to take?** You want them to send money, but giving money can take many different forms, and it is important to know which you are dealing with. Are you asking existing donors to renew support? Approaching new donors? Writing to a certain group you have identified as likely prospects? All these, or many other possibilities, require a different approach.

- **How much money do you want them to give?** What is your goal amount for each donor to send? Having clearly defined monetary goals from the outset will aid in your planning and evaluation of the success of the campaign.

- **What is the minimum you want from each donor?** This is a vitally important question to answer and to get right. The amounts you ask for will determine how much you receive. Think back to the last time you got a fundraising letter. You probably looked at the reply card to see what the suggested donation amounts were. If they fell into the price range of what you felt was reasonable and that you felt you could afford, you might have been more likely to send money. If you ask for too much, you might turn new donors off. However, long time donors might be offended by asking for too little. It is very important to know whom you are writing to and figure out an appropriate amount.

- **Are there additional actions you want them to take?** Do you want them to attend an event? Refer a friend? Call their congressman? Sign up for a newsletter?

WHY ARE YOU APPEALING TO THEM NOW?

Are there special circumstances that have prompted this fundraising plea? An emergency or a need for disaster relief? An urgent pending legislation? You need to identify the specific problem or service your organization needs funding for. Donors like to know exactly where their money is going.

WHAT BENEFITS WILL DONORS GET?

First, list the tangible benefits, such as membership,

special services, and discounts. Are you offering a freebie or premium such as a T-shirt, tote bag, calendar, or book? Then list the intangible benefits. Your donor will feel good about himself or herself and his or her contributions in the world. Donors can also be motivated by the desire to feel a part of a special group.

WHO IS GOING TO SIGN THE APPEAL LETTER?

This question takes us to a different focus. We will talk much more about this in the next chapter, but for now, bear in mind that every fundraising letter should be written as a direct one-on-one appeal. This means you will need to find an appropriate personality to "write" the letter and sign it. This, in turn, will dictate the content and voice of the letter. A celebrity writing an appeal letter will be much different from a sports star or business figure. Therefore, you can see why it is important to know who will be writing and signing the letter before you write a single word of copy. Consider the following questions:

- **What is Your Letter Signer's Name?** Who has agreed to sign the letter? Is it someone from your organization, such as the president or chairman of the board, or is it an outside person, such as a concerned celebrity?

- **How is He or She Connected to the Nonprofit?** This may be evident, in the case of the signer being a member of the organization's staff or board. If you have an outside person signing the letter, you will need to be sure to make their connection clear.

- **How is He or She Connected to Potential Donors?**
  Do they share common experiences? A common
  demographic? A common love for a region or activity?
  Are they well known for their love of something
  connected to our organization?

- **What are the Signer's Feelings about the Nonprofit
  or Cause?** If you are using a bigwig or celebrity to
  sign your fundraising letter, you might not know the
  answer. Ask them. They may have a very specific
  story or memory that will bring your letter to life. (We
  will learn more later on using story to write letters.)

Expert Alan Sharpe also recommends adding the following
questions to the line-up:

- **What hot buttons can you push?** Are there buzzwords
  or phrases that will motivate your donor to action?

- **What proof can you offer?** Can you find a human-
  interest story to make what you do come alive for the
  reader? Are there facts and statistics you can offer as
  supporting evidence? A good story supported by facts
  is powerful. What can you tell your reader about your
  past successes and goals achieved?

Now that you have gotten your creative juices flowing and
started thinking about what you will be writing and whom
you will be writing to in your fundraising letter, let us turn
our attention to the content of fundraising packages.

Chapter 5

Key Elements of the Successful Fundraising Package

Successful fundraising packages do not happen by accident. They are crafted lovingly and sometimes laboriously down to the last detail, with fundraisers even planning what kind of postage they will use in a direct-mail appeal. In this chapter, we will look at the key elements of a successful fundraising package, and then examine techniques for incorporating those elements into every package you create. Finally, we will look at the essential components of every fundraising package: the envelope, the letter, the reply device, and the reply envelope.

VOGELE'S DIRECT MAIL RESPONSE RESEARCH

Look at the decision process a reader goes through when opening a direct mail fundraising letter. This has been studied thoroughly. One master of the psychology behind direct mail fundraising packages is a German professor by the name of Siegfried Vogele. He has conducted extensive research, using equipment such as machines that measure skin chemistry and cameras that track eye movement to monitor people as they hold a fundraising letter in their hands.

Vogele maintains that you, the fundraising letter writer, have only a few seconds to engage the reader, starting with encouraging him or her to open the envelope in the first place. His research shows that those fundraisers who engage their reader in a dialogue, answering their questions in the letter, will be the most successful. As your potential donor opens the envelope, skims through the letter, and checks out the reply card, many questions range through her mind. If you skillfully answer them, you have hooked her. Here are some of the many questions that may flit through your reader's mind as he is perusing your fundraising letter, beginning with holding the envelope in his hands:

- Where is the letter from?

- Who wrote this letter?

- How do they know about me?

- Where did they get my address?

- Why are they writing?

- Should I open it?

- What do they want?

- Does it require action?

- Have I seen this before?

- Did my name get stuck on a mailing list?

- Should I just throw it away?

And those are just some of the questions that go through you donor's mind as he holds the envelope. Let us say he decides to open it. Here is the next round of questions:

- What is this organization?

- Have I heard of them?

- Have I given money to them before?

- Why do they need my help?

- What difference will my contribution make?

- Will I get many solicitations from them?

- Now will they expect money from me all the time?

- How much of this donation goes to people in need?

- How is this group different?

- How long have they existed?

- Are they local?

- Can I trust them?

- Does anyone famous support them?

- Is there a deadline?

- How easy is it to donate?

Leave these questions unanswered, and you will not get the donation. Now let us look at Vogele's research into what makes a reader reject your plea. He says there are four waves of rejection.

What Vogele calls the "first run-through" is the most important, because if your letter passes this test, you have a good chance of engaging the reader farther. However, the first run-through lasts only 20 seconds, and this includes opening the envelope, glancing at what is inside, and deciding whether to read farther. If the writer fails to engage the reader or prickle her curiosity, or does not manage to answer her initial questions, the letter will reach the recycling bin without another thought.

If you have managed to engage the reader, however, then you move onto wave two, and your chances of nabbing that donation have improved significantly. You are not out of the woods yet, however, so do not start celebrating. Now the donor reads more carefully, asking yet another set of questions in her head. In wave one, she just scanned the highlighted headlines. Now she is reading the beautiful words you wrote so laboriously. Will they induce her to action? Vogele says that if your copy manages to produce many little "yeses" as it is read, you have a good chance of reaching the final, big, yes.

However, next we reach wave three. So far, you have engaged the attention of your donor and gotten her interested in taking action. But here is another crucial point — does she take action immediately? Or, more likely, does she succumb to what Vogele calls the "filing-away or archive wave?" We love to procrastinate, and when we are opening mail at the end of a long day, the last thing on our mind is opening our checkbook in response to an appeal for money. Unfortunately, archiving your letter can be the kiss of death. Weeks later, when she comes upon your appeal again, she may wonder what she saw in it. Instead of a yes, you have gotten another no, and into the recycling bin the letter goes.

Wave four is what Vogele calls "putting to one side," which is subtly different from the archiving of wave three. It is all in the intention. If you have induced your reader to put aside your letter, rather than archive it, you have gotten them to resolve to respond. Maybe she does not want to sit down and write a check now, but will put the letter with her bills. Maybe she wants to wait until her next paycheck, when she has a bit more money to spare. The good news is that you have hooked her enough that her intentions are pure. The bad news is that 50 percent of letters that are "put to one side" are eventually thrown out.

The moral of Vogele's waves of rejection is clear: the faster you can engage your reader and get him or her to respond, the better chance you have of securing that donation. The first 20 seconds of his or her engagement with the mailing are crucial. The first phase of opening the envelope takes eight seconds. The second phase, looking at the contents of the envelope, takes four. The third phase, in which the reader scans headlines and highlighted text, takes another eight. You have those 20 seconds in which to accomplish your goal of getting the reader to read more of your copy, and ultimately, to get her to say yes to your donation.

Now that we understand the process a reader goes through in opening your letter, let us examine what will get her to read it. What are the main characteristics of a successful letter?

CHARACTERISTICS OF A SUCCESSFUL LETTER

- **A successful letter is personal.** It is not written by some vague, unidentifiable entity, or even an institution. They are written from one person to another, and they sound like it.

- **A successful letter offers a two-way exchange.** It gives the donor a chance to gain something in return for their support.

- **A successful letter moves the reader to action.** Period. If the letter does not accomplish this, it is not successful.

There are tried and true writing techniques that will set you on the right path.

THINK OPERA WHEN YOU GET STUCK

The first technique we will look at is one borrowed from professional copywriters. It is called the AIDA formula, and one easy way to remember it is to think opera — Aida, by Verdi, is one of the most famous operas ever composed. So if you are stuck while writing your fundraising letter, put a little opera music on. Maybe it will get you going again. It will at least remind you of the following formula:

- **A**ttention. You want to grab the reader's attention with an arresting opening, headline, or sub-headline. You might ask a compelling question, present a grabber of a story, or tell a joke.

- **I**nterest. Your letter must immediately arouse interest in the reader. You have grabbed them with a great headline or opener, now you need to hold their attention. Follow through with some gripping content. Show your donors why your letter is of pertinent interest to them.

- **D**esire. You must create in your potential donor a desire to respond. You can do this through listing product benefits, case studies, and testimonials. It is also done by offering the reader a chance to make a difference, which they can do easily and efficiently by responding to your letter.

- **A**ction. The A in our acronym stands for Action, or sometimes, Ask. But it does not matter which word you choose, the result is the same — you ask your reader to take action and he or she responds by writing a check, or filling out a form to charge a donation.

Before we move onto taking an in-depth look at every component of the fundraising letter package, it is important to continue on our examination of the common qualities of all successful appeals. Bear in mind that these qualities apply to every sort of fundraising letter that you will write, but there are many different types of fundraising letters, such as acquisition letters, special appeals, welcome packages, and thank-yous. We will go through all these different types in chapter eight, but for now, be aware that these content features are the hallmark of every type of letter. Master these techniques and you cannot go wrong.

QUALITIES OF SUCCESSFUL LETTERS

Personal, Please. Successful fundraising letters sound like you are writing to a friend or family member. You can sense a personality behind the pen. They are not dry, sterile, and boring. Good fundraising letters are conversational.

You and I. Your fundraising letter is from an individual, so make it sound that way. Various studies have shown that the use of the words *you* and *I* are the most powerful way to engage the reader because it appeals directly to him. Even though telling stories, relating anecdotes, and the use of common names have also proven to be effective, the use of *I* and *you*, particularly *you*, has the most impact.

We Know You are a Friend, But… A successful fundraising letter addresses the donor by name. *Dear friend* is out. Nothing turns off the donor faster than a form letter, especially one beginning, *dear friend*, when it is clear you are not friends.

Use Human Terms to State Your Case. Do not get bureaucratic and institutional. Make your need human. Donors do not give money to help institutions or organizations; they give money to help humans. For instance, do not say, "We are raising $20,000 for our capital fund," say, "We are raising money to provide ten artists with studio space on campus."

Always Ask For Money. This may seem obvious, but there is a temptation to ask for the ever-vague "support" rather than a specific dollar amount. Donors like to know exactly where their money is going to go. Tell them.

Ask Often. It no doubt goes against the grain, but the request needs to be repeated over and over again in your letter. People will not give unless they are asked, period, and it helps if they are asked repeatedly.

Benefits, Not Needs. Maybe we are a selfish species, but donors give money because they think they will get something in return. Maybe it will be only an emotional lift, but they want to feel they are getting something. Describe what they will get in return. Will they be feeding the hungry? Providing water to a child in Africa? Education to a deprived child? Helping to rebuild a home after an earthquake? Only break this rule in a genuine emergency.

Educate Them. When your donor is done reading your letter, he should understand the shape of the crisis, the needs of your organization, and how you help your constituents. Donors like to feel they know something about the causes they support.

Heart, Not Head. Even though you are educating them, do not forget to appeal to the heart. The head makes up reasons not to give. The heartstrings are tugged, and you have a donation.

Ponder the Package. The whole package counts, not just the letter. You need to consider the impact of the envelope, the reply card, and the reply envelope. We will talk more on this soon.

It is Not the King's English. Use good grammar, but go for the snappy over the sophisticated. You want it to sound punchy and emotional, not dry and distant.

Send Money Now. Or at least give your reader a reason to. It is very important to create a sense of urgency in your copy, without being phony. Do you have a deadline for a matching grant looming? Is important legislation being considered that you need to mobilize against? Is there some kind of budget deadline? Always tie your appeal to an upcoming deadline. It is too easy for donors to procrastinate. However, do not overuse this gambit. And be aware if you are using the bulk mail at the post office that it can take longer for your mail to be delivered, thus negating the effectiveness of this approach.

Format Your Letters. Nothing is worse for readability than big chunks of type with no "entry points," indentations, or spaces. Always indent paragraphs. Use bullet point lists when possible. Use subheads, and consider underlining or highlighting them.

Take as Long as You Need. Do not be afraid to write a long, informative letter. Some will read it carefully, though most will scan to get the pertinent details.

Now that you have some ideas on how you are going to approach your writing, look at all the components of the fundraising package. The package is really quite simple and practical. For starters, you will have the envelope and you will need to plan a design for that. Next is the letter itself, then some kind of reply card, and finally, a reply envelope. The entire package should feature one unified design and have an underlying theme that matches. You can look back at the work you did on your marketing concept to figure this out, and we will talk in much more detail about how to write each aspect of the package soon. First, let us look at each component, piece by piece.

THE ENVELOPE

Remember Vogele's waves of rejection? You have approximately eight seconds to convince a reader to actually open the envelope and get to your letter. It is for this reason that many experts consider the envelope to be the most important part of your fundraising package.

Sometimes called the carrier envelope, the outer envelope, or the mailing envelope, in order to distinguish it from the reply envelope, it is the vehicle that carries your fundraising letter into a home or office, and it is the first thing your potential donor will see. Thus, the outer envelope conveys the initial impression to your reader, and the way it is designed and the words that appear — or do not appear — on it will affect whether the envelope is opened or tossed in the trash.

Bypass this issue of an envelope and saving time and money by sending prospective donors a postcard, or even a flyer, is not a good idea. As we have mentioned, the effective fundraising appeal is an entire package, which also includes the letter, a reply card, and a reply envelope. Studies have shown that all these components are necessary for a successful campaign, therefore, anything less than an envelope containing these elements will be a waste of money. Bear in mind that postcards are even easier to ignore than a fat envelope, stuffed with information and maybe even some freebies.

Let us look at the kinds of competition your envelope faces in its quest to be opened. First, your prospective donor is busy. He has probably just arrived home after a long day's work, and he takes a quick glance at the mail before heading to the kitchen for a beer and a snack, or perhaps heading to the bedroom to change to get to the gym. Maybe your prospective donor is a young mother, looking through the mail after getting her toddler down for a nap because she feels she should. All she really wants is to take a nap herself. Unless your envelope is vitally compelling, odds are good that each of these prospective donors is going to lay the envelope aside.

Not only does your envelope face competition from you donor's busy schedule, that same batch of mail might contain solicitations from other charities or nonprofits. Most donors who support charities support more than one. This gives you opportunity, but it also gives you a challenge — how are you going to set your nonprofit apart and persuade your reader to put your organization on his list to support? Also, since much of our mail falls into either the bills category or the junk mail category, it is easy to classify a fundraising appeal with the latter and pitch it. Most readers are trained to watch out for bills in their daily mail and little more, since so few of us receive personal letters.

Equally important is the competition from other media. There are telephone callers asking for money, door-to-door canvassers, and even telethons on television or radio. There are also Web sites asking for donations to various causes. This account only details the fundraising pitches your donor is exposed to, which he does not actively invite into his home. We have not even yet mentioned the fact that he or she often just wants to set the mail aside without looking at it and go plunk down in front of the television or the computer.

The benefits of writing and designing an envelope that readers rip open are many, starting with the obvious fact that if your reader does not open the envelope, you have no chance of getting a donation. If he does open the envelope, at least you have some chance. With well-written envelope copy, you accomplish several goals at once. You will boost your response rate, reduce your cost to receive a gift, improve renewal rates, and reduce the number of your letters that are thrown away without even being opened. That little envelope carries a lot of responsibility on its shoulders. In truth, while many fundraisers write "teaser" copy on the outer envelope, some schools of thought hold that this is not even necessary, and in some cases, might be a distraction. The job of figuring out the envelope might fall as much to design and style as writing. If you are confused about how to design an effective envelope that compels donors to open it, do not worry. In the section on content, or how-to, we will give you tips and techniques for designing an effective carrier envelope for your fundraising letter.

Besides carrying the responsibility of encouraging the recipient to open your letter, the outer envelope also performs another important and very basic task. It must get your letter and the accompanying enclosures to your prospective donors with the contents intact. This fact can affect the design decisions you will eventually make, and we will touch upon it in more depth in the upcoming section on content.

THE LETTER

The standard letter format is, of course, 8 ½ by 11 inches, and in nearly all cases this is the size you will select for your design. There may be times when you will want to choose a slightly different size for effect. Monarch size, which is 7 by 10 inches, feels more like personal stationery, and thus it might be used when you want to evoke a more personal feel. The letter may vary in length from one page to a multi-page missive, and it can be one-sided or two-sided. As you might guess, there is a variety of opinions on which of these options is the most effective, which is a subject that will be covered in the content chapter. The most important thing to remember is that a fundraising package contains a fundraising letter. No, you cannot throw in your latest newsletter and call it good. Neither can you use the brochure you developed for clients, or any other piece of copy you might have. A fundraising package contains a fundraising letter, period.

THE REPLY DEVICE

You need to include a reply device, which is some kind of form on which the donor can write their information and make a donation. This can be full sheet of paper, or a half-size sheet. It can be printed on card stock or some other thicker paper, in order to make it less easy to lose. You might see the reply device referred to as a coupon or a reply coupon or a memorandum. Whatever name you decide to call it, the reply device is vitally important, because the donor will look for it for guidance as to how much to send and how to send it. This can be by check or credit card, and your reply device will contain all that information. Some reply devices also invite donors to visit the organization's Web site for an easy way to donate.

REPLY ENVELOPE

You want your donors to send you money, because that is the point of the fundraising package, right? In order for them to accomplish this, you will need a reply envelope. It is usually a little bit smaller than the outer envelope, so that it fits inside it easily, and it will be addressed. Many organizations will also include postage on the reply envelope. However you decide to design it, a reply envelope is an integral part of the overall package.

OPTIONAL EXTRAS

The outer envelope, letter, reply device, and reply envelope are the core essentials of every successful fundraising package. You might want to include a few of the following extras, too. Consider each of these extras as a part of your marketing concept for the package in order to decide whether they will fit.

BUCKSLIP

The "buckslip" is a piece of paper that is often configured in the size of a dollar bill, or a buck. The buckslip is included with all of your other enclosures, and it is your chance to write a bit extra. Do you have a planned giving program you would like to promote? Or do you want to encourage a monthly membership? These are ideal uses of the buckslip. You can also use it to feature testimonials, detail the way you spend your funds, or show off a celebrity sponsor. The uses of the buckslip are many, and it can be very effective as a boost to your message. While the buckslip should be designed to coordinate with your overall package, you can have copy printed on one side of it or both, you can use color or black and white text, and you can use photos or images or not. Despite the cost of printing an extra slip of paper, with certain design choices the buckslip can be an inexpensive way to add luster to your message.

FREEBIES OR FRONT-END PREMIUMS

Alan Sharpe calls these "freemiums," which is an acronym of free and premium. Some fundraisers have been using the front-end premium with great results for years. Think the Christmas address stickers that a variety of organizations send out. Some even send out Christmas cards as front-end premiums. One organization devoted to the welfare of Native American children sent out small Dream catchers that could be used on a key ring. A freebie is included as part of the fundraising package and requires no action on the part of the recipient. They can be very persuasive, if only because of the guilt effect. If you receive a package of Christmas address labels and begin using them, does it not make you feel at least a little bad that you have not contributed some money to the people who sent them to you? This basic fact of human psychology is the idea behind many freemiums.

How to choose what sort of front-end premium you will include in your fundraising package? Here are some guidelines:

- **It is a Free Gift!** Nothing more, nothing less. Even though the idea is, of course, that you would like the recipient to send money (see the guilt effect above) it is important to emphasize that your front-end premium is a gift with no strings attached. Remember that the word free works like magic in direct mail, as consumers have been conditioned to react positively to it. Who would not? We all love the idea that there is still a free lunch. Whatever you do, do not imply that the potential donor must contribute simply because you gave her a gift. It is free.

- **Make Connections.** Your front-end premiums need to have some connection with your organization and the text of the letter. The Dream catcher example mentioned above is a good example, as it has immediate symbolic and visual connections to the organization. Museums may include small reproductions of pieces from their collection or a literacy organization may send a small free pencil or bookmark.

- **Three-Dimensional Bulk is Good.** It may seem counter-intuitive, since adding additional weight will cost you more in postage, but front-end premiums that have some heft to them have proven to be very effective in getting recipients to open the envelope. Just think how you feel when you get an envelope with some heft to it. Are you not eager to open it and see what is inside? This is especially true if the words "Free Gift" appear somewhere on the envelope. Examples of freebies that create bulk are address labels, small books, rulers, or sets of cards. One organization even sent out packets of seeds to signify that donations "seeded" their activities. Use your imagination to come up with ideas.

- **Think Long Life.** Some front-end premiums end up working very hard for their organizations by keeping its name in front of the donor for lengthy periods. This works by using freebies that the recipient will want to keep around. Premiums such as calendars, address labels, or pens can all serve this purpose. Every time your prospective donor uses the freebie you have chosen, it is another chance for them to see you name and think about your nonprofit.

PREMIUMS OR BACK-END PREMIUMS

So how does a back-end premium differ from a front-end

premium? While a front-end premium arrives with the fundraising letter package, the back-end premium is an enticement to get the recipient to donate. Back-end premiums tend to be of higher value than the freebies offered up front. Think T-shirts, tote bags, or DVDs, to name a few time-honored favorites. Back-end premiums give a value-added benefit to the donor. Not only does she get to feel good by donating to your cause, she also gets a special book or other item. Here are some guidelines that will help you choose back-end premiums:

- **Link to Your Cause.** As with front-end premiums, some sort of connection to your organization is essential for an effective back-end premium. For instance, PBS is a master at this, offering back-end premiums such as DVDs of favorite programs during their fundraising drives. They also offer packages, which might include a DVD, a tote bag, and a T-shirt and bumper sticker, or other such combinations. Back-end premiums can be useful for garnering repeat donors if they are linked to your cause.

- **Tell Them Early.** Mention the back-end premium as soon as possible in your fundraising letter. We will discuss this more thoroughly when we get to the chapter on various types of fundraising letters, but it bears mentioning here. Let the donor know early on that you are offering him a desirable premium and you will have his attention from the outset.

- **Think Exclusive.** If your back-end premium is available all over the Internet and in retail stores, it will not be much of an enticement. However, if you can offer your potential donor something she cannot find anywhere else, she will be more inclined to send you money. A tote bag emblazoned with your organization's attractive logo is a useful one-of-a-kind premium, for instance.

- **Make Fulfillment Easy.** A small glass ornament may be the perfect premium to send from your small art-and-craft college, but not if it is impossible to ship to donors without breaking. Make certain that your back-end premium will be easy and relatively inexpensive to ship.

LIFT LETTER, OR LIFTNOTE

The lift letter is an enclosure that is so named because they are designed to lift response. It has become a standard fixture in many direct mailings today. You are familiar with the lift letter. It is the envelope that reads, "Please read this if you have decided not to donate today," or something along those lines. Inside is a letter from someone other than the person who signed the main fundraising appeal. The lift letter was first used in the publishing industry as a plea to people to subscribe. Its success in the publishing world has caused it to be picked up in the nonprofit arena as well. Think creatively when it comes time to write the lift letter. You might want to include a heartfelt plea from your executive director, or testimonials from people who have been helped by your program. You will find specific examples and more ideas for lift letters in a future chapter.

BROCHURE

Some fundraising experts will advise you to include a brochure about your organization; others will tell you to avoid it at all costs. The best advice you can heed is to test your results when using a brochure and when not using one. However, if you have to make a decision without the luxury of time and money to test the best outcome, you will want to fall on the side of not including the brochure. It is going to cost more money, both in printing and postage, and if its eventual efficiency is in doubt, there is little reason to use it.

SURVEY OR QUESTIONNAIRE

This extra works on the time-honored policy of giving your donors something to do. People like to be engaged and active.   These are sometimes called involvement devices because they involve your potential donor.   Other involvement devices include petitions to sign or postcards to mail to your Congressman or representative.

Now that you have a good idea of the possibilities for what to include as enclosures, it is time to turn to the meat of the topic and take a good strong look at content of fundraising letters. First, review some guidelines, and then, in the following chapter, you will take an in-depth look at types of fundraising letters and how to write them.

CASE STUDY: FLOYD CRAIG

Floyd Craig- President and Senior Consultant,

Craig Communications

FACraig@aol.com

3188 Boxley Valley Rd.

Franklin, TN   3706

As president and senior consultant of my own communication firm, I write several fundraising letters a year. I've been working in the nonprofit arena for 45 years and I've written all kinds of fundraising letters through the years.

I've learned that the more a writer knows about the dreams and goals of the clients, and the more one can know about the audience, the better the outcome. When I've had fundraising letters that weren't as successful, it was often because the timing was off. The appeals were sent either too early or too late, or sometimes it was because there was not sufficient time for me to get to know the client and/or the audience.

When I begin working on a fundraising letter, I first want to see all past appeals, including the letter, enclosures, envelopes (outgoing and incoming), the follow-up letters, responses, mailing schedules (first, second, third mailings), type of postage, etc. I also look at what other promotion was done during the appeals, and I arrange a face-to-face meeting with the CEO or president of the organization. The most important tip to write a successful fundraising letter is to know the audience, and speak with, not to, the readers. One good way to do this is to picture in your mind a single prospective donor and write to them. Also, don't forget the P.S.! As for what not to do, don't forget those who will receive the appeal! And don't worry about writing long. If the writing and content of the letter is great, two or three pages should not be ruled out.

The entire fundraising package is very important.   Always remember that first impressions must communicate being "personal." All of the details of the package are important, and oversight of the printing and mailing is vital. For the fundraising letter itself, the best advice is to rewrite, rewrite, rewrite! After you have finished the first draft ask three or four of those who would be part of the audience to read it out loud to you. And then, once again, rewrite, rewrite, rewrite!

CASE STUDY: FLOYD CRAIG

The best source of ideas is reading other appeal letters. Every direct mail item I receive I study. For years, I have collected appeals from all different categories from capital fund raising to ongoing alumni support and I've done research on all the mail I received. This helps to spark ideas. By the way, just because I liked an appeal does not always mean it will work.

I also ask business associates what has worked for them and what has bombed. One of the most successful appeals I ever did was handwritten by a "retired person" and was hard to read. Types of appeals change from year to year but I always try to remember that folks respond to appeals for basically two reasons—to get a benefit they want and to protect a benefit they already have.

Content of Fundraising Letters

I t is time to get to the significant part, and that is the actual content of the letters you will be writing. Begin by looking at some of the techniques professionals use to produce successful fundraising letter packages.

First, writing successful fundraising letters is not about writing award-winning literary prose. It is, however, about writing clearly and simply and in a friendly, colloquial manner. Many people think that fundraising letters need to be written in a dry, official manner in order to highlight the organization's seriousness. Nothing could be further from the truth. Study the following guidelines for effective writing and learn to utilize them in every letter that you create.

GUIDELINES FOR EFFECTIVE LETTER WRITING

1. **Write the Way You Speak.** This is the number one most important technique for writing effective fundraising letter. Strive to write and structure your letter in a natural, flowing manner that mimics actual speech.

The idea here is that you are carrying on an actual conversation with your potential donors. You want to engage them the way an actual conversation would, not put them to sleep like a dull, boring lecture from their college days. Think about the way you would write an e-mail to a friend, or the style in which you pen a letter to a family member. Strive to write in such a personal style. This is easy to say, and yet harder to achieve if you have been trained to write in an academic, legal, or business style. The following considerations will help to keep you on track.

- **Use you and I.** Remember, the fundraising letter is a conversation, and what is a conversation? It is an exchange between two people. Your conversation takes the form of an appeal. This makes it even more important to be friendly and readable. Studies have shown that the use of the word you is the most effective technique at creating interest and readability. What using you repeatedly does is switch the focus of the conversation from the organization to the donor. We will take this a step farther in the segment on donor-centered copy.

- **Use Contractions.** Yes, we know that you were taught that proper English never uses contractions, but we are writing conversational English here. In informal, spoken English, we use contractions. Rarely would anyone say, "I am going to the store." Instead, you say, "I'm going to the store now." The same is true with contractions such as you're, don't, and can't. If in doubt, say your words aloud in a sentence to hear what flows in a natural speech pattern. If you are really in doubt, use a contraction. Trust us. It's friendlier.

- **Use colloquialisms.** Those who you who took many English classes are really squirming now. However, the rules of copywriting are very different from the rules of Standard English. Remember, we are writing for results here. We are writing for a donation, not a prize for correct grammar. Thus, we want to use everyday language, and specifically, everyday patterns of speech. Remember, your goal is to mimic a personal letter or an exchange with a friend here. So, go for it — do not be afraid to use a colloquialism in your fundraising letter.

- **Use simple sentence structure.** By simple, we do not necessarily mean correct in the traditional manner of every sentence containing a subject, verb, and predicate. No, in copywriting, fragments and sentences that break the rules are okay, as long as they result in a natural-sounding flow. Good copywriting sentences are short. They are also to the point.

- **Use italics and underlining.** Okay, so obviously we do not speak in italics and with underlining. But, wait a minute. Perhaps we do. Italics and underlining are traditionally used to emphasize a word or phrase. When we speak, we use tonal variation to emphasize one word over another. Using italics and underlining can help you to mimic a natural flow. Do not be afraid to use italics.

2. **Write to Your Reader's Point of View.** So, you have sat through one or two meetings during your time as a fundraiser, right? In those meetings you have probably tossed around a bit of nonprofit lingo, right? After a few years or even months in the nonprofit world terms like mission statement, case study, and constituent readily roll off your tongue. That is fine. But confine those words to the fundraising meetings with your peers. There is no faster way to turn off a potential donor than to indulge in bureaucratic-ese. Save the lingo. Put yourself in your donor's mind and write accordingly.

3. **Let it Rip!** Ask any professional writer about their process and odds are good they will tell you the most important thing is to allow yourself to write a really awful first draft. The novels, articles, and professionally written copy you read in print or on the Internet did not come out of the author's brain fully formed. No, the professional writer knows the value of writing multiple drafts. The trick is to get something, anything, down on paper. Then you have raw treasure to work with.

4. **Learn to Edit Yourself Effectively.** Once you have digested all the information in this chapter, you might want to create a checklist to follow as an editing guide. This can serve as a handy reminder of things you want to look at before you send the letter out. You will want to include the following.

   • **Simple sentences.** We discussed using simple sentences in the segment on writing in a conversational style. It is easy to get caught up in your message and forget this. After you have written your letter copy, scan it for sentence length. See if there are sentences that can be broken down into component parts. Simplify, simplify, simplify.

- **Passive voice.** Successful fundraising letters are written in active voice. You want your donor to act, not be acted upon. You yourself want to act, not be acted upon. Thus, "a total of 500 meals were served by our organization," becomes "We served a total of 500 meals." If in doubt, the easiest way to avoid passive is to start with the subject.

- **Extra words.** Do not be wordy. Wordiness detracts from your message and makes it difficult for the reader to grasp what you are saying. Go through your copy and edit it for extra words. Now do it again.

- **Clichés & Metaphors.** In Standard English, clichés are bad and metaphors are good. We are going to turn that advice on its head here. While we do not advise overdoing the clichés, judicious use of them can add to the conversational tone of your copy. The reason clichés are clichés is that they work. They are shorthand for expressing common sentiment. A well-chosen cliché can put instantly put you on the same page as your donor. Conversely, most metaphors belong in novels or short stories. In a fundraising letter, a metaphor or simile will sound forced.

- **Humor.** Use it sparingly. What is funny to one man might not be funny at all to the next. What makes one woman double over in laughter might leave her friend puzzled. It is also very easy to offend accidentally when using humor. Be wary.

5. **Study Good Writing.** Professional copywriters maintain what they refer to as Cheat Sheets. This is nothing more than a file full of effective copywriting or other admired pieces of writing. Perhaps there is a particular turn of phrase that you admired, or a stellar opening sentence. Stash the letter in your cheat file and emulate it on your next fundraising letter. Every fundraising letter writer should also have a couple of indispensable references on their bookshelf. The old standard, and still the favorite, is Strunk and White, which comes in at under 100 pages and will teach you everything you need to know about the rules of good writing. Check the bibliography page for specific information and other suggestions.

Now that you have learned a little about how to write effectively, it is time to look at what you will write about it. We will go into the process of writing a letter step by step in just a bit, but first let us look at some general guidelines:

Write About People. Do not tell your reader about the program that teaches young mothers how to parent effectively, tell them about the mothers and how the program helps them. You may specifically need money to print the manuals these young mothers read, but you will get your donor excited by writing about the mother who will use this manual. Alan Sharpe says it simply: "Donors give to people, not to programs." Always remember to state your needs in human terms. Your donor is a person who wants to help another person. Tell him how his donation will accomplish that, not how it is going to pay for a new roof. To this end, Alan Sharpe recommends asking yourself the following questions:

- What is the client's need?

- What do we lack to meet that need?

- How will the client benefit once the need is met?

For instance, if you need money for a new roof to replace the leaky one that currently covers your soup kitchen, you might answer the questions as follows:

- The client needs a warm, dry place to eat a nourishing meal.

- We lack a warm, dry place because the roof leaks.

- With a new roof, the client has a warm, dry place to get off the street and eat a meal.

In your copy, you would emphasize how your homeless clients spend most of their time outdoors, and much of it hungry. You provide them with not only a warm meal, but a warm place to eat it, and somewhere to go for at least a brief time to take a break from the streets. But because of the leaky roof, or the general disrepair of your building, or the lack of money in your general fund, you are unable to serve the needs of your client. Always, always, always tie the appeal back to the person you are helping.

Write Donor-Centered Copy. What you, the fundraiser, need to do is learn why donors give and then give them that reason. The result will be a donation. This is why your letters need to appeal primarily to your donor's needs, not yours. Some simple re-thinking and re-phrasing will do the trick. If your nonprofit runs a soup kitchen, for instance, your first inclination may be to write something along the lines of, "We feed homeless people a warm, nourishing breakfast five days a week." However, it would be much better — and far more donor-centered — to write, "You can feed a homeless person a warm meal by sending us a donation." Another common fundraising ploy is to use the word help. This might result in a sentence such as "Help us save the whales." Instead, a donor-centered letter would say, "You can help save the whales by sending money today." See how simple the restructuring can be, and what a difference it makes?

Make It Relevant. You need to make your message relevant to your donor. Your donor has a lot of competition for her attention. You need to make your message interesting, and you need to make it mean something to her. When what matters to her and what matters to you match up, you have yourself a donation. Expert Alan Sharpe says it is important to "speak to the donors where they are now." He gives the example of diabetes. Nearly everyone knows someone who has diabetes, he points out, and many people might be severely impacted by a family member or other loved one who has the disease. Yet a major organization sends out fundraising letters citing the "two million people" who have diabetes. How much more effective those letters would be if they made the disease relevant to potential donors by personalizing it.

Hit Their Emotions. Writing fundraising letters is all about appealing to the heart first and the mind second. First, you want to engender feelings of compassion, empathy, and altruism. Then you want to inform them about your activities. Use your heart, then your mind. It is important to appeal to both. Your donor may feel an emotional tug toward your organization, but if you do not give them logical reasons to donate, you have lost the "sale." The logical, rational brain of your donors will appreciate the information you give them about tax deductions, how much of the gift goes to cover administrative costs and how much to programs, and any other rationales you can muster to support your cause.

Use Quotations. Let someone else do the talking, at least for a line or two. Do not overlook the power of using a quotation, which can inspire and motivate. Quotations become noted and repeated quotations in much the same way that clichés become clichés — because they are appreciated and valued enough to be repeated. You can search through quotation books or numerous online resources for quotes on a particular topic. Be sure always to use the name of the person along with the quote. Quotations add color, and they can add humor or pathos to your letters. They lend authority to your words.

Use Testimonials. Another way to let some other people do the talking is to use testimonials. These can be gleaned from comments made by volunteers, staff, or clients, either spoken or written. The testimonial can put words of praise into the mouths of people from whom it will mean the most, such as people your nonprofit has helped. You can use testimonials all throughout your fundraising package, including the envelope, as the first line of the letter, as a headline or subhead in the letter, or on the reply device. Testimonials are appropriate and effective to use nearly anywhere.

Emphasize Benefits. As we have pointed out elsewhere, donors become motivated to give money when they feel they will get something in return. That something might be warm, fuzzy feelings about having contributed, it might be a tangible premium, such as a tote bag, or it might be both. Many donors would like to think they give money only for altruistic reasons, but it simply is not true. So instead of emphasizing how much you need, think about emphasizing how much they will benefit.

Talk About Past Gifts. Along the same lines, a powerful motivator can be for the donor to see how past gifts have made a noticeable difference. Tell a story about how the money they sent last time contributed. For instance, how many extra meals were you able to serve? Showing donations in action can make a donor feel useful and good, and that, as we have seen, can motivate them to send more money. The one time you probably do not want to do this is when you are sending an emergency appeal letter.

Ask For Money. Well, of course you are going to ask for money, you say. However, you would be surprised how many people are tempted to ask for the more vague, less direct, "support" in their letters. Be clear in what you are requesting, and repeat your request often throughout the letter. Remember the reason you are writing the letter is to ask for money, period. The one time to go easy on the money emphasis is during a membership campaign.

Give Reason to Send Money Now. It is important to create a sense of urgency in your fundraising letter. This can be a challenge, granted. Do not make up a silly, sham reason, but work to find a genuine one. Do you have a budget deadline looming or a deadline for a matching grant? Can you tie your appeal to an external or societal event such as an upcoming election? Is there a special holiday that will increase your needs approaching? Your soup kitchen will want to serve an extra-special meal on Thanksgiving and Christmas, for instance. You can also create urgency through the premiums you offer by emphasizing that the supply is limited.

Write as Long as You Need To. Do not be afraid to write long letters. Yes, people tend to have shorter attention spans these days and we have already seen that competition for attention is fierce. But those people who are not inclined to read a long letter will scan the headlines and sub-heads, or maybe read a P.S. Yet others will sit down and read every word, as you repeat your argument for donation. Remember, you want to answer all their questions and give them no reason not to donate.

Format Letter for Easy Reading. Successful fundraising letters give the reader a way into the copy with indented paragraphs, bullet points, and headlines and sub-heads that are centered and underlined. In this way, both careful readers and scanners can find the information they seek. It is also important to keep paragraphs short. If you must write a lengthy paragraph, make sure you indent it, and set it off with a headline that is highlighted in some way.

WRITE YOUR LETTER, STEP BY STEP

Now that you have read and digested the general guidelines of successful fundraising letter writing, it is time to get down to it and actually write a letter. This section will give you advice on how to approach the task, going systematically through the various parts of a fundraising letter. We have referred to writing headlines and sub-heads and using testimonials and asking for the gift. Now, it probably all sounds like an alien language to you, but never fear, by the time you finish this section you should be able to draft a basic fundraising letter.

Remember back in the previous chapters when we discussed marketing and talked about developing the marketing concept? Now is the time to pull that out and review it. Do your ideas for the overall theme of the letter still seem to work? Have you had more thoughts since you wrote it? Review the marketing concept and see where you stand. If it is not already committed to paper, now is the time to write it down. Decide on your overall theme and be sure to note the following:

- What kind of letter is it?

- What amount of money will you be asking for?

- What will you do with this money?

- Who will sign the letter and be its voice?

- Is your request time sensitive?

- What organization successes or programs will you include?

- Are you offering premiums or donor involvement devices?

- What will the package include?

- What will the package look like?

Once you have answered these questions on paper, you are ready to begin.

STEP-BY-STEP: THE OUTER ENVELOPE

Are you surprised that we will be starting with the outer envelope? Should we not write the letter first, so we know what is inside the envelope? The answer is no. Most experts advise beginning with the envelope. Consider what we have learned about the outer envelope and its importance: if your potential donor does not open it, your letter will not be read, period. So it is vital to take some time and ponder the envelope copy, if any, first.

You have a matter of seconds while your reader sorts his mail and briefly holds the envelope in his hands. Should he recycle it, read it later, or open it? All he has to go on to make his decision is the appearance of and the words on the envelope he holds in his hands. Here are some ideas for ways to ensure the envelope is opened.

Make it Look Unusual. Fundraisers often use either over-sized or under-sized (such as the Monarch) envelopes so that they will stand out in the crowd of mail you receive each day in your mailbox. You might consider using an unusual paper. Instead of white, think of a color that reflects your organization. Use recycled paper, which can be very thematic for environmental groups. Also, consider if you will want to use a window envelope, which looks more business-like, or a closed-face. Some groups have even used envelopes with two window faces, which really make a statement!

The Personal Letter. This is the anti-copy approach. Instead of coming up with a clever teaser line or other come-on, you do not write anything on the envelope. Instead, you design it to look like a personal letter from a friend. This is arguably less effective in these days of the Internet when very few people receive or expect personal letters. However, it is still a common approach.

The Clock is Ticking. The use of a deadline can be very effective. However, remember to keep the deadline focused on the benefit for the donor, not on the benefit for you. Copy along the lines of, "We need you to reply by June 1st" will not be particularly effective. The reader will probably shrug and toss the envelope in the recycling container. After all, what is in it for him? However, copy that says, "Grab your free T-shirt by June 1st" may well motivate her to open up the envelope.

Tell a story. Well, you will not be able to tell a whole story on the outer envelope, obviously, but you will be able to begin one. We humans are hard-wired to not only tell but also to read stories. Starting a story on the outer envelope is often an irresistible teaser. Use a provocative image or beginning words of a story. Here is a hint: stories begin with conflict. Therefore, for instance, an outer envelope for your soup kitchen might show a photograph of a client with the quote, "My hunger was a living, growing thing, until..." The reader must open the envelope to discover the "until." A disaster relief agency might use a teaser along these lines: "We didn't even have time to run." Accompanied by a picture of a ruined home, this would be a strong lure. The reader wants to know, who did not have time? Why did they need to run? Was their house ruined? What happened? The "what happened?" is the most powerful question a storyteller can evoke. It is deeply ingrained in us to want to know the answer to that question. If you can evoke it on the outer envelope, you will have people ripping it open to read more.

Riddle Me This. Present a mystery to your readers on the envelope. Get them scratching their heads to figure out what your teaser copy means, and you will have them ripping open the envelope. To do this, start by stating a fact about your organization and then turn it around to create a paradox. Think along the lines of old moral sayings such as "it is better to give than receive," which play to the benefit the donor will receive.

Curiosity Opened the Envelope. Are you offering a premium or a freebie inside? Tease the reader with a bit of information about it on the outer envelope. An organization offering free pens or pencils might say, "What will you draw with the pencil inside?" Or perhaps your soup kitchen has decided to include a free recipe for soup. You might write the following on the envelope: "Who will you feed with the free recipe inside?"

Write On Both Sides. You can also use both sides of the envelope, starting your teaser copy on one side and continuing on the back. Used with arresting images, this can be very effective at getting readers to open that envelope.

Postage Counts. Carefully consider what kind of postage you will use. The postal indicia are printed on the envelope along with the teaser and the image. It presents an official image and indicates you have used bulk mail. Think about what kind of image you are presenting and if this is part of it. If you are going for a friendly, community type feel, you probably do not want to use the indicia. However, if budget is a concern, it will save you time and money. You can also use metered postage, which has a very business-oriented feel to it. Meters have the option of dates, which adds urgency, and some even allow you to add a line of copy. This can make it look less business-like and friendlier. Finally, there is the good old-fashioned stamp. Any direct mail expert will tell you that a postage stamp raises response rates. Why? It is the human element. Stamps just look more personal and friendly. Truth to tell, they are, because someone has taken the time to actually place the stamp on the envelope, rather than running it through a machine. Choose a commemorative stamp or some other special stamp that reflects your organization. Some experts even recommend using multiple stamps. The theory on this is that they are eye-catching to the potential donor.

REPLY DEVICE AND REPLY ENVELOPE

While you might be eager to get onto writing the letter, take a few minutes to begin roughing out the reply device. This is not going to take you nearly as long as writing the letter itself, so you might as well get it out of the way. In addition, it is on the reply device that you will be writing out the various levels of donation. As you figure these out and write them down, you may come up with more ideas to add to your letter. Moreover, it is an excellent idea to have all of this information firmly in mind as you write the letter. You will need to know whether you are asking for a small donation or a large donation and what the different levels of giving are in between. All of this information will figure into the letter that you write. Remember to keep the reply device in line with the overall marketing concept you have planned. If you have decided on recycled paper for the outer envelope, you will probably want to use it for the reply device and the reply envelope as well. Writing the reply envelope will be straightforward. You will not need to worry about teaser lines or arresting images, because your outer envelope has already done all the hard work of getting your reader to open it. All you will need on the reply envelope is the name and address of your organization, though it is an excellent idea to check that you have all of that information correct. You do not want all of your donations going to the wrong address!

THE LETTER, STEP BY STEP

Okay, now the hard work — and the fun — begins. Sharpen your pencil, make certain your pen has lots of ink, or open a file on the computer. Close the door and tell your secretary you will not be taking any calls. Now, consider, first, the overline.

The Overline

What, you might be asking, is the overline? Think of it as a headline. It is the sentence that will appear above the salutation, and, like all headlines, it needs to be succinct and attention getting at the same time. The one and only goal of the overline is simple: it exists to get your potential donors to keep reading your letter.

Not all letter-writers utilize the overline. Writing an overline is optional, and dependent on the preferences of the organization. Some fundraising letter-writing experts swear by the use of an overline, and others never bother. Study the following ideas for writing an overline, and review your marketing concept to decide whether you will use one or not.

Something else that will help you make a decision is to look at what others have done. Open your cheat sheet file and look at some of the fundraising letters you have collected. (You can also refer to the sample letters in the next chapter of this book.) Some will have an overline and others will not. On the letters that do use one, read it carefully. Does it compel you to keep reading, or does it feel like more wordiness to wade through before you get to the point? Would the letter have been better off without the overline? Do you like the look of a letter with an overline? Answering these questions according to your own personal preferences should aid you in deciding whether to use a headline or not.

Let us say you have decided that you want an overline on your letter. Now all you have to do is write a knockout sentence that will grab your donor and propel them into the letter. The following ideas may help you do this.

Use a Handwritten Overline. Go back to your sample letter file. One trick you may have noticed in other fundraising letters is the use of a hand-written overline. This gives the appearance of someone from the organization having had a last minute thought and scrawling a note on the letter before it went in the mail. A conceit, for sure, but an effective one. This technique increases the personal feeling of your letter. A highly effective technique is to get the signer of the letter to handwrite the overline, and include their initials. "We need your help," "We're counting on your," or "Please read about how you can make a difference" are all overlines that can compel your reader to keep reading. This leads us to the next point.

Keep 'em Reading. Yes, we know, it is not that easy, but there are tried-and-true techniques to aid you in this. Think about when you sit down with a novel or a book. What keeps you turning pages? Odds are good you are seeking an answer to a question. What will happen next? This is the fine art of creating suspense, and you can utilize it in your letter writing. Think in terms of telling a story, and remember the most important element of story is conflict. By hinting at a conflict, you can entice your reader to keep reading. You have conflict inherent in your organization because you exist to fill a need that is not being met elsewhere. The hungry homeless man and the pregnant teacher both have big problems — conflict. Begin by thinking about conflict as the basis of presenting a story now and you will have a head start on writing the body of the letter copy. The key to keep readers guessing is to withhold information. Do not tell them everything upfront. Give them a teaser line that will compel them to read further on into the letter. For starters, here are some specific ways to do this in your overline.

1. **Pose a Question.** Do you know what it is like to feel true hunger?

2. **State a Paradox.** We live in the wealthiest country in the world, yet hundreds go hungry every day.

3. **Begin a Story.** She was so weak and hungry she did not think she could survive any longer.

4. **Use a Predicament.** She needed food for her hungry children, but she had no money.

Your Overline Can Be Linked to the Envelope Teaser. This is a powerful technique. You might pose a question or a paradox on the envelope, for instance, and then answer it in the overline, being careful to leave an opening so that donors will read further. While this can be very effective, there are a couple of things you need to watch out for. First, bear in mind that the envelope teaser is just that — a tease to get the donor to open it and read further. If you engage their curiosity with the envelope teaser and then immediately satisfy it with the overline, they will not read any further. If you have asked a question on the envelope, for example, and then fully answer it in the overline, there will be no reason for anyone to read the letter. Also, bear in mind that the donor may hang onto the letter to act upon later, but odds are good that he has recycled the envelope. If he re-reads your letter a few days later, ready to act, but the overline makes no sense without the envelope teaser, you may lose the donation.

Note It! Another technique that experts say works wonders is the use of the Post-it Note. Your mailing house can affix these to the top of the letter for you in a cost-effective way. Use the same principles we have already discussed to write an overline, only write it on the Post-it Note that will adhere to the top of the letter. You will want to hand-write this note, preferably using the same person who signed the letter and the same ink. This increases the feeling that the donor is receiving a personal appeal and can be very powerful. Because the Post-It Note will be a different color, it is visually arresting and will more easily catch the reader's eye. Be certain you have a compelling overline to propel them further.

The Date

When writing a fundraising letter, you must consider every single word that you put on the paper. Decisions must be made every step of the way, and this includes what date you will use. Seems like such a simple thing, but the way you choose to write the date can make the difference between setting a personal or impersonal tone. Many copywriters go for a general personal tone by simply naming the day: Wednesday. Some go a step further by also stating the time of day: Wednesday afternoon. Both of these convey a sense of personal warmth, as if the president of the organization has closed his office door and sat down at his desk to write you a letter personally.

How to Write the Date. Alan Sharpe goes even further and makes a distinction between the ways the date is written. If you use all numerals, such as 03/08/10, for instance, he says this immediately conveys the impression the letter was generated by a machine. It can also be confusing if you have Canadian donors, who transpose the numbers in the European style. Readers in the United States will read the above date as March 8th, while Canadian readers will read it as August 3rd. Another impersonal date is to use the month and the year, as in March 2010. Adding a date to this makes it a bit more personal, such as March 3, 2010. To make it yet more personal, try adding the day and the date, such as Tuesday, March 3, 2010. Sharpe says this increases the personal feel because of the way we communicate about days. For instance, you might tell someone you left him or her a message last Wednesday, or that you e-mailed him or her on Friday. Finally, the most personal of all the uses of dates is to add not only the day, but also the time of day, such as Tuesday morning, March 3, 2010. Little changes like this can make a huge difference in how your fundraising letter is perceived.

The Salutation

Many copywriting experts rant and rave about the use of the words "dear friend." They will tell you that the single most important thing to remember about the salutation is to never, ever use the words dear friend. You do not write an e-mail or a letter to a friend and address it "dear friend," do you? Of course not. Using a salutation of "dear friend" is a sure sign that you using bulk mail, and it is impersonal to boot. This can create some difficulties because what if you cannot afford to personalize your letters and are using bulk mail? Some fundraising letter-writing experts would go so far as to suggest that the extra cost of personalizing letters will be more than made up for with the boost in your return rate. This is something to consider. If you are absolutely adamant in using bulk mail, you will need to find ways to make "dear friend" sound less impersonal. One way around it is to add more to it. If you are doing a local mailing, for instance, you can use "dear friend and neighbor," which gives your letter more of a community feel. You can also add a phrase that makes them special. For instance, "dear friend and art lover," or, "dear friend and supporter of the arts." If you want, you can even dispense with the "dear friend," and use only, "dear art lover," or "dear animal lover." The thing to remember with your salutation is to make it sound as personal as possible within the budget that you are working with.

Developing the Copy Platform

We talked in an earlier chapter about the importance of finding a marketing platform, or unifying idea for the fundraising letter package. Go back to that now and pull it out, because it is time to translate it into an idea that will guide your letter-writing efforts. The copy platform is the structure upon which you will hang all the words and sentences and paragraphs of your letter. It will affect how you write your lead and all the text to follow. It is important to commit to a unifying idea before you begin writing the letter. Follow through with it throughout and see how it works. If it is not flowing right, you will know it early on. Do not be afraid to start over with a different copy platform. You have already answered questions about specifics, such as who will sign the letter, what, if any, kinds of premiums you will offer, and what you will be asking for. Distill that down into one succinct statement, which notes the need, what will be done to correct it, and what a gift will accomplish. This statement will become your north star, to which you return if you are stuck. You will also be writing this information repeatedly in the letter, mentioning it within the framework of the story or idea you have selected to present the information. Now it is time to decide on a structure through which you will present those specifics. Was there any idea that leapt out as you made notes about those things? Do you want to tell a story that you will weave throughout the letter? Will it be a story about a client, volunteer, or something else? Do you have a series of facts and statistics that you want the potential donor to know about, or is the main thrust of your letter going to be about the workings of your organization? Coming up with a copy platform will give you a starting point and a structure to guide your efforts towards writing a first draft of the letter. It will give you a way to present your message in an appealing format to your potential donor. It might also help you come up with some ideas for the lead.

The Johnson Box

The Johnson Box is a term often used in the direct mail industry. It refers to a box at the top of the letter that contains the key message of the letter. The Johnson Box is named after Frank Johnson, a direct-marketing expert who designed his box to improve the response rate of a campaign for American Heritage magazine. Some people think that the use of a Johnson Box looks too gimmicky or glossy when trying to achieve a personal feel. These experts thus believe that using Johnson Box may not be a good idea for fundraising sales letters. However, there are ways that you can adapt the Johnson Box and take advantage of the intent behind it to highlight your message. You could use a Johnson Box at the top of your letter with a touching story, or you could put a Johnson Box in the middle of the letter. In this case, you might want to use it to set off a testimonial or other aspect of the letter you wish to feature. Most Johnson Boxes are set off in a centered rectangular box, but you can also set off selected bits of your copy with parallel lines above and below it. In these days when we are constantly bombarded by information from a variety of sources, the Johnson Box can be an effective way of getting your donor's attention.

The Lead

What is the lead? It is the opening paragraph of your letter, and, according to many different studies, it is the most-read element of your fundraising letter. (The other highest read elements are the outer envelope copy and the P.S. We have already discussed the outer envelope copy and we will get to the P.S. soon.) Research has repeatedly shown that if your reader is not interested in the lead, she will not continue to read the rest of the letter.

Whew! That is a lot of pressure for one measly collection of words. but never fear, you have done your preliminary research and by now you should have a fairly good idea of what information you want to include in your letter. From here on out, it is simply a question of shaping the material to best capture the minds and hearts of your readers.

The first line of your lead is the most important. Your first sentence needs to grab your reader's attention in such a way that it will be impossible for him not to read on. He will be so curious, so emotionally engaged, or so stunned by what you have written that he will simply have to keep reading. Accomplishing this is not as difficult as it might seem.

Keep your first sentence simple, and keep it focused on one central thought. Up until now, you have been engaged in gathering information from a variety of sources and writing as much down about every aspect of your organization as possible. Now it is time to distill those divergent facts and ideas into one strong central thought. This should contain the crux of the vital message you have chosen to communicate. Take your time with this, and allow yourself to write several versions. Professional writers know that writing is mostly rewriting. The first sentence is so important that it bears lavishing attention upon it. What you are looking for as you write and rewrite is an attention-grabbing sentence that will clearly state your message. Do not muddy the waters by trying to write everything you want to convey in one sentence or paragraph. Remember, you have the whole letter yet to write. Keep it simple, direct, and clean, and your donors will reward you by continuing to read your leader and ultimately pulling out their checkbooks or credit cards.

One hint from professional copywriters is to allow yourself to write fast as you write the lead and the text. Then after you have completed a rough draft, go back to the beginning. You will no doubt see that your lead sentence needs work. Now read your copy until you get three or four paragraphs down — odds are good that you might find your lead buried there. Professional writers know that the first few paragraphs are warm ups and that the good stuff does not happen until a ways in. Using this trick may help you find your lead sentence with a minimum of stress.

There are some tried and true ways to arouse a reader's desire to keep reading, based on the techniques professional writers have been using for years. Let us take a look at some of these:

Tell a Story. We humans are hard-wired not only to be storytellers, but also to respond emotionally to a well-told story. Stories tug at our heartstrings and once our heartstrings are pulled, it is an easy next step to open our wallets. The key in using a story in the lead of your letter is to introduce it. You will not have room to tell the entire story in your lead, nor do you want to. You want to begin the story and engage the reader's curiosity so that she will continue reading your letter to find out what happened. Once you have started a story, you can then move into presenting information about your organization and its needs, perhaps returning to the story once or twice throughout the letter, and then finishing the story near the end of the letter. With this technique, your donor will be avidly reading the letter to find out what happened, and along the way be digesting the information that you need to present. The use of storytelling is a powerful technique, which can keep you donor reading until he has no emotional choice but to open his checkbook.

Use a Quote. Quotes engage us because they are another person speaking directly to the reader. A pithy quote can say more in one sentence than many people can state in a paragraph. Alan Sharpe calls quotes zingers and advocates their use in a method similar to storytelling: "The secret to using zingers well is to think of them as bait. You are fishing for donations. The zinger is the lure on the end of your line. You want supporters to take your lure so that you can reel them in." You can use this "bait" in two ways. The first way is to search through collections of quotations for an apt zinger to use in your letter. There are many internet reference sites but you might also want to invest in a good book on quotations, which will serve you well through not only writing fundraising letters but other pieces as well. Another way in which you can use a quote is to find one from somebody connected to your organization — a volunteer, caseworker, or client, for instance. Using a quote in this way can often be paired with the storytelling technique to create a powerful opening.

Ask a Question. Asking a question at the head of a fundraising letter is an effective technique because it is human nature to need to find the answer. Your potential donor will read further in order to discover the answer to the question you are asking. To make the best use of this technique, do not use a question that can be answered with yes or no. One way to generate questions is to go back to the old five Ws and one H: who, what, when, why, where, and how. Starting a question with one of these is a nearly sure-fire way to create a powerful question that will provoke a reader to think — and keep reading. Remember, just as with story telling, you want to raise the reader's curiosity and compel them to find out the answer by reading further.

Present a Fact. Our brains love facts, as long as they are presented in an easily digested manner. We love to learn and starting your letter with a fact can engage this aspect of human nature. It also has the advantage of evoking curiosity to learn more, thus compelling your donor to keep reading.

Tell a Joke. This works well if you use it to poke fun at yourself. This technique creates an immediate bond because, if used correctly, it can be personal. Many public speakers begin their talks with a joke because they know it is a powerful way to get their audience to relax and feel a connection with him. You can utilize this in your fundraising letter writing also.

Be Honest. This opening works because it creates the feeling that you are confiding in the donor. And you are — you are telling them that your organization has a need that they can help fulfill, while fulfilling their own sense of purpose and charity as well.

Surprise Them. Marketers do this to you all the time. They construct headlines, which imply one thing and then lead you in a different direction when you actual read their copy.

Show Immediacy. It is so easy for your donors to set aside your letter, as we have discussed earlier. Creating a sense of urgency will compel them to read further in your letter. You want them to feel that there is an urgent need to keep reading the letter to find out more about how they can help.

THE TEXT

All right, you have a gorgeous lead with a fabulous opening sentence that you are certain will compel readers to peruse the rest of the fundraising letter. Now it is time to write the text. What, specifically will you write? While the task might seem overwhelming, even with all the prep work that you have done, just remember to take it gradually and one paragraph at a time, and you will be fine. First we will discuss what, precisely, you will write, and second, how to write it.

What to Write

You have opened the fundraising letter with a provocative statement or story or question. Now it is time to get into the meat of the letter. Besides the all-important asking for the donation, after you have the donor's attention, you have many options to use to convince them to send you money.

Write a Rough Draft

Once you have gotten the idea behind the letter in your head, you have passed a huge hurdle. With your copy platform as you guiding light, you can now approach writing your letter by simply going through these sub-heads, one at a time, and writing corresponding copy about your organization. By the time you get to the end, you will have a rough draft of a letter written. Should any of the sub-heads not seem applicable, feel free to ignore them. However, it is also important to remember that pushing yourself to write something that may feel uncomfortable can often result in powerful copy. Sound good? Let us get started. Remember, the best way to write is to dive in. Do not over-think it. Writing is a generative process, and the more you write the more ideas will spring forth. One last tip before we get started: Do not worry about writing long letters. Research has shown that long fundraising letters are the most effective, though this may seem counter-intuitive. Your donor will naturally think up questions and objections as he reads along. Your job is to answer these thoroughly, so thoroughly that there is no doubt by the time he gets to the end of it what your organization does, how he can help, and how he can donate money immediately.

Inform Them. Tell them either about the organization or the crux of the problem, preferably both. You may want to cite facts and statistics to back up your statements. A fundraising letter for a group dedicated to educating the public about climate change, for instance, might want to cite some statistics about the effects of global warming. Once you have come up with a catchy opening that has aroused their interest, following it with information about your cause or organization makes a powerful one-two punch.

Ask Early. Also, ask often. Many fundraising letter writers make the mistake of going on and on about this and that before getting to the heart of the matter. Your reader will be scanning the copy, looking for the "catch." Why not make it easy and give it to them upfront? You do not have to ask for a specific amount early on, but do ask. Get the donor in a giving mood as soon as possible and let them know that you are going to be asking for money. You are not just sending them this letter to be neighborly!

Tell How It Will Be Used. Your donors like to give money to organizations that will use it responsibly. They like to know for what, exactly, you will use the money. Be honest. Do not assume that you can tell them you are going to use it for a special program for clients when it is really going into the general fund. Be upfront and be specific. Some big-name organizations have learned the hard way that it is important to be scrupulously honest about where the money is going. In the months after the terrorist attacks of September 11, donations poured into the Red Cross. However, it was later revealed that money people sent assuming it would go directly to disaster relief for victims of the attacks had actually gone into a general administrative fund. This damaged the good name of the organization and the good will of the public towards it. The organization had to do some quick damage control and later painstakingly rebuild its image.

Share Past Successes. Think about sharing some past successes in the letter. If you have chosen to highlight a story about one of your clients as the copywriting platform, for instance, you might end the story by focusing on a successful outcome. (Just be sure to save this successful conclusion until the end of the letter to keep the donor reading.) Everyone likes to be associated with a winner. In particular, people like to give money where they think it will actually do some good. Reassure them they are doing so by highlighting your past successes.

Highlight Your Volunteers. Another thing you might want to write about is your volunteers. Perhaps in the story about a client you might also be able to mention a special volunteer who got involved with that client and made a difference in his life. Highlighting volunteers adds a personal touch to your fundraising letter. It also helps to bring the letter to the level of the donor, particularly if a celebrity or other well-known person signs it.

Give Them Reason to Trust. Just as your donors will want to know exactly how their money is being spent, they will also want to know that they can trust you with their hard-earned money. This means that you need to show them that you can be trusted. One area of concern for many potential donors is the proportion of money spent on administrative costs. Your donors want to feel that their money is going to the cause, not the administration of it. So be sure to share these figures if they are good ones.

Describe Future Needs. If you have big plans for the future, share them. If you know you have a capital fund campaign coming up, let your donor know about it. If you know that you will soon be outgrowing your space and need a new one, tell this to your donor. Remember, the old adage information is power still rules the world. The more information you can give your donor, the fuller picture they will have of your organization. The fuller picture they have of the organization, the more likely they will be to donate. So do not hold back.

Offer Hope. Do not get so caught up in the story of how deep the need for your services is and give the impression that the outlook is bleak. Potential donors do not want to contribute to a doomed cause. Be sure to show some reason to hope in your letter. Point out the strides you have made in the past, or highlight a specific story about one individual to show hope.

Show Appreciation. A simple thank you can work wonders. Repeat it often. Make it heartfelt.

Promise A Benefit. Do not forget the primary reason that most people are motivated to donate — because they perceive a benefit to themselves. Keep this in mind as you write and remember to mention it. The benefit can be tangible or intangible and either can be a powerful motivator. Intangible benefits, such as feeling good about themselves or feeling they have made a difference, can have an enormous impact. Tangible benefits, such as premiums, should also be mentioned.

How Much Should You Ask For?

Many organizations will have tried and true dollar amounts that they have asked for and received, either in membership or fundraising campaigns. However, if you are writing your first fundraising letter package, or your organization has recently gone through some changes, you may need help deciding how much you should ask for. Fundraising experts will ask you to remember one vital point: the level at which you start your donors giving will have a direct bearing on how much you can upgrade then to in the future. In other words, start them as high as you can so that you can continue to raise their levels of giving. Also, be mindful of the 80-20 rule, which states that 20 percent of your donors will give 80 percent of the contributions. Once you can convince this core group of contributors to give at higher levels, you are reaping substantial fundraising rewards. Expert fundraiser Roland Kuniholm, author of *The Complete Book of Model Fundraising Letters*, offers some good tips in his book.

Research Competitors. How much are they asking for? If you ask for substantially more or less than your nearest competitors, it may raise alarms with potential donors. It is a rule of human behavior to want neither the cheapest nor the most expensive. Match your gift-giving levels to similar organizations for the best shot at success. If you do decide to ask for a higher amount, do it for a reason. Perhaps you are offering a special gift as an enticement, or maybe your group has plans for a special new program.

Research Mailing Lists. If you are using a purchased mailing list, find out the average gift size and match your asking donation to it. It is important to learn as much information about the donors on your list so as possible so that you can make good use of it. Start your donors out in their giving comfort zone. If the average donation on your list is $25, do not start out asking for $50 in your fundraising letter.

Testing, Testing. Keep careful notes on what the best level of asks are from campaign to campaign. You can test to see what levels of asks create the best response, and test different letters in your campaigns.

Offer a Range. For the first-time donor, it is most effective to give a range of suggested giving levels. You can present them in increments of $10, for instance, $15, $25, and $35. This is desirable for the first-time donor about whom you have no information on what to expect in terms of giving.

Motivate to Give More. A good way to do this is to offer a premium. Of course, be aware that if you are offering a first-time donor a premium they will be expecting a premium in all future offers.

HOW TO WRITE

Now we have gone through and given you numerous ideas about what to write about. If you have been following along and making notes and writing, you may even have a rough draft put together by now. Of course, having a rough draft is not the same thing as having a polished piece of writing that will motivate donors to run to find their checkbooks. However, having a rough draft does give you something to work with; material to shape into raw treasure. With at least some words on the page, you can put to use some copywriting techniques that will spiff your prose up and make it shine. Here are some tips that should help you.

Make It Personal. We have said it repeatedly, and we will return to it before we are done. One of the most important techniques you can learn is to make the letter sound as personal as possible. Dry, formal, or stilted language does not a good fundraising letter make. Remember, your donor want so feel as if she is helping people, not a program. So personalize your letter when you go back to rewrite it. We've talked about the importance of using the words "I" and "you" already. We humans like to be acknowledged, and most of us do not get enough acknowledgment in our lives. So use the word "you" and make your donor feel valued. Because most of us are trained to write in a more formal style, using "you" may feel a bit awkward and unnatural at first. This is so often the case that experts like Mal Warwick even present lists of ways to use the word "you" in their books. (You can peruse Warwick's list in his book, *How to Write Successful Fundraising Letters*, details of which are listed in the bibliography.) Remember that even familiar phrases like "thank you" contain the word you, for starters. Think in terms of writing the way you would talk to a trusted friend. "How are you?" "How are you feeling?" Clearly, you will not be writing these phrases to your potential donors, but simply thinking in those terms will help you to begin injecting the word "you" into your copy. Another helpful trick that copywriters often use is to read their copy aloud. Hearing the words as opposed to seeing them on paper immediately points out any leftover formalities or awkwardness. Fundraising expert Tom Ahern recommends going through your letter and circling all the "yous" in red ink. If you can look back over the page and see tons of red circles staring back at you, then you know you have used the word "you" enough! Before you know it, you will be writing personal-sounding copywriting like an old copywriting pro!

Use Simple English. Short sentences rule in copywriting. Do not go in for long sentences separated by many commas. Avoid the use of semi-colons and colons when possible. The semi-colon in particular gives off the air of formal, academic language. Avoid it. Do not use big words or foreign words. If your reader has to stop and puzzle over the meaning of a word, you have probably lost him. Remember, the point is to keep the reader reading. You want to keep his attention engaged. Clear, simple writing is the best way to do this. Do not confuse simple writing with un-intelligent writing. Our best writers utilize simple sentence structures and words. Use punchy verbs when possible and look for words that communicate emotion. While it is important to make your reader think, what you really want him to do is feel! Avoid the use of adjectives and adverbs, which often are space fillers but add little to the copy.

Use Good Transitions. Part of the art of great copywriting is to use effective transitional sentences. What are transitional sentences? They appear at either the end of one paragraph or the beginning of another. Transitional sentences guide the reader through the letter and help it to flow. Good transitional sentences are like cliffhangers at the end of chapters in a novel — they keep the reader wanting to read further. How do you write good transition sentences? One effective way is to keep mentioning things to come. Your reader will read onto the next paragraph to find out what is coming. Do not give her all the information in one paragraph. Mention most of it, but leave some for the next, which will motivate her to keep reading to find out what she is missing. You can also end your paragraph with phrases such as "but that's not all," or "and there is more to the story," or something similar. You can also begin a paragraph with the word "another," which is an invitation to read further. Another what? A surefire way to keep the reader reading is to begin the paragraph with the reader's favorite word, "you." Another word that keeps readers hooked is "and." When "and" is used at the beginning of the paragraph it leads the reader right into the sentence. Finally, one of the most effective transitional devices is the question. How to most efficiently use the question as a transition? Simple. Ask a question at the end of one paragraph and then answer it in the beginning of the next. A word of warning, here. Vary the use of these devices. You do not want to end every paragraph with a question, for instance. And you certainly do not want to start every paragraph with "and," "you" or "another." Sprinkling these devices through your letter can motivate your reader to keep reading to the end of your letter.

Write Sub-heads and Highlight. The average letter reader does not sit down and read your wonderful prose word for word. Oh, no. Remember that the recipient of your letter is busy, just like you. If, by chance, or luck, or good teaser copy, you have managed to get your potential donor to open your letter, do not count on her reading it line by line. Instead, she is more apt to skip down the page, attempting to grasp the key concepts of the letter. She will do this first to see if it is worth reading more carefully. It is up to you to make certain that those key concepts stand out so that she can grasp them easily. Decide in advance which key words you want to stand out. This should be relatively easy, as you have worked hard to distill your message. You have also learned to ask for it repeatedly. A word of caution here. Do not make the mistake of choosing words to underline or chunks of text to put beneath a sub-head by what looks good, or even by what would be considered good writing. Make your selections based on what will convey an emotional appeal to the reader. Here is a hint as to what appeals to readers: donor benefits. These can fall into the tangible or intangible categories. You may feel that highlighting is a bit too, well, lowbrow, for your particular cause, that it looks flashy and garish. If this is the case, there is still a way that you can arrest the attention of your reader as her eyes skip about the page. That way is to utilize underlining, which is a bit more understated yet still effective in drawing attention to itself.

Italics. Along the same line as underlining or highlighting, you can also make use of italics to create emphasis. Italics are nearly universally denounced by editors and writing experts, but they are nearly universally loved by copywriters. Why? Because italics add emphasis to writing. When your reader's eye scans along a line of type, the italicized line will capture her attention first because it looks different. Second, she will assume that there is something of special importance in that sentence, because it has been italicized. So do not underestimate the power of italics to help you underscore your important message.

Repetition can be effective. You have a few main points that you want to hammer home. You have developed a message that you want to convey to your reader. In addition, you know that it is important to be clear and focused in your letter. You can achieve all of these goals using repetition. Whether through one key word, such as "dream" or "hope," or a whole phrase, do not be afraid to utilize repetition to tell your story. On the other hand, unless you are using repetition for effect to underline your message, it is a good idea to push yourself to look for the fresh word or a new way to phrase a sentence. The result will be a livelier letter that your recipient will want to keep reading.

Write with a Sense of Urgency. As a fundraiser, your worst enemy is the human tendency to emulate Scarlet O'Hara, and say, **"I'll think about it tomorrow."** You want your potential donor to be roused to take action now. It can be difficult to think up a way to motivate your readers to send money now that does not sound contrived. Look at your calendar for the upcoming year and note any events, deadlines, or special considerations. Is it an election year? Perhaps you run a political organization that will have obvious ties to the political calendar. Maybe your organization is not overtly political but, in looking at your calendar, you note that an upcoming legislative session will affect your group. This is an excellent reason to send a fundraising letter. Perhaps you have a budgetary deadline or a special event coming up for which you need funds. The one time to be wary of creating a sense of urgency is when you are using bulk mail. Depending on the volume of mail the post office has when you drop your bulk mail off, it may take up to two weeks for your mail to be delivered. So if you have asked your readers to mail in their responses within 14 days because of a specific need, but the post office has not mailed your letter for two weeks, by the time your donor gets the letter the deadline will have passed. Do not forget to repeat your deadline request in the P.S, if you are using one, and on the reply device as well.

Before and After. One powerful copywriting technique to consider is the before and after. Glance through any woman's magazine and odds are good you will see before and after features in which women's looks are updated. Look through the January issues of popular newsstand magazines such as People or Us Weekly and you will notice before and after features about people who have successfully lost weight. Turn on the television and you will find shows that show how to change your wardrobe or your home completely. Why are these articles and programs so popular? It is because, as Alan Sharpe points out, they show us both a problem and a solution. Right there, on the page, in living color, are examples of how people have changed themselves. As a fundraiser, you can capitalize on this basic aspect of human nature and share with readers how your organization has helped a client to change. You can do this through painting vivid word pictures of how your organization has affected people. By offering before and after copy in your fundraising letters, you give your potential donors hope that they, too, can influence the world for good.

Testimonials. What could be more positive than presenting testimonials from clients your organization has helped? A testimonial is any compliment your organization has received, or any tribute that has been paid to you. Odds are good you have received testimonials unsolicited from clients or others. All you need to do to include those in your fundraising letters is to get permission from the person who made the testimonial. Also, consider asking for testimonials from volunteers who have had good experiences working in the field, or from other donors. Testimonials are the ultimate in the personal appeal, as they are compliment originating from a real, live person. It can be a powerful motivator to a potential donor to see that people just like him — perhaps neighbors or friends — have found the organization worthy and donated money. Your reader may read a testimonial from a client and be impressed with how your organization has helped to change a life. A testimonial does not have to be long. A sentence or two can be powerful. The best way to find testimonials is to start looking for them. Make a file for testimonials. Tell your staff to be on the lookout for them, and you keep your eyes open, too. If you receive a letter or e-mail with any kinds of praise or thanks, be sure to keep it or a copy of it in your testimonial file. If you lack submitted testimonials, you could also go directly into the field and talk to clients and volunteers yourself.

Write a Story. Research has shown that utilizing the power of story can help nonprofits boost their response rates to fundraising letters. You have heard the word story repeatedly, probably from the time you were a small child. After all, one of the first things most of us remember is begging an adult, "Tell me a story!" The capacity to tell, and in turn, appreciate, a story, is hard-wired into us from birth. It is part of what make us human and sets us apart from the mammals that are next closest to us. However, you may have heard the word story so much that you do not know exactly what it means. Here are a few tips to help you define and write a story. For starters, all stories start with conflict. If you do not have any conflict, you do not have a story. It is that simple. Conflict comes from several potential sources — man versus society, man versus. man, man versus himself, or man versus nature. In the nonprofit world, odds are good that your clients may fall into the man vs. society or the man vs. man category. For instance, if you service homeless people, your clients have a conflict with a society that does not offer affordable housing to its citizens. If you deal in some sort of counseling or addiction services, your clients have a conflict within themselves that makes it difficult for them to quit drinking or taking drugs or whatever. It should be easy for you to identify the conflict, since you work in a nonprofit agency. An excellent starting point for telling any story is to begin with the conflict. For instance, a mother cannot afford to buy food for her starving children. A young woman sticks a needle in her arm once again. After you have identified the conflict, then look for the solution. What happened to the mother who could not afford food for her children? Did they starve? No, she discovered the food bank that you run. Write a story with your organization as the hero and you will touch readers' hearts and boost response rates. Here are some additional tips to utilize stories successfully in your fundraising letters.

1. **Write About People.** Odds are good that you chose the latest bestseller off the shelf because it featured a character that intrigued you. Emulate the bestselling writer when you write your fundraising letter and focus on people when you decide to tell a story. The lofty idea or moral principle simply does not have as much power to motivate us as a story about people.

2. **Enliven with Detail.** One or two well-placed details can make your story spring to life. For example, "The young mother clapped her raw, red hands together in the cold," is more powerful than, "The woman's hand were cold." Beginning writers often feel they must write in general terms to capture the interest of the most people, but in reality, the opposite is true. The more details you can provide in your stories, the more they will resonate with your readers.

3. **Make it Relevant.** To overstate the obvious, if you run a soup kitchen, do not write a story about an addict — unless that addict is someone you have helped toward recovery with a nice hot meal in his stomach. The key here is to understand your audience and write to them. This should not be a problem. After all, you did an enormous amount of research about your target donor early on. Go back to that information that you collected now and refresh your memory about your donor. Use it to create a compelling story.

4. **It is all About the Message.** Even your story should support the underlying message you have decided to share with your potential donors. The woman with the cold hands that we mentioned earlier had red, raw hands because she needed to stand in the chilly weather in order to eat dinner. But at your soup kitchen, there are no long lines of people waiting outside. The message? Donating to your soup kitchen will not only satisfy hunger, but other needs as well, and donors can feel good about contributing to the whole person.

Turn Facts and Statistics into Stories. It is okay to use facts and statistics, desirable even. But bring in the facts and statistics after you have told a story, or as a part of one, to make your letters more appealing.

How to Write the Ask. We have discussed how to calculate how much to ask for. But, how, precisely, should you go about asking for the money? The best advice is do not be afraid to be blatant. Ask early and ask often. Remember, your reader is busy. Your reader is distracted. You may have him engaged in a lovely story, but he wants to know why you are telling him the story. Alan Sharpe recommends asking at least three times in a two-page letter. Ask once on the first page, once near the top of the second page, and once again on the second page, near the end. If you use a postscript, ask again in that. You can use hard asks, such as "send money now," or soft asks, like "your generous gift will ensure the survival of the whales." You can use a combination of hard and soft asks. Just be certain to ask early and ask often. Asking for money is the point of the letter, after all. Let the reader know early on why you are writing.

The Close. Make it simple and straightforward, and tell the recipient what you want him or her to do. Keep it focused and direct. "Send money now." "Help save the whales today." Note, you have moved from asking to telling here. You are no longer requesting, you are directing. You have been polite long enough, and the reader has had enough opportunity to read and process your message. In the close of the letter, you want to state clearly and succinctly exactly what you want him to do.

The P.S. You have probably read numerous sales letters, either ones that have arrived in the mail or perhaps on the internet, and one thing you will have noticed in all of them is the heavy use of the P.S. What is the point of this? In many cases, you will see not just one P.S., but multiple ones, with P.S.S. and P.S.S.S. Why does everyone use a postscript? There is one simple reason for this. It is because study after study has shown that the reader's eyes move down the page to read the end first. Research has proven that the postscript is one of the most effective parts of the sales letter. This holds true for fundraising letters as well. Often the recipient is seeking to learn the point of the letter, to find out what the "catch" or "ask" is, or simply to learn how much. Utilize this basic fact of human nature and use the P.S. to restate your case. You can also use the P.S. to restate the benefit, or state some other inducement to action in it. Writing a strong call to action in the P.S. can boost your response rate dramatically. You will hear a few dissenters who take issues with the common wisdom about using a postscript in your letters. Alan Sharpe is one. He feels that the "P.S. in fundraising letters is stupid and belongs in another millennium." He explains that the postscript is a leftover from the days when people wrote letters by hand or sometimes typed them. With either of those methods, if you had a thought you wanted to add, there was no way to insert it easily into the body of the letter, so the use of a postscript made good sense. However, we live in the computer age when these concerns are no longer valid. Sharpe says that word processors make the postscript obsolete. He also contends that the P.S. is contrived and designed only to lift response and that because of this it turns the recipient off. The P.S. has been used so heavily in sales letters, with so many people overdoing it, that Alan Sharpe makes a compelling point. The use of the P.S. thus should be a matter of either personal preference or something that you will test for results.

HOW TO FORMAT

We have mentioned the importance of formatting your

letter in a way that will make it accessible to your readers. How, precisely, should you accomplish that? A few simple guidelines will help you. Always indent paragraphs for an informal look. If you are going for a more formal aura, skip the indenting and format all paragraphs flush left. You will also want to format the letter ragged right. This again is more personal, as it emulates the look of a hand-written letter. Official reports and formal business communication are all fully justified. This is not the look you are going for! Format your fundraising letters in ragged right. Finally, this is a letter you are writing, not a brochure or newsletter. It is thus advisable to skip the photographs or sidebars or the use of other graphic design elements. Keep it simple. Keep it looking like a letter. If you have photographs you want to use, include them as an enclosure (see below), but do not use them in the body of the letter. Remember, the idea is to make your fundraising letter look as much like a personal letter as possible. Rarely does a personal, handwritten letter include photos or sidebars. These simple how-tos should help you to format your fundraising letter. If you are stuck, go back to the idea of what a personal, handwritten letter looks like and judge against that.

A Few Additional Writing Tips

Here is a selection of extra writing tips that may help you as you write your fundraising letters.

The Rule of Threes. Particularly in the American culture, we are used to having things presented to us in threes. For example, think about the following: red, white, and blue.

The stars and stripes forever. Think also of Goldilocks and the Three Bears, or the Three Little Pigs. We like things in threes. If we are presented with a list or phrase of two, it may not seem like quite enough. On the other hand, four may seem like too many. This trick is so ingrained in professional writers they rarely even think about it. Get in the habit of writing things in threes, and soon you will be doing it automatically.

End With the Important Part. This is true for both sentences and paragraphs. Put the most important part of your thought at the end, where it will have the most impact. We tend to gloss over the first part of a sentence or paragraph, seeking the point of it. So make certain that your important point is at the end, where your reader's eye will fall upon it.

Put Yourself in the Reader's Place. This is another trick of professional writers, who understand that it is all about the audience — who they are writing for. Do one last read-through of your letter before you give it final approval. It might be a difficult trick, but put yourself in the mind of the recipient. What is he or she doing as she opens the letter? Out of all the distractions pulling on her, what is the one thing that will garner her attention? Now look at your opening. Does the first line arrest her immediately? Continue through your copy as you pretend that you are the reader. Gauge what his reaction will be.

Read it Aloud. Reading aloud is not just for children — it is an excellent way for you to get a feel for what the copy sounds like. People often "hear" things they read. Help them out by reading it aloud. You will be surprised at how many little errors and things that simply do not sound right you will catch.

Writing is Rewriting. Any professional writer will agree with this statement. That beautifully crafted piece of brochure copy you just marveled over did not come straight from the writer's head through his hands onto the page. Well, it did, but the first time out the words were probably a mishmash that would not make sense to anybody but the writer himself. Writing is a process, and the process is one of going back over the words to achieve clarity and then to polish and hone them.

Avoid Passive Voice. This is the cardinal rule of all writing, the first lesson that professionals learn in Writing 101. However, many lay people are unfamiliar with the rule. What is passive voice? It involves the subject of the sentence being acted upon rather than acting. For instance, the man walked his dog, is an example of a simple active sentence. The passive version might read, the man was walking his dog, or the dog was walked by the man. The latter is a bit of a ridiculous example, but you would be surprised how often the extreme passive voice surfaces. Here is a hint for uncovering passive voice: it has some version of the verb "to be" in it.

THE REPLY DEVICE, STEP BY STEP

It may not seem particularly important to lavish attention on the reply device. But remember, in fundraising letter writing all copy is important. Consider that the reply device may be separated from the letter itself, or that the donor may set the package down, and, when returning to it later, pick up the reply device first. The reply device may end up being the only piece of the fundraising package that a potential donor actually reads. Therefore, the reply device needs to be clearly written. Alan Sharpe points out that the reply device is actually the conclusion of your request for funds, so if it does not work, your letter itself has failed. The reply device may seem like just another piece of copy that you are going to have to find time to write, but in reality it is one of the most important aspects of the package. Let us look at some of the things your hard-working reply device can accomplish.

- Support all the other parts of the package in their primary intent — asking for the gift.

- Get the donor involved. Research bears out the notion that people are more likely to donate if they actually have to do something, like fill out a reply device.

- The reply device is where you list the specific amounts you are asking for. Giving your donors specific amounts helps to motivate them further as they will not have to waste time thinking up a gift amount on their own.

- Verify the names and addresses of your donors.

- Gather other information, such as e-mail addresses.

Remember that your reply device is a small, but hard-working piece of paper that has four primary functions, which are as follows:

1. A record of the donor's name and address. If you are using a mailing house, you will also include the donor number.

2. If using an outer envelope with a window, the reply device may carry the address of the recipient.

3. It is pre-printed with the donor's name and address.

4. By coding the reply device, it can help you track the effectiveness of your campaign. This "key code" will tell you what is working and what is not. The use of a key code will help you to distinguish a successful campaign from a failed one.

Here are some initial guidelines to follow in writing your reply device:

Make it Clear. Be transparent in what you are asking for and make it consistent with the offer of the main fundraising letter. Make certain that your suggested gift amounts are listed in an easy-to-read format.

Remind Them of the Benefits. Next to the gift amounts, list the benefits in a succinct, easily digested fashion. The reply device is where donors look to grasp the heart of the matter — what is in it for them? How much are they expected to give? What will they get in return for their donation? List these benefits in as clear a fashion as possible and you will reap the benefits in a high response rate.

Appearance Counts. Make the reply device clean and uncluttered. Make it easy for the donor to check off an amount, write out a check, and send in the envelope. Many are the donor who has been motivated to donate to an organization only to be presented with a confusing reply device that completely turns him off.

Keep It Focused. This is a reply device, which asks for a donation, period. Do not ask for volunteers on the reply device, and do not ask them if they are interested in receiving a newsletter. Do not take an entirely new direction on the reply device. Make certain that it fits in with the overall theme you have developed in the rest of the package. Keep the reply device centered on its one main chore — asking for money. You can solicit volunteers in a follow-up letter.

Convince Yourself. Pretend it is the only piece your recipient will read. This will force you to treat the reply device as another piece of copy to be well written, not just an after-thought.

Make it Easy. Yes, donors like to get involved by doing something, but if it requires too much thought, you will lose the donation. Do not make the donor do too much.

Keep Selling. Restate the reason you are asking for funds now on the reply card to remind the donor of what motivated her. Ideally, the donor will read the letter, be convinced to donate, and pick up the reply device in order to do so. However, it is the job of the reply device to motivate the donor to actually write the check and put it in the reply envelope. Another reason to restate the appeal is that this may be the only piece of the package your reader might see, should it be separated from the package contents.

Use an Acceptance Statement. This is a simple statement written in the voice of the donor, something like, "Yes! I want to contribute to saving the whales. Here is my donation."

Include the Organization's Name and Address. Again, assume that the reply device and the letter might get separated.

Call it something grand. This is especially useful advice if you are soliciting large gifts. Come up with a name for your reply device that sounds a bit grander. Alan Sharpe recommends "Memorandum of Acceptance."

Information for Check Writers. Tell them who to make their checks out to, as even a small hang-up such as this can prevent a donor from sitting down to write out the check.

Do Not Keep Using the Same One. As mentioned above, the reply device should reflect the overall theme and feel of the fundraising letter package itself. So using the same reply device repeatedly will not serve your fundraising campaign well. Because reply devices are small, they can be printed several to a sheet, and are thus inexpensive to produce. Take the time to design one for each new campaign.

Keep it Separate. Do not attempt to keep things simple by printing both the reply device and the letter on the same page. Research has shown that this simply does not work. The reply device is a vital part of the fundraising letter package and you will get much better results by using one.

OPTIONAL ENCLOSURES

One of the first things that comes to mind when deciding upon optional enclosures is a brochure. It always seems like a good idea. Why not enclose a brochure to include more information about the organization? As a, do not include a brochure unless you have extra information you need to impart that will not fit in a letter. Brochures will add to your mailing costs, and they are often discarded without a second glance, which is a waste of your organization's money. Here are some circumstances in which you might want to include a brochure:

Extra Information. Perhaps you have material that does not fit into the letter, but you feel is vital in buttressing your case to donors. Put it into a brochure and include it in the package.

Illustrate a Premium Offer. If you are offering high-end or otherwise special premiums that are complex to explain, a brochure is the correct place to provide that information.

Detail a Membership Package. Explain the benefits of membership in a separate brochure.

Illustrate a Specific Project. Are you asking for funds for a special new program? A new facility? You might want to include all the pertinent info on it in an accompanying brochure.

Testimonials. Upon occasion, some organizations have had success featuring a brochure with testimonies from either clients who have been helped or others who have given.

When writing the brochure, bear in mind that, it, too, is a fundraising piece of copy, and it must work extra hard because it also has one of the above intents in mind. Also be aware that the recipient may pick up the brochure first, or that the brochure might be separated from the rest of the package. Because of this, you will want to re-state the key message you have decided on for your fundraising package. The brochure is not the only other enclosure you may be considering.

Newspaper Clipping. Using a clipping from an external source lends extra heft to its impact. The fact that the media has paid attention to your organization also adds legitimacy.This will need to include a message that is overprinted or printed above the text to inform the recipient of the original source and significance of the article. It is also vitally important to include another request for money on this (and all) enclosures.

Photos. A picture is worth a thousand words, but is it worth the money you will spend to add one to your package? Quite possibly. Fundraising letter-writing experts will tell you that using a photo as an enclosure adds not only a personal touch, but it can also add a sense of urgency. Including a photo creates the feel that the letter-writer took the picture himself and included it, much as you would include a packet of photos to a friend. When using a photo, be sure to include a copy message on the reverse side. You know by now what else you need to include — another appeal for funds.

Lift Letter. We defined the lift letter at the start of this chapter, and talked about its beginnings in the world of magazine publishing. The reason a lift letter is so successful at "lifting" response is that it often answers an objection. The donor has decided not to donate for a specific reason, but by opening and reading the lift letter, there is a good chance that the objection will be overcome. Another way the lift letter might work is to play on the donor's emotions by presenting another selling point. When writing the lift letter, think short, engaging, and attention getting. You can use it to highlight special programs, testimonials, or some other special aspect of your organization. And, of course, ask for the donation again.

DVD or CD. Internet users are flocking to watch videos on You Tube. Society today is accustomed to receiving information through video presentations and you can turn this to your advantage by including a DVD with your letter. The catch is, of course, that you will need to motivate the recipient to watch the presentation. Using a DVD presentation lends a special feel to the appeal, as if it was so important that the organization went to the extra time and trouble to produce a video. As such, this might be an especially effective enclosure to include for the high-end donors.

Test. In an upcoming section, we will discuss testing the results of your fundraising package in detail, but it bears mentioning here that testing the effectiveness of enclosures is important, and easy. Do a mailing with and without. If you get a high enough return on the "with" mailing to justify the cost, you will have your answer. Remember, that with all of the enclosures you are considering, they must carry their own weight. In other words, they produce more in donations than it costs to produce and mail them. If sending extra enclosures is not lifting your response rate, then simply dispense with them.

Testing. Not every single one of your fundraising letter packages is going to hit the mark. Would that it could be otherwise, but the sad truth is that some of your fundraising letters are going to fail, despite your best efforts. However, even a failed fundraising package can provide you with excellent information that you can use to write a successful letter next time. It all depends on your attitude — and your ability to test the results. After all, if you do not test your results, how will you know what works and what does not work? If you continue to send out untested fundraising letter packages, you might as well just throw your money into the wind. You will simply be repeating mistakes you may not even realize you are making.

Sample Book. One easy way to begin testing is to compile a sample book. This should contain copies of every fundraising package you send out. Make certain to retain copies of every piece of the package, from the outer envelope, to the reply envelope, reply device, enclosures, and the letter itself. Along with the fundraising package, you should also keep notes on the results achieved. Then if you want to test various elements of the package in the future, you will have results to compare with your returns. For example, you may be wondering if you want to pay extra to include a lift letter in the next mailing, and if you have information on the rate of return when you used a lift letter you will be able to calculate how well it worked without one.

Themes and Copy Platforms. Another useful byproduct of keeping a sample book is that you can track the effectiveness of various marketing themes and copy platforms. With your sample book, you will build up a storehouse of knowledge about which themes work best for your organization. You will be able to see, for instance, that all the letters you sent out featuring a story about the success of a client netted a high response rate. Conversely, those letters you designed around a fact-based presentation did not perform as well. Once you have hit on a successful presentation, do not mess around with changing it unless you have an excellent, well thought out reason. And by excellent, we do mean excellent. It would be silly to change themes when you have discovered one that works. You can still achieve variety by featuring different clients or different aspects of the program. The best thing to do is keep mailing out the successful fundraising letter package until you notice a drop-off in your rate of return. What if you worry that you need to educate your donor more about your organization? Do not worry about that. The task is first to acquire the donor. After that, you can take on the job of educating them through newsletters and annual reports. For now, focus on getting the donor in the first place.

Cheat Sheet. Earlier we mentioned the practice of compiling fundraising letter and other pieces of written copy in what copywriters call a "cheat sheet." This should be an ongoing practice that you are constantly compiling. Every time you see a direct mail piece or a bit of written copy that you admire, save it. Create a special binder or folder to put it in, and then when you are stuck for ideas you can pull it out and get ideas. Another way to utilize a cheat sheet is to track the evolution of another organization's fundraising packages. Save each one with a date, and then you will have a record of what they have been doing. If an organization is sending the same basic package out repeatedly, you can be certain that they are achieving success with it. On the other hand, if you notice a shift in theme or emphasis, it is a good bet that the original campaign was not successful. Look at the work of other groups and learn from their successes and failures. Take what you have learned about fundraising and keep it in mind as you review these other letters. Look for the features we have discussed in this book and see how others have put them to use.

What to Test. Some aspects of the campaign will be self-evident and you can use your own judgment for them. However, most fundraising experts agree that the following aspects of the campaign are what you should pay attention to in the testing process:

The Ask. The amount of the ask can make a tremendous difference. For instance, you might get completely different results when the smallest amount is $35, as opposed to $75. The only way you will know this is if you keep good records and test. You might also see different results when you offer a gift as a premium when the donor upgrades his donation. Through testing you will be able to see if offering the premium is worth it in higher donation amounts.

The List. If you are purchasing new mailing lists on a regular basis, it is imperative that you test them to learn their response rates. Things to test for include how recent you received a contribution, how frequently the donor gave, and, of course, the amount of the gift.

The Copy. When testing copy it is important to control the test by changing only one thing at a time. If you change the copy, the premium, and the ask, how will you know which one gave you more success? Test one variable at a time. If you are going to test copy, change the wording of your letter, but leave the ask and the premium and everything else the same. Another aspect of the actual copy that you might want to test is long versus short. It is common wisdom that long copy works better, and most organizations will find this is true. If you are writing letters for a well-known organization, however, you might find that long copy is not needed. The donor will already be familiar with the activities of your organization, and it will not be necessary to spend time explaining what you do. In that case, you can concentrate on the specifics of the campaign and your letter may be considerably shorter. The advantage of shorter copy is that your letters will cost less and you will achieve a more efficient rate of return.

Enclosures. It is always a good idea to test optional enclosures such as brochures, lift letters, newspaper articles, or photos. This is especially true because adding these to the fundraising letter package increases the cost of both printing and postage.

The Letter Signer. Are you using a celebrity as your letter signer? Or perhaps the president of the organization? Or someone else? The person who signs the letter can have a huge impact on the success of your campaign. You might be surprised at the difference between a letter with a celebrity signer and one without. The only way you will find out is through testing.

Outer Envelope. This is an easy thing to test. First, note the difference in a campaign in which the outer envelope contains teaser copy verses one in which it does not. Another thing to look at is the difference when you use various lines of teaser copy. Remember, your major goal is to get the donor to open your package. If the recipient does not open it, you have no chance at getting a donation. Thus, the teaser copy on the outer envelope is crucial and it bears testing. Another approach that professionals often take is to vary the teaser copy on the outer envelope while keeping the contents of the letter intact. This is a way to give the package a fresh look without changing a letter that is proven to work. The old adage holds that you will get bored with the copy long before your donors. So freshening up your outer envelope copy can be a way to combat your own boredom if nothing else.

One Last Look Before You Send it Out. Santa Claus makes a list and checks it twice, and it is a good idea to emulate the fat guy and do the same. Create a checklist that you will follow religiously of things to inspect before you send the fundraising package out the door. Your list should include:

The Internal References. This means, when you say, "return your gift in the postage-paid envelope" you really did include a postage-paid envelope. Or that when you say in the letter, "For just $25, you can support our soup kitchen," that the $25 level of ask is included on the reply device. You would be surprised how often little errors like this are made.

The Pitch. We have told you repeatedly, so that you should know it by heart. Ask for the donation on every piece. Before you send the package out, check to make sure that this is so. You are sending out this letter to ask for funds, so make sure you do it repeatedly.

Personality Plus. Does your letter have that personal touch? Does it look attractive and have a nice "feel" to it. You want your recipient to want to spend time with your package, because the longer you've got them hooked into reading it, the better chance you'll have of securing a donation.

Easy Reading. Does it make sense? This may sound like a silly question, but when a writer gets close to her work, as happens when she is writing over a long period, it becomes impossible to judge even the simplest of sentences. Give the package to an objective reader to scan for clarity and focus.

The Fit. It may sound silly, but it has happened many times: you are using a window envelope and as volunteers begin the process of stuffing, it becomes apparent that the addresses do not line up with the window. Or, just as you are about to insert the reply envelope, you learn it is too big to fit into the outer envelope. It is a good idea to check all of these things well ahead of time.

Keys and Codes. Check that you have coded the mailing correctly. For testing purposes, this is vital.

The Big Picture. Spread out every piece of the fundraising letter package and look over them to make certain that they all cohere with one another. Also, ask yourself if every single piece is needed. Could you do without that lift letter?

Would the overall package suffer if you did not use the photograph?

That is it! Once you have checked over everything in your package you are ready to send it out, sit back, and wait for the results.

CASE STUDY: ADAM SANFORD

Adam Sanford- Development Associate

Oregon College of Art and Craft

8245 SW Barnes Road

Portland, OR   97225

I'm a development associate with twelve years experience in and around non-profits, and I write fundraising letters every single day.

I write the letters myself, and then they are submitted to management for approval. Most of the letters that I write are thank-yous, but I also helped write the year-end appeal letter. We send that one out about once a month.

It is important to make a connection between you cause and the constituent's interests.

If you can focus on programming success or membership benefits that relate in a positive way to each specific constituents interests, that connection will increase the possibility that they will make a donation or support your efforts in some way. I also think it is important to acknowledge any previous participation and thank them for their support and encouragement. Finally, share with them how their contribution will impact the lives of others. People need to feel that their support is making a difference.

Many of the letters I generate serve as templates and are distributed through merges to a wide audience. We get a good response from most of our letters, but not everyone who receives a letter makes a contribution. I think one of the reasons this might happen is that some letters can feel impersonal. In today's world of mass marketing and cookie-cutter mailings, it is easy for a potential donor to feel disconnected from the purpose of the non-profit. If you can find small ways of personalizing letters, even though it may take extra time, I think it can pay off.

CASE STUDY: ADAM SANFORD

For pre-planning, I try to get a general sense of the purpose of the correspondence. Always do some research and ask around about exciting things happening for the non-profit that you can share with the public.

The best tip I can give for successful fundraising letters is to be honest. I think people connect best with simple, clear messages. There's no need to be exclusively wordy and convoluted. Don't be afraid to ask for their support. Things you should never do are make up statistics or stories to enhance your image. Keep it real because if you don't, it may end up harming you in the end.

It is always good to keep an eye out for what other organizations are doing. Also, the purpose of the letter or appeal often lends a framework for the development of materials (the look, feel, and general presence of the fundraising package). I get ideas for letters from colleagues, and other mailings in the mail. I mostly rely on my sense of what people will respond to best.

The importance of the overall fundraising package depends on the non-profit and their constituency. As a non-profit art college, I think we encounter more pressure to have an elevated sense of design and presentation. Other organizations might not deal with such scrutiny. No matter what, though, you want your materials to stand out in the crowd. With so much junk mail out there today, an eye-catching envelope can make all the difference.

The best advice is to be personable. Don't get too technical and wordy. Speak simply and let the message or cause speak for itself.

Types of Fundraising Letters

Up until now, fundraising letters have been covered in a general sense, giving guidelines for writing that will apply to all sorts of fundraising letters. But in the course of your career as a fundraising letter writer, you will be called upon to write many different kinds of letters from the straight contribution letter to the thank-you letter to the sustainer letter. This section will talk about the different kinds of letters you might run into and how to approach writing them. It will also give examples of each of these letters.

STRAIGHT CONTRIBUTION OR SOLICITATION LETTER

The straight contribution letter is the granddaddy of all fundraising letters, the oldest and most well-known of all the different types of letters you'll run into. It is the basic fundraising letter, the one that you'll use simply to ask for funds for your organization. In essence, everything that we have thus far written about fundraising letters applies to the straight contribution letter. Master writing the straight contribution letter and you will go far because all other types of fundraising letters are variations on this theme.

When should you use the straight contribution letter? When you have a readily identifiable cause that does not need a lot of explanation or convincing that you are performing a worthy cause. Organizations that feed or clothe the hungry, help the homeless, or aid in disaster relief are all typical groups that regularly send out straight contribution letters. They do good work that is easily grasped, and they have a built-in emotional appeal inherent in their work. As a reminder, you will want to cover the following bases when you write a straight contribution letter:

- Grab the donor's attention with a strong lead

- Ask for the gift as soon as possible

- Ask for the gift often

- Use stories to convey emotion

- Tell what the gift will accomplish and put it in human terms

- Be personal and use the word "you"

- Create urgency with a deadline

- Inform the donor about your work

- Share Past successes

- Show appreciation

- Offer hope and a sense of satisfaction

Following is an excellent example of a straight contribution letter.

STRAIGHT CONTRIBUTION LETTER EXAMPLE

November 8, 2007

Name

Address

City, State, Zip

Dear _____,

Many of us are fortunate to have quality healthcare available to us and to our family members; some of us may even take it for granted. We may not have to seriously consider the cost when we schedule an appointment, order a prescription or contemplate hospitalization. However, for some families in our community, a child's accident or illness becomes a budget decision as well as a health concern. Necessary healthcare may be delayed or not received at all due to family financial constraints.

During the recent wildfires in Southern California, a mother called the Glendale Healthy Kids office seeking help for her child who was having difficulty breathing due to the very poor air quality. She explained that she had applied for Healthy Families insurance coverage, but due to a clerical error, her application had been misdirected and she was told to start the process over again. It was plain that the child could not wait so our case manager scheduled an appointment with one of our physicians and also provided the inhaler necessary for the child to breathe.

GHK helps hundreds of children who are unable to access timely healthcare every year. These are the children who fall through the cracks of our healthcare system. Typically, their parents work but do not have employer-based health coverage or do not have dependent care. They may not qualify for MediCal or Healthy Families insurance and cannot afford the increasingly high premiums for private health insurance. For families like this, Glendale Healthy Kids may be the only avenue to get the help they need for their children.

A former Glendale Healthy Kids client wrote, "…there is not a day that goes by that I am not thankful for all that you have done for me. My life changed, and I learned that there are people and organizations that care about kids like me. Your work and kindness not only saved my life, but it saves so many others."

STRAIGHT CONTRIBUTION LETTER EXAMPLE

So today, whether you've had a long-term relationship with us, or are just starting out – give from your heart. Your donation will make a difference in the lives of children who are suffering with illness or injury.

With gratitude,

President

Board of Directors

Because the straight contribution letter is the basis of all the other fundraising letters you will be writing, it is worth it to go back over this sample and deconstruct it. Let us look at some of the elements of this letter and what makes it successful:

Dear _____

The salutation is temporarily left blank in order to be personalized. No impersonal "dear friend" or "dear neighbor."

Many of us are fortunate to have quality healthcare available to us and to our family members; some of us may even take it for granted. We may not have to seriously consider the cost when we schedule an appointment, order a prescription or contemplate hospitalization. However, for some families in our community, a child's accident or illness becomes a budget decision as well as a health concern. Necessary healthcare may be delayed or not received at all due to family financial constraints.

This first paragraph clearly states the need—there are people in this very community, perhaps even people the letter recipient knows, whose children need medical care.

This paragraph also reminds us of how lucky most of us are to take quality healthcare for granted.

During the recent wildfires in Southern California, a mother called the Glendale Healthy Kids office seeking help for her child who was having difficulty breathing due to the very poor air quality. She explained that she had applied for Healthy Families insurance coverage, but due to a clerical error, her application had been misdirected and she was told to start the process over again. It was plain that the child could not wait so our case manager scheduled an appointment with one of our physicians and also provided the inhaler necessary for the child to breathe.

This paragraph is set off in italics so that is attention-grabbing, and it couches the work of the organization in human terms, telling the story of one mother battling for her child. It also ties the letter to a recent news event—the Southern California wildfires.

GHK helps hundreds of children who are unable to access timely healthcare every year. These are the children who fall through the cracks of our healthcare system. Typically, their parents work but do not have employer-based health coverage or do not have dependent care. They may not qualify for MediCal or Healthy Families insurance and cannot afford the increasingly high premiums for private health insurance. For families like this, Glendale Healthy Kids may be the only avenue to get the help they need for their children.

Information about the organization and its past successes.

A former Glendale Healthy Kids client wrote, "...there is not a day that goes by that I am not thankful for all that you have done for me. My life changed, and I learned that there are people and organizations that care about kids like me. Your work and kindness not only saved my life, but it saves so many others."

Testimonial from a satisfied client.

So today, whether you've had a long-term relationship with us, or are just starting out – give from your heart. Your donation will make a difference in the lives of children who are suffering with illness or injury.

Closing and the Ask.

With gratitude,

President

Board of Directors

The letter is signed by one person, the president of the Board of Directors.

Once your potential donor has read your fundraising letter and turned into an actual donor, what do you do next? Ignoring him or her is not an option. Just as your mother taught you years ago, it is always proper and necessary to write a thank-you letter. It is simply the polite thing to do. Consider your new donors as new friends with whom you are going to build a long-term relationship. Not only that, but as your new donor becomes better familiar with the good work that you do, you may also be able to persuade her into giving larger and larger donations as time goes by. Communication is the key to repeat donations. Additionally, many donors will require a thank-you letter for tax purposes.

The thank-you letter will be also be used when you need to thank a donor or volunteer or board member for a cash donation that does not include membership, for donations of in-kind services or goods. As mentioned in the section on welcome letters, it is vitally important to acknowledge and thank donors for all different kinds of donations.

Bear in mind that every donor, no matter how small, deserves a thank-you letter — even if they have only contributed $5 or $10. You should write a form letter that each and every donor will receive. However, donors who give large amounts of money should receive individualized letters.

Guidelines for thank-you letters at every level include expressing gratitude in a warm way. You want your donors to be glad they decided to donate to you, not feel unappreciated. Remind them how they, along with their fellow donors, will have an impact on whatever issue it is you deal with, and praise their decision to donate. You might also want to share recent successes in the thank-you letter, especially if you did not make this part of your solicitation letter.

Some organizations also use the thank-you letter as a place to ask for another donation, however, research has shown that the amount of money netted from this practice is not enough to cover any costs of mailing and production. However, research has shown that the amount of money netted from this practice is not enough to cover any costs of mailing and production. However, research has also repeatedly shown that thank-yous have several important functions (besides the basic bottom line one of politeness):

- A thank-you will boost response to future asks.

- A thank-you will boost donor loyalty.

- A thank-you will allow you to begin building long-term relationships with your donor.

These are all benefits that go way beyond a simple cost analysis and make writing a thank-you worth the time and effort.

Following are several different samples of thank-you letters.

SAMPLE HIGH-END DONATION LETTER

The following letter is an example of a thank-you for a high-end donation. Note also the information at the end of the letter concerning tax records.

Dear_____ ,

On behalf of Oregon College of Art and Craft, I would like to thank you for your generous **annual fund gift of $1,000.00.** We truly appreciate your commitment to the College. Your leadership, dedication, and munificent contribution of your time and energy sustain and strengthen the unique, quality craft education programs the College brings to the community.

Again, thank you for your partnership and investment. Your support fosters our mission of providing the highest quality professional training to tomorrow's artists and craftsmen.

Sincerely,

Development Associate

SAMPLE HIGH-END DONATION LETTER

This letter is provided for your tax records. We confirm that you did not receive any goods or services in exchange for your donation, making the entire contribution tax deductible to the extent the law allows. Please consult your tax advisor for further information regarding deductibility. Our tax ID number is _____.

The next letter sample is an example of a thank-you to a corporation for sponsoring a table at a special event. Note also the listing of the benefit to the corporation:

SAMPLE SPECIAL EVENT SPONSOR THANK-YOU LETTER

Date:_____

Dear _____,

On behalf of Oregon College of Art and Craft, thank you and _____ for your gracious support of the College through a $2,500 event table sponsorship at Art on the Vine 2008 to be held on Saturday, March 15, 2008 at the Oregon Convention Center. We greatly appreciate your generosity!

Your table sponsorship merits the following benefits:

• Recognition in the College's newsletter and publicity materials

• Recognition in the auction catalog

• Acknowledgement on the Donor Wall in the College's Centrum

We also ask that you list the names and addresses of your guests for the evening on the form enclosed. Collecting this information ahead of time allows for a quick, smooth check-in and check-out at the auction for you and your guests.

Again, thank you for supporting Oregon College of Art and Craft. Sponsoring a table at Art on the Vine is a great way to demonstrate your support of fine art and craft education. If you have any questions, please do not hesitate to call me at 503-297-5544, ext. 146.

Sincerely,

Auction Coordinator

SAMPLE INDIVIDUAL MEMBERSHIP THANK-YOU LETTER

The following is an example of an individual membership thank-you that gives a personal feel because it mentions a current exhibit.

Dear_____ ,

On behalf of Oregon College of Art & Craft and especially our students, I want to thank you for your recent _____ contribution. Your new membership at the Individual Level helps us maintain unique educational programs that serve thousands of artists and art patrons each year. As we move into an exciting new phase of planning and expansion, we are grateful more than ever to our community for its sustaining generosity.

If you provided your e-mail address to us, you will receive our short and colorful monthly e-newsletter. Or check our Web site **www.ocac.edu** for event updates.

We invite you to join us for our current exhibition in the Hoffman Gallery. Showcasing over seventy alumni participating, the Alumni Centennial exhibition through February 22, 2007, you'll have an opportunity to see the work of the next generation of craftspeople, artists, makers, designers, and crystalline thinkers. Featuring both two- and three-dimensional work in contemporary art and craft media, the invitational exhibition honors the college's alumni and their realization of becoming professional, working artists.

Thank you again for helping us to ensure that the College thrives.

Sincerely,

Development Director

A similar letter from the same organization takes the opportunity to inform the member about the college's upcoming auction—the most important fundraising event of the year. This is an example of how a thank-you letter can do double duty.

DOUBLE DUTY THANK YOUR LETTER SAMPLE

Dear_____ ,

Thank you for your $35 contribution to the Oregon College of Art & Craft. Your gift at the Individual Level helps the College maintain our unique educational programs, serving thousands of artists and art patrons each year. As we move into a new phase of planning and expansion, we are more than ever grateful to our community for its support.

Spring is a busy time here at the College. Saturday, April 30 is the date of our only fundraiser, our Art on the Vine auction. Tickets are $150 each. The auction features both silent and live bidding, full dinner with champagne and dessert, and hosted bar with appetizers. We work hard to procure wonderful, collectible art in all price ranges, along with wine, nice travel packages and fun parties to bid for. Call us if you would like to attend.

If you provided your e-mail address to us, you will receive our short and colorful monthly e-newsletter.

I hope you'll visit us often to see the new exhibits and to look over the remarkable hand-crafted works which make our gift shop one of the most colorful and unique in the area. Don't forget that the Hands-On Café offers a delicious Sunday brunch – nothing is more enjoyable than a leisurely meal away from the hustle of the city!

Thank you again. We look forward to seeing you soon.

Sincerely,

Development Director

If you offer a membership as part of the donation package, you will want to write a special form of the thank-you letter called a welcome letter. This may be a letter or an entire package, welcoming the member to the fold, thanking him or her for his or her donation, and offering information on all the programs the organization offers.

If you think that skipping the welcome letter might be a good way to keep down costs, think again. More and more, the welcome letter is becoming an important part of a fundraising campaign. Think about it: if you give money or time or effort to a person or group, you expect a thank-you in return. Perhaps a better way to look at this is to turn it around: if you do not receive a thank-you, you would feel a bit snubbed. You do not want your donors to feel snubbed. On the contrary, you want to make them feel pleased with themselves for choosing such a great organization to donate to — and a welcome letter can accomplish just that. If you make a donor feel appreciated, the odds that he or she will donate again increase dramatically.

Also bear in mind that immediately after his or her first donation is the best time to approach your donor for other options, such as sustainer programs. Take advantage of this by making your welcome letter do double duty by describing some of these options. Many experts feel that the immediate aftermath of the first donation is the best time to build a long-lasting relationship. You have convinced him or her to donate once, after all, and so once he or she begins to see not only the benefits of the organization, but other ways to contribute, you will be on your way to hooking a star prospect.

The welcome package is also an excellent opportunity to share information about your organization with new donors. This, in turn, will get them more excited about the group they have decided to give money to and may help turn them into long-term donors. Odds are good that your welcome letter may be only the second or third piece of information about your organization that your donor sees, so make it count. And, while you are providing donors with this information, you can also provide them with information about other giving or volunteer opportunities and see if they express an interest.

THINGS TO INCLUDE IN THE WELCOME LETTER

- A large and readily visible indication that the letter is about welcoming the new donor to the organization. Something as simple as the word welcome in big letters will do.

- A form which will enable new members or new donors to request more information about specific programs. This is an excellent place to feature special programs.

- A donor option form which gives information on opting out of mailing lists.

- A form, which will allow them to request information on other giving options—such as a monthly giving program.

- Information about programs the organization offers which the donor might want to participate in—volunteer opportunities, upcoming special events, grass-roots campaigns, future lobbying, or protest events.

POSSIBLE ENCLOSURES FOR THE WELCOME PACKET

- Brochure about member benefits and services

- A member survey (keep it brief, you don't want to overwhelm them).

- Information on volunteer opportunities

- Information or brochure on planned giving opportunities.

- Information or brochure on monthly giving programs

- Information or brochure about how the organization works — here is another place where all that inquiry you did into your nonprofit will come in handy!

- A membership card. Some nonprofits like to briefly state the member benefits on the back.

- Information about any merchandise you might sell, along with the amount of discount a member will receive on it.

While creating the member or new donor welcome kit may seem like a lot of extra work and expense, in the long run, it will improve your retention rate dramatically. And every organization is looking for ways to improve their long-term standing. Even if you only create an abbreviated version of the above suggestions for a welcome packet, come up with something. It will give your new donors an excellent impression of you.

SAMPLE NEW MEMBER WELCOME LETTER

Dear Member,

Welcome! And thank you for joining Environment Northwest.

We are so pleased that you have decided to support our commitment to creating models for green, sustainable businesses throughout the Northwest. Together we can foster a new way of doing business that will be a model for companies throughout the world.

SAMPLE NEW MEMBER WELCOME LETTER

With your membership, you are supporting a network of concerned activists and business people who share a vision of a sustainable life style on this green and blue planet of ours. As a member of Environment Northwest, you are an environmental as well as an economic activist. This marriage of environment and economy is the wave of the future, and no longer do the two need to be seen as mutually exclusive.

We pledge to bring you the most up-to-date information possible on all economic environmental strategies. We'll keep you informed of the latest in sustainable ventures, and offer you many opportunities to get involved at various levels.

With your membership, you are eligible for all the following benefits:

Environment Northwest Monthly, our award-winning newsletter which, as part of our commitment to sustainability, will be e-mailed to your inbox unless you specifically request a paper copy. Every issue of Environment Northwest Monthly contains tips for wedding the environmental and economic on a business as well as a personal level.

Access to the Environment Northwest Database, our online compendium of resources on all things environmental and economic.

Annual Directory of Sustainable Northwest Businesses. We make it easy for you to put your money where your mouth is with this yearly directory sent to you in pdf format.

Twenty percent Member discount on all books and merchandise for sale on our Web site. Show your loyalty to the cause by sporting one of our green T-shirts or carrying a tote bag.

In order to keep you as informed as possible about our organization, we've enclosed a brochure with more information about all of our activities. We invite you to peruse this form at your leisure, and please feel free to contact us with any questions or concerns. We have also included information about our planned giving and monthly sustainer programs.

Again, welcome. And thank your for your support. We look forward to working with you in the continuing fight for our green planet.

Sincerely,

Executive Director

Environment Northwest

SPECIAL EVENT LETTER

In the course of your fundraising career, your organization may decide to sponsor special events either to raise money or to raise awareness of the nonprofit in the community. Or, you may have an annual event such as an auction that will require you to write letters asking for specific types of donations. Things to remember for the special event letter:

- State why help is needed

- Appeal to emotions

- Give a deadline—which will no doubt be easy because special event letters are time-sensitive

- Always make it easy to respond

The following letter succeeds in informing the recipient not only about the work of the organization, but tells them about a special event — a holiday party with toys for clients — and how their contributions have in the past and will in the future contribute to such important work.

SPECIAL EVENT LETTER

December, 2007

Dear Neighbor:

If you thought you knew what the "typical" Foothill Unity Center client looked like, you would have been surprised to meet Jane. She looked like a woman you'd see across a crowded aisle at Pavilions or Trader Joe's — not someone gripped by quiet desperation.

SPECIAL EVENT LETTER

She only stopped by to sign up for a discount on her electric bill. But the income range she marked on the form qualified her family for all our services. As we talked, her story came out.

In a stroke of appalling luck, Jane and her husband — parents of three — lost their jobs at the same time. As they scoured the market for work, bills and expenses piled up. Things got desperate so fast. Now they weren't even sure they could hold onto their home.

Still, when we suggested Jane might want to sign up for food and services, she resisted. "Oh, no!" she exclaimed. "We donate to you!" We eventually talked her into accepting help.

There is no "typical" client at Foothill Unity Center. The truth is, most of us are just a paycheck or two away from Jane's dilemma. We hope it never happens to us. But if it does, we know we have a place to turn to get the help we need.

Thanks to caring local people like you, Foothill Unity Center is always there with a range of services unmatched across Los Angeles County. Last year, we distributed nearly 1.2 million pounds of food to 2,071 unduplicated very low-income local families. We also provided clothing, limited motel vouchers, and referrals to the homeless and people in crisis. Our clients meet stringent income guidelines and are requalified annually. Over 70% are children and seniors.

Although there's no time limit for using our services, many families only need help for a short time to get back on their feet. Three or four months after we first met Jane, she came in to give each of us a hug. "This is the last time we'll be using your services," she announced, tears in her eyes. "My husband and I have both found work."

During the holidays, coping with the stresses of hunger and economic hardship becomes more difficult than ever. Please help us make sure no neighbor of ours spends this special season without food, hope, and caring hands. Send a generous holiday gift to Foothill Unity Center today. As always, we promise we'll use it well.

YES! I want to help local families in need have

a brighter holiday season and greater hope for the New Year.

SPECIAL EVENT LETTER

My tax deductible donation of $ _____ is enclosed 0

Please charge my donation of $ _____ to my MasterCard ☐   Visa ☐

Account # _____-_____-_____-_____

Expiration Date: _____

Name on Acct._____

Signature: _____

Zip: _____

Because the holidays are such a difficult time for families in need, our annual Holiday Gift and Food Distribution is always one of the season's brightest moments, especially for children.

On December 16, we'll take over Ayers Hall at Los Angeles County Arboretum to treat our clients, including well over 1,500 children, to a warm, colorful Christmas celebration. Each family will receive a generous holiday food box, gifts, and toys for their children. There'll be festivities galore, including new books from Monrovia Reads; a host of fun activities for kids; and a chance to socialize with the guest of honor, Santa Claus himself.

We will be welcoming low-income neighbors we serve from eleven local cities: Altadena, Arcadia, Azusa, Baldwin Park, Bradbury, Duarte, Irwindale, Monrovia, Pasadena, Sierra Madre and South Pasadena. Volunteers from all these communities will be on hand to make sure it's a day to remember.

This event, and all of our programs, would not be possible without the generous support of neighbors like you. While the Center receives some grant monies, the help we give is primarily funded by donations from local organizations, businesses, and individuals. We're proud to say that for the past five years, over 90% of those funds have gone directly to client programs.

Please join us this holiday season in giving your neighbors in need the best possible help: not a handout, but a hand up. We only send out an appeal once a year, and this year your support is vital to keep our programs going. Your gift to Foothill Unity

SPECIAL EVENT LETTER

Center now will make life better for so many — for the holidays and in the coming year.

My thanks for your caring support, and warmest wishes for a season of joy to you and your loved ones.

Sincerely,

Executive Director

P.S.: There are many ways to help! Of course we always welcome your donation by check or credit card. A gift of appreciated securities can offer you tax savings. Including us in your estate plans is an especially meaningful choice. Volunteering or making in-kind donations like food, toys, and clothing enable us to give more. Donating to or shopping at our thrift store, the Rainbow's End, helps, too. Whatever form your generosity takes, know that we're deeply grateful for your support.

Foothill	Foothill	Rainbow's End
Unity Center	Unity Center	Boutique and Thrift Store
Distribution and Administration	Distribution Site	346 W. Huntington Dr.
415 W. Chestnut St.	191 N. Oak St.	(King Ranch Center)
Monrovia, CA 91016	Pasadena, CA 91107	Monrovia, CA 91016
Telephone: 626 358-3486	Telephone: 626 584-7420	Telephone: 626 303-3040
Fax: 626 358-8224	Fax: 626 584-4722	

Another type of special event letter you may need to write involves asking for donations for an event such as an auction. In this case, you will want to include suggestions for donations, the date of the event, deadlines for donations, and pick-up and delivery of the donated item. Here is an example of such a letter:

SAMPLE SPECIAL EVENT DONATION LETTER

Name

Address

City, State 97210   June 23, 2008

Dear _____,

As OCAC embarks on its 101st year of fine craft education, we invite you as a local wine shop to investigate "Craft 101" with us by donating a selection from your inventory to the College's major fundraising auction, Art on the Vine 2008. Art on the Vine celebrates exceptional art and wine, so donating excellent wines for bid allows you to get your company's name in front of a large group of local wine aficionados. Thus, we are offering regional wineries the opportunity to feature their wines at this event which attracts _____.

Past donations have included cases of wine, verticals, magnums, catered winetastings and tours, and extremely rare and/or valuable single bottles of wine. If your donation is valued at $1,000 or more, you will also receive on complimentary ticket to Art on the Vine. If we receive your donation form by the deadline outlined below, you'll be recognized for your donation in the auction catalog, which is mailed to more than 4,500 people.

Please keep in mind the following, important information:

- Art on the Vine 2008 will be held on March 15, 2008 at the Oregon Convention Center.

- Arrangements for pick up or delivery of your donation will be made upon receipt of your donation form.

- DEADLINE for donation form (to be included in catalog listing) is December 1, 2007. After this date all donations will be listed in the catalog addendum.

- DEADLINE to deliver/pick up donation is March 1, 2008.

Thank you for considering this request. Please don't hesitate to contact me with any questions you may have. Your donation to this event helps ensure OCAC's future as the nation's preeminent craft institution.

Sincerely,

Auction Coordinator

SPECIAL APPEALS LETTER

Similar to the special events letter is the special appeal letter. When will you use a special appeal letter? When you need donors or members to focus on any of the following:

- **An individual program.** Perhaps you have a certain program that needs funding or a special event coming soon.

- **A specific issue.** Is the government considering legislation that will affect your constituency? Issues that affect your organization may crop up at any time.

- **A specific need.** Perhaps you have suddenly discovered a budget shortfall or some other issue that requires you to ask for more funding.

- **A specific opportunity.** A new way to expand your program, participate in an event, or partner with another organization are all opportunities that might call for a special appeal letter.

- **A certain season.** For instance, winter coming on is a crucial time for groups serving the homeless or those who offer help with heating bills. The approach of hurricane season in the south is a time to make certain poverty-stricken populations have home repairs finished.

- **Holidays.** Come Thanksgiving and Christmas, people really do start to turn their attention to helping others

— and this can translate to increased donations for you. Also think about other holidays throughout the year that you can key a special appeal letter to.

- **A financial challenge.** Perhaps you have a Capital Campaign, or a debt which needs retiring. Or maybe there is a sudden need to find a new location or purchase the building you currently rent. Financial challenges happen to everyone. Be certain to be clear about what you need the money for and how much, exactly, you need.

Bear in mind that even though you are appealing for help based on a special need, most organizations make it clear that the funds collected through these campaigns will be undesignated. This is so that they can decide where the best use of the donor's money will be.

Because special appeals letters are most often mailed only once, they will have specific time references in them. This is a great, legitimate way to emphasize urgency. Another difference with special appeals letter is that the ask amount may vary. With your regular solicitations for general donations or memberships, you will have a set string of donation amounts. But because your special appeals letter is keyed to a specific need or program, you may be asking for different and specific amounts. Along the same lines, you will also be far more specific about the programs or events you are asking the donor to support. Special appeals letters may be shorter than the straight contribution letter and it is even more likely to have a warm and friendly tone.

The following example of a special appeal letter keys the Ask to a specific request—money for a back-to-school shopping spree. It also has a unique focus in that it utilizes a personal appeal-asking each recipient to send it on to ten other people.

This letter also clearly states the need and asks for a very specific and doable amount of money to donate—$25.

SAMPLE SPECIAL APPEALS LETTER

Dear Friend,

I have been asked to help raise at least $10,000 to assist in the Mervyns/Jaycees Back-To-School Shopping Spree Program.

The Back-To-School Shopping Spree Program helps underprivileged kids in our community buy new school clothes when they start back to school in September. It offers kids and parents a dignified way of getting the clothes they need for their upcoming school season. The more money raised on the part of the Jaycees, the more Mervyns will match our funds, and the greater number of underprivileged kids whose needs will be met in a compassionate and professional manner.

In order to help reach this goal, we ask that you kindly do the following:

1. Please forward a check for $25 (no more) made payable to "The Pasadena Jaycees," 471 Walnut Street, Pasadena, CA 91105

2. Please retype this letter on your letterhead and send it to ten friends or individuals in your company who you know personally and know will be able to help. With your letter, please send the names of those who receive it along with the enclosed list of recipients to date.

All contributions are fully tax deductible. No goods or services have been offered or received by you in consideration of your gift. Thanks for joining me in supporting this worthwhile endeavor.

Best regards,

Past President

Pasadena Jaycees

MAJOR DONOR APPEAL LETTER

As the returns from you fundraising letter campaigns begin coming in, you will notice one thing — most of the donations are relatively small, in the $100 or less range.

However, it is possible to raise larger amounts of money through the direct-mail fundraising letter, it just takes a slightly different approach. These appeals are called either "major donor" or "high-dollar gifts." A few years back, these high-dollar appeal letters were relatively rare, but as organizations become more successful with them, their use has increased.

These letters may be targeted as a special appeal to your file of most generous donors, or they may be used in mailings to specially identified groups. The major donor letter will promise a certain level of benefits in return for the higher level of donation, so only take this route when you are ready to follow through on your promises.

Consider some of the things that set major donor letters apart from the garden-variety fundraising letter. For starters, and most obviously, the ask amount is high. Major donor letters feature a high-ask string - while you may offer several levels of giving, they are all much higher than that ask amounts in the standard letters.

The major donor fundraising package will also look different. It will be printed on more expensive paper with a stylish, elegant design that appeals to a high-end donor. The way you phrase the letter will be different, too, to appeal to a different income level of donor. You might offer membership in a special "President's Circle" or some other type of club. These offers of membership in an exclusive club are designed, honestly, to motivate through good old-fashioned snob appeal. Along the same lines, the major donor appeal will always, always, always, be personalized. Your high-dollar donors do not want to open a beautiful package and find it addressed to "dear friend." That is tantamount to a slap in the face.

Besides those differences, the major donor appeal may have an entirely different marketing concept behind it. While you will want to provide your major donors with information about your organization, you will also want to consider providing them with an entire package of benefits. Some of these might include:

Membership in an Insider's Club. You might want to name the club the President's Circle, the Founder's Club, or The President's Club. Some organizations also create several levels of club membership, such as the gold, silver, or bronze levels.

Invitations to Special Events. These may include receptions with the president, a dinner at a board member's home, or a similar event.

Recognition through Plaques. This may be done in an annual report or, in the case of a school or museum, in an actual physical location. Of course, the highest-end donors may be honored by naming a building or wing after them.

Special Gifts. You might consider books or pieces of art, perhaps some sort of specially commissioned piece. Keep it relevant to the goals of your organization.

Since listing these benefits could take up the entire fundraising letter, a good approach is to write the fundraising letter and include a separate brochure that will list the benefits you have decided to offer. In the letter itself, you will want to make sure the tone of the letter befits the people you are addressing, and in most cases, it is wise to have the letter signed by a peer of the major donor. You might also want to specify a special use of the funds that will be collected from your major donors.

SAMPLE MAJOR DONOR LETTER

Dear (Major Donor Name),

I want to personally thank you for your past support of Homes For All and offer you an opportunity to join our prestigious President's Circle.

As a member of this exclusive group, you will enjoy certain privileges and benefits. You'll be invited to the annual President's Circle dinner, where you'll receive a briefing on the organization from the president and meet our board of directors. You will be a special guest at Homes For All groundbreaking ceremonies. Members of the President's Circle will have their names inscribed on a plaque at Homes For All headquarters. Finally, you'll receive invitations to special events throughout the year, including members-only lectures and teas, and meetings with the new homeowners that make up the client base of Homes For All.

But most important, as members of this special group you will enjoy the biggest benefit of all: the satisfaction of knowing they've helped a deserving family own a home. As a President's Circle donor, your funds will go directly toward the purchase of a home for a family in need. Your generous gift will be put to use immediately toward sponsorship of a new home. This is a unique opportunity to see your donation put to use immediately.

Building houses for previously homeless families is not cheap, even with our access to discount materials and a commitment to recycling materials. Despite this, over the last five years, Homes for All has placed 120 families in new homes. Nearly all

SAMPLE MAJOR DONOR LETTER

of these 120 families remain in their homes and have perfect payment records on the reduced mortgages we offer them. Clearly Homes for All has found a formula that works to aid families find stability through home ownership.

However, there is a crying need for more homes for poverty-stricken families. As a President's Circle supporter, you'll help to fill a huge gap that exists between those of means and those who struggle to get by.

Once again, thank you for your support in the past. We look forward to welcoming you to our President's Circle club.

Sincerely,

Executive Director

RENEWAL LETTERS

You may also see this referred to as writing renewal letters or writing a renewal series letter. Any time you write a letter to an existing donor it is called a renewal letter. Often renewal letters fall into the category of an annual gift letter. What, precisely is an annual gift letter? It is a fundraising letter that solicits a donation given annually, and to receive donations, you will be sending out a series of letters on an annual basis. Sending the annual letter is an excellent time to remind people of their long-term commitment to your cause, and get them excited about re-committing. The good news is that the renewal letter offers a high rate of return.

You will be sending renewal letters to people who have already shown a high degree of interest in your organization. If you offer memberships or other kinds of tangible benefits, such as a magazine subscription, then you will want to send out a renewal letter on the anniversary of the date of their original contribution. In this case, you can send a renewal letter that is closely related to an invoice, which will jog your supporter's memory that it is time to re-up his or her membership.

The other time that you may send an annual letter is at the end of the calendar year. This, then, is a letter that would go to all prior donors. With this option, though, be aware that you do not want to send a letter to donors who have recently sent money for the first time as this may do more harm than good. You will want to establish some sort of cut-off date for asking for renewals and a three-month time period is considered appropriate. With this type of annual renewal letter it is important to let the member know that it is standard procedure, with the letter being sent to everyone, so he or she does not think he or she is being singled out.

You may be wondering if sending a renewal letter is appropriate if you are also sending a variety of other letters throughout the year. The answer is yes, however, during the time you are sending the renewal letters, refrain from sending out any other types of fundraising letters.

Non-profit organizations have traditionally approached the renewal letter in two different ways. The most common is the short reminder letter. This is a simple letter which tells the donor that her membership will soon be up for renewal, or that the anniversary of her first contribution is at hand and she may want to consider donating more.

Another type of renewal letter tends to be lengthier and presents a recap of what the organization has accomplished in the last year. This kind of "annual report" letter is especially appropriate when you are sending a year-end letter rather than an anniversary re-up letter. The following guidelines will help you write an annual renewal letter:

- **State the Benefits to Renewal.** If membership includes a magazine subscription, for instance, make it clear that this subscription will lapse if there is no renewal. It is important to mention other benefits, too. For instance, membership in a museum offers free admission to the museum and a discount on all purchases at the gift store. These are important benefits to remind members about.

- **State the Renewal Request Clearly.** Some experts recommend stating the renewal request in the very first sentence or paragraph. Remember, you are writing to people who already support your organization. Therefore it is not so much necessary to sell yourself as it is to remind them why they support you. It is customary to send out a series of renewal letters and the letters will typically get more and more urgent as time goes on. Do not place blame on the donor; instead mention busy schedules and overwhelming commitments. Make them feel good about themselves as you remind them of their commitment to you.

- **Upgrade!** The annual renewal letter is an excellent place to ask for an upgraded donation amount. You will be preaching to the choir here — you know these members or donors have already contributed and appreciate your work, so why not push them (gently) to donate more? The donors who respond to the first renewal letter you send out are the best prospects for this and will be most responsive to upgrading. Be sure to ask them.

- **Share Successes.** The annual renewal letter is a great place to update members on the victories and successes you have enjoyed over the past year. Remember, donors like to feel they are making a difference, and they will appreciate reading about your triumphs over the past year.

- **Simplicity Rules.** This is especially true with a year-end annual letter. We are all busy, and around the holidays, we are even busier than usual. Compounding that is the issue that lots of other organizations will be sending out year-end letters, too. Competition for the time of your donor is even fiercer at this time of year. So keep it simple.

- **Future Forecast.** No, you do not know what the future will bring — but look to it with anticipation in your letter. Everyone likes to feel hopeful, and your donors are no exception.

Another way to approach writing the annual renewal letter is to think about what your goals for it might be. The obvious, bottom-line goal of any fundraising letter is to seek donations. A renewal letter can accomplish that, and, as we have seen, it may also help you to upgrade your donor's gift. But in the case of a renewal letter, there is another goal at play and that is to constantly renew your donor's commitment to your cause. The savvy fundraiser regards donor loyalty as a long-term occupation and has that goal in the back of her mind with every contact she makes to the donor, be it by letter or phone or e-mail.

Yet another goal that a renewal letter might net you is converting your donor to a monthly giver. The ideal donor is the one who happily gives a check once a month, be it from his checking account or a credit card. An annual letter can be the perfect place to broach this topic with your donors. Another great idea is to make use of the liftnote concept. Include one of these smaller size pieces of paper along with the main letter, and use it to explain the details of the monthly giving program you would like to promote.

SAMPLE RENEWAL LETTER

December 1, 2007

Dear ,

First and foremost, on behalf of Oregon College of Art and Craft, and especially our students, we wish to thank you for being a valued supporter of this vital educational and cultural resource. Your collaboration and involvement is extremely important as we continue to accomplish our mission of contributing significantly to the continuity of contemporary craft as an artistic expression.

I'm contacting you today to remind you that your membership will expire in 30 days. As the College moves into a new phase of planning and expansion, we are grateful more than ever to our community for its continued loyalty and generosity. A membership form is enclosed with the hope that you will renew or perhaps consider increasing your membership level in honor of OCAC's commitment to providing students and our surrounding community with the highest quality art and craft educational resources and experiences. We can also process your membership with a credit card (Visa/MC/Disc) by phone at (503) 297-5544 ext. 177.

In addition, we invite you to visit the Hoffman Gallery's upcoming exhibition entitled Interlaced. The exhibit will showcase a number of textile processes that incorporate alternative media. The show will run from January 24 through February 24, 2008, with an opening reception on Thursday, January 24 from 4:00 – 7:00pm. Anne Amie Vineyards, our featured local vintner, will pour specially selected wines during the opening event. Regular gallery hours are 10am-5pm, Monday through Sunday.

SAMPLE RENEWAL LETTER

Thank you again for your commitment to the arts; to OCAC. Your further investment will help to ensure that the College continues to flourish as one of Oregon's finest educational, cultural and community resources.

Sincerely,

Development Associate

The Year-End Contribution Letter

What do non-profits organizations have in common with retail businesses? While on the surface the similarities may seem to be miniscule, there is one large commonality. Retail businesses earn much of their yearly income during the last month of the year and nonprofits garner a large share of their donations during the end-of-the-year holiday season also. The holiday season engenders a feeling of generosity and hope in many people and it is at this time of year that their thoughts turn to giving.

Because of this, successful nonprofits have made it their habit to write and mail a year-end appeal to donors and other supporters. What makes these letters different from the standard solicitation letter and how should you approach writing them? The following guidelines should help.

- A reference to the year's end or the holiday season should be made in the first paragraph if not the first sentence.

- Use special papers with a holiday theme and consider offering premiums such as holiday greeting cards or mailing labels.

- Offer hope for the new year. Explain the successes of the past year and look forward to continuing success in the future.

- Use all of your mailing list. This is not a time to be selective.

- Do not forget to mention the all-important tax deduction. Emphasize the benefits of a year-end tax deduction. Businesses and individuals may be looking for deductions at this time.

SAMPLE YEAR-END CONTRIBUTION LETTER

December, 2007

Dear Friends,

As winter approaches and 2007 comes to a close, so does our year-long celebration of a century of fine art and craft education at Oregon College of Art and Craft. Entering our 101st year, OCAC is poised to be at the center of next chapter of the contemporary craft movement. I am writing today to ask that you consider OCAC in your year-end giving plans. Your much needed support can be directed to fund tuition assistance for the next generation of professional craft-focused artists, provide Art Adventures scholarships for economically disadvantaged children, or ensure our Studio School programming remains vibrant. Your tax-deductible contribution will help the College maintain its unique educational programs, serving thousands of artists and community members each year.

We are proud to continue our tradition of exceptional craft education. In 2007, over 900 students from 100 schools throughout the US and Canada competed in the NICHE Awards, which celebrate excellence and innovation in the American craft industry. OCAC students won three of fifteen total student awards, and received a greater number of awards than any other college in the country. It is wonderful to see our students gain national recognition.

Community participation in our Studio School program is at an all time high. Our campus comes alive as students explore their creativity. OCAC also invigorates the artistic community through Artist in Residence fellowships to emerging and mid-career artists. Since its inception, the College has brought approximately 200

SAMPLE YEAR-END CONTRIBUTION LETTER

artists to Portland to participate in the program; 50% of these artists have chosen to remain in the region.

One of our most successful programs is *Journeys in Creativity*, an immersive art education and cultural appreciation program for Native American teens. 100% of Journeys participants rely on scholarships in order to attend. This year workshops will include a hands-on canoe design and construction project. OCAC will strive to reach thousands more through new outreach initiatives to Southern and Central Oregon Tribes, offering free hands-on craft events to entire communities. We are proud to announce that Journeys student artwork will be on display at the Smithsonian Museum of Native American Art in Washington D.C. in March 2008.

During the summer of 2007, nearly 1100 children participated in our popular Art Adventures program - 20% of whom relied on community scholarship support in order to attend. Youth participants engaged in workshops that included ceramics, wood, metal, and drawing/painting. Additionally, more than 100 teenagers participated in workshops that offered in-depth study and coaching towards production of portfolio-quality work in subjects such as painting, fashion design, jewelry and ceramics. All programs concluded with an enthusiastically attended Art Walk for family and friends, where students were given the opportunity to show pride in all they had accomplished.

We are excited for the opportunity to increase access to the finest contemporary art and craft educational resources for students and community members in the Portland metro area and beyond. As we move into a new phase of planning and expansion, we are extremely grateful to our community for its continued loyalty and generosity. Thank you for considering making a fully tax-deductible gift to support our efforts. A contribution form is attached. To request additional information, or to arrange a tour of our campus, please call us at 503-297-5544 ext177.

Sincerely,

President

LAPSED DONOR

When does a donor become a lapsed donor? This will vary according to whether you offer memberships or simple request donations, but most organizations consider a donor to be lapsed when they have not contributed over the past year. Some nonprofits extend this to include anyone who has not contributed in up to three years. Beyond that, your donors are not lapsed, they are former donors—and discuss when to give up on them in the next section.

Lapsed donors are almost as good at current donors at giving money, and they are way better than strangers to your organization, so they are worth cultivating. Some experts believe that you may net an 11 percent response rate from a lapsed donor mailing.

One of the simplest and most effective things you can do in the lapsed donor letter is to ask the donor to come back. The key is to get the donor involved so that they will take action to send you a gift. Be sure to tell your donor how much you miss him, too.

Another key thing to consider is that the longer the period of time is since the donor gave you money, the less likely is it that they will give again. Because of this, many fundraising experts recommend dividing your lapsed donors into three segments. First deal with the most likely to re-donate, those who have lapsed for only a year. The next level should be those donors who have not given for two years. And finally, you will send a mailing to those for whom it has been three years. Because of the differences in these groups, you will also want to send each of them a slightly different letter. The one-year lapsed donor will likely respond to a casual "we miss you" appeal, since it is likely he or she has simply forgotten to mail his or her donation. You will want to get progressively more vociferous as the time since the last donation lengthens.

Besides scrutinizing the length of time since the last donation, also look at how many times your lapsed donor has given in the past. There is a world of difference between the donor who has given repeatedly and suddenly quit giving, and the one who as donated once and quit. The more times a donor has given, the more personal you will want the letter to be. You also have decisions to make about how much you will ask for. It is appropriate to ask the one-time donor for the same amount she originally gave. For the repeat donor you can ask for the amount of the most recent donation, or figure an average of all his donations, or begin with the smallest on the theory that it is better to lure him back.

SAMPLE LAPSED MEMBERSHIP LETTER

Dear,

The Oregon College of Art and Craft turns 100 years old this year, and it is impossible to think that we could have come this far without the generous support of community members like you. OCAC counts on dedicated groups and individuals as we continue to contribute significantly to the continuity of contemporary craft as an artistic expression.

Our records show that your annual membership has now expired. Given your proven commitment to our mission, I hope that you will renew, and perhaps consider increasing your membership support in honor of our centennial and 100 years of teaching and inspiring students of all ages. I have enclosed a membership form so that you may choose a giving level that is right for you. Or, fill out our new Century Circle form. Contribute $100 or more and choose either a limited edition OCAC hat or tote bag as our special gift to you. I hope you'll take a moment to write a check and complete the form. Consistent support is central to our ability to serve the community of Portland from this vital and much-loved educational institution.

In addition, we invite you to visit the Hoffman Gallery's upcoming exhibition entitled Interlaced. The exhibit will showcase a number of textile processes that incorporate alternative media. The show will run from January 24 through February 24, 2008, with an opening reception on Thursday, January 24 from 4:00 – 7:00pm. Anne Amie

SAMPLE LAPSED MEMBERSHIP LETTER

Vineyards, our featured local vintner, will pour specially selected wines during the opening event. Regular gallery hours are 10am-5pm, Monday through Sunday.

Craft's relevance to the modern world has never been more vital. In an increasingly electronic, technological, and impersonal society, the core human inclination to make and create has only become more acute. A contribution to OCAC ensures that the values of craft and fine art remain active and open to discovery by each subsequent generation.

Thank you so much for your participation as a valued member of the Oregon College of Art & Craft family. We're truly grateful for loyal and dedicated friends like you who appreciate the importance of having this essential cultural resource in the community. We hope to hear from you soon.

Sincerely,

Development Associate

SAMPLE LAPSED DONOR LETTER

Dear Former Supporter,

Have you forgotten us?

In the past, your generous contributions have helped Hot Dinner Delivered to provide delicious and nutritious dinners to senior citizens and shut-ins who otherwise might not have a decent meal all day. Thanks to gifts such as yours, we have been able to provide not only food but a bright spot in an otherwise lonely day to hundreds of seniors.

The need for these meals is greater than ever. Hot Dinner Delivered volunteers report that many shut-ins are unable to cook for themselves and without access to our meals, they would be forced to eat a cold meal from a can, or worse, un-nutritious snack food. For many of the seniors who are served by our program, a visit from a Hot Dinner Delivered volunteer may be their only human contact all day.

One thing our society does not seem to be able to master is basic quality-of-life care for geriatric patients. Hot Dinner Delivered works to solve this problem on the most basic of levels — with a delicious and nutritious hot meal. Most of our clients cannot afford to pay for this service on their own. It is through generous donations like yours that we are able to provide this vital service.

SAMPLE LAPSED DONOR LETTER

Last year we served an average of 100 hot dinners every day. In the upcoming year we have plans to add on a lunch service also. But all of this takes money, of course. As you read this letter, think about your own parents, grandparents, or great-grandparents. Perhaps they live far away from you, or perhaps a busy career prevents you from checking on them as much as you like. Certainly few of us have time to cook meals every night for an elderly relative. Wouldn't it give you comfort to know that somebody was not only looking in on them, but providing food as well?

Please remember your elderly relatives as you decide to renew your gift. It is up to all of us to contribute to the well-being of the oldest members of our society.

Sincerely,

Executive Director

PS. We appreciate your generous support in the past. Please help us to feed the elderly by donating again.

PREVENT LAPSED DONORS

One of the best ways to deal with lapsed donors is to prevent them from lapsing in the first place. For members, send out a renewal letter, as detailed in the previous section. But for non-membership organizations, it is also a good idea to send out a letter before your donor's support wanes. Most computer programs have sort features that should allow you to flag donors whose last gift falls right before the lapsed donor cut-off. You will want to lavish special attention on these soon-to-be-lapsed donors to lure them back to the fold before they have wandered off for good.

Why all the attention to the pre-lapsed donor? Experts say that it is in the neighborhood of five to eight times more cost effective to get a donation from a current donor than a stranger. Your current donors know your message and are comfortable with your work — perhaps they have just forgotten to send in their donation. Give them the benefit of the doubt and work a little harder to retain them.

To write the pre-lapsed donor letter, begin by acknowledging the donor's past gifts and thanking the donor for his or her support. Tell the donor how much his or her support means. Be specific here. If you can point to figures such as "Your $25 donation means five dinners for a homeless man" so much the better. Also consider offering a premium or other incentive to renew his or her support.

Lure back with a survey letter

One ideal way to lure lapsed donors back is to send them a survey letter. You will learn much more about survey letters in the next section, but for now look at how they apply to the issue of lapsed donors.

You have learned that the value of giving donors something to do and one of the best things they can do is give you a piece of their mind. Ask them why they have stopped donating. It is that simple—just ask. You can do this through a survey with pre-ordained questions or leave room on the reply device for donors to give their answers. At the very least, you will receive valuable feedback on your fundraising campaigns. Odds are good that you will also get some donations along the way. Then take this information and put it to work making sure your donors do not lapse in the first place.

Add a Note to an Existing Package

Yet another way to appeal to your lapsed donor is one of the simplest and most cost effective: add a note to the package you are sending to everyone else. This can be a note on a smaller piece of paper, like the liftnote or buckslip, and it can simply state: "We miss you. Please come back."

WHEN TO GIVE UP ON A DONOR

All your efforts notwithstanding, there will still always be some donors who simply do not respond to your efforts to get them to start donating again. When is it appropriate to give up? The line is a bit different depending on whether you offer a membership or ask for straight donations. For a membership organization, if repeated contacts have not netted a renewal, the donor's lack of interest is clear. However, for a donation system, the line is not so clear. You could keep asking forever—or until you receive a request to no longer send information. The point is, you just never know. However, most experts recommend slacking off the mailings after a year and a half to two years and stopping them completely after three years.

Also, please remember that it is bad form not to remove the names of the deceased from your mailing lists. If you get a request from a relative to stop sending because the donor has passed away, please honor it promptly.

The exceptions to the guidelines mentioned above are if the donor has made large gifts, if they have given gifts for a long time, or if they have personal ties to the organization. In the case of the donor who has given large gifts in the past, you might want to try a personal visit, either by phone or in person, or an invite to a special event. For the donor who has given a long time, it is wise not to abandon them immediately. And those with a personal tie to the organization should be kept on the mailing list indefinitely.

SURVEY LETTER

Many of us feel powerless and at times, like we don't have a voice in the world. So what could be better than somebody actually soliciting our opinions? People love to talk and they love to offer up their ideas for the world. It is in this spirit that the survey letter works. Besides the fact that people love to share their views of the world, they also love to help. This is one reason that an involvement device works so well—because it allows people to participate. There is also an element of flattery involved. After all, who does not like to be asked for their opinions?

Survey letters may not be appropriate for every organization, but they can be powerful tools for certain kinds. For instance, a group that promotes a cause that provokes an emotional reaction, good or bad, is a natural to use survey letters. Groups behind hot-button issues can make excellent use of the survey letter. But how does a survey letter actually work to net donations? The questions start out simple, and centered around the actual issue, and then they become more centered on the needs of the organization. This is when you ask for the gift.

Here are some guidelines for writing the survey letter:

Tell the Recipient Why He's Been Chosen. This implies that the reader has some special insights that might benefit the organization. A person who is an environmentalist might be chosen to answer questions about the threat from global warming. A person who works in the food industry might be called upon to respond to queries about nutrition for seniors,.

Give Reasons for the Survey. How will you use the responses? Why is it important that the recipient answer you? Will you present the information to government figures? Use the survey answers to decide upon future educational programs? Share results with the media to boost interest in the cause?

Do Not Make the Questions Too Hard. If they are too complicated, your reader may lose interest part way through.

Pair Facts with Emotion. Many survey letters are longer than basic fundraising letters because they present numerous facts for the reader to chew on. After all, this is part of what makes the survey letter work—you have got a chance to present a picture of the situation to your potential donors. At the same time, you want to get an emotional zinger or two into the letter. Clearly identify your own feelings about the subject. Allow yourself to get fired up so that you can communicate those feelings to your audience.

Do Not Forget the Ask. The survey letter always ends with an ask. It helps to create a sense of urgency in the survey questions and then it is a natural step to make the pitch for a donation.

SAMPLE SURVEY LETTER

Dear _____,

You've been chosen to receive this survey because of your support of environmental causes in the past.

Here at *Environment Northwest*, we've noticed an increasing feeling of helplessness among environmentalists. Sometimes it seems as if everybody but our politicians is getting the message about global warming and the dangers tour environment.

While more and more citizens become outraged at the blatant destruction of our planet, our elected officials continue to ignore our pleas for green legislation.

It's enough to make the most peaceful environmentalist blazing mad. So we at *Environment Northwest* have decided to quit fuming and do something about it—and this is where you come in. We've devised the enclosed survey as an attention getting device. The results will be tabulated and sent not only to our elected officials, both locally and nationally, but also the local and national news media.

We aim for no less than a raucous chorus of voices informing our government what citizens really think about the environment.

Can we count on your help? It will only take a few minutes of your time. I've also enclosed a brochure titled 50 Ways to Save the Planet, which lists easy changes you can make to live a greener life style. Consider this our thank-you for taking the time to complete the survey.

And while you're at it, won't you consider sending Environment Northwest a generous contribution? We foresee a future in which every government official considers the environment before making any decisions. You can help us achieve this future by making donating money today.

I urge you to complete the survey and send it back along with a donation today, and I thank you in advance for your help.

Sincerely,

Executive Director

SAMPLE SURVEY LETTER

PS. If you would like extra copies of the survey for friends or family to fill out, please call _____ and we will rush them to you. The more of our voices that are heard the better! Thanks for your support.

FRONT-END PREMIUM

As you might recall from our earlier discussion, a front-end premium letter is a fundraising package that includes a free gift in the mailing. This gift is usually something relatively small and easy to mail, such as address labels, note or gift cards, a religious medal, or small book. Front-end premiums cost more to produce, of course, but the extra cost is worth it because of the higher rate of donations you will net from the mailing.

Following are some guidelines for writing the front-end premium letter:

Connect the Dots. Make certain that your front-end premium relates to your organization in some way. You do not, for instance, want to send out a religious medal if you are an arts organization. A literacy organization would find a natural pairing in a bookmark. Whatever premium you choose, be sure to note the connection in your letter. For instance, a museum enclosed gift cards adorned with an image from their collection might note the name of the painting and that it is among the most popular to be viewed, then mention that members have the pleasure of seeing the painting whenever they like because admission is for them is free.

Don't Tie Gift to Premium. Guilt does not motivate people to give, it just makes them feel guilty, and that makes them want to forget the thing that made them feel that way. It is also unethical to imply that because you sent a gift, the recipient is required to send money.

The Premium is a Gift, Period. Let us face it — there is no free lunch, but we all persist in desiring one. However in the world of fundraising the free premium does truly exist. Emphasize repeatedly that the premium is free.

Choose Long Life Premiums. Ideally, it is good to find a premium that will be used repeatedly and cause the recipient to remember your nonprofit every time she uses it. Calendars, note cards, bookmarks and address labels imprinted with the organization's logos all work well for this.

SAMPLE FRONT-END PREMIUM LETTER

Dear _____,

Every avid reader knows you can never have enough bookmarks. Please accept the enclosed bookmark as a free gift to mark your place in the next book you read. When you sit down to read in your favorite chair, or open a book before you fall asleep tonight, think for a moment about the pleasure you get from reading. Now ponder a world without that ability—and what a different world it would be.

Many live in just such a world—shamed by their inability to read, doomed to a life of making do and hiding their problem. But at Reading Round-Up, we're proud to proclaim that we've taught thousands of adults how to read, so that they too can know the joy the use of a simple bookmark can bring.

So while this bookmark is a gift to you, it contains a very important reminder, that not everyone is lucky enough to be able to enjoy the gift of reading. At Reading Round-Up, we envision a world with 100% literacy. Ambitious? Yes, indeed. But would you deny the gift of reading a great book to any human being?

SAMPLE FRONT-END PREMIUM LETTER

Won't you help us make this dream a reality and make a financial contribution to our organization? Then, the next time you sit down to read you'll know you've made a difference to someone who struggles with a shameful secret. And every time you use the enclosed free bookmark you'll feel good about the donation you've made.

A gift of just $25 will buy textbooks to start one adult on her way to becoming a reader $50 ensures that we have workbooks for three adults. And your generous donation of $100 will start four people on their way to the wonderful world of reading. In our busy world, it is difficult to know how to make a difference. But at Reading Round-up, we see lives change every day. Wouldn't you like to be a part of that change? You can, and it is simple to do. Just send your generous gift today.

I thank you, and so do all the future readers of the world. Enjoy your free bookmark!

Sincerely,

Executive Director

BACK-END PREMIUM LETTER

How does the back-end premium letter differ from the front-end premium? The back-end premium offers a gift with donation, and often the ask string is affiliated with different groups. Public broadcasting is a master at the back-end premium, offering viewers a variety of different gift packages for their donations. Back-end premiums also are response boosters, but again will cost more money to produce because you will need to pay for the gifts to be given away.

Here are guidelines for the back-end premium:

Talk About it Early. As always, lead with your strength. Let the reader know about your premiums up front. Highlight the gifts as early as possible, which is an attention getter anyway.

Relate it to Your Cause. Just as with the front-end premium, it is important to have your gifts relate to the work your organization does. Again, the public broadcasting system does this well. They often offer DVDs of favorite shows, or packages, which might include a DVD along with a book or other related item. It is even more beneficial if you can find an exclusive premium of some sort to offer. This might be a magazine that you or your parent organization publish, or a reprint of a book.

Emphasize the Benefits. When writing the back-end premium copy, it is wise to build desire just as a marketer would through relating the good things that happen through owning the premium. A little flattery never hurt, either. Something along the lines of how the recipient will understand the value of the potential gifts.

Remember, it is Free. While the back-end premium does require a donation, it still is technically free and you need to emphasize this in your copy.

SAMPLE BACK-END PREMIUM LETTER

Dear _____,

If you were one of our clients, the free gift we're offering would be of little use to you.

Why is that?

Because the free book we want to send you is an exclusive cook-book filled with the

SAMPLE BACK-END PREMIUM LETTER

best recipes from local government officials, television stars, and other celebrities. The recipes were collected exclusively by Cup of Soup Kitchens for this benefit cookbook.

Purchasing the cookbook would cost you $25.95 in the store—if you were able to purchase it. But you can't, because we've printed it for the express purpose of giving as a free gift with a donation of $50 or more. Cup of Soup Kitchens Recipes is full of luscious recipes and beautiful photographs of local landmarks. Wouldn't you like to wake up to Rise 'N Shine Muffins tomorrow morning? That is local reporter Sharon Dalton's contribution to the book. Or how about trying Beefeater's Stew for dinner? It's a favorite of city councilman Bryce Trumbull's (though he admits it is his wife that cooks it).

You'll be delighted and amazed at the wide variety of delicious and nutritious recipes in *Cup of Soup Kitchens Recipes*, but the book has a very serious message. People in this community go hungry every day. Families go to bed with their stomachs growling every night.

At *Cup of Soup Kitchens*, we serve hot meals to people in need every night. Over the past five years since we opened, we have served over 150,000 meals, which means 150,000 people (many of them children) have gone to bed with food in their stomachs, full and content.

What started as a few concerned citizens preparing food at home and offering it to the hungry at local parks has grown into a full-fledged operation with our own kitchen and serving room. Our success has been rapid and we're proud of this. But all of this comes at a price. And even though we are have very low overhead and strive to keep our costs low, like all nonprofits, we still are constantly in need of funds.

This is where you come in. With your donation of only $50, you'll be contributing the full stomachs of 10 people. Not only that, but you'll be the proud owner of a beautiful cookbook, too. And every time you make a recipe from that cookbook, perhaps you will stop to be grateful for the simple bounty of food that you might take for granted.

Thank you in advance for your generous gift and I sincerely hope you enjoy your gift.

Sincerely,

Executive Director

NEWSLETTERS

A newsletter is not technically a fundraising letter, of course. But if you do send out a monthly newsletter and if so, do not overlook it as an opportunity to ask for donations or volunteer help, as the following sample demonstrates. This newsletter not only informs people about the work of the organization, it also succeeds in discussing a specific kind of donation, asking for volunteers, and asking for help in spreading the word about their work. And it includes a testimonial.

SAMPLE NEWSLETTER

It's almost February — Kids Dental Month!

At GHK, we are getting ready for Give Kids A Smile Day — when children who are low income, underinsured can receive a free dental exam, cleaning, sealant and minor treatments from a participating GENEROUS dentist. This year we are processing over 400 applications for qualification, of which almost 100 children qualify to date. 18 dental offices are volunteering their services. Thanks to Sullivan Schein and the American Dental Assn, we have goodie bags with toothpaste, brushes, floss, etc, for the projected 200 children. Thanks to everyone for this opportunity to change lives! Have you asked YOUR dentist to help GHK?

I know we have lots of volunteers out there, not just for GHK, but other organizations as well. For those of you who itemize taxes: 2008 charity mileage deduction is 14 cents per mile, while medical mileage is 19 cents per mile.

Did you know — ????

Many folks don't think of donating appreciated securities to charities. (68% to be exact) Not only are there tax advantages, but you also don't have to worry about lots of paperwork.

If you haven't yet heard of the Ruth Charles Challenge (she will match up to $5,000 any amount donated for our brand new endowment fund) here's your chance to participate. Simply designate your donation to the fund. It's a great way to tell people about GHK and why it is SO important to ensure our future. and you can do it through a securities contribution, too!

SAMPLE NEWSLETTER

Yes, I know that we are all waiting for the health plan which will cover all the needs of our kids. A suggestion on the desk now suggests cutting vision and dental care from Medi-Cal, which means more kids for GHK. And February is National Heart Month, too. Stress puts strains on the heart.

Our healthy tip for the month: Stress often causes breathing to be shallow, which nearly always causes more stress because it puts less oxygen in the bloodstream and increases muscle tension. The next time you feel uptight, take a minute to slow down and breathe deeply, in through your nose and mouth through your mouth. Do this several times.

We are in need of a few good volunteers to help with a variety of "one day" tasks: labeling the newsletter, filling provider "thank you" bags, delivering provider "thank you" bags, etc. Many times, things come up between newsletters, so if you'd like to volunteer to be on our "Spur of the Moment" volunteer list, just let me know. I understand that you may not be able to do everything that comes up, but even a one-time is great!

April is being designated as "Glendale Healthy Kids Month" Do you belong to a club, church, organization, book club, etc? During April, tell them about GHK and our services. We have a great fact sheet and also parent brochure we can send out.

Mark Your Calendars:

Taste of Downtown Glendale is May 14

GHK Annual Appreciation Reception is June 26

"Dear Dr. Thank you for everything. You helped me see with my glasses. You are a good doctor. Now I see everything clear. Thank you again,_____"

Thanks for helping all our kids

USING E-MAIL

When, if ever, is it appropriate to use e-mails as fundraising letters? There are times when using e-mail is not only appropriate but also desirable, but consider the guidelines for using it carefully and do not overdo it. E-mail is cheap and fast and nearly everyone in the developed world is accustomed to using it. However, it is also an informal medium and you run the risk that your message will not be taken seriously. It is also extremely easy to hit the delete button before your letter is even read, so choose not only your words but also the frequency with which you send them carefully.

Choose e-mail for short messages (this is not the place for your two-page appeal letter) that have a timely quality. Experts recommend using e-mail in the following ways:

- **To Update.** Keep donors and other interested parties abreast of any news or developments that affect your organization.

- **To Issue Alerts.** This would be anything that requires member action, such as an upcoming demonstration, or a letter-writing campaign, a petition drive, or movements to contact government officials.

- **Requests for Help.** When you have special need of volunteers, an e-mail blast can be very effective at finding people to sign up.

- **Surveys.** E-mail lends itself to surveys of all kinds, which can also easily be set up on your Web site.

You can see that these uses of e-mail fall most readily into the category of keeping people informed and maintaining donor loyalty—which, as we have seen, is a vitally important practice. Each one of the above types of e-mail can of course be accompanied by a brief recap of the organization's goals and a quick appeal for funds. Never miss an opportunity to ask for money. And do not forget that e-mails have a way of getting forwarded. Some even end up going viral—which means, like the virus that attacks the human body, they run rampant across the web and suddenly everyone is talking about them. Because of this you always want to make sure to include at least basic information on your organization. Assume that people who have never heard of you before may see your e-mail.

E-mail is a very different beast than regular mail and different guidelines govern its use. We listed suggestions as to what kinds of messages are best sent via e-mail. What follows are guidelines as to how best to use it.

- **Mail to Current Members or Donors.** It is important to send e-mails only to current members or people who have expressly said they are interested in receiving mailings from you. Today's computer users are concerned about spam and viruses and most of us are slammed with a lot of excess e-mail. It is easy to delete unwanted e-mails unread, and if a particular organization sends a high volume of unwanted e-mail, they run the risk of alienating the potential supporter, not encouraging loyalty.

- **Include an Opt-Out Option.** Give recipients the chance to opt out, or no longer get the e-mails, with every message you send. And when somebody does opt out, take him or her off the list immediately. Nothing is more frustrating than asking to be taken off a list and continuing to receive e-mails (or direct mail for that matter).

- **Share Policies.** Inform your supporters of your policy on sharing e-mail addresses. Most organizations opt for a policy of never sharing addresses unless they have the supporter's permission.

- **Get Their Attention with a Subject Line.** Your subject line is the equivalent of the carrier envelope in direct mail — it is the single most important element of the mailing because it is what will convince the recipient to open the e-mail. No catchy subject line and odds are good the e-mails will go directly into the trash bin. What makes a catchy subject line? Capture their interest with news, or an interesting twist — but remember to keep it simple, too.

- **Maneuver Around Spam Filters.** You have gone to great effort to craft a compelling survey for supporters, and you have headlined it with a catchy subject line. But, alas, your work is all for naught if the e-mail goes right into the junk file. Spam filters do e-mailers a great service, but sometimes they collect mail we actually do want. How to avoid this? For starters, watch out for subject line words and phrases that will alert the filters. Words and phrases to watch out for are anything remotely sexual, anything related to getting out of debt, or health remedies. The other thing that spam filters do is assess spam by volume. So if you are sending out a large number of e-mails at once, your mailing may register as spam. One way to deal with this is to talk to your e-mail provider and ask for an exemption for your organization.

- **Pay it Forward.** As mentioned earlier, it is relatively common for e-mails or videos to go viral on the Internet these days. If your message is one that will impact or resonate with a wide variety of people, ask people to forward it to other interested parties.

- **It is a Two-Way Street.** The Web and e-mail are two-way mediums, and users are accustomed to instant communication. Be prepared to cope with supporters or other interested parties who hit the reply button with comments and questions. At the very least devise an automatic reply that thanks them and informs them you will get back to them as soon as possible.

- **Consider an E-mail Marketing Service.** Companies like Constant Contact (**www.constantcontact. com**) can help you to send out professional-looking communication on a regular basis at a reasonable price. These businesses offer templates for newsletters, surveys, greeting cards, and other theme mailings.

Now that you have mastered the mechanics and logistics of e-mailing messages from your organization, here are few final tips on how to actually write the e-mail:

- **Include Information About Your Organization.** This is a good idea for two reasons. First, because you never know when an e-mail will get forwarded to others who have never heard of your group and have no idea what you do. And second, it is always a good idea to remind current donors of your mission. Remember, the average person is deluged with e-mails, mail and images from radio and television every day. With the constant stream of information, it is easy to forget who is who in the nonprofit world.

- **Check It Over Carefully.** You would be surprised how many people forget to use the spell check function on e-mail. Just because e-mail is an informal medium, it does not mean it has to be full of typos and grammatical and spelling errors. Use your spell check function and check over it several times.

- **Include Links to Web site.** You are going to be keeping the e-mail communication short and sweet. One way to get more information to e-mail readers is to include links to your Web site. Interested parties will click through to learn more. Encourage this practice by offering them a reason to do so.

- **Be Wary of Asking for Money.** For starters, e-mail is not the most effective medium to use to ask for donations. If you do decide to mail an e-mail solicitation, send it only to current donors who have provided their e-mail addresses. And only use e-mail as a solicitation if you are set up to take donations via either credit card or PayPal on your Web site. You will only alienate readers if you do not have such an option set up. Supporters may expect to write a check for a direct-mail solicitation, but they expect to be able to donate instantly if contacted by e-mail.

DEALING WITH THE MAILING LIST

One last subject we need to deal with before getting onto talking about writing tips, and that is dealing with the mailing list. You have written exciting, compelling solicitation letters, have your thank-yous prepared—you are ready to go. There is just one problem, and that is, who are you going to mail the letters to?   This is when it is time to turn your attention to finding a mailing list. What follows are information and ideas on how to develop a successful mailing list.

Develop your own list. As an ongoing practice, you should be constantly collecting names, addresses and e-mail addresses of interested parties and supporters. Every time you have an event or appear at a trade show, collect names for your mailing list. Add the names of all board members and volunteers. Go through old records to find names of former donors and former volunteers. With these options, you will have the basis of a mailing list.

Trade with another organization. Find another nonprofit organization and negotiate a deal to swap mailing lists. Study after study has shown that most people who donate to one organization will also donate to others. To best utilize this option, do not trade with another group whose goals are exactly similar to yours. Instead, look for a group whose aims may be complementary. Your soup kitchen may look to a homeless shelter to trade lists with, for instance. Or an organization focused on diabetes may want to partner with one who works to prevent childhood obesity.

Rent a mailing list. If the above two options do not net you enough names, your next step is to look into renting a mailing list. The way most mailing lists are rented is through a one-time agreement. Sources for these rental lists include other non-profits, schools, museums, businesses, and publications. As with the trading option, look for companies that have similar interests or goals, and be creative, too. Rental fees will vary widely. This is because the value and quality of the lists themselves will vary widely. Find out when the list was last updated and who updates it—go for a professional here, if possible. You are renting this list, so you will not get direct access to it. Instead, you will have your mailing handled by a third party.

Working with a list broker. A list broker will handle the transactions of renting a mailing list. To best assist them, be prepared to tell him what your target audience is, your budget, the timing of the mailing, and the results you are looking for.

CASE STUDY: LINDA TAUBENREUTHER

Linda Taubenreuther- inwords

inwords@earthlink.net

Currently I'm a partner in the freelance writing and editing business, inwords and I've been working in the nonprofit arena for 30 years. Writing fundraising letters represents bout a third of my freelance writing business. I write appeals letters frequently.

The best fundraising letters have the following hallmarks: Immediate capture of interest. Conversational yet compelling tone. Case built logically in an order that makes the reader want to keep reading.

The less successful letters usually result from the client's insistence on a formal "businesslike" tone. Also letters that are a) too short to state the case persuasively or b) too crammed with facts and information are not as effective.

Before I begin a fundraising letter, I do extensive research on the organization, its goals, its target audience, and what their resistance points are likely to be. My best advice for writing fundraising letters is to write with one person in mind. Envision someone you know who is like the letter's target audience. What one thing could you say to that person that would persuade him/her to respond?

Never do any of the following: write in passive tense or use a stiff tone. Not plan a logical flow in stating your case. Try to include too many messages. Bury the key message far into the letter.

I come up with ideas for letters by thinking of the key message, then giving it an intriguing spin that will make the target open the envelope. The outer envelope is very important. The reply must be friendly and easy to complete, and should reinforce organization's personality and tone.

If time permits, soak up all the information you can, and then put the entire project out of your mind for a day or more. Your brain will process and organize the information for you during this time, and you'll be much more ready to craft the piece than you would be if you started writing immediately.

CASE STUDY: LINDA TAUBENREUTHER

I get inspiration and ideas from the stories and information the people in the organization provide me. There are no templates. The best letters are organic to the organization I'm writing about.

Writing Tips

Now that you have familiarized yourself with fundraising letters you may be called upon to write, it is time to go back to the basics and talk again about writing. All the information in the world about the different forms of letters will not help you at all unless you can convince yourself to sit down at your desk and write. So for starters, you will learn about ways to overcome the fear of the dreaded blank page.

CREATIVITY NUDGERS

The most important thing is to convince yourself to write something — anything. This sounds easy when you are lying on the couch reading a book about writing. But it may feel difficult when you actually sit down at your desk, turn on your computer, and are ready to begin to write. You wait and wait and wait....and no words come. How to prevent this from happening? How do you overcome the fear of the blank page? What follows are some tried and true ideas from professional writers and other creative types.

- **Do Warm-Up Exercises.** At the end of this chapter, you will find a full section of writing exercises. Choose any or all of these and do them for five or ten minutes before you begin working on your fundraising letter.

- **Work for Ten Minutes.** This falls into the category of tricking your brain. Tell yourself all you have to do is get started and work for just a few minutes. Odds are good that once you have written for that long, you will be engrossed in the work and able to keep going.

- **Set a Time Limit.** Set a timer for one hour, turn off the iPod, the radio or the TV, vow to not answer your phone and close down all Internet portals. Close your office door. Focus fully on the letter. You will be amazed at how much you can get done in one concentrated blast of work. Reward yourself with a break or a cup of coffee or tea at the end of the hour.

- **Allow Transition Time.** If you have been in a board meeting all morning, or on the phone with donors, do not expect to finish that chore up and switch right over to writing. Allow yourself to ease into it a bit. Stand and stretch, go outside and take a walk around the block if possible, or simply close your eyes and breathe deeply for five minutes or so. Let your mind drift and relax before you begin writing.

- **Write Regularly.** It is all about the momentum. Novel writers will tell you it is much easier for them to keep the flow going if they connect with the work in one way or another on a consistent basis. They may not have hours to work on it, but novelists will find a way to read the pages they worked on the day before, or scrawl some notes. Emulate them and find a way to look at your letter on a regular basis. It will keep it fresh in your mind and allow your subconscious to work on new ideas while you are sitting in the boring meeting.

- **Write Badly.** It may seem like writing badly is counter-intuitive to this whole book, but in reality writing badly is not a bad idea at all. Most people freeze up when they face the blank page because they feel they have to be perfect. To the contrary — it is helpful and freeing to allow yourself to write badly. Tell yourself you must write the worst sentence ever, and then another, and then another. By allowing yourself to be bad you allow yourself to get words on the paper — and once you have words on the page you then have something you can work with in the writing process, which we will discuss next.

THE WRITING PROCESS

It may also help you to remember that writing is a process. Professional writers know this, and they do not expect to sit down and have a perfect and full formed fundraising letter spring forth onto the page. They use the above-mentioned creativity nudgers to get themselves to the page on a daily basis, and then they look at writing as a process. Everyone approaches the writing process a bit differently to suit his or her individual needs, but it may help you to find a strategy you are comfortable with if you understand the basic flow of the writing process.

BRAINSTORMING

This is the idea gathering phase, the time when you want to start committing possible directions to paper. There are many ways to brainstorm, either alone of with others. If you create ideas and energy better with other people, then by all means do what you do best. Invite colleagues or volunteers or board members to a brainstorming session in which you toss ideas around. You can use a white board and have someone lead the session, or you can simply ask for help brainstorming at the end of a meeting, and write down ideas on paper.

If you prefer to work on your own, there are many ways to brainstorm also. Grab a pad of paper and pencil or open a computer file. Start by assigning yourself some prompts (see the writing exercises section for more on this). For instance, you might write at the top of the page, "The perfect fundraising letter for my organization includes...." Then either set a timer for ten minutes or number the page from one to fifty and write down as many things as you can possibly think of. The essence of brainstorming is to be wild and crazy and simply let the ideas flow. It does not matter how goofy the things you come up with are, what matters is that you are getting ideas on paper. These ideas will make is much easier to write the letter. Which leads us to the next step, writing the first draft.

FIRST DRAFT

The first draft is also sometimes called a rough draft. During this phase, your ideas for the letter start to take shape on paper. Perhaps you have an opening sentence that is just short of attention grabbing. Write it down. Follow the above-mentioned idea that it is okay to write badly and have at it. Let the words flow without worrying about how they sound. Put thoughts of grammar and spelling out of your mind and let it rip. Once you have some words on the page you can set about revising and polishing them. But the most important thing is to get something, anything, onto the page.

COMPOSTING

When you have a completed first draft, set it aside for a bit. If time allows, set it aside for a few days to give your brain a rest and allow your subconscious to process what you have written. This is sometimes called composting, and just like the process, which creates gorgeous rich soil full of nutrients, your mental composting will break forth all sorts of riches. You may find yourself coming up with the perfect headline while driving to work in the morning, or a stellar lead will pop into your head during your evening jog. One caveat: do not take too long away from the work, because then it may just be difficult to return to it. The brain will get bored, quit composting, and move onto something else.

What if you are under a serious time constraint and do not have time to set it aside for a few days? Take as long a break from it as you possibly can. Get up from your desk and go to lunch or take a walk. Professional writers often notice that the perfect solution to a writing problem comes when they step away from the work for a moment. It is as if the brain engages in another activity and this allows the thought that has been embedded deep in their subconscious to pop up.

SECOND DRAFT

The second draft is where you are going to look at the "big stuff." It is not the time to fuss with grammar or spelling. Use the second draft to look at issues of flow, organization, voice, and logic. Check on transitions — do they keep the reader's eye moving down the page? Have you conveyed the emotions you desire? Is there a personal voice behind it? Would the third paragraph read better if it came second? Rearrange and see how it reads. The great joy of working on a computer is that you can easily put it back the way it originally was. So do not fear making major changes. Approach the second draft in the spirit of experimentation and openness, much the same way you approached the brainstorming and you will be rewarded with many insights.

THIRD DRAFT

Once you have a second draft you are happen with, now it is time to move onto the third. In this draft, you will now look for the little things that you purposely ignored in the second draft. Check on grammar and spelling. Edit on the micro-level, looking at word choice and clarity of sentences. Do your words carry a sense of precision that also conveys emotion? Since you have settled the big issues of organization and flow, in this draft you can tinker and polish, making each word and sentence gleam.

SEND OUT FOR EDITS

You have gotten your letter as good as you possibly can, and you are happy with it. Now it is time to find another set of eyes to take a look at it. Find a colleague or volunteer or board member to read it. Keep an eye out for someone with whom you can establish an ongoing editing relationship. Finding someone to trust in this process is invaluable. It is so useful that you may want to consider budgeting money for an editor to either take your work and help you shape it, or one to be the last reader who makes certain that all is well written.

If you have specific concerns about the letter, be sure to note them for your editor. You might be unsure if the story you have chosen to use conveys emotion or falls flat. Maybe you are uncertain of your grammar or word choices. Be clear about what you are looking for — do you want your editor to concentrate on big-picture aspects or focus on grammar and spelling? Or perhaps you do not have any specific concerns. Whichever, there is no substitute for having another set of eyes look at your writing. Your editor will catch inconsistencies, sentences that are unclear, and stories that fall flat.

When you have gotten your edited draft back, take another look at it. You are the ultimate authority on this letter. You may agree with every change that your editor recommends, or you may not agree with all of them. Read the edited copy carefully and decide whether or not to make the changes. Get your letter into what you think is perfect shape. And then it is time for one more step.

SEND OUT FOR PROOFING

Lastly, you will want to send the edited and rewritten letter out to a proofreader. Is there someone in your organization who always has an eagle eye for errors? Some people are simply naturally adept at proofreading. It will be a huge boon to you to find and make use of these people. After you have taken your letter through all the stages of the writing process, you will be so close to it that you will no longer be able to see if there are any mistakes. So you will need to rely on others to check through it for errors or typos — all those little glitches that the spell-check would not catch.

Now you have made it through the entire writing process and you have a stellar fundraising letter to show for it. Follow this process whenever you have a fundraising letter of any type to write and soon you will be cranking them out like a pro.

But what happens if you are cruising along on your first or second draft, and suddenly you get stuck? Writer's block is a familiar problem to many. Some of the things that have already been covered will help to mitigate it. But just in case they do not help, here are several suggestions.

BLOCKBUSTERS

Step away from the computer. Humans are stubborn. When individuals encounter a problem, they sometimes think they can solve it through sheer force of will. Many a writer has stared at the blank page for long minutes on end, willing the words to come. In truth, an opposite approach is more fruitful. Get up from the computer and take a break. You will be surprised how often an idea pops into your head the minute you leave your desk.

Take a break. Similar to the above suggestion, taking a break can be your best bet for replenishing your writing muscle. Go have a cup of tea or eat an apple. Take a walk. Think about anything except the letter you are attempting to write. You will return to your desk refreshed and renewed, and that is the best state through which to receive creative ideas.

Do something repetitive. For some reason, the creative depths of the brain seem to get released when one engages in a repetitive activity. Weeding, sewing, mowing, the lawn, knitting, walking, showering, and lifting weight— any thing that involves repetitive motion often nudges creative ideas loose.

Mix it up. Sometimes you get into a rut. You start at the beginning and keep powering on through—until you cannot power anymore. And then you stay stuck where you are, willing the idea for the next sentence to come. But jar your thoughts a little and mix things up. If you are looking for an idea for the start of the letter, go to the end and read backwards. Or start in the middle of what you have written. Print out what you have and attempt to read it when the page upside down. It might sound ridiculous, but jarring creative thoughts loose is sometimes only a matter of looking at the work in a different way.

Cut and paste. Print out what you have so far, and cut it up into paragraphs or even sentences and rearrange it as random. It might not make any sense at all — but then again the unexpected juxtapositions may also give you fresh ideas.

The main thing to remember when you hit a roadblock in your writing is not to keep doing what you have been doing. If you have been working at your computer, sitting at your desk, take a pad of paper and a pen, and move to a new location. Switch between writing by hand and working on the computer. Keep the energy flowing by taking lots of little breaks. The creative mind craves variety and change, so feed it that and it will feed you ideas in return. Remember the famous quote from Albert Einstein, "Insanity: doing the same thing over and over again and expecting different results." Take a hint from one of history's great geniuses ,and try something a little out of the ordinary.

So now you have gotten comfortable with the writing process and learned how to overcome blocks. Perhaps you would like to go a step further and now seek some help with the actual writing itself. Look at ideas from two disparate writing worlds — the profession of copywriting and the world of literature.

HELPFUL HINTS FROM THE WORLD OF COPYWRITING

Copywriters rely on their ability to sit down at the computer and create lively copy on a daily basis. Uncertain what, exactly, a copywriter writes? The term is often used to refer to those who write advertisements, but in truth, it has a much broader base than that. According to Wikipedia, "Copywriting is the process of writing the words that promote a person, business, opinion, or idea." In the course of your day, you read the results of a copywriter's handiwork all around you, on Web sites, in business or medical brochures, in newspapers or magazines, in the direct-mail pieces you read, or the catalogs you peruse. You also hear it on the radio and see it on television. Copywriters are responsible for writing a lot of words on a daily basis, and thus they are excellent professionals to emulate when it comes to producing your own work. Take a look at some of their ideas.

Know your subject. Go back to the notes you took about the organization. Review them again and again until you are certain you know everything there is to know about it — even more than you thought it was possible to do. A copywriter who is hired to write about a company and sell its products will begin by learning every single thing about the business—from all angles.

Clarity. It is not possible to write compelling copy without clarity. You must know who you are, what you want, what you are asking for, and what you will be asking for in the future. Get clear about every aspect of your fundraising campaign.

Taking AIDA a step farther. In an earlier section, we discussed an acronym beloved of copywriters called AIDA, which stands for the process that occurs when a product or service is being marketed. (Make no mistake about it, when writing a fundraising letter, you are engaged in selling yourself and your organization to potential donors.) AIDA stands for attention, interest, desire, and action—the steps a potential customer goes through as they decide to make a purchase. Nowadays, the traditional AIDA has been update to include other letters. One common version adds an S for satisfaction on the part of the consumer or donor. You might also be interested in taking a look at the BOSCH formula, which is as follows:

- **Be inquisitive.** Ask questions. You need to know your organization and your donor to write effective letters.

- **Offer solutions.** Talk about the end result — i.e., the great feeling your donor will have after giving money.

- **Stimulate the senses.** Let your customer test the product, or add premiums or freebies to entice them.

- **Cross your sales.** Market accessories. In the case of non-profits, this equates to getting your donors to donate up or decide to volunteer in addition to giving money.

- **Hit the closing point.** Make the sale, or get the donation.

The BOSCH formula was created by sales expert Peter

Hubert as a tool for international sales trainings. The point of using either the AIDA or the BOSCH formulas is that it is an easy memory jogger which will enable you to keep in mind the steps you need to convince your donor to take on the way to making that donation. These formulas act as handy mental guideline shortcuts to light your way as you work. Print them out and tack them on a bulletin board or somewhere near your work area so that they are encoded in your brain as you write.

Swipe File. Copywriters are famous for maintaining bulging swipe files. These include samples of advertising and other copy pieces such as direct mail letters that have been proven to be successful. These samples may be ones they have written, or pieces they have read and admired from others. The swipe file becomes a reference source for ideas and inspiration. As a fundraising letter writer, you might want to emulate the copywriter and begin your own swipe file of fundraising letters that you have admired. Sometimes reading another written piece is the best way to get your ideas going.

Technique for Producing an Idea. A well-known process that many advertising and copy-writing executives rely on to produce ideas follows recommends that you fill yourself up with as much information as possible. Cram your brain full of every bit of information related to the topic that you can find. When you cannot fit another bit of byte of information into your mind, take a break. Put the topic out of your mind and go do whatever it is you like to do to relax — read a book, dance to music, swim, garden. Go about your business without worrying about your project, and before you know it — poof! into your brain will pop the first line of the letter or the perfect headline. The idea is similar to the concept of composting that we discussed earlier, with a bit of front-loading of information at the start. Give your brain some seeds to ponder and it will reward you with many new shoots of ideas.

HINTS FROM THE WORLD OF LITERATURE

Yes, we have made the point over and over again that writing fundraising letters is not about writing award-winning literary prose. You want your style to be direct, not descriptive and flowery. However, just as the successful fundraising letter writer can learn from the profession of copywriting, so too can she emulate some techniques from the world of literature. These techniques include the art of story, and utilizing voice.

The Art of Story

The capacity to tell stories is one of the things that separates humans from other species. People tell stories to make sense of the world, or to entertain. The ability to tell and understand a story is hard-wired into the human brain, and accordingly, people are predisposed to process information given in story form. To relate back to the previous discussion, copywriters are very familiar with the art of story and use it in their copy all the time. It is one of the most powerful techniques available to the person who wields words. The fundraising letter writer has much to learn from the techniques of writing a story.

Elements of Story

Put simply, within the dramatic structure of a story, a character or situation is moved from one state to another. In other words, the character or situation effects a change. Common patterns of change include a fall from grace, or the opposite, such as a poverty-stricken person making a fortune, or a loner falling in love.

What makes a story work well?

Humans innately relate to story because story is lived every day, in one way or another, and people use stories to shape their lives and explain them to themselves. Stories have a beginning, middle, and an end. Often in a person's life there may be situations that are in the middle that do not change—an endless, repetitive job, for instance. Reading a story in which a character similar to yourself gives you hope. It is human nature to respond to a character who changes. The secret ingredient of all stories is conflict. Quite simply, there is no story without a conflict. If all were rosy and right with the world, there would be no impetus for the story character to want to change. The conflict sets the story in motion by becoming a situation the main character can no longer tolerate. Then he or she sets out to change either the situation or himself or herself.

How can you apply these concepts to your fundraising campaign?

It may seem a bit of a leap to think about applying the concepts of story to your fundraising letter writing. After all, you are trying to convince people to donate money or time, not worry about change and dramatic arc. However, there is not such a chasm as you might think. After all, you are attempting to get your donor to change her behavior—you are asking her to move from being a non-donor to a donor. The fastest way to move a donor to action is to inspire them and the quickest way to inspire is through showing an example of someone who has changed. By highlighting your client who clawed his way from homelessness to being a homeowner, with your help, you are using the techniques of dramatic structure—moving a character from situation to situation.

The best way to utilize storytelling techniques in writing fundraising letters is to think character, conflict, and change.

- **Character.** Tell the human story. Humans relate to other humans, not numbers or generalities. Tell a human story in order to capture the attention of potential donors. Think of clients or volunteers whose stories you can tell, and think about beginning those stories with conflict. Think beyond the typical story, also. Do you have a volunteer who felt lonely and disconnected before she began helping your organization? Highlighting her change to a connected, happy member of society may also be a powerful way to demonstrate the value of your organization. As a general rule, if you have a program or a success you want to share, find a person to tell the story through. To use another metaphor, ponder the snapshots from your most recent vacation. Remember when you shared them with your good friend? Recall your friend leafing through the photos, lingering over some while glossing over others quickly. Odds are good that the ones your friend lingered over were shots that had people in them. The ones she set down quickly were simply landscape or cityscapes, without people to enliven them.

- **Conflict.** It cannot be repeated often enough—all stories start with conflict. Yours should, too. Besides the anecdotes you choose to put in your fundraising letter, think in terms of starting with conflict to frame the message of the letter also. For instance, the fact that your organization is short of money for necessary operations is a conflict that needs solving. The potential donor has the means to help you effect change in the situation through a donation. Frame your letter starting with conflict and the potential solution to that conflict and you'll be well on your way to writing successful letters.

- **Change.** Demonstrate the change your clients or volunteers have witnessed, share the change from to feeling good that your donors will experience, emphasize how potential donors can be a part of positive change. One of the main constants of human lives is change, yet unless it is good change we resist it. So give your potential donors some good change to wrap their brains around.

VOICE

Another aspect of literature that you can utilize in fundraising letters is voice. What is voice? It is the way an author tells a story, the way they express themselves in the world.   An author's voice reflects her way of seeing the world. Voice is what makes one piece of fiction stand out from another; it is what makes you want to read everything the author has ever written. Perhaps you feel that the author's take on the world is similar to your own, and this gives you a sense of comfort. Or maybe the author's voice is so very different that you are fascinated by his unique take. Either way, it is often voice which compels you to keep reading. Voice sounds natural and easy. More than anything, a strong voice in literature sounds unique. Think Holden Caulfield in The Catcher in the Rye, Rabbit Engstrom in the Rabbit books by John Updike, or the character of Scout in To Kill a Mockingbird. Each of these characters have a unique and compelling voice which makes you feel as if they are real live characters. There is a sense of personal knowledge—that you know these characters intimately. Because you know them so well, you grow to care deeply for them.

How does Voice Apply to Fundraising Letters?

Here is a hint: it is all about making it personal. Just as we respond positively to a well-drawn character in a novel, so too will we respond well to a fundraising letter that is written as if by a real person. A letter that has the feel of a living, breathing, human behind it will go much farther to tug at the heart-strings of your potential donor than one that is written in dry, boring language.

How to use voice in your letters? By allowing your fundraising letter to have a personality and sound like it is from a real person. This may seem to be much more easily said than done, but in truth, after a few tries, you'll be able to produce natural and engaging copy. The secret is that the more you write the easier it is to write, and the easier it is to write, the more natural your words will sound. So take advantage of the exercises we offer below to loosen yourself up and get in the habit of writing, at least a little, every day.

How to Write With a Sense of Urgency

This may seem like an impossible task or a mysterious process that magically occurs. But it is not. It is entirely possible to learn how to write with a sense of urgency and still sound natural. The first key is to keep in mind the magical "C" word: conflict. If there is not a problem to solve, it is rare to have a sense of urgency. If all is happy and serene, what need is there to rush? To the contrary, consider the problem of a homeless man with nowhere to go when the weather falls below freezing. Or the mother with a feverish child who has no medical insurance. Or the woman who is so hungry she runs the risk of fainting. These are all urgent situations and you can write about them or others in your letter in order to rouse your donor to action. The other key is to create some sort of deadlines. In the world of fiction, thrillers do this all the time. It is such a common plot device it has a name: "the ticking clock." In a thriller, the hero may be racing to find the bomb and disarm it before it blows up the entire city. The suspense is heightened by the author always keeping us informed as to how much time is left before the bomb explodes. You can use the ticking clock technique to create a sense of urgency. For starters, find a deadline. It could be that winter is coming on and temperatures are dropping. It could be that an important piece of legislation is about to be passed. It could be that a special event is coming up.

Once you have decided on the deadline, do not let the reader forget about it. Keep reminding him or her how many minutes are left on the bomb. Repeat the information about the upcoming legislation, or the fact that winter is bearing down and some of your clients face illness or even death if he or she does not get shelter. Constant repetition of the ticking clock may seem unnatural at first, but after awhile it will become second nature. Do not be afraid to go overboard with this technique — you can always edit out excess later.

WRITING EXERCISES

You may find it easier to enjoy a productive writing session if you start each one with writing exercises. Many people fire up the computer or pull out their writing pad, fully expecting brilliant thoughts to burst forth with no warming up. But, think about it: musicians practice scales, athletes run laps, and even the most casual of exercisers will do a few stretches before heading out. So it should not be a surprise that some writers do the same and use writing exercises for a few minutes at the start of each writing session. Warming-up with exercises gets the brain working, and it allows you to sink deeply into the words — the building blocks of your letter. Writing exercises also help keep the fonts of creativity going.

The best way to utilize writing exercises is to use them for a few minutes at the beginning of each writing session. Set yourself a time limit of five to ten minutes, fifteen at the most. The problem with going too long is that you might find the exercises so much fun that you will never get any work done on your fundraising letter. You might want to set a timer to facilitate this. After you have done your ten minutes of warm-up exercises, switch immediately to your writing. This is not the time to take a break or get up to use the bathroom. An athlete would not stretch and then wait an hour to run because his muscles would go back to their unstretched state in the interim. The same is true with your writing exercises. Do not do them and then go wander around and chat with colleagues for a half-hour. Do the exercises and allow them to move you directly into the writing of the letter — the true point of your writing session.

Many people like to keep a spiral-bound journal or some sort of writing notebook handy so that they can keep all of their writing exercises together. It is important to remember that the point of writing exercises is to warm up—not to generate ideas and material for your fundraising letters, unless you choose to. However, you may also find that your time doing writing exercises naturally produces great material for your letters. The value of maintaining a writing notebook is that you have one place in which to corral all your exercises and journal entries. However, do not let worrying about having just the writing notebook stop you from getting going — grab a legal pad or some computer paper and stuff all your exercises into a file if need be.

Ready? Let us get started with one of the easiest ways to begin, writing in a journal.

Writing in a Journal. You have chosen a spiral-bound

notebook to use for your writing exercises, so why not begin filling it by writing a journal entry? Journal writers of today go way beyond the old "Dear Diary" entries of old. You can write whatever you want — be it a list of your daily activities, all the people you saw over the course of a day, your current gripes, things you love — anything that occurs to you. Some creative types like to do a variant of journal writing popularized by Julia Cameron in her best-selling book, *The Artist's Way*. She advocates writing "Morning Pages," which are three hand-written pages completed first thing upon rising. Writing Morning Pages is a way to clear out the gunk and get the cobwebs out of the brain. You might want to vary the process a little and write Morning Pages at the start of your fundraising letter writing session. But what if you have the desire to write but open the spiral and the blank page blares at you like a neon light, preventing you from even getting a start? If that is the case, it is time to begin collecting prompts.

Prompts. One of the cornerstones of free writing is the use of prompts. What are prompts? They can be a word, phrase, or sentence, and they are used to jog your mind and get your writing juices flowing. You can use prompts that are related to the subject matter you want to write about, or you can use totally different ones. You can use prompts to help ease yourself into a journal entry, or you can use them as a wonderful warm-up tool. Prompts have a way of surprising you and leading you in directions you might not imagine. You may start with a prompt about the clock and end up writing up about your date the night before. Prompts are all about delving deeply into your sub-conscious where the good stuff is stored. For this reason, many writers choose prompts randomly, and some feel that it is better not to choose them because of interest in the subject or through an emotional connection with the topic.

- **Choosing prompts.** Maintain a list of prompts in your writing notebook or file. There are many sources for writing prompts, including books and Web sites such as **www.creativewritingprompts.com**, **www. writingfix.com** or **http://www.creativity-portal. com/howto/writing/writing.prompts.html**, which features many useful links. You can also make up sentences off the top of your head or take old fundraising letters you have written and cut them up and rearrange them into new sentences. They really do not even have to make much sense. Open a dictionary and choose a word or two, or make a whole list of them for future reference. You can even choose several words from different sections of the dictionary and arrange them into a string of words, which may or may not constitute a sentence. The prompt really does not matter so much as the writing it jogs you to produce.

- **Grab a Photo.** If you are a visual person, you might enjoy using a photo as a sort of prompt. Find a photo or a reproduction of a painting and gaze at it for a minute or so, then begin writing. You might begin, "This photo makes me think of..." or, "When I look a this photo, I see..." You can find images by doing a Google Image search (go to **www.google.com** and click on the Image link) or by visiting the Web sites of major museums. The Museum of Modern Art (**www.**

moma.org/collection) and The Smithsonian (**www. si.edu**) are great places to start.

- **Make it Project-Specific.** You can also collect prompts that relate either to your organization or your current letter-writing project. For instance, you might want to write a list of attributes of your organization: helpful, caring, successful, and so on. Or list specific things you do: feed the hungry, help the poor, provide temporary shelter, etc. Using prompts specific to your organization or project can be incredibly helpful in jarring loose a barrage of ideas.

Free Writing. One of the oldest and best-known of all writing exercises, free writing was popularized by writer and educator Peter Elbow many years ago, though it is a practice that has been around as long as humans have set their thoughts on paper. Teachers of all topics have taken Elbow's ideas and modified them for their own use, but the basics of free writing remain the same. The idea is to bypass the censor that prevents us from expressing our thoughts on the page by keeping the hand moving.

To engage in a session of free writing, begin by setting a timer for 15 or 20 minutes. Choose your topic or prompt, and begin. While you are writing, keep writing, no matter what. Keep moving the pen across the paper, even if you cannot think of anything to write, even if you are repeating the same word over and over again, even if you are writing, *I hate this exercise, I hate free writing*. Eventually your mind and hand will return to the topic or some other one and you'll be back on your way.

Free writing can be used as a warm up or as a way to free thoughts that might be stuck. Do a free writing session if you simply cannot seem to come up with thoughts for your fundraising letter. You can use a line from it for a prompt, or even write something like, *I don't know how to begin my fundraising letter* as a prompt. Free writing is a simple exercise with minimal rules, but you might be surprised at how effective it can be.

OTHER WRITING EXERCISES

A to Z. Pick a letter, any letter and write as many words that you can think of that start with it for five minutes. Or pick a letter and write a series of sentences that begin with that letter. For example: B — bat, boy, bag, buddy, basket, bucket, battle, and so on. This may seems like a silly exercise but it has the effect of pulling you right into using the language. It gets the brain oriented to the use of words. You can also do this with sentences, which will take a bit more thought. For instance: C — Can't find a book, Could you help me? Carrots are good for you, Casting about for an answer, she had none.

6 Questions. 6 questions can be a fun way to get your juices flowing. It utilizes the classic 5 Ws and 1 H: who, what, when, why, where, and how to get your brain going. Make this a project-specific exercise by answering the questions in relationship to your organization or the current campaign. Or combine this exercise with an entry from your list of prompts. For instance, choose a noun such as computers and ask yourself the 5 Ws and 1 H: who uses a computer, what do they use it for, when do they use it, why do they use it, where do they use it and how do they use it. Yes, this is another simple exercise, but again, the idea is to get yourself to sink deeply into the use of the language.

Interviews. You can also use the 6 Questions exercise on people — either yourself or your donor. Begin by asking yourself the questions and answer them quickly. You might want to design an interview around your reasons for working for your organization, or what you feel the chief benefits of the non-profit are. This can be an excellent way to come up with material for your letter while warming up. You might want to take it a step further and do this exercise with an imaginary donor. Use it to get inside their head and learn their motivations. Pretend your donor is a character in a novel and ask questions to learn more about him or her. This is what fiction writers do to create characters; no reason you can't do it to create a donor profile.

An Ordinary Day. This is an exercise that will appeal to the closet fiction writer. Screenwriters and novelists often imagine what an ordinary day for their character might be in order to get to know them better. What do they do when first they wake up? Do they have to have coffee first thing, or do they drink tea? Do they go right to the shower or linger over the paper? What kind of car do they drive to work? Where do they work? You might want to design ordinary days for your clients, your volunteers, and your donors. It can be an excellent tool for gaining understanding of everyone that you work with — and it is fun, too!

Make lists. Making lists is a fun, easy way to get warmed up. Many writers have used list-making as a substitute for a journal entry if they are too busy to write a full entry.

List everything you ate today. Or list what you are wearing. List everything you can see in the room you are sitting in. List all the sounds you can hear. List what you see outside your window. Take it a step further and make lists about your organization or the current campaign. List 10 ideas to market your non-profit. List 20 ideas for letter leads. The best way to write lists is to do it fast, and don't-over-think it. Number your page from 1 to 20, decide on your topic, and write fast.

Outside, Looking In. Just for fun, describe your organization as an outsider might see it. You can focus on the physical aspect of it, or the programs you offer, or the people who work for you. Pretend you are an outsider visiting your offices for the first time. What do you see?

The Elevator Pitch. Business people are taught to write and refine an elevator pitch. What is an elevator pitch? If you get in an elevator with another person and they ask you what you do, you have only a minute or two to tell them before the elevator reaches their floor. What do you say? How do you succinctly tell the story of your organization? People often approach this assignment with great seriousness but have some fun with it and play around on paper. You might want to come up with elevator pitches for yourself, your donor, your volunteers, and your clients — just for fun, and just to get to know them better.

Modes of Description. Another great warm-up is doing a description exercise. The idea is to take one object and describe it in three different ways: literally, metaphorically, and abstractly. This really gets your brain working on various levels. For instance you might choose an object such as a coffee mug and describe it exactly as you see it, noting color, shape, and size. Next describe it metaphorically: does it look like something else? For instance, you might describe the handle of the coffee mug as donut-shaped. Finally, go for the abstract, which is the process of describing one object to something that is totally unrelated.

OTHER WRITING TIPS AND TOOLS

Talk it Out. If you find yourself really struggling with the writing, consider using voice-activated software. You can find this software for sale very inexpensively on the internet, and some people find it to be very useful in freeing themselves to express words naturally. Once you purchase the software, you need to train it to recognize your voice, but this is easily accomplished. Voice-activated software is one of those love it or hate it things — people either take to it very naturally or they simply don't seem to be able to get the hang of it. But if you are having a difficult time with the words, it might be the answer for you. If using voice-activated software does not appeal to you, but talking your letter out does, then consider buying a digital voice recorder. These small devices are a vast improvement over the old tape recorders and are very easy to use. Keep your digital recorder with you to record ideas for your fundraising campaign as they occur to you and experiment with speaking the letter into the recorder. The only drawback is that the process of typing the notes from the recorder can get tedious, but perhaps your organization has administrative assistants that can help with that. Finally, don't forget the good old-fashioned way of finding a person with a sympathetic ear and talking your ideas out.

Computer Versus Hand. In this day and age, nearly everyone heads right to the computer when it is time to begin writing. But you may have better luck with the good old-fashioned pen and paper. For some, the flow of words onto the page comes much more naturally than typing into a computer (or for some, a typewriter).

Chunk it Out. You may see references to the practice of "chunking" information, which is a technique that is often used on the web and includes arranging your words in such a way that they are easy to read. Chunking makes good use of bullet point lists, subheads, and short sentences and paragraphs — all techniques we have talked about earlier in the book. But there is another way to look at chunking, also, and that is as a way to make your writing easier. One problem that writers often have is getting overwhelmed by the big picture. They look at the entire letter that they must write and get discouraged before they even begin. Try breaking up your letter into chunks. Tell yourself that you will begin by working on the headlines. In your next writing session, commit to writing the subheads, and so on. Also do not limit yourself to following any particular order in the writing. If you feel like working on the ending first, go ahead and work on the ending first.

Clustering or Mind-Mapping. This is a popular technique for organizing information and can be very useful in preventing writer's block. Begin by writing the topic of your letter (or any word that reminds you of it) in the center of a blank piece of paper. What ideas does the topic present to you? Draw a line out from the center word for each thread. Some sub-heads will have separate lines, while others will relate and can be placed on the same thread. This process gives you an image of your mental map — what your thoughts are on the subject at hand. From here it is a simple step to either write a traditional outline or begin writing. To begin writing, simply choose a thread and launch into it.

Words Out, Words In. Sometimes you have to refill the available supply of words in your brain in order to write more. The cure for this problem is simple and enjoyable — read. It will be especially useful if you read other fundraising letters or material put out by other non-profits, or even that put out by you. Read whatever will get you in the mood to write your fundraising letter.

Act a Role. It can be very helpful to pretend you are someone else when you are writing and you get blocked. Pretend that you are one of your organization's volunteers, or perhaps a client. Or pretend that you are an historical figure connected to your nonprofit. For instance, if you are an organization devoted to helping the blind, pretend you are Helen Keller. Or if your nonprofit is working to eradicate obesity in children, pretend you are a famous athlete. Role-playing is not only fun, it can be very useful in jogging ideas out of your brain.

Print it Out. The brain responds differently to words read on a computer screen than to those on the page. If you have been reading your letter solely on the computer, try printing out a copy. You might be surprised at the new ideas that occur to you.

Switch it Up. Have you been at your desk in your office, working for hours? Grab you pen and paper and head to the coffee shop for a change of pace. Or go sit outside if it is nice out. Go work in the conference room, or downstairs in the lobby. The idea is to change locale, which often lends a fresh perspective on things.

Stop in the Middle. Ernest Hemingway used to end every one of his writing sessions in the middle of a sentence. Why? Because that way he had an automatic starting point the next day. Many are the authors who have pushed themselves to finish a whole chapter or important segment of a project, only to find themselves at a loss the next day — when they have to face starting a new chapter. This can be almost as intimidating as starting at the beginning. So get in the habit of ending at a high point, in order to keep the momentum going and give yourself and easy entry the next session.

Relax. Finally, do not forget the value of simply relaxing. Before every writing session, sit quietly for a couple minutes and take deep, cleansing breaths. Run through your body, looking for places of tension and discomfort. Focus attention on those spots, consciously relaxing them. Then take one final deep breath and turn on your computer or pull out your pen. Your mind will be much better prepared to engage and send you just the right words if you clear it of stress and negativity.

Following these suggestions for approaching the task of writing should help you complete your fundraising letters with a minimum of stress and a maximum of efficiency. You will be producing top-quality, successful fundraising material in no time at all. Just remember not to allow yourself to get stuck in a rut. If you reach an impasse or something is not working, move on — or better yet, refer back to this section and find a technique that will help you move past it.

CASE STUDY: CRAIG VALINE

Craig Valine- The (Former) Struggling Consultant

Enhanced Marketing Performance

556 S. Fair Oaks Avenue, #469

Pasadena, CA 91105

www.craigvaline.com

info@craigvaline.com

I was president of the California Junior Chamber and Marketing Director for the California Jaycee Foundation for a total of 12 years, and in these positions I wrote. fundraising letters periodically.

I write fundraising letters using direct response techniques and methodologies Primarily, I write Appeals where other letters have failed. My letters have been "back ups" or secondary appeals when there has been a previous lack of response.

The hallmarks of successful fundraising letters are: 1. Simplicity, 2. A great heart-warming and dramatic story, 3. A compelling call to action and deadline, and 4. A free gift/bonus/incentive for taking action now.

In my opinion, a letter only fails if it doesn't produce a response. Lack of response is feedback only. My experience: We once did a multi-step letter campaign asking for donations for a program called "Operation Santa Claus". The letter was modeled after a successful campaign written by a well-known copywriter. The first letter failed to get any response. The second letter written a little differently got a couple of responses. And, the third letter got no responses. My opinion is that our letters didn't have a strong enough emotional appeal and lacked urgency. It was a good lesson to learn.

When it is time to start the pre-planning process, I use a multi-part questionnaire to organize my thoughts. I gather anything and everything that can help me understand

CASE STUDY: CRAIG VALINE

the project and primary purpose (past promotions letters, memos, etc. I interview anyone important relating to the project. I post index cards up on my wall to prioritize core features and benefits. Then, I write. The best tip for a successful fundraising letter is to find and craft the best emotional and dramatic story related to your appeal. Conversely, don't try to sell your readers on anything using traditional selling methods. Grab them in heart and gut – then make it easy for them to say, "Here. Take my money."

To find good ideas for a letter, I ask the people involved in the project or previous donors, relative to the organization or the project at hand, "What makes you cry?"

Depending on what action you want them to take, I think every aspect of the overall package is important. But, beware. A personal looking letter has to match the envelope that carries it. It can't look "all corporate", and then try to be personal inside. My general thought is, anything that will help aid them saying "yes!" is good for a direct mail package.

Write like you talk. Be simple. Use your personality in your copy. Ultimately, people buy you and the way you tell your story. Don't try to sound like a Professor of English.

People are people and they speak everyday language.

I keep a swipe file of appeals used on me every day. I ask my neighbors and business acquaintances to keep their mail for me. I get my ideas from watching TV (Oprah and, Dr. Phil, etc.). I listen to my friends when they have a problem.

Conclusion

And now, at last you reached the end of your journey through the world of successful fundraising letter writing. You have taken a thorough look at your organization and its goals, and also delved into the mind of your donor. You have walked through the world of marketing and perhaps decided that the "M" word is not so bad after all. You have learned about the various elements of fundraising letter package, including the outer envelope, the reply device, the reply envelope, the lift letter, and the actual fundraising letter itself. You have learned about and seen samples of all different types of fundraising letters and gleaned some pretty good tips for writing, too.

What is left? Absolutely nothing. All that remains is for you to go forth and write successful fundraising letters that will have your organization's accountants grinning from ear to ear. But please bear one thing in mind as you write your fundraising letters. Writing fundraising copy for organizations working their hardest to do good in the world is a noble pursuit. At heart, it is an act of philanthropy. The word philanthropy means, at its core, "a love of mankind." You will see variations on this definition, such as the "voluntary promotion of human welfare" or "a desire to help mankind." But at its heart, philanthropy means a love of humankind. And what more noble occupation could there be than serving mankind with all the love you can muster?

So keep this noble definition in mind as you write your fundraising letters. Post it near your desk in a place where you will see it often, and if you get stuck, or the words simply will not come, glance up at it to remind yourself what you are doing and what is important to you. Just as we learned that knowing your organization inside out is of vital importance to writing fundraising letter, so too, is knowing yourself.

The most important thing you can know about yourself is that you are a philanthropist, a lover of humankind, working to better the world.

Bibliography

BOOKS

Bray, Ilona, J.D., *Effective Fundraising for Nonprofits: Real-World Strategies That Work*, USA: Nolo, 2005

Clinton, Bill, *Giving: How Each of Us Can Change the World*, New York: Alfred J. Knopf, 2007

Kuniholm, Roland, *The Complete Book of Model Fundraising Letters*, Paramus, New Jersey: Prentice Hall, 1995

Rosso, Henry, *Rosso on Fund Raising: Lessons From a Master's Lifetime Experience*, San Francisco: Jossey-Bass, Inc., 1996

Sharpe, Alan, *Breakthrough Fundraising Letters*, London: Andrew Spencer Publishing, 2007

Warwick, Mal, *How to Write Successful Fundraising Letters*, San Francisco: Jossey-Bass, Inc., 2001

WEB SITES

Communication

Constant Contact   **www.constantcontact.com**

Donor Information Research

Amazon **www.amazon.com** For information on book authors

American Medical Association **www.ama-assn.org** For information on doctors

First Source **www.firstsourceonl.com** For information on architects

Forbes **www.forbes.com** For information on business people

Fortune **www.fortune.com** Also for information on business people

International Movie Database **www.imdb.com** For information on entertainment figures

Fundraising

Alan Sharpe **www.raisersharpe.com**

Mal Warwick **www.malwarwick.com**

WRITING INSPIRATION

Prompts

Creativity Portal **www.creativity-portal.com/howto/writing.prompts.html**

Creative Writing Prompts **www.creativewritingprompts.com**

Writing Fix   **www.writingfix.com**

Images

Google   **www.google.com** (Click on Images)

Museum of Modern Art   **www.moma.org/collection**

Smithsonian Institute **www.si.edu**

Author Biography

A long-time free-lancer for magazines and newspapers, Charlotte Rains Dixon has recently concentrated on writing copy for businesses and Web sites. She is also a prolific ghostwriter. Visit her Web site at **www. wordstrumpet.com**.

Glossary

The world of non-profits and fundraising is no different than any other—there are all kinds of specialized lingo used by professionals who practice in the field. You have read most of these words at various points in the text. We have also added a few from the world of direct mail that might not have appeared in this text, as you might run into them as you continue your fundraising letter writing. Refer to this list of commonly used terms if you get confused by any of the language.

AIDA. An acronym designed to help you remember the stages of marketing—Attention, Interest, Desire and Action.

Active donor. A donor who has recently given money to your organization. Many nonprofits consider the time period to be within the last 12 months, but others will stretch it to 18 to 24 months.

Annual fund. Money which supports the general operation of the organization and its yearly budget.

Ask. The request for money in a fundraising campaign.

Ask string.   The listing of monetary amounts on a fundraising letter reply card that allows donors to select how much they want to donate.

Attrition.   Donors lost to the organization.   This can happen for a variety of reasons, including death, moving, job loss or other reasons.

Attrition rate. Usually given as a percentage, this is the rate at which donors do not renew their gifts.

Average gift. This is the average amount of gift received across all donors.   To find this number, divide moneys received by number of gifts received.

Back end. All the activities that your organization must do to get, process and disburse a gift after it has been received. Not to be confused with:

Back-end premium. A freebie offered to donors with their donation.

BOSCH Formula.   Copywriting formula to help with marketing ideas.

Buckslip. Piece of paper in the size of a dollar bill which is included with the fundraising letter package when it is mailed.   The buckslip either repeats the main message or talks about a related point such as monthly giving programs.

Business Reply Envelope. Self-addressed envelope with the postage paid by the organization sending it.

Caging. Recording the gift amount and other pertinent

data from the donation. This is an old term, taken from a post office practice of sorting mail into wire bins.

Call to action. The part of the letter that urges the reader to respond and also tells them how to do so.

Carrier. The outer envelope which carries the contents of your fundraising package.

Charity mentality. The mind-set a nonprofit organization sometimes finds themselves stuck in, whereby they consider themselves in a "poor us" charity light, rather than taking pride in their programs.

Cheat sheets. Also called Swipe Files, these are collections of successful and engaging fundraising letters that others have written. They can be used for inspiration and ideas.

Clickthroughs. In e-mail campaigns, this refers to the people who have clicked on a link in an e-mail message.

Closed-face envelope. And outer envelope without a window.

Control package. Your best performing fundraising letter package. You will measure all others against the success of this one.

Cost to raise a dollar. The cost effectiveness of your fundraising campaign, which measures how much it costs to raise each dollar donated. You can easily figure this by dividing fundraising campaign costs by gross income.

CPM (Cost per thousand). How much you have to spend to get your message to one thousand people.

Decoy. The practice of inserting a name into a mailing list in order to ascertain that the list is being used as per the agreement.

Donor acknowledgement. Your responses to your donors should be a thank-you or a receipt, or both.

Donor acquisition cost. How much is costs you to get donors through your fundraising campaign.

Donor conversion. Convincing one-time donors to become repeat givers.

Donor cultivation. The ongoing process of nurturing your donors to become regular supporters and higher levels of giving.

Donor retention.   Keeping your donors active and supportive.

Dupe. Duplicate. Refers to duplicate names appearing on the same mailing list.

Dupe rate. The number of names that are found to be duplicated on one list.

External analysis. External factors beyond your organization that might have an impact on your work, such as social and political.

Frequency. How many times a donor has donated to the organization within a specific time frame.

Front end. Everything you have to do upfront in order to get a gift. Not to be confused with:

Front-end premium. A free gift mailed with your fundraising letter which is intended to encourage donations. Often this takes the form of address labels or note cards.

Fulfillment rate. Number of people who actually give money after pledging to do so.

Involvement device. Any element in a fundraising package that potential donors must manipulate with their hands. This can be a sticker to peel off, something to cut out, or a place to sign, and involvement devices are known to boost the rate of giving.

Johnson Box. Copy at the top of the letter which is surrounded by a box or some sort of eye-catching element. It is designed to get donors to keep reading and was pioneered by Frank Johnson who started using the Johnson box to sell magazine subscriptions.

Key code. A code of letters, numbers or other marks which is placed in the fundraising package to help gauge the effectiveness of the campaign.

Lapsed donor. Any giver who has not given a donation in the last year or longer

Liftnote or lift letter. A secondary letter, often on a smaller piece of paper, which is included in the fundraising package. It is often signed by a celebrity and repeats the salient points of the main letter.

List. Short-hand term for mailing list. The names and addresses of the people to whom you will send your fundraising letter.

List broker. The middle man who arranges for a nonprofit organization to rent or buy a mailing list from the owner. The list broker will typically be engaged to research and recommend the correct mailing list for the nonprofit.

Marketing concept. The details of your fundraising package—what aspects of the organization you will feature, who you will be asking money from, and what benefit that person will derive from their donation.

Mission statement. Your organization's vision and reason for being.

Niche marketing. The practice of defining a narrow slice of market, or niche, in which to operate.

Nixie. A fundraising letter returned to the sender because of an incorrect address.

Open rate. In an e-mail campaign, the number of e-mails that are actually opened.

Overline. The uppermost headline in a letter. It is most often placed above the salutation

Package. All the elements of your fundraising package, including the letter, the outer envelope, the reply envelope, the reply card, and the premium.

Personalization. Customizing each letter. For instance, using the name of the recipient on the letter, or the amount of the previous gift.

Piggy back. One offer accompanying another.

Postage-paid envelope. Also known as a Business Reply Envelope, this is a self-addressed envelope with postage paid by the organization sending it.

Premium. Any item offered to a donor to encourage them to donate. Usually premiums are free, but they can also be linked to a donation. When premiums are free and arrive with the package, they are called front-end premiums. When they are tied to a donation, they are called back-end premiums.

Prospect. A recipient of the fundraising letter who is a good bet for donating, but has not yet made a donation.

Prospect mailing. A fundraising package sent to prospects. You might also see this called an acquisition mailing.

Renewal mailing. A fundraising package sent to previous donors or others who have supported the organization.

Renewal Window. The period of time during which an annual renewal letter is sent out; traditionally no other fundraising letters will be mailed during this time.

Reply card. The card in the package which the donor completes and returns with the donation.

Response rate. Number of responses the mailing has elicited, calculated as a percentage of the total number mailed.

Salutation. How the donor is addressed at the beginning of the letter.

Smart goals. An acronym designed to help you remember

how to create goals. Make them specific, measurable, agreed-upon,

Special appeal. A fundraising letter mailed to existing donors which asks them to contribute to support a specific program or event.

Special event letter. A special event letter is a fundraising letter keyed to a specific event such as an auction or other fundraiser.

Straight contribution letter. The granddaddy of all fundraising letters, this general letter asking for funds is the basis of all the letters you will write.

Strategic fundraising plan. Your overall plan for fundraising.

Survey letter. A letter, which includes a survey or questionnaire as an involvement device.

Sustainer program. You may also see this referred to as a Monthly Giving Program. Either term refers to a program, which allows a donor to make regular donations on an automatic basis. This is usually done via direct withdrawal from a checking account or credit card once a month.

Target donor. A specific profile of the average donor you are going after.

Teaser. Any image, phrase or headline placed on the outer envelope to arouse curiosity and encourage the recipient to open the envelope.

Thank-you letter. Letter to the donor, acknowledging his or her gift.

Upgrade. Persuading donors to increase the size of their gifts, or their frequency.

Window envelope. An envelope with a window cut in it. The window will be covered with clear acetate, which allows the mailing address, the return address, or a special message to be seen on the enclosed materials.

Index

109, 112-114, 117,
122, 123, 126, 136,
141, 158-160, 163,
166, 168-170, 244,
245, 249
Donor 18, 22, 24, 25,
46-56, 59, 68, 75-81,
84-86, 88-91, 93-95,
97, 99, 100-104, 108,
110-116, 118-122,
124, 126, 127, 130,
131, 133, 134-139,
141-143, 145, 147,
148, 151, 157-160,
163, 165-168, 170,
174, 178-180,
184-186, 194,
196-203, 206-208,
210-213, 223. 244,
245, 248-251, 258,
259

E

Event 35, 40, 41, 42, 79
Exercise 256-259
Exclusive 101

F

Fundraiser 22
Fundraising 27, 28, 32, 33,
35-37, 39-43, 46-50,
52-56

G

Gifts 116, 160
Giving 20, 22
Goal 21, 22, 24, 27, 35,
36, 38, 39, 41, 42,
195, 202, 203
Government 46, 193, 214,
215, 220, 223
Graphic 154
Grants 45, 46

I

Idea 235-237, 241, 243,
246, 256, 258, 259,
263
Impact 179, 226
Income 45, 46, 49
Interest 89, 108, 137, 150
Issue 223

L

Letter 234, 235, 236, 237,
239-241, 244-247,
249-254, 256-262,
264, 265
List 141, 143, 155, 157,
158, 168, 181, 195,
198, 205, 213, 222,
224, 225, 228, 229
Loyalty 180, 187, 202,
203, 206, 223, 224